Porter Scobey, PhD and Pawan Lingras, PhD
Saint Mary's University

WEB PROGRAMMING *and* INTERNET TECHNOLOGIES

An E-Commerce Approach

JavaScript
CSS
XML
(X)HTML
PHP
MySQL

JONES & BARTLETT
LEARNING

World Headquarters
Jones & Bartlett Learning
5 Wall Street
Burlington, MA 01803
978-443-5000
info@jblearning.com
www.jblearning.com

Jones & Bartlett Learning books and products are available through most bookstores and online booksellers. To contact Jones & Bartlett Learning directly, call 800-832-0034, fax 978-443-8000, or visit our website, www.jblearning.com.

Substantial discounts on bulk quantities of Jones & Bartlett Learning publications are available to corporations, professional associations, and other qualified organizations. For details and specific discount information, contact the special sales department at Jones & Bartlett Learning via the above contact information or send an email to specialsales@jblearning.com.

Copyright © 2013 by Jones & Bartlett Learning, LLC, an Ascend Learning Company

All rights reserved. No part of the material protected by this copyright may be reproduced or utilized in any form, electronic or mechanical, including photocopying, recording, or by any information storage and retrieval system, without written permission from the copyright owner.

Web Programming and Internet Technologies: An E-Commerce Approach is an independent publication and has not been authorized, sponsored, or otherwise approved by the owners of the trademarks referenced in this product.

Production Credits
Publisher: Cathleen Sether
Senior Acquisitions Editor: Timothy Anderson
Managing Editor: Amy Bloom
Director of Production: Amy Rose
Production Editor: Tiffany Sliter
Marketing Manager: Lindsay White
V.P., Manufacturing and Inventory Control: Therese Connell
Permissions & Photo Research Assistant: Lian Bruno
Cover and Title Page Design: Kristin E. Parker
Composition: Northeast Compositors, Inc.
Cover and Title Page Image: Laptop: © Redshinestudio/ShutterStock, Inc.; Button: © Chad Baker/Digital
   Vision/Thinkstock; Keyboard: © Andrey Priyatkin/ShutterStock, Inc.; Screen: URRRA/ShutterStock, Inc.
Printing and Binding: Courier Corporation
Cover Printing: Courier Corporation

Library of Congress Cataloging-in-Publication Data
Scobey, Porter.
  Web programming and Internet technologies : an E-commerce approach /
Porter Scobey and Pawan Lingras.
     p. cm.
  Includes index.
  ISBN-13: 978-0-7637-7387-8 (pbk.)
  ISBN-10: 0-7637-7387-5 (pbk.)
1. Web site development. 2. Business enterprises—Data processing. I.
Lingras, Pawan. II. Title.
  TK5105.888.S388 2012
  006.7—dc23
                         2011038345

6048

Printed in the United States of America
16 15 14 13 12   10 9 8 7 6 5 4 3 2 1

Dedication

To the memory of my mother and father, who likely would not have read it, but would have liked a copy for their coffee table; and to Patricia, who might even read it, but would insist that its sojourn on our coffee table be short-lived.

—Porter Scobey

To my family, who may have a similar vague and equally short-lived sense of joy and pride.

—Pawan Lingras

Contents

Preface

Web Programming and Internet Technologies: An E-Commerce Approach is designed to be used as a textbook for first or second year Computer Science or Information Technology courses. It can also be used for independent study by anyone interested in getting a broad introduction to a useful subset of the many technologies commonly used to develop commercial and recreational websites.

It is the authors' hope (and belief) that if a student exercises due diligence by working through all of the questions, exercises, and other activities that this book provides, he or she will be well on the way to becoming a competent web developer. Because such a diverse set of technologies is required to create anything beyond a trivial website, it is not possible for any book to provide in-depth discussion of every topic without overwhelming the reader with the sheer volume of information. Therefore, this is not a full text on any of the technologies described. However, each chapter has a section at the end entitled *What Else You Might Want or Need to Know*, which contains material that, if pursued, can take the reader well beyond the text material, as well as a References section containing annotated links and other references that point the way to further professional development. A developer must always try to be aware of alternative technologies, but our main focus here is to develop a single cohesive example that illustrates a particular collection of open source and widely used technologies.

Chapter 1, Setting the Scene, is the first of two foundational chapters. It provides an introduction to the Internet and the World Wide Web and the relationship they share. A discussion of web servers and browsers helps us understand the nature of communication on the World Wide Web. The chapter also discusses some essential Internet concepts, including the *Internet Protocol (IP)*, *IP addresses*, *domains*, and *domain name servers*. Knowledge of these basic Internet terms and concepts will help us understand how to establish a presence on the Web. At the end of this chapter we get a feel for where we are going by looking at a real-world commercial website and identifying the features that we will explore at some length in subsequent chapters.

Chapter 2, **Establishing a Web Presence**, provides us with the first of many "hands-on" experiences to come. We begin with a discussion of *Internet Service Providers* and some of the tools one can use to begin web page development. Then we discuss the creation of a very simple web page and how to "put it up on the Web," using the occasion to introduce the notion of a *MIME type*. Our goal in this chapter is to get a first web page "up and running" in the simplest possible way.

Chapter 3, **XHTML for Content Structure**, begins the development of an e-commerce website that will expand in functionality with each succeeding chapter of the text. This is a unique feature of our approach: a strict policy of applying each new topic discussed to a single, extended example. This example will show the development of a website for a real commercial enterprise, and will run throughout the text. The initial version seen in this chapter is a very simple website that uses only basic features of eXtensible HyperText Markup Language (XHTML). A very important point that we emphasize here is that XHTML is concerned *only* with the *structure* of the content, or information, contained in our web pages, and *not* with the presentation or behavior of the content on those pages. We have chosen to use XHTML as our markup language because it imposes a stricter discipline on the web developer and encourages more consistency in web page construction than the less restrictive HTML.

Chapter 4, **CSS for Content Presentation**, immediately addresses one of the problems we ignored in the previous chapter, that of the *presentation* of our web page content. We continue to emphasize how important it is to keep structure and presentation separate as we think about and build our web pages. This will be particularly important as our site becomes more complicated and populated with a larger number of pages. We want our users to experience the same "look and feel" as they "surf" from one of our pages to the next, and we need a mechanism to provide this consistency. The use of Cascading Style Sheets (CSS) allows us to define a presentation style that can be applied consistently to all the web pages on our site and also permits us to easily change any aspect of the presentation that we wish to modify.

Chapter 5, **XHTML Forms for Data Collection and Submission**, extends the XHTML of Chapter 3 to provide the forms and associated "widgets" that allow our users to enter data on a web page. Generally that data is then submitted across the Web by the browser to a server, where it may be stored in a database or processed in some other way. The submission process and server-side processing will be discussed in more detail in later chapters. Here we are focused on just the forms themselves.

Chapter 6, JavaScript for Client-Side Computation and Data Validation, introduces the JavaScript programming language, which we use here to perform some simple arithmetic calculations and to check the data entered by our users into our forms for validity. The language is relatively easy to learn and use, even for nonprogrammers. We also learn about the *Document Object Model (DOM)*, an *Application Programming Interface (API)* that provides a programmer with access, via JavaScript in our case, to various parts of a web page for examination and manipulation. These features are part of what we need to know if our business is to carry on a successful and secure two-way communication with our users.

Chapter 7, JavaScript for Client-Side Content Behavior, discusses additional capabilities of JavaScript and the DOM. There are many ways in which JavaScript can be used to add some "dynamic" activity to our web pages, which have been quite "static" up to now. In particular, we learn how to place a rotating sequence of business-related images on our home page, and how to implement a simple dropdown menu.

Chapter 8, PHP for Server-Side Preprocessing, introduces another programming language, PHP. Unlike JavaScript, which works on the client side, PHP is a server-side technology. Our web pages up to this point have essentially been served from the server to the user's browser in the form they were created. This chapter changes all that. PHP is a programming language in which programs[1] can be used to create or modify web pages "on the fly." This means that the user receives an XHTML document that has been created using instructions from the PHP program, possibly based on input that has previously been received from the user on the client side. A single PHP program can potentially be used to create an arbitrary number of different XHTML pages. We will see how an existing web page can easily be enhanced with the addition of a simple "embedded" PHP script, and then we will move on to perform more sophisticated actions like providing e-mail feedback to users when they submit form data.

Chapter 9, MySQL for Server-Side Data Storage, introduces MySQL,[2] one of the most widely used (and open source) database systems on the Web. Any business will sooner or later need to make use of a database of some sort to keep track of inventory and customer contact information, as well as customer preferences and

---

[1] The "programs" written in both PHP and JavaScript are also frequently called *scripts*.

[2] At the time of writing, Sun Microsystems had purchased MySQL, after which Sun itself was acquired by Oracle. Since Oracle is the vendor of one of the world's most successful enterprise database systems, some concerns have been raised about the long-term viability of MySQL, which began life as an upstart, open source alternative to Oracle's product. In the way these things happen on the Internet and the World Wide Web, MySQL is likely to survive in some form, with a dedicated group of support volunteers, even if an attempt is made to kill it off.

similar kinds of information. Furthermore, the information stored may be represented in various formats. Users browsing the website of the business will often need access to this database in order to see information on a product or service, to provide information about themselves to the business, and to conduct transactions such as placing online orders and paying for them. This chapter discusses some of the most fundamental database concepts in the context of the MySQL database.

Chapter 10, PHP and MySQL for Client-Server Database Interaction, once again proves the old maxim that sometimes the whole is greater than the sum of its parts. The real power of PHP programs to dynamically generate an unlimited number of pages that change over time without the web developer changing the program can be exploited with the help of web databases. These databases can be continuously updated through automatic or human-assisted data collection programs. For example, the website of amazon.com makes suggestions such as, "Those who purchased this item also purchased the following items." Such purchase-inducing suggestions can be generated using information retrieved from a database consisting of all purchase records. Or, we can have a store manager enter new products and information about them, such as their descriptions, prices, and pictures of the items. A PHP program can then read the information from a database and dynamically create an online catalog, prepare an invoice for a user's purchase order, accept payment from the user and provide the user with a comforting confirmation of payment, and then (finally) send the order information to the warehouse for processing. An introduction to the interaction of PHP and a MySQL database is covered in this chapter.

Chapter 11, XML (eXtensible Markup Language) for Data Description, introduces XML, the high-level, data-driven markup language that is fast becoming the "lingua franca" of the World Wide Web. One of the difficulties in web communication is the wide variety of formats that have been (and still are) used to represent the many kinds of data that appear all over the Internet. XML represents the best attempt yet to provide all web users with a standardized way of representing most, if not all, forms of data. We have already discussed how HTML was "rewritten" as an XML "application" and became XHTML, for example. This illustrates how XML may be regarded as a *metalanguage* for describing a wide variety of other languages. Business applications can use those languages to communicate and exchange data on the Web. We may also use it in a similar way to describe the kind of data we deal with in our online business. In this chapter we will again study just some of the basics of this powerful new technology and then suggest how you may wish to employ it to describe your own business data.

Chapter 12, **Collecting, Analyzing, and Using Visitor Data**, discusses some techniques, such as the collection of web logs for collecting information about the browsing and buying habits of your customers. That information can be put to use in various ways, from enhancing the experience of users when they visit your website, to encouraging your customers to explore other parts of your website and perhaps make additional purchases.

The text is designed to be most useful for students who enjoy a hands-on learning experience, with a need-to-know approach to the introduction of new topics. This is consistent with our view that the bulk of what we discuss should be directly applicable to the development of the website for our simple sample business that proceeds throughout the text.

All the web pages and programs have been tested and appear on the accompanying CD-ROM. Many of the programs require certain facilities on an actual web server. With each sample web page and program we explicitly point out what is new and useful about that particular program, and often add extra material to summarize, or place into context, the feature(s) currently being illustrated.

There are also some files provided on the CD-ROM with the book that cannot be viewed in the browser as they require server-side computing that includes execution of PHP programs as well as database manipulations. Some readers may be ready to install the necessary software packages, copy the CD-ROM files to appropriate directories, import the database, and start experimenting with all of the programs and web pages. Others may want to keep their existing system intact and would like to have a sandbox to play in. For these readers, we recommend installation of VirtualBox: https://www.virtualbox.org/. VirtualBox is an open source product from Oracle Corporation that allows people to run another operating system in a virtual environment within their existing operating system. In the context of this textbook, readers can run our fully setup Linux system from their Windows or any other operating system. The website for the textbook, go.jblearning.com/scobey, provides instructions on how to install VirtualBox.

The use of a real-world commercial enterprise will help students understand the importance of using these features in an e-commerce environment. The website also includes links to the additional resources mentioned in the exercises, as well as links to the necessary public domain and proprietary software.

Each chapter has five important end-matter sections:

1. ***Quick Questions to Test Your Basic Knowledge*** is a group of questions that have short answers that can be found in, or deduced from, the current chapter material. Instructors may download the answers to these questions at go.jblearning.com/scobey.

2. ***Short Exercises to Improve Your Basic Understanding*** are short activities that usually involve some hands-on effort and are based on the material in the current chapter. Not all of these exercises have "answers," because some of them simply direct students to perform certain actions to gain familiarity or see the result, but those that do have a "solution" of some kind are also available to instructors at go.jblearning.com/scobey.

3. ***Exercises on the Parallel Project*** are activities involving the project each student will have chosen to run in parallel with the one in the text, and in which he or she implements, in that chosen project, the same (or similar) features seen in the sample project of the text. These exercises are designed to be open ended in the sense that they do not have specific answers, nor will each student or team of students (as the case may be) come up with the same "answer." Indeed, these exercises are posed in such a way that different solutions are practically mandated.

4. ***What Else You May Want or Need to Know*** contains material that should help students consolidate and extend their knowledge and understanding of the current chapter. This material, combined with links from the References, can serve as a springboard for the instructor or student who wishes to go beyond what is presented in the text. An instructor may wish to use something from this section for an additional short class presentation or as the basis for additional assignments or projects for students.

5. ***References*** will contain, for the most part, links to websites that give further details or explanations of the topics covered in the current chapter.

With the book organized into twelve chapters, an intense three-month course could cover the entire text at the rate of approximately one chapter per week. The first couple of chapters could easily be covered more quickly, depending on the background and maturity of the audience, and individual instructors may want to spend more than a week on one or more of the later chapters.

In any case, a course delivered at this pace would necessarily need to omit much of the material in the *What Else You May Want or Need to Know* sections. However, if most or all of this material is used to supplement the core material, and a more leisurely pace is followed, there is enough material in the text for two courses that would span two semesters, with the split occurring at the end of either Chapter 6 or Chapter 7. If an instructor desires to cover fewer topics in greater detail in a single course, Chapters 11 and 12 could be omitted, and this is an option that has worked well for one of the authors during class testing of the text material. Information technology courses could use the same sequences, but focus on the e-commercial design and perhaps leave some of the programming-based activities to their more technically-oriented compatriots.

Additional resources are provided for instructor download at go.jblearning.com/scobey. These include PowerPoint Lecture Outlines, Answers to End-of-Chapter Questions and Exercises, a Test Bank, and a PowerPoint Image Bank.

Constructive criticism of any kind is always welcomed by the authors. In particular, specific suggestions for clarification in the wording, changes in the order of topics, or the inclusion or exclusion of any particular items that would contribute to the overall goals of the text are appreciated.

Porter Scobey and Pawan Lingras
Department of Mathematics and Computing Science
Saint Mary's University
Halifax, Nova Scotia
Canada   B3H 3C3

Porter Scobey   Voice: (902)420-5790   E-mail: porter.scobey@smu.ca
Pawan Lingras   Voice: (902)420-5798   E-mail: pawan.lingras@gmail.com
For either author   Fax: (902)420-5035

Acknowledgments

The authors would like to thank the many colleagues, family, and friends who have supported and encouraged them during the writing of this text. In particular, we thank the students who helped us class test the text and provided helpful feedback. Special thanks are due to Sanjiv Jagota and Nature's Source for the images and data that were helpful in modeling the e-commerce website. Thank you also to the following reviewers who provided valuable feedback on the manuscript: Stephen Brinton,

Gordon College; Lixin Tao, Pace University; David Tucker, Edinboro University; and Venkat N. Gudivada, Marshall University. Finally, to Tim Anderson, Senior Acquisitions Editor; Amy Bloom, Managing Editor; and Tiffany Sliter, Production Editor, of Jones & Bartlett Learning. We extend our gratitude for their patient help and understanding during the preparation of the book.

Typographic and Other Conventions

This section contains a summary of the typographic styles we use throughout the text to identify various entities, including a list of our file extension conventions.

1. A *slant font like this* is used for *technical terms* (and possibly variations thereof) that are appearing either for the first time, or later in a different context, or perhaps to call your attention to the term again for some reason.

2. An *italic font like this* is used for emphasizing *short* words, phrases, and occasionally sentences of a *nontechnical* nature.

3. A `typewriter-like monospaced font like this` is used for all code, for showing input to and output from programs, for links, and for showing contents of text files.

4. **A bold font like this is used from time to time for a longer passage that is of particular importance, either in context, or for the longer term.** It may also be used to emphasize the name of a software program, like **HTML-Kit**, or the name of an organization or company, like **W3C** or **Microsoft**, and help it to stand out from the surrounding text in a particular context, if required. This font is also used to refer to other sections of the text, such as **References**.

5. Table 1 shows the file extension conventions that we will follow in this text. Most source code files will have the name of the file in a comment as the first line of the file, unless such a comment is not permitted to be the first line in a file, which may be the case for XML files. This first comment line may be followed by a second comment on one or more lines, indicating briefly the

File contents	File extension
Ordinary text files	`.txt`
(X)HTML markup	`.html`
Cascading Style Sheet rules	`.css`
JavaScript code	`.js`
XML markup	`.xml`
PHP code	`.php`
A textfile of comma-separated values	`.csv`
An image file, usually a screen capture	`.jpg`

Table 1

File types and their corresponding file extensions.

contents of the file or the purpose of the code in that file. Exceptions to this convention are those very simple files we use to begin the discussion of some topics.

6. Each figure in the text that shows either the full or partial contents of a file, or the display of a file as it would appear in a browser window, is accompanied by two pieces of information:

- The full pathname of the relevant file (including the files that are display images)

- A caption detailing the (possibly partial) contents of the file (or what the display image is showing you)

All of these files are provided on the CD-ROM included with the text. For these files there are two relevant subdirectories at the root level of the CD-ROM:

- **graphics**, which contains all of the browser display images (in **jpg** format) that are used in the text to illustrate the discussion. (It should be noted that all browser display images are presented in minimalist form, with all browser toolbars collapsed, except the main menu toolbar, to minimize the display area required in the text.)

- **cdrom**, which contains all of our website XHTML and CSS files, image files, JavaScript and PHP Scripts, and data for our MySQL database.

CHAPTER 1

Setting the Scene

CHAPTER CONTENTS

1.1   Overview and Objectives

While the *Internet* has been around for more than four decades, its usage has exploded since the advent of the *World Wide Web* in the early 1990s. From a web developer's point of view, the web technologies of that time were very simple, mostly consisting of *HyperText Markup Language* (*HTML*) in its most basic form. Almost everything that one needed to know could be explained in a book of modest size. The technologies have since proliferated beyond anyone's expectations, and it is now impossible for any individual to be an expert in everything that is used in website development around the world.

In this book we will make an attempt to capture the essential features of several technologies one can use to launch a career as a web developer. The aim is to provide sufficient information about web development without overwhelming the reader. We will use the example of an e-commerce business and demonstrate that the core knowledge contained in this book can indeed be used to develop credible websites.

At the end of this chapter, we list the various technologies that will be covered in this book, and also mention a few alternate competing technologies that we will not discuss, just to give you a sense of what is "out there."

Beginning with this one, each chapter of this text ends with a collection of activities to be performed, and other follow-up material. The first of these sections contains "short-answer questions to test your basic knowledge" (of the material directly covered in the current chapter). Next comes a section of "short exercises to improve your basic understanding" (of the procedures discussed in the current chapter). These exercises will be mostly of the hands-on variety.

Then there is the key section covering "exercises on the parallel project." This will be an ongoing project throughout the text, which will allow you to develop a website whose content will be of your own choosing, but whose functionality will parallel that of the major example we introduce in the text and continue to develop from chapter to chapter.

There is also a section on "what else you may want or need to know." This section provides additional material, however brief, on some topics that were not covered, or perhaps merely mentioned, in the chapter itself, and either directly supplements that material or suggests follow-up action that you might take to extend and consolidate your knowledge. Pursuing these additional resources can help you to achieve a higher level of sophistication in the use of those technologies described in the chapter, or to explore some of the alternate competing technologies. Time constraints may not permit you to complete all of the suggested activities in this "what else" group, but we hope to provide sufficient direction so that the book will not only help you ramp up to the information superhighway, but also give you pointers on going the distance if you wish to do so.

A final section on references will contain links to websites of interest, where you are most likely to find the most up-to-date information on any particular topic.

In this chapter we will do the following:

- Distinguish between the Internet and the World Wide Web

- Explain client-server architectures, illustrated by web browsers and web servers

- Discuss how web browsers and servers communicate

- Take a brief look at a real-world e-commerce website

- Outline the technologies we will discuss in this text, and mention a few of the competing technologies that we will not discuss

1.2 What Is the Internet?

The *Internet* is a world-wide collection of computers and other devices connected by various means such as copper wire, fiber optics, and wireless communications of various kinds. Businesses, governments, organizations, schools and universities, private homes, and "people on the go" are all "connected to the Internet," or "wired."

The Internet came into existence at the end of the 1960s, driven by a cold war desire of the U.S. military to have a secure means of communication in the event of nuclear war. Initial development was under the auspices of the ARPA (Advanced Research Projects Agency), and what eventually became "The Internet" was called ARPANET in the beginning. The first developments were performed by a small number of research institutions funded by ARPA, but by the late 1970s and early 1980s several other networks had been developed. With the growing interest of businesses and private individuals, over one million computers had been connected by 1992. The Internet has continued to expand at rates that are difficult to measure, but it has clearly become ubiquitous, in much of the "developed" world at least.

1.3   What Is the World Wide Web (WWW)?

The *World Wide Web* is a "software infrastructure" consisting of many different communication standards for gaining access to, and exchanging information over, the Internet. Many different kinds of computer software applications that run on computers connected to the Internet use those communication standards to provide that access and/or make those exchanges. The presence of a *web browser* is the most familiar sign that access to the World Wide Web, or just "the Web," is available.

The development of what eventually became the World Wide Web was started in the late 1980s by Tim Berners-Lee and others at CERN (the French acronym for the European Laboratory for Nuclear Research). The idea was to use the notion of *hypertext* so that scientific documents could be made available over the Internet to anyone who had a connected computer. The term *hypertext* refers to the "linking" of documents to one another in such a way that one can easily go from viewing one document to viewing another related document via a "link" to that other document that appears in the first document. The *HyperText Markup Language* (*HTML*) was developed for the purpose of describing the structure of documents that would be made available, and "browsers" with simple text-based interfaces (Lynx being one of the better known ones) were used to retrieve and display the documents. It was not until Mosaic, the first widely used browser with a *Graphical User Interface* (*GUI*), was developed that the World Wide Web really took off. The rest, as everyone now knows, is history.

1.4   What Is Meant by a Client-Server Architecture?

The *client-server architecture* is one approach to communication between two software applications that usually (but not always) reside on physically distinct machines. In typical client-server communication a *client machine* first sends a request to a *server machine*. The server then either honors the request by returning to the client whatever was requested, or returns an error that indicates why the request could not be honored. At least this is the ideal response, and when an error is returned it is up to the software (and perhaps a user) on the client side to decide what happens next.

1.5 How Do Web Browsers and Web Servers Fit the Client-Server Model?

In the client-server context of the Web, a "web browser" is a "client program" that a user employs to contact, over the Internet, other computers that are running "server software" and are therefore capable of responding to requests sent by a browser for information to be displayed in the browser window. At the time of writing (2010) Microsoft®'s Internet Explorer™ is still the most widely used web browser, but Firefox™, Opera™, and Safari™(among others) are also widely used. Google®'s web browser, Chrome™, has also entered the competition, and by the time you read this there may well be other new arrivals.

The term "web server" is potentially confusing because sometimes it refers to a software program, and sometimes it refers to the computer on which that program runs. Just knowing this should help you to tell from the context which one is being referenced in any given situation. In either case, the "web server" is the server side of the client-server architecture in the context of the Web, and it is the program (or the machine) that responds to requests from browsers. At the time of writing the most popular web server is the open-source Apache, but Microsoft's IIS (Internet Information Server™) is widely used by those in the Microsoft camp.

1.6 How Do Web Browsers and Web Servers Communicate?

In this section, we will look at a number of concepts that are necessary to understand if we are to get a sense of how web browsers and web servers communicate with each other.

1.6.1 Web Protocols and Layered Communication Architectures

Communication protocol A *communication protocol* is simply an agreement by two or more parties about what rules will be followed when communications between or among the parties take place. Humans use (mostly informal) protocols all the time when communicating. Think for example, of making a simple telephone call: A caller dials the number, the phone at the other end rings, a person picks up the receiver and says "Hello," the caller identifies himself or herself and states the purpose of the call, the recipient responds, the caller says "Thank you. Goodbye." and hangs up, and the recipient then hangs up as well. That's a "protocol" in action.

Web protocol A *web protocol* is, similarly, an agreed-upon set of rules and data formats to be used when two or more computers or other devices, or application programs running on those machines, wish to communicate across the Internet, usually but not always on behalf of human users. In any given communication it is likely that there will be several different protocols involved.

Common web protocols There are many protocols in use on the Web. Here is a very short list of some of the more common ones:

- *TCP/IP*, a two-part protocol (*Transmission Control Protocol/Internet Protocol*) that underlies pretty much everything that travels over the Web. This is the low-level "lingua franca" of the World Wide Web. If TCP/IP went away tomorrow, the Web would cease to exist. One of the reasons it is so widely used is that it guarantees delivery of the information that was sent.

- *UDP*, another protocol (*User Datagram Protocol*) that can also be used as the underlying transport protocol for information, and though it may be faster to use if you are moving large multimedia files (for example), it does not guarantee that all of the information will arrive safely. This may not be an important consideration if you do not care that your final photograph is missing a pixel or two.

- *HTTP*, the *HyperText Transfer Protocol* that browsers use to send requests for information to servers and that a server uses to send the requested information back to a browser.

- *FTP*, the *File Transfer Protocol* used to transfer files from one computer to another across the Internet.

- *TELNET* and *SSH* are both protocols that can provide "terminal emulation" when used to connect, over the Internet, to a remote computer and log in to an account on that computer. TELNET (*TELephone NETwork*) has been around for many years, but its use is discouraged these days because of security concerns, in favor of SSH (*Secure SHell*).

Layered communication architectures One difficulty with trying to understand how things happen on the Web is that there are so many of these web protocols, and often it is not clear which ones are in play. A second difficulty arises from the fact that all these protocols are just parts of a much "bigger picture."

In a nutshell, any communication over the Internet between two computers can be viewed in the following way: Data starts in an application on the first computer, "trickling down" to the actual hardware on that machine, passing over the Internet to the hardware of the second computer, then "bubbling up" to the application running on that second machine that is expecting it. If the second application replies, the process is reversed. On each machine, the data passes through several communication "layers."

There are different models of these layers, including the seven-layer *Open Systems Interconnect Model* and the four-layer *Internet Model*. Much more could be said about these models, and the many protocols that are found at the various layers within them, but it would take us too far afield. The average web developer does not need to know any more about them than you now know (but see the suggestions for follow-up in the end-of-chapter material).

1.6.2   Web Addresses and Address Resolution via DNS

Just as a letter being sent by regular mail needs to have the address of its destination affixed if it is not to go astray, so does a request for information sent from a browser out on the Internet need to supply the "address" of the recipient to which the request is being sent.

> **IP addresses** Every computer attached to the Internet has a unique *IP address*, which has the form `a.b.c.d`, where each of the values `a`, `b`, `c`, and `d` is a positive integer in the range `0..255`, and the intervening periods are a required part of the syntax. Since this allows for just over 4 billion different 32-bit addresses, we are soon to run out, and another scheme must be implemented (the IPv6 scheme, which is currently under development, and which will provide many more Internet addresses). Organizations, businesses, educational institutions, governments, and even countries are issued blocks of these IP addresses, which are then redistributed "internally" by the recipients.

> **Fully qualified domain names** So, though a computer will find it very convenient to work with a numerical "address" like `123.234.235.236`, humans prefer names to numbers since they are usually easier to remember. Thus a

computer with the preceding address may also have a name, or, more accurately and completely, a *fully qualified domain name* or *FQDN*, which could be something of the form

```
www.mysite.yourhost.com
```

if it's a commercial website, or

```
someschool.downyonder.edu
```

if it's an educational site.

Host machines and domains The characters following the last period of an FQDN indicate the largest "domain" to which that name belongs, and can be a country code, such as `ca` for Canada, or one of a small number of specific designations, such as `.edu` for an educational institution, `.com` for a commercial enterprise, `.gov` for government, or `.org` for an organization (essentially noncommercial) of some kind. The name at the left of the domain name (i.e., to the left of the first period) is generally the name of the host machine, and as one proceeds from left to right through the domain name, the succeeding names represent larger and larger domains to which that host machine belongs.

The domain name system and domain name servers Because humans tend to use FQDNs and computers will use the actual numerical IP address when communicating with one another, there has to be a system to convert addresses from one form to the other. This is the *Domain Name System (DNS)*, and the machines connected to the Internet that perform the service of "resolving" any FQDN to its corresponding IP address are called *Domain Name Servers* (for which the acronym is also *DNS*), or simply "name servers." Although it is possible to use IP addresses directly when "surfing the Web" few humans would do so, so this process of "address resolution" is a very important part of what goes on as part of the traffic over the Web.

1.6.3   URLs, URNs, and URIs

The most frequently encountered of these three acronyms is (probably) URL, then URI, and finally (and much less frequently, if at all) URN, though this may be changing.

Uniform Resource Locator (URL) A URL is, as its name suggests, a *uniform* (or "standard") way of referring to the *location* of a web document (or, more generally, to the location of a web *resource* of whatever kind). Naturally, therefore, the fully qualified domain name of the host machine on which the resource is located forms an integral part of the URL for that resource. However, it is not enough to know *where* the resource is located. One must also know, and be able to specify, *how* the resource will be accessed (i.e., the method, or *protocol*, that will be used to access the resource). After all, not every web "resource" is just a page to be displayed. So, a URL quite often has the form

```
scheme:address_of_resource
```

in which `scheme` is, more often than not, the familiar `http` (though it could very well be something else, such as `ftp`), and `address_of_resource` itself has the following form:

```
//fully_qualified_domain_name/path_from_document_root/
   name_of_resource
```

Thus, if you enter something very typical, like

```
http://cs.smu.ca/jobs/2011/current.html
```

into your browser's "address window" and click on Go or press Enter, you are saying you want to retrieve the document `current.html` using the `http` protocol scheme, from the server whose fully qualified domain name is `cs.smu.ca`. The forward slash (`/`) immediately following `cs.smu.ca` refers to the directory on that host which is the host's *document root* (the main directory where the web server stores files that it can serve to requesting browsers). This directory may, of course, also have lots of subdirectories that also contain "servable" files, and which help to keep the website organized. The rest of the path (starting from the document root, wherever it might be located, which is something we cannot determine from the URL) is `jobs/2011/`, and the final item is the name of the actual desired resource, `current.html`. Sometimes you will see a URL that looks like

```
http://cs.smu.ca/~porter/jobs/2011/current.html
```

in which the *tilde* symbol (~) indicates that the name `porter` is the name of a user on the host system and that `cs.smu.ca/~porter/` is the *home directory* (or *personal document root*) for this particular user on this server.

Uniform Resource Name (URN) A URN is a name that has the same form as a URL, but may not identify an actual location on the Internet. So, a URN can be used to talk about something without implying its location or indicating how to get at the particular resource referenced by the name.

Uniform Resource Identifier (URI) A URI is a more general concept than either a URL or a URN. According to Wikipedia®[1], the "contemporary" viewpoint is that URLs and URNs are both "context-dependent aspects of a URI and rarely need to be distinguished." In fact, it is suggested in the same Wikipedia article that the term URL may be falling into disuse, since it is "rarely necessary to distinguish between URIs and URLs," and the more "user-friendly" term "web address" is now more frequent in any case.

1.7   A Real-World E-Commerce Website

The bold prediction from the 1990s that "If your business is not on the World Wide Web, you will soon not be in business" still contains a certain ring of truth today. A lack of web presence may not drive a small business with a loyal clientele and ongoing word of mouth advertising out of business. However, many such businesses have established a web presence to communicate information to their clients and attract new customers. This book will discuss technologies that can be used to add increasing levels of sophistication to the web presence of a business.

Let us look at the well-developed e-commerce site of Jones & Bartlett Learning (publisher of this book) to understand various aspects of an e-commercial website.

Figure 1.1 shows the home page of Jones & Bartlett Learning. The top-left corner has the logo of the company and at the top-right is a "search window" that allows the user to search for items of interest on the website.

A menu of various options appears on the toolbar below the logo. These options are typical of most commercial websites. They allow you to get more information about the company, contact the company, shop for their books, and obtain help. The rest of the page includes information about the products and links to obtain more information about them.

---

[1]See `http://en.wikipedia.org/wiki/Uniform_Resource_Identifier`.

FIGURE 1.1

graphics/ch01/jbHome.jpg
The home page of Jones & Bartlett Learning (publisher of this text) at
http://www.jblearning.com/.

The graphics and layout of the page are specified using HyperText Markup Language (HTML) or Extensible HyperText Markup Language (XHTML). We will be studying the essential features of XHTML in Chapter 3. If you choose different options, you will notice that the basic layout of the site remains consistent as you move from one part of the site to another. Such a consistent presentation is best achieved by the use of Cascading Style Sheets (CSS), which are described in Chapter 4. If you hover your mouse over any one of the menu options, the bar below shows you submenu items. Usually, such dynamic behavior is achieved with JavaScript®, the topic of Chapter 7. JavaScript also allow us to provide simple animations such as rotating images that appear under the "Featured Titles" on the J&B home page.

If we click on any one of the categories and choose a book title, we will be entering the realm of e-commerce, as shown in Figure 1.2. Not only can we get detailed information about the book, we can also add it to our "shopping cart."

If we decided to buy multiple titles, we would get an invoice such as the one shown in Figure 1.3. We have decided to purchase two copies of one of the books and one

FIGURE 1.2

graphics/ch01/jbBook.jpg
A web page display showing one of many book titles from Jones & Bartlett Learning.

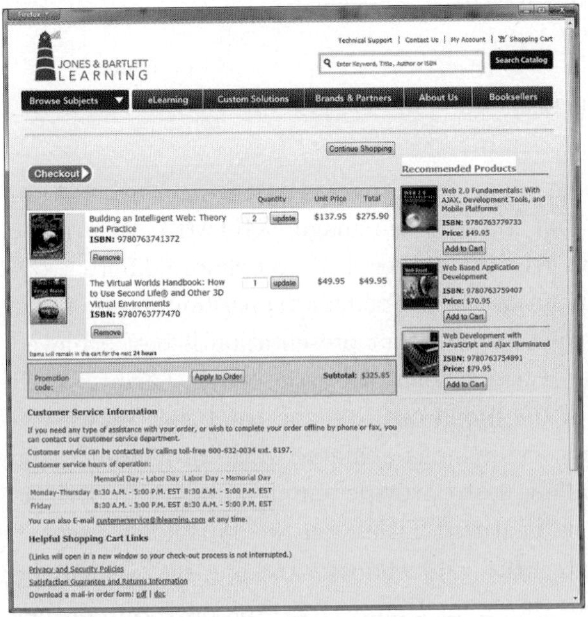

FIGURE 1.3

graphics/ch01/jbCheckout.jpg
An invoice page from the Jones & Bartlett Learning site showing the purchase of two titles.

copy of another book. The web page has several fields that allow us to enter values, such as "Quantity" of each book. This kind of "form processing" will be discussed in Chapter 7. An invoice like this is dynamically generated using web programming with languages such as Perl or (in our case) PHP. The information used to create an invoice comes both from the user and from a database that is internal to the J&B website. We will see how PHP and a popular database package called MySQL®can be used to generate such invoices for our fictional business in Chapters 9 and 10.

1.8   What Are the Technologies We Will Discuss?

Our goal in this text is to familiarize you with most of the basic principles underlying website development. At the same time, you need to be aware that the implementation of those principles on an actual website can be performed in various ways, and we will have the time and space to introduce only some of the implementation technologies.

Our approach is to take the *open-source* route, which means that we shall have the distinct advantage of being able to use a lot of "production quality" free software applications and utilities. This kind of software should never be regarded as inferior for the simple reason that it is free. In fact, software often tends to be one of the great counterexamples to the old saying, "You get what you pay for." With open-source software, history shows that you often get much more than you pay for. And the hard truth is that you may get bad software no matter how much you pay for it. As always, the safest rule to follow is: Buyer beware! This applies, of course, whether or not you have actually "bought" anything.[2]

After our brief introduction to the Web in this chapter, and once we have dealt with the nitty gritty of actually "getting onto the Web" in the next chapter, we will start our discussion of the following web technologies, in the order listed:

- *HTML* (*HyperText Markup Language*) and *XHTML* (*eXtensible HTML*) will provide us with a way to describe the *structure* of each document we wish to place on our website.

- *CSS* (*Cascading Style Sheets*) will allow us to give each of our web documents a presentational style.

---

[2]Software that is actually free should not be confused with *shareware*, which is software that (usually) you may use without restriction for a while, but you are required to pay for it eventually if you continue to use it. This requirement is often based on the honor system, and whether the developer gets paid is thus dependent on the integrity of the user.

- Web forms give our website visitors a chance to enter data that we can use in conducting business transactions with those visitors.

- *JavaScript* is a "client-side" programming language for performing computations and input data validation, as well as user interactivity, in the browser context. (See the next two items as well.)

- *DOM* is the *Document Object Model*, which provides a tree-like structural model of a web document, and an API (*Application Programming Interface*) so that languages like JavaScript can access and modify parts of a web page during and after its display, often under user control.

- *DHTML* (stands for *Dynamic HTML*, which is what the combined usage of XHTML, CSS, JavaScript, and the DOM is generally called) is another acronym you will often encounter in the context of producing interactivity for the browser user, but it is not really a separate technology.

- *PHP* (*PHP: Hypertext Preprocessor*, originally *Personal Home Page*) is a server-side programming language that permits the creation, on the server, by running a PHP program (or *script*), web pages whose content can vary each time that page is created.

- *MySQL* is the implementation of a relational database system, which can be used to store virtually any kind of business data, and that we can access and use on our websites.

- Web access to a MySQL database on a server can be performed by a PHP program on that server and controlled from our website.

- *XML* (stands for *eXtensible Markup Language*) provides a text-based and very flexible way of describing data of any kind and, together with some associated technologies, permits such data to be easily transferred between all manner of applications, on and off the Web.

- *DTD* stands for *Document Type Definition*, a frequently used method for validation of XML documents.

- *XSLT* stands for *eXtensible Stylesheet Language Transformations*, a language for transforming an XML file in various ways, including into XHTML for display in a browser.

- Collection and analysis of website visitor data on the server via such techniques as web logs and cookies.

Some of the above technologies are absolutely essential for any web developer to know (XHTML, or at least HTML, CSS, and JavaScript, for example). Others simply represent one of several alternatives among competing technologies, albeit ones that are widely used and excellent choices to do what they do. For example, we have chosen to discuss the PHP programming language but another excellent choice would be *Perl*, which is an older, but very powerful and flexible, programming language that uses something called the *Common Gateway Interface* (*CGI*) for performing the same kinds of actions for which we will use PHP.

All of the technologies we will discuss are freely available, either automatically simply because you have installed a web browser, or by downloading the appropriate software from the Internet. There are many additional options we will not discuss that are also freely available (including Perl). However, there is an equally large number of proprietary solutions available from companies like **Microsoft** (*Active Server Pages*™, or *ASP*) and *Flash*® from **Adobe**®. Flash was formerly a Macromedia product, but Adobe has acquired Macromedia.

1.9 Summary

In this chapter, we looked at some of the key concepts of interest to those approaching web development. These included the Internet, the World Wide Web itself, web servers, and web browsers. We also gained some insight into communication on the Web and discussed some of the major protocols, such as TCP/IP and HTTP. We also learned about IP addresses, Fully Qualified Domain Names, and how Domain Name Servers are used to convert one to the other. We also distinguished between URLs, URNs, and URIs. Finally, we got a glimpse of an actual e-commerce website. We closed the chapter by summarizing the technologies that will be used to develop various features that one encounters in many e-commerce websites, including XHTML, CSS, JavaScript, MySQL, PHP, and XML.

1.10 Quick Questions to Test Your Basic Knowledge

In this section of each chapter you will find questions that invite short answers, and you should be able to find those answers directly in, or at least infer those answers directly from, the material in the current chapter.

1. What are three different ways computers can be "connected" to one another? The fact that "connected" is enclosed in quotes is a hint to one of the ways.

2. What is the difference between the Internet and the World Wide Web?

3. If each decade is divided into two "periods," an "early half" and a "late half" (early 90s and late 90s, for example), in what period was the Internet "invented," and in what period was the World Wide Web "invented"?

4. If a friend tells you she has just used `ftp`, what has she probably done?

5. What are the names and brief descriptions of each part of the URL shown below?
   `http://cs.smu.ca/~pawan/opinions/comments.txt`

6. What does the acronym ARPANET stand for, and what is its relation to the Internet?

7. What is the acronym for the underlying protocol that is used nearly universally these days to move information across the Internet, and what does that acronym stand for?

8. When and why might you find it useful to use UDP?

9. What are the two web browsers that currently have the most users?

10. What is the difference between a URL, a URN, and a URI?

11. What was the name of the first widely used text-based browser, and the name of the first widely used GUI-based browser?

12. What is an FQDN, and how does it relate to an IP address?

13. Can you give an example of a valid IP address and an invalid IP address and state why the first is valid and the second is not?

1.11   Short Exercises to Improve Your Basic Understanding

In this section of each chapter you will find short, mostly hands-on, exercises that ask you to perform activities based on the material of the current chapter.

1. Find a computer connected to the Internet with at least two web browsers installed on it. Choose several different websites (the home pages of Microsoft,

Google, Adobe, and YouTube®, for example). Use each browser to visit each of those pages and note any differences between the appearance of each page from one browser to the next. This is a good way to convince yourself that the "web experience" is not yet as consistent as we might like it to be. It is also a good way to convince you at the outset that we must always be vigilant in constructing our web pages to be as certain as we can be that we have minimized any differences that will be seen by visitors to our web pages who happen to be using different web browsers.

2. On the basis of the preceding exercise, formulate a *best practice* that you (and *all* web developers) should follow consistently.

3. Locate a real-world e-commerce website (other than the Jones & Bartlett Learning site of this chapter) that actually sells products online. Browse the site as though you were going to be an actual customer, choosing items and placing them in the site's "shopping cart," perhaps deleting some items along the way, and then proceeding to check out before canceling the transaction. This will give you a sense of where we are heading in our discussions in the rest of this book.

1.12   Exercises on the Parallel Project

Since this is the first chapter, and the first group of exercises of this type, we need to say a few words about what we mean by the "parallel project."

Beginning in Chapter 2 we will be using the example of a business that sells health products online to illustrate all of the topics for web development that we discuss. This example will extend throughout the text, and we want you to develop your own "parallel business" and its corresponding "parallel website" by implementing the same functionality for your business and website that you see in our text example.

So, let's get started.

1. The first thing you need to do is think about what kind of "business" you would like to run, and for which you would like to develop a website. Our only restrictions[3] are that it cannot be an online store for health products (our own main example) or for books (we also use the publisher of our text in a few early examples). It is worth giving some thought to this choice, since you will

---

[3]The institutional environment in which you are working may have other restrictive criteria of which we cannot possibly be aware, but of which *you* should be aware. Decency, for example, or political correctness.

be committed to it for the rest of your work with this text, unless you want to make major and time-consuming changes mid-stream. If you know of an actual existing business that does not have a website and would like one, that too is a possibility to consider.

2. Having chosen the type of your business, you now need to "flesh it out" by making at least these additional choices:

   a) A name for your business (Think of this as something that would eventually go in the header of the home page of the website for your business.)

   b) A short "mission statement" for your business, perhaps including a short "back story" as well, telling how your business got started (a chance to let your imagination run wild) (Think of this as something a visitor might find under the "About Us" link on your site.)

   c) A short list of some of your products and/or services, which will eventually be made available for purchase online (This item speaks for itself.)

   d) A short descriptive paragraph or list of phrases designed to catch the attention of potential customers (Think of this as something that might eventually appear as part of the main content area of the home page for your business.)

3. Once you have made the above choices, enter them into a text file called `my_business.txt`. Make sure that the file content is well organized from a conceptual point of view, and pay particular attention to spelling and grammar. You can never assume that your viewers (and potential customers) will not be put off by bad spelling and poor grammar. Also, be prepared to submit this file for approval in some way that will be described by your instructor if you are required to do so.

1.13   What Else You May Want or Need to Know

This section of each chapter may contain items that simply extend or enhance material in the chapter in some way, questions for which you may need to search elsewhere for the answers, or further exercises to help you consolidate and extend your knowledge and understanding of the chapter material and possibly how it relates to the material of one or more other chapters. A Google search may often be useful.

1. There are probably more web browsers than you thought there were. Try to name ten different web browsers and the platform(s) on which they run (since some browsers are available on more than one platform).

2. During the early days of the Web, many people used things that had names like Gopher, Veronica, Archie, and Jughead. What were these "technologies" and why are we no longer using them today?

3. What does the acronym W3C stand for?

4. What is the IETF and what does it do?

5. In the context of the Internet, what does the acronym RFC stand for, and what role does an RFC play in the ongoing development of the Internet?

6. The two HTTP *request methods* that are most often used in communication between web browsers and web servers are GET and POST. Describe briefly the main difference between them. We will come back to these much later in the text, but you may wish to explore them now for a sneak preview.

7. What are some of the other, less frequently used, HTTP request methods and for what purpose is each one used?

8. When an HTTP request is made by a browser to a server, a *status code* is returned by the server to the browser. Often the user does not see, and may not even be aware, of these status codes. But ... what is (probably) the most commonly encountered HTTP status code that an average user will actually see?

9. Name the seven layers of the *Open Systems Interconnect Model*, as well as the four layers of the *Internet Model*, and indicate where the two models "match up."

10. We mentioned that the part of a URL to the right of the rightmost period in the URL is the "largest domain" in that URL and is generally either a two-letter *country code*, like ca for Canada or au for Australia, or a three-or-more-letter designation like gov for a government department, com for a commercial enterprise, or edu for an educational institution. Newer designations in this last category are gradually being accepted, such as mobi for mobile-compatible sites and travel for travel and tourist industry-related sites.

11. The full syntax of a URL is actually somewhat more complicated than we showed in this chapter. In all its glory it can look something like this:

```
scheme://username:password@domain:port/path?query_string#anchor
```

Here the `username:password@` will be required if the resource is password protected, though the more usual approach is to have the user fill in a *login form* that requires a username and corresponding password. The `:port` part of the URL may be required to indicate the *port number* on which the server is "listening" for requests to access a particular resource. By default, web servers generally listen on port number 80, and other standard services have their own assigned port numbers, so whether this part of the URL is required depends on the situation. The `query_string` that is separated from the `path` portion of the URL by a question mark (**?**) represents some information that is being sent to the server from the browser, and will likely be "processed" by the destination resource on the server. This information might be data from a web page form, for example. We will come back to this later in the text as well. And finally, the `#anchor` represents a special marker on a web page that tells the browser to go to that part of the page and start its display from there rather than from the beginning of the page. If you keep an eye on your browser's address window as you surf the Web, you may see some or all of these features in the URLs that you observe.

12. As you browse the Internet you will of course be using the `http` URI protocol scheme as you visit various sites. But sometimes you wish to open, in your browser, a document or some other "resource" that is located on your own computer. In this case, the corresponding file is not being "served" by a web server; instead it is simply being opened in the browser in much the same way it would be opened by any other program running on your computer. However, there is another protocol scheme that the browser uses to deal with files in this situation, the `file` URI protocol. For example, if you have the file `test.html` on your Windows PC in the location

`C:\MyWork\web\test.html`

and you open this file in your browser and then check your browser's address window you will likely see this:

`file:///C:/MyWork/web/test.html`

Here `file://` corresponds to `http://` in the sense that the general syntax of a URI requires that it start with the name of the protocol scheme, followed by a colon (**:**) and two forward slashes (**//**). The third forward slash may be interpreted as the "top-level directory" of your computer and the rest is just the path down to the file. Note that even though Windows® uses backslashes (\) to separate portions of a path, these have become forward slashes, which is the Linux/Unix way of doing things, and is also the generic format for paths in this context. You may also type a `file` URI directly into your browser address window if you know the local path to the file.

1.14 References

Most of our references are links to Internet sites, including many to Wikipedia. Keep in mind, though, that the Web is a very dynamic place, and sites come and go, or change their URLs. Thus some of the links we provide may have changed or even disappeared when you try them. If this turns out to be the case, you can probably find the new location of the site or a different but comparable site by going to Google and providing a few appropriate search terms. Such is the wonderfully convenient nature of today's World Wide Web. As for Wikipedia itself, we have found it to be a reasonably reliable source of useful and up-to-date information. It is, of course, always a good policy, which we try to follow ourselves and which we recommend to you, to verify the accuracy of any information you get from the Internet or any other source, by comparing what several different sources say about it.

1. You can read about the history of the World Wide Web at this location:

   `http://en.wikipedia.org/wiki/History_of_the_World_Wide_Web`

2. "The World Wide Web Consortium (W3C) is an international community that develops standards to ensure the long-term growth of the Web." This is a quote from their website, which you can find at:

   `http://www.w3.org/`

   From here you can follow links to read about all the Web-related standards the Consortium has approved or has under development.

3. You can find a great deal of information that allows you to compare many different browsers in various ways at the following site:

   `http://en.wikipedia.org/wiki/Comparison_of_web_browsers`

4. The Web Standards Project has prepared some "Acid Tests" browser users can employ if they wish to see how well their browser of choice does in handling web standards. If you're interested, check out this link:

   `http://www.acidtests.org/`

5. The acronym *gTLD* stands for *generic Top Level Domain*. Why is it a small g? Who knows? But you can find a list of country codes for top-level domains that are countries, and a list of the other top-level domains as well, at this location:

   `http://en.wikipedia.org/wiki/List_of_Internet_top-level_domains`

   This should remain a relatively dynamic site, as newer top-level domains get added to the growing pool.

6. For further information on the URL/URN/URI question, check out the following site:

   `http://en.wikipedia.org/wiki/Uniform_Resource_Locator`

7. You can probably find more details on URL syntax than you will ever need to know at this site:

   `http://www.w3.org/Addressing/URL/5_BNF.html`

8. For more information on the `file` scheme for accessing files on your computer with your browser, see:

   `http://en.wikipedia.org/wiki/File_URI_scheme`

CHAPTER 2

Establishing a Web Presence

CHAPTER CONTENTS

2.1   Overview and Objectives

In order to create a professional website, we will have to take time to learn some things about many of the technologies listed in the previous chapter. However, most computing types like to get their feet wet by getting a crude product "out there," and then systematically learning how to make it better. In this chapter, we will get a quick start by creating a website containing only a simple text document. The focus of the chapter is to learn some of the basic steps involved in getting a website "up and running" for the whole world to see, but in the simplest possible way. The following two chapters will focus on content organization and presentation details.

So, in this chapter you will learn the following:

- What an Internet Service Provider is, and what services you can normally expect from one

- What web development tools you need to get started

- How to create a simple, text-only web page

- How to display and test a web page before "going live" (putting your web page on the Web)

- What's involved in putting your web page online

- A little bit about *MIME types* and how browsers use them to determine the kind of document they are asked to process

2.2   What Is an Internet Service Provider (ISP)?

An Internet Service Provider (ISP) is a business or an organization that provides Internet connections for its customers or members by enabling data transmission between computers in workplaces or homes and other computers on the Internet. In most populated areas, these data transmissions take place through physical cables or wires. On the other hand, customers who reside or work in remote locations, or who are "on the road" a lot, may be served using wireless data transmission.

It can be very confusing to read about the various technologies that may be used just to connect to the Internet. It is a world of mysterious acronyms and other arcane terms. Though we will not discuss any of these technologies in detail, and you do not need to know anything about them to become a web developer, you might find it useful to be able to put at least some of them into context if you encounter the terms. We therefore include a sampling of some of the acronyms you might encounter, with brief descriptions of the technologies for which they stand.

Wired Internet service provided by an ISP may come in a variety of technological forms, including:

- Simple dial-up through ordinary phone lines via a modem

- Cable modem service, often provided by the same company that supplies your TV

- *Integrated Services Digital Network (ISDN)*, a set of communication standards that are used for simultaneous digital transmission of voice, video, data, and other network services over the traditional circuits of the public switched telephone network and which has been around since the late 1980s

- *Asymmetric Digital Subscriber Line (ADSL)*, a data communications technology that utilizes frequencies that are not used by a voice telephone call and which enables faster data transmission over copper telephone lines than a conventional voiceband modem can provide

- *Fiber-To-The-Premises (FTTP)*, a generic term that may be used as a generalization of several possible configurations that use optical fiber deployment instead of metal wire for a broadband network architecture to homes or small businesses

And, of course, wireless voice and data communications are evolving on a continuous basis. Access choices of this form include:

- *WiFi*, generally used by PCs or other appropriately enabled devices to access the Internet in homes and offices, or at "Wi-Fi hotspots" in public places, provided a wireless network connected to the Internet is within range

- *Code Division Multiple Access (CDMA)*, a technology that allows several users to share bandwidth of different frequencies (a concept called *multiplexing*)

- *Global System for Mobile* communications (*GSM*), the most popular standard for mobile telephone systems in the world

- *Worldwide interoperability for Microwave Access (WiMAX)*, a telecommunications protocol that provides both fixed and fully mobile Internet access

These options vary greatly in terms of *bandwidth* (rate of data transmission), accessibility, and cost.

As well as providing data transmission, most ISPs provide additional services, which may include e-mail, network data storage, and the opportunity to create a website and "put it up on the Web" so that people around the world may view it if they wish. This ability to create a website is provided by giving you an exclusive URL and a file repository for your web documents. If you are working in a school, college, or university environment, your system administrator can also provide you with a similar ability to create your own website. You will need to consult your ISP, or system administrator, or instructor, or knowledgable friends for more information on your particular local situation.

2.3   What Tools Will You Need to Begin Your Web Development?

Beginners may be surprised at how little one needs to get started with web development. All you really need is a simple text editor and a web browser. You don't even have to be connected to the Internet to get under way.

Many novices who start to work with simple web pages tend to use *What-You-See-Is-What-You-Get* editors. You may have seen their acronym (*WYSIWYG*) in print, or overheard the term in conversation ("whizzy-wig"). These editors allow you to use a graphical user interface to type in the content and press buttons to specify the formatting. The formatted document is saved in a form that is commonly referred to as *HyperText Markup Language*, or *HTML*. HTML was the original specification for creating web pages. However, although HTML is still in widespread use, it has been superseded by a newer standard called *eXtensible HyperText Markup Language* (*XHTML*), and an updated version of HTML itself is currently under development. We will discuss the history of HTML and XHTML in Chapter 3. Also, though we will write our code in XHTML, much of what we say and do will apply equally well to HTML. In fact, unless it is necessary to explicitly distinguish the two, we may even refer, somewhat loosely, to either XHTML or HTML simply as "HTML."

The HTML markup created by WYSIWYG editors[1] tends to be very complicated. It is difficult to modify and enhance such documents at the source level. Therefore, we will be using (and we recommend using) tools that enable us to directly type in both the content and the formatting markup for any given page. One can use any basic

---

[1]Microsoft's FrontPage™ is a good example of a WYSIWYG editor that we would not recommend using, for the reasons that we mention here.

text editor, such as **Notepad**™, **Notepad++**™, or **EditPad Lite**™on Windows®, and **Vim**™or **Emacs**™, or even **pico**™on Linux™or UNIX™systems.

However, there are other text editors that cater to the HTML document family, such as **Bluefish**™, which is available for both UNIX-like systems (including Linux) and Windows, and **HTML-Kit**™[2] for Windows. In addition to helping us create our HTML documents, a text editor will also help us write web programs in different programming languages such as JavaScript and PHP. And while we will not be explicitly discussing the creation of multimedia documents, we will discuss how to embed them in our website. There are many easy-to-use programs for creating image, animation, audio, and video files, and a lot of them are freely available as well. Since new and better ones are appearing all the time, if you need such a program the best thing to do is search the Web using Google or some other search engine to determine what is currently available and recommended.

2.4   How Do You Create a Simple, Static Web Page?

Throughout this text we will be using a running example involving a vastly simplified version of an actual business named **Nature's Source**[3] that serves customers who seek a naturally healthy lifestyle. Our goal will be to present just the essential features of the development of such a website, but you may wish to compare our simplified development with "the real thing" as we proceed.

A typical website consists of a number of documents of various kinds. It is very important to make sure that they are properly organized in a logical directory structure. For example, on our CD-ROM, web documents discussed in this chapter will be in a directory[4] called `web02`.

We start our web development exercise with a document containing simple text only, which we can produce with any text editor. This first document will be called `first.txt` and its contents are shown in Figure 2.1. The line numbers shown in Figure 2.1 are not part of the actual file. They are provided when a file is displayed in the text to make it easier for us to refer to various parts of that file.

---

[2]One of the authors has used the justly renowned "Build 292" of this program extensively and found it very useful. In fact, HTML-Kit was used to format most of the XHTML files you see in this text. We have chosen how we wish to format our XHTML markup, and then had this program do it for us as we compose and test our files. The program is freely available for individual academic use, so students may want to try it.

[3]See `http://www.natures-source.com/`.

[4]We will use the words *directory* and *folder* synonymously.

```
 1                Welcome to the Website of
 2                      Nature's Source
 3
 4    This is our first foray onto the World Wide Web.
 5    We are a small company dedicated to the health
 6    of our customers through natural remedies.
 7
 8    We have a wide range of products that include:
 9
10      - books, and multimedia documents that help you get
11        healthy and stay healthy
12      - herbal medicines
13      - equipment for injury free body toning exercises
```

FIGURE 2.1

cdrom/web02/first.txt

The text file that will be used as the first web page for **Nature's Source**.

As simple as this file of plain text is, it still conveys the basic information we want our potential customers to see. All we have to do now is "put it up on the Web." We will see how to do this shortly. We should point out, however, that this file will not provide very exciting viewing. In fact, it will simply be displayed in the browser window looking just as we typed it in. Also, it will not provide any interaction with the user. For this reason, it is called a *static web page* (as opposed to a *dynamic web page* which *does* provide interaction with the user—by allowing user input or by retrieving and displaying data from a database, for example—and which we will discuss in later chapters).

So, our next task it to make sure we *can* display this file in a browser, which we do in the following section.

2.5   How Do You Test a Web Page "Offline" Before "Going Live"?

It is always a good idea to test a web page before actually putting it on your website, and this can easily be done with most simple documents that do not require computation from a web server by viewing them directly from your hard disk. If you launch your favorite web browser and click on the `File` menu, you will see an option for opening a file. If you choose that option, a "file open dialog box" will appear. Navigate through your directory structure and choose the file `first.txt` from the `web02` directory on the CD-ROM.

Note that we have explicitly said here that you should open your browser first, then navigate to the file and open it from within the browser. In particular, you should *not* double-click on the file to open it. This will almost certainly cause a program other than your browser to open the file (perhaps even the editor you used to create the file). This is because the file has a .txt extension, and most operating systems will try to open such a file with an editor, not a browser, when the file is double-clicked.

File extensions are often used to indicate the MIME type of a file. MIME is an acronym for Multipurpose Internet Mail Extensions, a protocol that was used in the early days of the Internet to help distinguish the various extensions that users wanted to attach to their e-mails. It has since grown to include designations for all of the many kinds of files that appear on the Web and that have to be handled by browsers and other web programs. An explicit MIME type is often sent as part of the communication between browsers and servers and is unseen by users, except for the fact that the kind of file involved in a transaction can often be inferred by looking at the extension (.txt for a text file, .html for an HTML or XHTML file, or .mp3 for an audio file containing a song, for example).

Figure 2.2 shows how first.txt will look in a web browser. The text file we have created looks the same as it did in the editor in which it was created, and there is a good reason for this. The file has a .txt extension, and the browser knows that a file with this extension should be displayed "as is." That is why we formatted the file reasonably well when creating it in the editor.

But even our best formatting efforts applied to a plain text file will leave much to be desired on our web page. For example, we might like to have the header appear in a large bold font at the top of the page. Including some graphics would be a nice

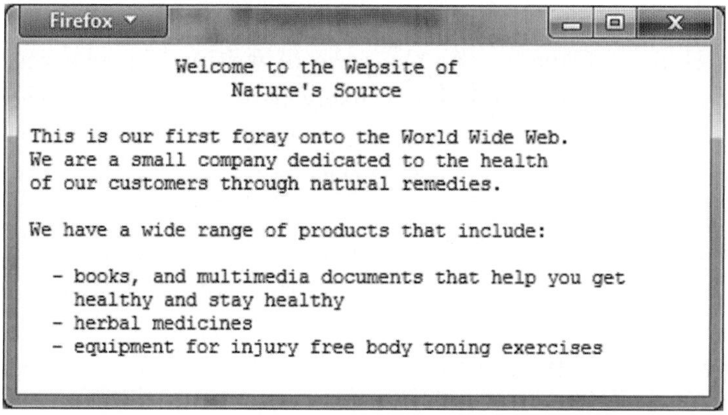

FIGURE 2.2

graphics/ch02/displayFirstTxt.jpg
A display of cdrom/web02/first.txt in the Firefox browser.

touch, and having *hyperlinks* to other documents would make it seem more like a "real" web page. None of this is possible with simple text, but we will look at all of these interesting formatting possibilities, and more, in the next two chapters. For now, let us focus on the mechanics of getting our simple text file to appear as a web page on the World Wide Web.

2.6   How Do You "Go Live" on the Web Once You're Ready?

In order to place our simple text file on the World Wide Web as a "web page," we will obviously need Internet access. This may be obtained through a private *Internet Service Provider (ISP)* or your academic institution. Both the ISP and the institution will have web servers that provide space for users to put their pages on the Web. You should contact your ISP or institutional system administrator to obtain the answers to two key questions:

1. How do I access the web space that is available for me to place my documents and allow me to "go live" on the Web?

2. What is the URL for the web space that is available to me?

Because there are so many possible answers to each of these questions, all we can do here is provide an example from our own experience to give you an idea of what is involved. Thus we describe the process of how we put our `first.txt` page on the Web. In our case we have a machine running the **Linux** operating system and the **Apache** web server at the Department of Mathematics and Computing Science at Saint Mary's University in Halifax, Canada. (At the time of writing, Apache was the dominant web server on the Internet, and this is likely to remain true for the foreseeable future.) The system administrator there has created an account for us called `webbook`. We can "log in" to this account in a variety of ways, such as:

- By using a program with a text-based command line interface. A good program to use for this purpose if you too have a Linux system that you need to access from a Windows PC is the freely available **PuTTY**. Figure 2.3 shows a PuTTY session from a Windows PC to a Linux server.

- By using a program with a *Graphical User Interface (GUI)*. This is probably the most convenient way to perform the login and do the file transfer or *upload*. Many utility programs that you can use for this are available. Two good ones

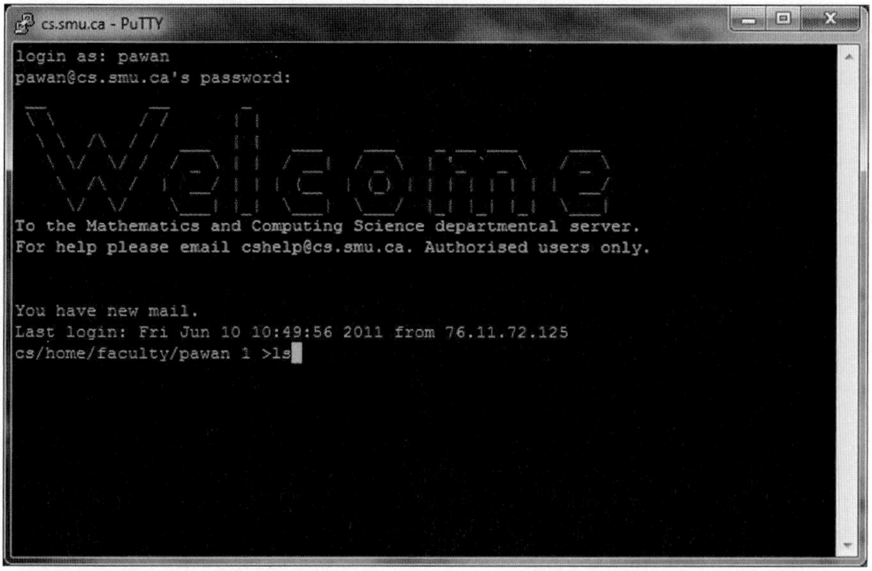

FIGURE 2.3

graphics/ch02/putty.jpg
A display of the command-line interface using PuTTY software.

that have free versions you can use in an academic environment are **WinSCP** and **WS_FTP**. Figure 2.4 shows a WinSCP session for transferring files to and from a Windows PC to a Linux server. The panel on the left shows a folder on the Windows PC, while the panel on the right contains a folder from the Linux server. One advantage of using a GUI-based program for uploading files is that it will let you "drag and drop" your files from your PC to the server. This, in turn, allows you to ignore most of the potentially confusing and trouble-causing details of the file transfer settings and procedure.

In either case we then use (either explicitly or implicitly) a file transfer protocol or program such as **ftp** or **scp** to do the actual file transfer. We need to log in to the account and gain direct access to it for the purpose of *uploading* files from our PC to the server, and hence to our "website."

Once logged in, we have to find or create the directory that will be searched by the web server for our files. On our Linux system running Apache, the standard location for storing web documents is a directory called `public_html`, which is located in a user's home directory. If such a directory does not exist, we must first create it, and then place a copy of our `first.txt` file in it.

Actually, in order to keep our website well organized, we will first create, within `public_html`, a subdirectory called `web02` (corresponding to Chapter 2), and copy

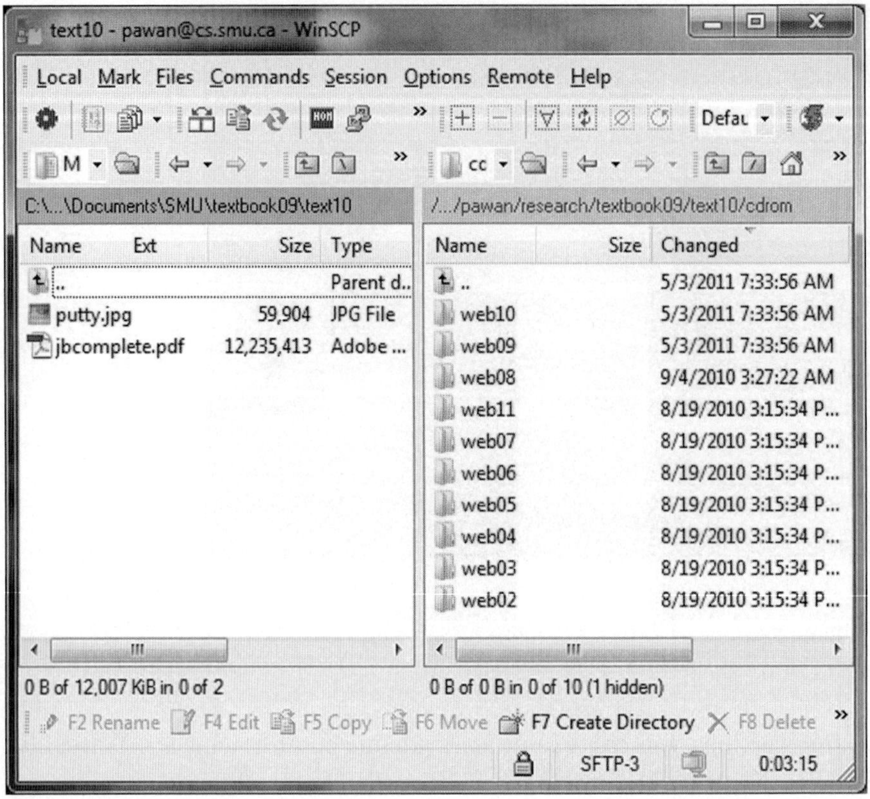

FIGURE 2.4

graphics/ch02/winscp.jpg

A display of the graphical user interface using WinSCP software for file transfer.

our file `first.txt` into that subdirectory. For simplicity and consistency (two goals we are always striving to achieve), it is a good idea to now begin constructing a directory structure that parallels that of the text. This will allow you to easily keep track of your own versions of the files you are working on that are text-related.

Next, before checking to see if the file can be seen by the rest of the world, we need to make sure that the web server will in fact be able to "serve" the file to the browser. This means that the directory path to the file must be accessible to the server and the browser, and the file itself must be readable by the browser.

How to set up the appropriate *directory permissions* and *file permissions* so that this will be possible will depend both on the system you are using and the interface you have chosen to log in to that system. If you use a GUI-based program to upload your files, that same program may allow you to create directories on the server and give both those directories and the files they contain the correct permissions.

However, let's come back to our own situation. Since similar situations will be reasonably common, it may be useful to point out that we used a text-based command-line interface to our Linux system, changed to our home directory, and gave the following command:

```
chmod -R 755 public_html
```

This is the "change mode," or "change permissions" Linux command, and a mysterious one it is, at least for anyone unfamiliar with Linux. What it does is this: It sets all necessary permissions for the directory `public_html` and (because of the **-R** option) recursively all the subdirectories and files underneath it.

The mysterious number 755 in the above command is an *octal number*[5] that specifies the nature of the permissions to be set. The first digit specifies the permissions for the user (owner), the second digit those for the group of users to which the user (owner) belongs, and the last of the three digits specifies the permission for all other users. The value 7 means "anything goes." That is, the user (the owner of the file) has all possible permissions for the given file (read, write, and execute). On the other hand, a 5 means "readable and executable, but not writable/modifyable," which is generally the kind of access a file owner wants the world at large to have for his or her website files. Thus we are allowing general users to read and execute our files, but not to write to (modify) them.[6]

This is way too much information if this is not your situation, but it gives you some idea of what is involved in making your website and its files accessible to the world at large.

Once a document is in the right place, and appropriate access permissions are set for the directories and the document, here's the next question: How do we (or how does anyone, for that matter) view the document? In this case, as you should be able to conclude from the URL discussion in Chapter 1, here is the correct URL to use for access to our first file from this web site:

```
http://cs.smu.ca/~webbook/web02/first.txt
```

If you type this URL into your web browser, or a web browser on any computer anywhere on the Internet, you should be able to see it as well. The file will be sent

---

[5] An *octal number* is a base-8 number that may only contain digits from the range 0...7. By way of comparison, decimal numbers, as you know, are base-10 numbers that use digits from the range 0..9.

[6] This is an oversimplification, of course, but will do for now. We have glossed over some details and subtleties that may puzzle you as well. For example, if a directory on a Unix-like system is "executable" you can read (display a list of) what's in it.

from the Saint Mary's University web server to your computer via the Internet. Keep in mind that even a simple document like this one may look different from what you see in Figure 2.2. For one thing, we have reduced the size of the actual display to get a figure that would fit nicely into the text as Figure 2.2, and you may be using a different browser.

2.7   Summary

In this chapter we extended the Internet and web concepts from the previous chapter by discussing some implementation level details. The discussion started with Internet Service Providers (ISPs). We then identified a decent editor and a web browser as the two basic tools a web developer needs to get started. We showed an example of the simplest kind of web document—a file of text—and saw how to view it through a web browser.

We introduced the idea of the MIME type of a file, and pointed out that browsers use this information about a file to deduce how they should handle the file. We also saw the relationship between the MIME type and the filename extension.

Finally, we looked at various issues involved in putting a web document on the Web. Depending on local conditions, the actual steps may vary widely, so we illustrated the procedure in the context of uploading a file from a Windows PC to an account on a Linux machine, from where it will be served by an Apache web server. This is likely to be a fairly common scenario.

Now that these basic implementation details are out of the way, we are ready to study the XHTML markup code that will allow us to provide more exciting web documents that include enhancements such as *hyperlinks* and graphics.

2.8   Quick Questions to Test Your Basic Knowledge

1. What is an *ISP*, and what are the main services you would expect an ISP to provide?

2. What is the major difference between *ISDN* and *WiMAX*, based on the little we have said about these things in this chapter?

3. What is the currently dominant web server on the Internet?

4. What are the two most basic tools you need to start your web development career, and what are specific examples of such tools on your particular *platform*? (This use of the term *platform* simply means some combination of computer, monitor, operating system, and perhaps other features.)

5. What does the acronym WYSIWYG stand for, and why do we recommend that you do *not* use a WYSIWYG tool for creating your web pages?

6. What is the difference between a *static web page* and a *dynamic web page*?

7. You should always "test" a web page before "putting it up on the Web." What does this mean, and how do you do it?

8. What does the acronym MIME stand for, and where were MIME types originally used?

9. How is a filename extension used by a browser?

10. What is meant by *uploading* a file, and, though we have not used the term until now, what do you suppose is meant by *downloading* a file?

11. Why is it important to have the correct permissions set on the files and directories of your website?

2.9   Short Exercises to Improve Your Basic Understanding

1. Most computing environments, even most home computers, will have a choice of editors. Explore your particular situation and make a list of all the editors you have to choose from. However, be careful not to confuse any word processor you might have with an editor. A word processor will put characters into your file that you cannot see and that will cause you no end of trouble when you are preparing a simple text file, or a file of HTML markup. You want an editor, not a word processor. On Windows, for example, **Notepad** is an editor, while **WordPad**™is a (very simple) word processor.

2. Do a little "research" to determine which of the editors you discovered in the previous exercise might be the best choice for creating web pages. You need to

look for editor facilities that deal explicitly with HTML. Make sure that you have full control of the code you enter into a file. It can be very frustrating if the software tries to be too "helpful."

3. Now explore your system and make a list of all the programs you might be able to use to upload files or copy files to your website. Once again check out the capabilities of each in your particular context, and try to decide which will be the best choice.

2.10   Exercises on the Parallel Project

In the analogous group of exercises from Chapter 1 you created a simple text file called `my_business.txt` containing some basic facts about your chosen business. That file should contain the name of your business, its mission statement, a list of some of its products and/or services, and perhaps a catchy slogan or two. Now you will reformat that file, possibly change its content, and "put it up on the Web."

1. First, make sure that your ISP is in place, you know what the URL of your website will be, and you have decided what software you will be using (editor, browser, and a program to upload files to your website).

2. Compare the content and formatting of your `my_business.txt` with the content and formatting of our file `first.txt` of Figure 2.1. Your file should contain a little more information than is in `first.txt`, but you can use `first.txt` and its display in Figure 2.2 to get an idea of the overall impression the first web page for your business should create. Revise your `my_business.txt` file accordingly.

3. If you do not already have the answers to the two questions posed in section 2.6, now is the time to get them.

4. Once you have those answers, upload your `my_business.txt` file to your website on your server.

5. Browse to your `my_business.txt` file on your website using at least two different browsers, and note any differences in the display from one browser to the next.

2.11   What Else You May Want or Need to Know

1. Although any editor will do for creating web pages, before long a typical web developer grows tired of typing in all those HTML tags over and over again. That's when the desire for something better grows too strong to resist. Every platform will have "something better," something that will let you enter HTML tags with the press of a key or the click of a mouse, for example, so you need to be prepared to check out the current state of affairs when the mood hits you. See the **References** in the next section for some suggestions.

2. Whether you use a simple editor or a high-powered IDE for web development, there is one problem you should be aware of, since it may rear its ugly head at any time. Or, you may never encounter it in a lifetime of web development. Life is like that.

    It's the so-called *end-of-line problem*, and it's caused by the fact that computing platforms do not agree on what character or characters should be used to mark the end of a line in a file of text. For example, Microsoft Windows uses a two-character combination, the carriage return and line feed (CRLF), while Linux and Unix use a single line feed (LF) character, and before its operating system became Unix-based, the Macintosh used a single carriage return (CR).

    The upshot of this disparity is that when text files are moved from one platform to a different platform, the transfer may take place in such a way that the end-of-file characters are not handled properly and as a result the file may not display properly on the destination platform.

    The reason that you may never encounter this problem is that nowadays many, if not most, programs are "smart" (at least smarter than they used to be) when it comes to dealing with this problem. A program used to transfer files may be smart enough to convert the end-of-line marker(s) on the source platform to the appropriate, and different, end-of-line marker(s) on the destination platform. A program used to display or edit a file at the destination may be smart enough to display the file properly even if the end-of-line character(s) are not the correct ones for that platform.

    One scenario in which you might see this problem is this. Suppose you have a file containing only text on your website, which is located on a Linux system, and suppose that file has proper line endings (the LF character). Suppose you need to make a change in the file and you download it to your PC with a program that does not convert the line endings. If you then open the file in a simple editor like Notepad on Windows, you will find that all the text in the file shows up as a single long line, because Notepad is not smart enough to handle the file properly.

So, now you know. Keep this in mind if you should encounter a problem that might be related to what we have discussed here. If you can (that is, if you have two different platforms available), try your own file-transfer program and editor to see if they behave properly in this regard, or to see if you can produce the problem we have described.

3. Earlier in the chapter we made the (unsupported) statement that, "At the time of writing, Apache was the dominant web server on the Internet, and this is likely to remain true for the foreseeable future." You should always take such statements with a grain of salt, at least until you have attempted to verify them independently. To confirm statements like this, you can do a web search for relevant information. And although much information on the Web is also to be taken with more than a grain of salt, one can get some idea of what the truth may be by looking at the same data or information on various sites. See the following **References** for some relevant links.

4. In this chapter we discussed some of the details that would be involved if you were setting up your website on a Linux server. You can, of course, also set up a web server on your Windows machine, provided you are connected to the Internet. You do not have to be connected to test your web pages, but to "go live" you need to be connected to the Internet via an ISP. As for the web server itself, you can set up **Apache** on your Windows machine, or use Microsoft's **IIS** (**Internet Information Services**). The following **References** contain links to further information if you wish to try either of these options.

2.12   References

1. Here are Wikipedia links to pages that provide more information on the various wired and wireless technologies used to connect to the Internet that we men-

tioned in this chapter, as well as a couple of wireless ones (*Long Term Evolution* (*LTE*) and *Wireless Mesh Networking* (*WMN*)) that we did not mention:

```
ISDN: http://en.wikipedia.org/wiki/Integrated\_Services\_Digital
      \_Network
ADSL: http://en.wikipedia.org/wiki/Asymmetric\_Digital\
      _Subscriber\_Line
FTTP: http://en.wikipedia.org/wiki/Fiber\_to\_the\_x
WiFi: http://en.wikipedia.org/wiki/Wi-Fi
CDMA: http://en.wikipedia.org/wiki/Code\_division\_multiple\
      _access
GSM: http://en.wikipedia.org/wiki/GSM
WiMAX: http://en.wikipedia.org/wiki/WiMAX
LTE: http://en.wikipedia.org/wiki/3GPP\_Long\_Term\_Evolution
WMN: http://en.wikipedia.org/wiki/Wireless\_mesh\_network
```

2. Here are links to the software tools we mentioned for establishing cross-platform connections and transferring files:

```
PuTTY: http://www.putty.org/
WS_FTP: http://www.ipswitch.com/
WinSCP: http://winscp.net/eng/index.php
```

3. It is always a risk to recommend a particular piece of software, but if you are creating your web pages on Windows and are permitted to install software on your system, you should check out a program like **HTML-Kit** or any similar software you can find that provides an IDE and will therefore allow you to easily create (and modify) HTML markup. Build 292 of HTML-Kit (the free version) is available from the following website:

```
http://htmlkit.com/download/
```

If you are running Linux or Mac OS-X, check out **Bluefish** (which is also available for Windows) at this site:

```
http://bluefish.openoffice.nl/
```

Two very powerful and flexible IDEs are **Eclipse**™and **NetBeans**™. Both are also free, but the downside is that each one has a fairly steep learning curve. Here are the relevant links:

```
http://www.eclipse.org/
http://netbeans.org/
```

4. The following are "just" editors, but saying that belies their usefulness, since they all have (or can be given) features that go far beyond those provided by a simple editor like Notepad for Windows. They are all available for the Windows platform, though Vim and Emacs "grew up" in the Unix environment and can be found on virtually any Unix or Linux system in some form. In fact, Unix and Linux users generally split into two categories—Vim (or vi, the original program) users and Emacs users—and sometimes you have to leave town in a hurry if you choose the wrong place and time to claim that one of these programs is better than the other.

```
Vim: http://www.vim.org/
Emacs: http://www.gnu.org/software/emacs/
Notepad++: http://notepad-plus.sourceforge.net/uk/site.htm
EditPad Lite: http://www.editpadpro.com/editpadlite.html
```

5. Here are a couple of sites to check for browser usage statistics:

```
http://www.w3schools.com/browsers/browsers_stats.asp
http://news.netcraft.com/archives/web_server_survey.html
```

6. The site

```
http://www.whatbrowser.org
```

will tell you what browser and what version of that browser you are using. It can also provide a few potentially useful tweaks for your browser of choice, as well as some informational links and some helpful links should you wish to try an alternate browser.

7. If you wish to use Microsoft Windows as your underlying platform, you may want to start here

`http://www.microsoft.com/web/downloads/platform.aspx`

for Microsoft's version of what you should have, or if you wish to have a nice Apache setup that includes the MySQL database software and the PHP server-side programming language (both of which we will be studying later), try this site:

`http://www.apachefriends.org/en/xampp-windows.html`

CHAPTER 3

XHTML for Content Structure

CHAPTER CONTENTS

3.1   Overview and Objectives

The time has now come to learn the essentials of the latest widely used incarnation of the *HyperText Markup Language (HTML)*, which is called *eXtensible HyperText Markup Language (XHTML)*. XHTML is very similar to HTML, but is an improvement over HTML because it requires us to be more careful and consistent when writing our markup code. This language will not only help us create the look of most of the web pages we see every day, but it will also provide the foundation for many of the technologies we will be using later on in this book. Our immediate goal will be to extend our simple website by incorporating some commonly used XHTML markup, adding more pages, and introducing the notion of *validation* of a web page.

So, in this chapter we will discuss the following topics:

- A brief history of, and the relationship between, HTML and XHTML

- The importance of maintaining both a conceptual and physical separation of the structure and presentation of our web page content

- XHTML tags and elements

- The basic structure of every web page

- Some basic XHTML markup, including the head, title, and body of a page, as well as headings, paragraphs, line breaks, tables, images, comments, tag attributes, and HTML entities

- Multipage websites and hyperlinks connecting the various pages

- A mechanism for inclusion of common material in several different website documents

- DOCTYPE declarations and web page validity

3.2   Once There Was HTML, Now There Is XHTML

The first documents on the World Wide Web were created using HTML. The history of HTML goes back to 1980, when Tim Berners-Lee, a physicist, began to create a system for sharing documents among fellow physicists. The first specification for HTML was published in 1991 by Berners-Lee. Though HTML subsequently evolved through several standards, its development was essentially frozen at version 4.01.[1] XHTML, which is essentially HTML rewritten to comply with the standards of XML (see Chapter 11) became the next stage in this evolution, and XHTML is now a commonly accepted standard for use by all web browsers and developers. The authors recommend that all new web page markup code (including yours) be written using XHTML, rather than HTML, at least until HTML 5 becomes widely supported.

3.3 A Very Important Distinction: Structure vs. Presentation

The purpose of the XHTML markup language (and of HTML before it) is to describe the *structure* of a web page. That is, XHTML is used to indicate which parts of the page content should be treated as headers, which should be ordinary paragraphs of text, and what should be placed in the rows and columns of a table, for example. Note that this notion of structure does *not* include any mention of such things as what fonts should be used for the various items of text, or in what color that text should appear. These are aspects of the *presentation* of the page content, and we will find it convenient to keep these two aspects of each web page separate in our minds as well as in the actual documents that make up our web pages. For one thing, doing so will make it much easier for us to change the "look and feel" of our page design, should we decide to do so.

Unfortunately, during the early days of web development, developers got impatient and "jumped the gun" by inventing HTML tags such as `<font>` to deal with presentational aspects of their web pages. This was not always done consistently from browser to browser, which was one problem, and it was eventually recognized as a bad idea in any case. The solution was to describe the presentational aspects of a web page using *Cascading Style Sheets* (*CSS*), which we will discuss in the next chapter.

3.4 XHTML Tags and Elements

An XHTML document, such as the one shown in Figure 3.1, contains nothing but text. In fact, it will contain "ordinary text" that you want to display on your web page, as well as *markup* (that is, "formatting commands" or, better yet, "structure-indicating commands") that describe the *structure* of your document. This markup is

---

[1]But now version 5 is in the works. See `http://dev.w3.org/html5/spec/Overview.html`. See the **What Else** and **References** sections at the end of this chapter for further information.

```
1    <html>
2    <head>
3    <title>Nature's Source</title>
4    </head>
5    <body>
6    <h1>
7    Welcome to the Website of Nature's Source
8    </h1>
9    <p>
10   This is our first foray onto the World Wide Web.
11   We are a small company dedicated to the health
12   of our customers through natural remedies.
13   We have a wide range of products that include:
14
15     - books, and multimedia documents that help you get
16       healthy and stay healthy
17     - herbal medicines
18     - equipment for injury free body toning exercises
19   </p>
20   </body>
21   </html>
```

FIGURE 3.1

cdrom/web03/first.html

The XHTML document for the first web page of **Nature's Source**.

specified using *XHTML tags*. An *XHTML tag* is a single letter or "keyword" enclosed in angled brackets <>, as in **<html>** or **<p>**. This "keyword" may or may not be an actual "word." More often than not it is just some (mnemonic) sequence of one or more alphanumeric characters. When referring to an XHTML tag, we may or may not include the angle brackets, depending on context. For example, we may refer to "the <p> tag," or simply "the p tag."

Usually, but not always, XHTML tags come in pairs. Each pair encloses the content to which that pair applies, and the tag pair together with its content is called an *XHTML element*. Thus we can also refer to a "p element" and mean some particular <p>...</p> tag pair and its content.

Often it is convenient to think of the opening and closing tags of the element as indicating the beginning and end of a formatting instruction for the enclosed text. Both tags in the pair use the same keyword. However, the tag that indicates the end of the element has a forward slash (/) before its keyword.

For example, we have a tag **<html>** that indicates the beginning of an XHTML document. It is paired with the tag **</html>** that indicates the end of the XHTML document. Everything included in this pair is the XHTML document, or, looked at another way, the entire XHTML document is an **html** element. Similarly, a **<p>** tag indicates the beginning of a paragraph, the next **</p>** tag indicates the end of that paragraph, and the two tags, together with the actual text of the paragraph between them, comprise a p element.

> **Any XHTML tag must contain only lowercase letters. HTML tags, on the other hand, are case-insensitive.**

An XHTML document file will typically have an extension of either .html or .htm.[2] Thus our first XHTML document file (shown in Figure 3.1) is called first.html. Note that the contents of first.html are just the contents of first.txt, with the addition of some HTML tags. Note as well that we have for the moment deliberately left the text formatted as it was in first.txt, and have placed all HTML tags at the left margin, except for the closing </title> tag.

With our next example we shall begin paying more attention to formatting to make our XHTML more readable (to human readers).

3.5 What Is the Basic Structure of Every Web Page?

Figure 3.1 gives us some idea of what goes into the making of an XHTML document. Every XHTML document must have the general form

```
<html>
  <head>
    <title> ... </title>
  </head>
  <body>
  ...
  </body>
</html>
```

in which the outermost <html>...</html> tag pair indicates the nature of the entire document. In this "skeletal" code we show as well, for the first time, the indentation level (two spaces) we will use to help make our code more readable.

Note that each XHTML document must be separated into a head element and a body element by the <head>...</head> and <body>...</body> tag pairs. The information enclosed in the <head>...</head> tag pair is general information *about* the web page that *is not shown* in the display area of the browser window, while the information enclosed in the <body>...</body> tag pair *is shown* in the display area of the browser window.

---

[2]So you can't infer from the extension whether a file contains XHTML or just plain old HTML.

Welcome to the Website of Nature's Source

This is our first foray onto the World Wide Web. We are a small company dedicated to the health of our customers through natural remedies. We have a wide range of products that include: - books, and multimedia documents that help you get healthy and stay healthy - herbal medicines - equipment for injury free body toning exercises

FIGURE 3.2

`graphics/ch03/displayFirstHtml.jpg`
A display of `cdrom/web03/first.html` in the Firefox browser.

Before continuing the discussion, let's take a moment to look at Figure 3.2, which shows how `first.html` will look in a web browser.

Notice that the top bar (the "title bar") of the browser window shows the name of the browser itself, and, depending on your browser and settings, it may show the "title" of the web page. This title is the one specified using the tag pair `<title>...</title>` that appears inside the `<head>...</head>` tag pair (in other words, it's the content of the `title` element).

The `html`, `head`, `body`, and `title` elements are all mandatory[3] parts of an XHTML document.

The `<body>...</body>` tag pair contains the content that is displayed in the browser window. But ... do you remember all the formatting we were so careful to insert in our text file `first.txt` (see Figure 2.1)? And do you remember how that formatting was preserved when the file was displayed in the browser as a simple text file (as shown in Figure 2.2)? All that formatting has been lost, now that the file is being viewed by the browser as an XHTML file. In other words, there is a different MIME type at play here (`text/html` rather than `text/plain`, because of the `.html` file extension), and the browser has its own ideas about how the content of such a file, containing ordinary text along with some markup, should be formatted. We can now see that this is different from how it thinks plain text, in a file with a `.txt` extension, should be formatted.

This is why we need to tell the browser how it should view the "structure" of our file, which we do using appropriate tags. In fact, we look at how to structure the content in the body of `first.html` in the next section.

---

[3]Exactly what "mandatory" means in this context will be discussed in section 3.12.

3.6   Some Basic Markup: Headings, Paragraphs, Line Breaks, and Lists

The body of our first XHTML document, shown in Figure 3.1, contains just two XHTML elements.

The first tag pair, `<h1>...</h1>`, is used to specify a first-level heading element. The number 1 that follows `h` indicates the heading level. An `h1` heading provides the largest display of its content, while `h2` provides the second largest display of its content, and so on, down to `h6`.

The second tag pair in our first XHTML document is `<p>...</p>`. The `<p>` opening tag indicates the beginning of a paragraph and the `</p>` closing tag marks the end of that paragraph. Even though we have typed the contents of the paragraph in the file `first.html` in Figure 3.1 with a format that seems reasonable, its display shown in Figure 3.2 completely ignores the formatting specified using our manually-inserted line breaks and indentations. The paragraph appears as "running text." If we want to break lines and provide an indented and itemized list, we will have to insert additional tags to indicate the desired structure.

In the `web03` subdirectory of your CD-ROM or the book's website you will find a version of the file modified in just this way. It is called `second.html` and contains the required additional formatting tags. The file itself is shown in Figure 3.3. Its display in a web browser appears in Figure 3.4.

The first thing to note about Figure 3.3 is the first line, which illustrates an XHTML comment. Comments in XHTML have the following syntax:

```
<!-- Text of the comment goes here. -->
```

Such comments can be single-line, multi-line, or end-of-line, but cannot be nested. In other words, one comment cannot be placed inside another.

The second thing to note about the file is that it has been formatted using our particular settings in **HTML-Kit**. We will continue to use this program to format our XHTML code throughout this text. There are many different formatting styles one could use for HTML source code, and this of course is just one of those styles.

```
1   <!-- second.html -->
2   <html>
3     <head>
4       <title>Nature's Source</title>
5     </head>
6     <body>
7       <h1>Welcome to the Website of Nature's Source!</h1>
8       <p>This is our first foray onto the World Wide Web. We are a small
9       company dedicated to the health of our customers through natural
10      remedies.
11      <br />
12      We have a wide range of products that include:</p>
13      <ul>
14        <li>books, and multimedia documents that help you get healthy and
15        stay healthy</li>
16        <li>herbal medicines</li>
17        <li>equipment for injury free body toning exercises</li>
18      </ul>
19    </body>
20  </html>
```

FIGURE 3.3

cdrom/web03/second.html

The XHTML document for the second version of the text-only web page of **Nature's Source**.

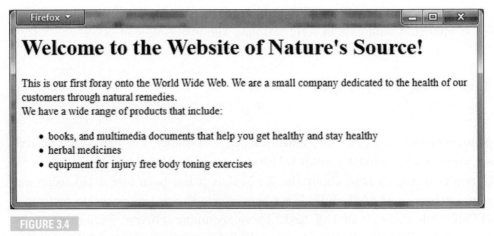

FIGURE 3.4

graphics/ch03/displaySecondHtml.jpg

A display of cdrom/web03/second.html in the Firefox browser.

It is a reasonable one,[4] however, and you could do worse than imitate it. Whatever style you use, or are required to use, be sure to use it consistently.

We also see three new XHTML tags in `second.html`. The first of these new tags is `<br />`, which is used to insert a line break into the text. This tag is different from previous tags we have seen. It does not come in a pair. Though the syntax of such tags does not require it, we format these tags by placing a blank space[5] and a forward slash after the keyword of the opening tag (`br` in this case), and omit the closing tag. Elements like this are also called *empty elements*, since they have no content.

The second new tag is `ul`. The `<ul>...</ul>` pair lets us create an *unordered list* by enclosing all the items in our list. Such a list is one in which the list items are not numbered; instead, each list item is preceded by the same symbol, which is often a "bullet" by default. Every item in the list is, in turn, enclosed within a `<li>...</li>` tag pair, which illustrates our third new tag (`li`).

As can be seen from Figure 3.4 the use of `<h1>`, `<p>`, `<br />`, `<ul>`, and `<li>` makes it possible for us to create a reasonably formatted web page, which is already much improved over the display of plain text.

But there is more to a web page than well-formatted text. We will take another step in the next section by adding to our web page a table with rows and columns, as well as images.

3.7 Tables, Images, and Tag Attributes

The images and other multimedia files that appear on a web page are in fact stored in separate files and embedded into the web page during the display process. When dealing with several such files, it is important to set up certain conventions for file organization. We have created a folder called `nature1` under the directory `web03` on our CD-ROM, which contains the web page and related files used in this section. If you look in that directory, you will notice that there are two items in the directory, a file called `index.html` and a subdirectory called `images`. The filename `index.html`

---

[4]Note that the main features of our formatting style include an indentation level of two spaces, and the fact that when one element is nested inside another, the inner element is indented a further level with respect to the outer. This can all be performed automatically by a program like HTML-Kit, but you often have to be prepared to do a little format-tweaking after the fact to get things just the way you want them.

[5]This blank space is becoming less and less necessary, but has been used for some time in empty tags because its absence has caused problems with older browsers.

has a special meaning. We are telling the web server that users should access the contents of the directory `nature1` through the file `index.html`. Let us find out what happens when we try to access the directory `nature1` on our website with this URL:

`http://cs.smu.ca/~webbook/web03/nature1/`

If you enter the above URL into your web browser, the web server will display the web page produced by the file `index.html` from the directory `nature1`. This file is shown in Figure 3.5. Note that we do not have to specify the filename `index.html`. This is because the Apache web server looks for a file with this name "by default" when you browse to a directory. In fact, most any browser can be configured to look for a specific file when the user browses to a directory, and though often the name of such a file is specified to be `index.html`, it may be something else, such as `home.htm`, or even `default.asp`.

The actual browser display of this file is shown in Figure 3.6. You can also load this file from your CD-ROM by opening the file `nature1/index.html` in the `web03` folder.

Let's examine Figure 3.5 a little more closely to see what's new in `nature1/index.html`. The display of this file in the web browser, as shown in Figure 3.6, shows that the contents of the web page are arranged in a table format. This table contains a total of four cells. The top-left cell contains the logo of our company. In the top-right cell, we have the address and other contact information for the company. General information about the company is in the bottom-left cell. Finally, an image that may convey what the company is all about—perhaps, in our case, this would be, "Use our products and develop a well-toned body!"—is embedded in the bottom-right cell.

There are four new tags in the XHTML markup of the file `nature1/index.html`, shown in Figure 3.5. Three of them are related to the table used to create the table of cells on our web page:

1. The `table` element itself is specified by the `<table>...</table>` tag pair and the complete contents of the table (its rows and columns) are the content of this element.

2. Each row of the table is specified by a `<tr>...</tr>` tag pair. Since this particular table has two rows, it has two `tr` elements.

3. Similarly, each column of the table is specified by a `<td>...</td>` tag pair. (Think of `td` as "table data.") In this table each row contains two columns, so each row has two `td` elements "nested" within it.

```
1   <!-- index.html -->
2   <html>
3     <head>
4       <title>Nature's Source - Canada's largest specialty vitamin store</title>
5     </head>
6     <body>
7       <table summary="Home Page">
8         <tr>
9           <td>
10            <img src="images/naturelogo.gif" alt="Nature's Source Logo" />
11          </td>
12          <td>
13            5029 Hurontario Street Unit 2<br />
14            Mississauga, ON L4Z 3X7<br />
15            Tel: 905.502.6789<br />
16            Fax: 905.890.8305
17          </td>
18        </tr>
19        <tr>
20          <td>
21            <h3>Welcome to Nature's Source - Protecting your health
22            naturally!</h3>
23            <p>Founded in 1998, Nature's Source was created to serve those who
24            use alternative healing methods. Offering only the highest quality
25            vitamins, minerals, supplements &amp; herbal remedies, Nature's
26            Source takes great pride in helping people live healthier, happier
27            lives.</p>
28            <p>Many Companies that talk about Customer Service fail to
29            deliver. Nature's Source exists to truly serve all the needs of
30            their customers. Each location features dedicated on-site
31            therapists along with knowledgeable staff who ensure that every
32            customer receives the best quality information available.
33            Continuing Education seminars are a regular event at Nature's
34            Source.</p>
35          </td>
36          <td>
37            <img src="images/outdoor4.jpg" alt="Eternal peace"
38          </td>
39        </tr>
40      </table>
41    </body>
42  </html>
```

FIGURE 3.5

cdrom/web03/nature1/index.html
A "default web page" for our business, with a simple (and temporary) table layout and images.

This is the first of our XHTML documents to display an image on its web page. This is done using an `<img />` tag. This is another empty tag like the `<br />` tag, since the `<img />` tag also has the space and a forward slash following its keyword, and has no content.

Of course, if we are going to display an image that is contained in a file, we have to specify the name of the image file, and possibly the full path to that file (if it is not in the same directory as the file that uses it). We have placed the images in a subdirectory called `images`. It is common practice to put all the images to be used in a given context in a single directory. While the directory name can be anything, `images` seems like an appropriate name and is a popular convention among web developers.

Now, if the `img` tag is not a pair, obviously we can't make the path to the file the content of the pair. So, what do we do? Well, now we get to see another aspect of XHTML tags, the *tag attribute*. Study line 10 from the `index.html` file in Figure 3.5:

```
<img src="images/naturelogo.gif" alt="Nature's Source Logo" />
```

This line shows *two* attributes of the `img` tag. One is called `src` and the other `alt`. Note the syntax: Each attribute is followed by an equals sign (=) and then by its *attribute value*, which is enclosed in quotes.

An XHTML tag attribute must always have a value, and that value must be enclosed in quotes (double or single). And tag attribute names, like tag names, are also lowercase.

The value of the `src` attribute of this `img` tag is the path to the file (`images/naturelogo.gif`) containing the image that we want to appear in the first column of the first row of our table. In other words, this `img` is the content of the first `td` element in that row. In a similar way, the image in the file `images/outdoor4.jpg` is made to appear in the second column of the second row.

The `src` attribute is mandatory for the `<img />` tag. Another mandatory attribute for the `<img />` tag is `alt`, whose value specifies the text to be displayed in case the image itself cannot be displayed for any reason. An image might not be displayed for any number of reasons. For example, the image file may be inaccessible, the browser may not support graphics, or a user with a visual disability may have the graphical display turned off. The text from the `alt` attribute value may also appear in a pop-up text box when your mouse hovers over the image (or may not appear, depending on the browser).

Figure 3.5 also shows another mandatory attribute, the `summary` attribute of the `table` tag, which is similar in purpose to the `alt` attribute of the `img` tag. That is, its value should provide a description of the table to users of non-visual browsers.

Actually, most XHTML tags have attributes, including the tags we have previously discussed. The reason we haven't mentioned them before is that, unlike the two we have seen for the `img` tag and the one for the `table` tag, most tag attributes are optional. All tags have "default behavior," and attributes are used to alter that behavior in some useful way.

Let's pause a moment for a key observation. In Figures 3.5 and 3.6 we have done something that you will see quite often on the Web—for the very good reason that at one time things *had* to be done this way—and which we will continue to do in this chapter (simply because we have not yet discussed the tools that will allow us to avoid it), but which you should see less and less frequently as time goes on.

What is it that we have done? Well, we have used the XHTML `table` element *for page layout purposes*, and this is now regarded as a design no-no. XHTML tables should only be used to display tabular data, like that shown in Table 3.1, and discussed in the next section.

To avoid having to use tables in this way, however, we need Cascading Style Sheets (CSS), which we cover in the next chapter. There we will show you how to achieve the same layout effect you see in Figures 3.6 and 3.8, but using CSS layout instead of XHTML table layout.

Unfortunately, browser support for many CSS features has been lacking (particularly in the case of Internet Explorer, the dominant browser), but this situation seems to be improving significantly. Even Internet Explorer, with luck, will become more and more standards-compliant in the near future.

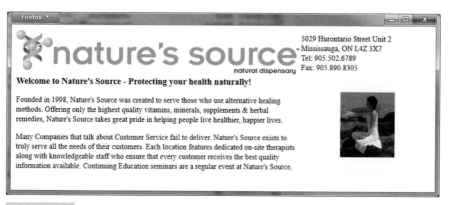

FIGURE 3.6

`cdrom/graphics/ch03/nature1/displayIndexHtml.jpg`
A display of `cdrom/web03/nature1/index.html` in the Firefox browser, showing a preliminary version of the home page for Nature's Source using XHTML table layout.

3.8   XHTML Entities

Another new XHTML feature we see in `nature1/index.html` is the use of the special character code `&amp;` (see line 25 of Figure 3.5), which produces the ampersand character (&) when the web page is displayed.

Some characters have special meanings in XHTML (the angle brackets enclosing tags, for example) and so if we want to simply display such a character we cannot just enter it into our file because it will be interpreted as its special meaning rather than appear as itself, causing the browser no end of confusion. Such special characters are often called *metacharacters* in general, and *XHTML entities* in our current context.

We need a special code to tell the browser to display such a character. Each such code starts with an ampersand (&), ends with a semicolon (;), and in between has a word or character string indicating the character in question. The fact that the ampersand is used in this way is what makes the ampersand itself a metacharacter. A short list of commonly used XHTML entities (metacharacters) is shown in Table 3.1.

XHTML code	Meaning	Actual symbol
`&amp;`	ampersand	&
`&gt;`	greater than	>
`&lt;`	less than	<
`&divide;`	divide	÷
`&plusmn;`	plus/minus	±
`&cent;`	cent	¢
`&euro;`	euro	€
`&pound;`	British pound sterling	£
`&yen;`	Japanese yen	¥
`&copy;`	copyright	©
`&reg;`	registered	®
`&trade;`	trademark	™

Table 3.1

XHTML entities (special characters or "metacharacters").

3.9 Adding More Web Pages to Our Site and Connecting Them with Hyperlinks

A fundamental characteristic of the Web is the ease with which we can navigate from one web page to another by clicking on a *link* to a second page that appears on the first page. We are now ready to develop a more elaborate website consisting of multiple pages, with links (or, more formally, *hyperlinks*) connecting them.

We have placed the files for this website in a directory called `nature2`. On your CD-ROM you can find this directory in the subdirectory `web03`. Once again the `index.html` file constitutes the "home page" of this simple website. The XHTML markup for this version of our `index.html` file is shown in Figure 3.7, and the browser display of the file appears in Figure 3.8. The browser display shows a typical website for a company, with the company logo at the top, followed by a row of menu links, then the main content area, and finally a footer.

In this new version of our `index.html` file we continue to use a table for layout, this time a table with four rows and five columns. Note that the first row (the logo row) and third row (the main content display area) contain the same content as the previous version of our `index.html` file, except that the contact information that appeared to the right of the logo has been removed and now appears on the page available under the `Our Locations` link, which you can reach, in turn, by clicking either the `About Us` link or the `Contact Us` link on the "home page."

3.9.1 A Menu of Hyperlinks

Row two (the menu links) and row four (the footer) are new to this version of our home page. The menu links we have chosen and placed in row two, and which will appear on *each* of the pages in this version of our website, include the following:

- `Home`, which will always return the user to the home page, and therefore links to the `index.html` file, so that clicking it will again display the view shown in Figure 3.8[6]

- `Buy Now`, which will eventually link to our complete e-commerce setup

- `Products and Services`, which will take the user to information about the products and services provided by our business

---

[6]Of course, if you are already at the home page of the website and click this link, you will see no change. If you are looking at any other page and click this link, you will be returned to the home page.

```
1    <!-- index.html -->
2    <html>
3      <head>
4        <title>Nature's Source - Canada's largest specialty vitamin store</title>
5      </head>
6      <body>
7        <table summary="Home Page">
8          <tr>
9            <td colspan="5">
10             <img src="images/naturelogo.gif" alt="Nature's Source" />
11           </td>
12         </tr>
13         <tr>
14           <td width="20%"><a href="index.html">Home</a></td>
15           <td width="20%"><a href="buy.html">Buy Now</a></td>
16           <td width="20%"><a href="products.html">Products and Services</a></td>
17           <td width="20%"><a href="yourhealth.html">Your Health</a></td>
18           <td width="20%"><a href="about.html">About Us</a></td>
19         </tr>
20         <tr>
21           <td colspan="3">
22             <h3>Welcome to Nature's Source: Protecting your health naturally!</h3>
23             <p>Founded in 1998, Nature's Source was created to serve those who
24             use alternative healing methods. Offering only the highest quality
25             vitamins, minerals, supplements &amp; herbal remedies, Nature's
26             Source takes great pride in helping people live healthier, happier
27             lives.</p>
28             <p>Many Companies that talk about Customer Service fail to deliver.
29             Nature's Source exists to truly serve all the needs of their
30             customers. Each location features dedicated on-site therapists
31             along with knowledgeable staff who ensure that every customer
32             receives the best quality information available. Continuing
33             Education seminars are a regular event at Nature's Source.</p>
34           </td>
35           <td colspan="2">
36             <img src="images/outdoor4.jpg" alt="Eternal peace" />
37           </td>
38         </tr>
39         <tr>
40           <td colspan="3">Nature's Source &copy; 2009 Porter Scobey and Pawan
41           Lingras</td>
42           <td><a href="contact.html">Contact Us</a></td>
43           <td><a href="sitemap.html">Site Map</a></td>
44         </tr>
45       </table>
46     </body>
47   </html>
```

FIGURE 3.7

cdrom/web03/nature2/index.html

The four rows of the table element in this file.

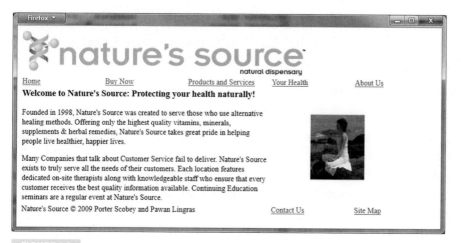

FIGURE 3.8

`graphics/ch03/nature2/displayIndexHtml.jpg`
A display of `cdrom/web03/nature2/index.html` in the Firefox browser showing a version of Nature's Source home page with links.

- `Your Health`, a business-specific link[7]

- `About Us`, which takes the user to a page giving information about the company

The footer contains some typical copyright information and two additional links that might be of interest to a site visitor: `Contact Us` and `Site Map`.

Let's begin our examination of the XHTML markup in Figure 3.7 by looking first at the second row (the second `tr` element). This second row is the only row that has all five columns, and that makes it convenient to use this row to specify the width of the columns. The `width` attribute for each column is set to 20% of the total width of the page. Each of these columns contains one of our "links" (the usual term for a *hyperlink* like those in our menu).

Links are specified using the `<a>...</a>` tag pair. The `a` tag is used to create hyperlinks, and also to specify a *bookmark*[8] on a page. On this page we use it for creating hyperlinks, and each `a` tag has an `href` attribute. The value of the `href` attribute specifies which URL to open when a user clicks on the link. In our case, all links are to files that reside in the same directory as `index.html`. In fact, the `Home` link takes us back to `index.html` itself. Therefore, we simply specify the names of the

---

[7]Since the business *we* have chosen is related to health, it is only natural to have more information on that topic available via a link like this.

[8]Usually when we click on a link and go to a new page, the display shows the top of that page, but a link can also be set up so that the display begins at a particular part of the page other than the top.

files. We can have more elaborate values for `href` such as `http://mypyramid.gov/` if we wish to link to some external site. The text between `<a>` and `</a>` is what is displayed in the browser. For example, with the XHTML code

```
<a href="buy.html">Buy Now</a>
```

the browser displays the text `Buy Now` as a link, and clicking on that text takes us to the file `buy.html`, which will then be displayed in the browser window, replacing the display of `index.html`.

Even though the table has five columns, we only specify one column in the first row. This column actually "spans" all five columns that appear in the second row. This is accomplished by using the attribute `colspan` for the `td` tag of this column, which specifies how many columns of the table this particular column is to span (or "extend over").

In the third row we have only two `td` elements, the first of which spans three of the five table columns and the second of which spans the remaining two columns. In the fourth and final row we have three `td` elements, with the first one spanning the first three columns of that row, and the remaining two occupying one column each.

As you might guess, the `td` tag also has a `rowspan` attribute (not illustrated here) as well, in case we need to have a table cell span more than one row.

3.9.2   Our Site Now Has Many Pages

There are quite a few other files that belong to our `nature2` website, and you will find them in the `web03\nature2` subdirectory on your CD-ROM. In fact, there is a file corresponding to each link on our "home page," so all of the links are "live." These files, and others reachable by starting from the links on this home page, form a skeleton of the website we plan to develop. Some of the additional pages will have additional links as well. These additional links will appear in the first column of the main content area row, under the `Home` link of the main menu, and will lead to pages related in some way to that content area.

We will not examine all pages of the site in detail here, but we will look at two additional page documents that contain some new features of XHTML. You should, however, take time to visit each of the pages of this very primitive website, and note how the "look and feel" is maintained from one page to the next. Keep in mind that for the moment we are not concerned with the presentational style of our pages, but only their structure and (abbreviated) content as we try to get a feel for what our site will eventually provide for our users.

If you click on the `About Us` link on the home page, you will be taken to the page `about.html`, a display of which is shown in Figure 3.9. This is one of the pages with

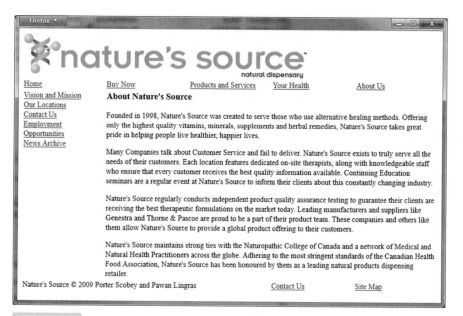

FIGURE 3.9

graphics/ch03/nature2/displayAboutHtml.jpg
A display of cdrom/web03/nature2/about.html in the Firefox browser.

additional links, seen to the left of the main content, of the kind mentioned above. These additional links provide, in effect, a submenu for the menu item About Us. In a later chapter of the text we will use JavaScript to create dropdown menus as a better alternative to this kind of submenu. All the XHTML markup we have used in the file about.html is based on the concepts we have already discussed.

The final page document from this group that we will look at now is sitemap.html, which comes up if you click on the Site Map link at the bottom-right corner of any page on the site. Every website should have a *site map*, since users may not know how to find their way through a labyrinth of menus and submenus to find what they are looking for. A site map should give them a good, concise high-level view of the structure and content of the site.

The browser display of the file sitemap.html is shown in Figure 3.10, and we can see that the top two rows of the web page, as well as the footer, are the same as for all the other page displays on the site.

The third row, however, has a number of interesting features. First of all, we see that this row contains another table, which has a border, one row, and two columns. This table is "nested" inside the third row of the table used to lay out the web page, and in fact illustrates the proper use of a table to display some data, in this case the site map data. This should be contrasted with our temporary, and not so proper, use

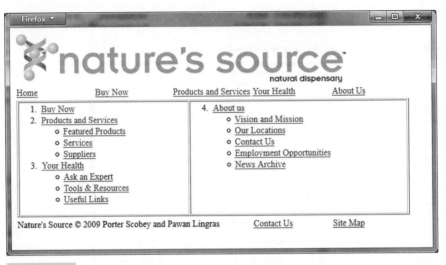

FIGURE 3.10

`graphics/ch03/nature2/displaySitemapHtml.jpg`
A display of `cdrom/web03/nature2/sitemap.html` in the Firefox browser.

of a table to lay out our pages in this early version of our site. Both columns contain numbered lists with bulleted sublists.

Let us focus on the markup for the third row of the layout table, which is the only thing shown in Figure 3.11. The `table` tag of the table that is nested in this third row has a new attribute called `border` that has a value of `"1"`. This begs the question: 1 what? And the answer is 1 *pixel*. This *pixel* unit of measurement can be thought of as a single point in an on-screen image. The word "pixel" is short for "picture element," and its actual size depends on your screen resolution. This is the default unit in XHTML whenever we do not specify the unit to be used for some measurement. However, even though the unit is often omitted, a better practice would dictate that we should not rely on the default, but instead always supply the desired unit explicitly with each measurement. In this case then we really should have `border="1px"`, with `px` being the required designation for the pixel unit. In any case, this is what gives us a border around all the cells in a table.

The ordered list is specified with the tag pair `<ol>...</ol>`. Each item in the ordered list is specified, in turn, with the tag pair `<li>...</li>`, just as we did previously for unordered lists. We nest an unordered list under three of the four ordered list items using the `<ul>...</ul>` tag pair we discussed before. Note in Figure 3.11 that we had to end the ordered list in the first column, and restart it in the second column. For restarting, we specified the starting number to be 4 using the `start` attribute.

```
   <tr>
     <td colspan="5">
       <table border="1" width="100%" summary="Page List">
         <tr>
           <td valign="top">
             <ol>
               <li><a href="buy.html">Buy Now</a></li>
               <li>
                 <a href="products.html">Products and Services</a>
                 <ul>
                   <li><a href="featured.html">Featured Products</a></li>
                   <li><a href="services.html">Services</a></li>
                   <li><a href="suppliers.html">Suppliers</a></li>
                 </ul>
               </li>
               <li>
                 <a href="yourhealth.html">Your Health</a>
                 <ul>
                   <li><a href="expert.html">Ask an Expert</a></li>
                   <li><a href="tools.html">Tools &amp; Resources</a></li>
                   <li><a href="links.html">Useful Links</a></li>
                 </ul>
               </li>
             </ol>
           </td>
           <td valign="top">
             <ol start="4">
               <li>
                 <a href="about.html">About us</a>
                 <ul>
                   <li><a href="vision.html">Vision and Mission</a></li>
                   <li><a href="locations.html">Our Locations</a></li>
                   <li><a href="contact.html">Contact Us</a></li>
                   <li><a href="employment.html">Employment
                   Opportunities</a></li>
                   <li><a href="news.html">News Archive</a></li>
                 </ul>
               </li>
             </ol>
           </td>
         </tr>
       </table>
     </td>
   </tr>
```

FIGURE 3.11

cdrom/web03/nature2/sitemap.html
The third row of the "outer" table element in this file. Note that this row contains a "nested" table.

3.10   Using Server Side Includes (SSI) to Make Common Markup Available to Multiple Documents

This section discusses a very important principle to keep in mind when you are developing your website, and one that we can illustrate quite nicely by taking a closer look at our simple "`nature2` website."

First, note that the "site" now contains `.html` files, and they all contain quite a bit of information that is the same in each file. That is, every page of this version of the website contains four "rows" of information (the logo row, the menu row, the main content row, and the footer row), and only the main content row differs from page to page. Of course, the markup for all four rows appears in each file, even though that markup is exactly same for the first, second, and fourth rows in each case.

If we carry on like this, we are potentially leaving ourselves open to a very serious problem down the road. For suppose that at some point we want to change the wording of a menu option or add a new menu item, or change one of the names in the footer. What does this mean? It means that every single one of our 17 files will have to be edited and modified. And what are the chances that all the changes that have to be made will be made correctly and consistently across all affected files? And then, if another change is required, we will have to do it all over again. If this happens, and it almost certainly will, you will have what is often called a *maintenance nightmare* on your hands, and you should be able to understand why it has this name.

So, what to do? The central idea is that we want to eliminate, as far as possible, duplicate markup, so that if changes are necessary we only have to make them in one place. One way of doing this is illustrated by the two files shown in Figures 3.12 and 3.13.

In Figure 3.12 (which is a third version of our `index.html` file for this chapter) lines 8, 9, and 29 have a similar syntax. For example, line 8 is

```
<!--#include virtual="common/logo.html"-->
```

and this line causes the Apache server to include the contents of the file `logo.html` in this latest version of our `index.html` file, in place of this line, before `index.html` is sent to the browser for display. This is the origin of the terminology *Server Side Includes*.

```
1   <!-- index.html -->
2   <html>
3    <head>
4     <title>Nature's Source - Canada's largest specialty vitamin store</title>
5    </head>
6    <body>
7     <table summary="Home Page">
8       <!--#include virtual="common/logo.html"-->
9       <!--#include virtual="common/mainmenu.html"-->
0       <tr>
1         <td colspan="3">
2           <h3>Welcome to Nature's Source: Protecting your health naturally!</h3>
3           <p>Founded in 1998, Nature's Source was created to serve those who
4           use alternative healing methods. Offering only the highest quality
5           vitamins, minerals, supplements &amp; herbal remedies, Nature's
6           Source takes great pride in helping people live healthier, happier
7           lives.</p>
8           <p>Many Companies that talk about Customer Service fail to deliver.
9           Nature's Source exists to truly serve all the needs of their
0           customers. Each location features dedicated on-site therapists
1           along with knowledgeable staff who ensure that every customer
2           receives the best quality information available. Continuing
3           Education seminars are a regular event at Nature's Source.</p>
4         </td>
5         <td colspan="2">
6           <img src="images/outdoor4.jpg" alt="Eternal peace"
7         </td>
8       </tr>
9       <!--#include virtual="common/footer.html"-->
0     </table>
1    </body>
2   </html>
```

FIGURE 3.12

cdrom/web03/nature3/index.html
The index.html file that includes from external files the text common to all pages in this version of the site.

```
1   <!-- logo.html -->
2   <tr>
3    <td colspan="5">
4      <img src="images/naturelogo.gif" alt="Nature's Source" />
5    </td>
6   </tr>
```

FIGURE 3.13

cdrom/web03/nature3/common/logo.html
The contents of this file are included in the preceding index.html file before that file is processed by the browser.

The contents of the file `logo.html` are shown in Figure 3.13, and as you can see, the file contains the first row (the first `tr` element) that appeared in the previous version of our `index.html`.

In a similar way, the contents of the second and fourth rows of our previous index file are brought in by lines 9 and 29 of the current file. By placing the content of these three rows in three separate files in a subdirectory called `common`, and including their content in `index.html` at the appropriate time, we have accomplished what we set out to do. Now each page document on our site can include this markup from the three files in the `common` subdirectory, and if any changes need to be made they need only be made in the files in that subdirectory and those changes will appear in each page of the site the next time the page is displayed. The remaining content of each file is specific to that file.

Our "nature3 website," found in `web03/nature3`, is a revision of our "nature2 website" in which each page on the site has been revised to include the markup from these three files. This, of course, is a "behind the scenes" effect, and if you start by displaying the `index.html` file for this version and then view any or all pages of the site you should see exactly what you saw in the previous version. We sometimes describe this kind of scenario as something that is "transparent to the user."

3.11   What Does It Mean for a Web Page to Be Valid?

So far we have been creating web pages more or less "on the fly," showing you as we go some useful XHTML features in context. You may have begun to wonder if we know what we're talking about. Our pages do show up in browser windows and have a reasonable appearance, but how confident does that make you feel?

Historically, browsers have been written to be very "forgiving" when displaying web pages. In other words, even if web designers were not very careful when designing their web pages, and didn't follow all the rules, a browser would often still be able to do a reasonable job of displaying such pages. That is one reason why the Web contains so many very badly constructed web pages.

We have a right to expect that a browser will be able to display any one of our web pages, so long as it is a *valid web page*. But what exactly does this mean? Simply put, it means that if we are using XHTML to mark up our web pages, then we must follow all the XHTML rules for creating those pages. Thus a web developer needs to know what these rules are, and needs to follow them.

This is not as bad as it may seem. We do not intend to provide all the rules at this point. In fact, a relatively small subset of the rules will suffice:

1. All tag keywords must be lowercase.

2. All attributes must be lowercase and have values that are enclosed in quotes.

3. Elements with content must have both opening and closing tags.

4. Tag pairs must be properly nested.

These are four of the most important XHTML rules that we must follow.

The last of the above rules, the "proper nesting of tags" rule, is one we have in fact followed, but not mentioned explicitly. It's easiest to show what this means by giving an example where tags are *not* properly nested. If we created a file in which the tags had the order shown in

```
<head>
<title>
...
</head>
</title>
```

then we would be violating this rule because the `title` element must be *completely* contained within the `head` element. In general, if the opening tag `<tag2>` *follows* the opening tag `<tag1>`, then the closing tag `</tag2>` must *precede* the closing tag `</tag1>`. This applies whether the elements in question are in the head or the body of the page.

We will say more about XHTML rules as time goes on, but for now you will be safe if you simply emulate the practices you observe in our sample files.

3.12   How Can We Determine if a Web Page Is Valid?

It is one thing to feel confident that you have followed all the necessary rules for inserting XHTML markup code into your web page files, but is there a way you can be certain you have done so?

The answer is *yes*. You can submit your file to an **online validator**, of which there are several. To do this you browse to the online validator site, enter the URL of the web page you wish to validate into the validator, and click a button that starts the validation process. The validator will then provide a feedback report telling you either that your page is fine, or that you have violated one or more of the rules.

Since online validators are usually capable of validating not only XHTML web pages, but also early and more recent versions of HTML, it is necessary to tell a validator what version of HTML or XHTML has been used in the construction of the web page you are validating, as well as some information about the *encoding scheme* (character set) you are using. To do this you need to add some informational lines at the beginning of your file. In particular, you need to do the following:

1. Add a **DOCTYPE** declaration to indicate the version of the markup language being used.

2. Modify the opening **html** tag by giving it an **xmls** attribute that provides a reference to the appropriate XML namespace.

3. Place a **meta** tag within the document **head** element to indicate the encoding scheme being used.

This sounds pretty scary, but fortunately you can easily turn it into a ritual, and then stop thinking about it. The file **third.html** is a copy of **second.html** modified to contain this information for the validator. Figure 3.14 shows the first few lines of this file, which contains the information listed above.

Having to do this for each file that you wish to have validated is the bad news. The good news is that you can treat the lines containing all of this additional information as "boiler plate" markup that you simply copy and insert into any new file you are

```
1   <!DOCTYPE html PUBLIC "-//W3C//DTD XHTML 1.0 Strict//EN"
2        "http://www.w3.org/TR/xhtml1/DTD/xhtml1-strict.dtd">
3   <!--third.html-->
4   <html xmlns="http://www.w3.org/1999/xhtml">
5     <head>
6       <title>Nature's Source</title>
7       <meta http-equiv="Content-Type" content="text/html;charset=utf-8" />
8     </head>
```

FIGURE 3.14

cdrom/web03/third.html

Lines 2, 3, 4, and 6 of this file contain information about the XHTML markup in the file, information that a validator will need.

creating. Then, as long as you "follow the rules" in the rest of the document (for the kind of document you said it would be), that document should validate without any problem.

Now, once we have prepared our document and inserted the validation information, how do we actually validate it? There are a number of validation sites on the Internet, but we recommend the one at

```
http://validator.w3.org
```

since it is maintained by the World Wide Web Consortium itself and is very easy to use. Just go to this site, enter the URL of the web page you wish to have validated into the window provided for that purpose, and then click on the button marked `Check`. You will then either be told that your page is valid, or be given an itemized report on the ways it violates the specifications of the document type (`DOCTYPE`) against which it was validated.

For example, Figure 3.15 shows a (partial) validator display just as the file `third.html` is about to be validated, and in Figure 3.16 we see a display (again partial) of the validator showing a successful validation of that file.

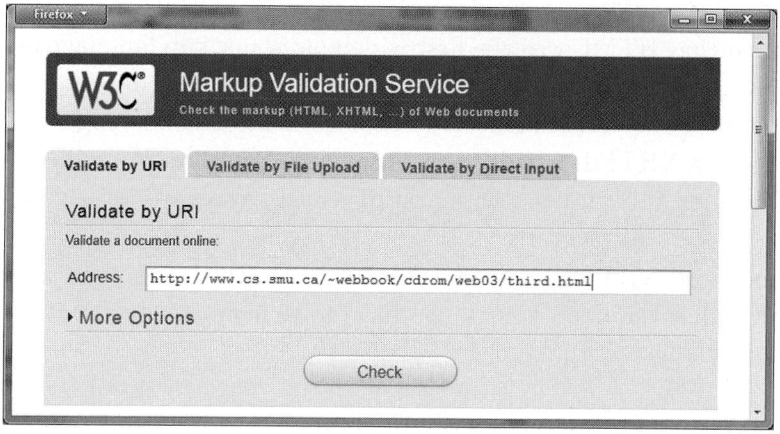

FIGURE 3.15

graphics/ch03/displayThirdHtmlToValidate.jpg
A Firefox browser display just before clicking the `Check` button to validate the file
cdrom/web03/nature2/sitemap.html.

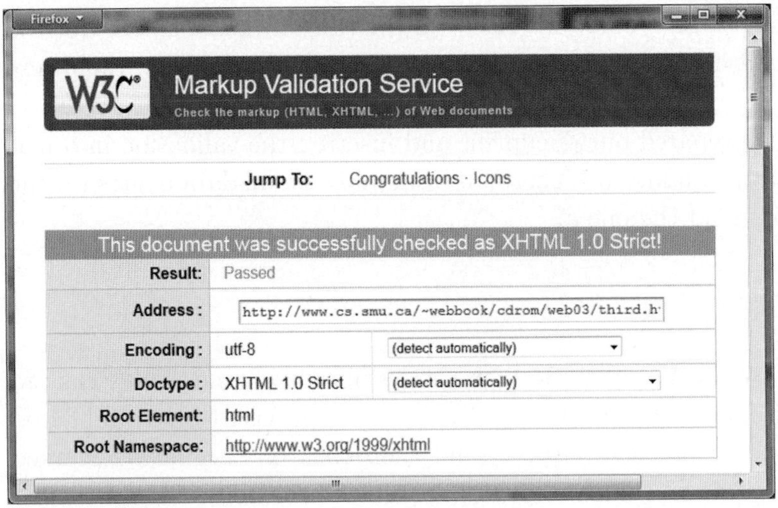

FIGURE 3.16

`graphics/ch03/displayThirdHtmlValidated.jpg`
A Firefox browser display showing a successful validation of the file
`cdrom/web03/third.html`.

3.13   Summary

In this chapter we learned that HTML was the first widely used markup language on the Web, and how it eventually was rewritten as XHTML. We stressed the importance of maintaining a distinction between the structure of the content on a web page and its presentation. HTML and XHTML should deal only with structure. We will use XHTML because it forces us to write better markup, which we regard as a good thing.

We distinguished between XHTML tags and XHTML elements (tag pairs and their content), and noted that the main things you have to remember when writing XHTML markup include:

1. Use only lowercase letters for tag and attribute names.

2. Make sure elements with content have both an opening and a closing tag.

3. Make sure empty tags have the right syntax and format, including the blank space before the forward slash.

4. Make sure tag pairs are properly nested.

5. Make sure that every attribute has a value, and that the value is enclosed in quotes (single or double).

We learned that the basic structure of any XHTML document includes at least the following four elements: `html`, `head`, `title`, and `body`.

We saw how to apply some simple markup to the content in the body of an XHTML document so that a browser can identify the structural divisions of the web page content and display them accordingly. XHTML elements allow us to mark such things as headings, paragraphs, and lists. An element can also be empty (have no content), like the tag for a line break, and element tags can have attributes that can be used to alter the display of the element content or the effect of the element.

Some characters, such as the tag delimiters < and >, cannot appear in an XHTML document except in their tag-delimiter context, so if we wish to have such a character in our document we have to use an XHTML entity, such as `&lt;` for <.

We saw how the `table` element can be used for page layout, even though it should no longer be so used, but with CSS not yet at our disposal we had little choice. Fortunately, we also saw a bona fide use of a table (on our site map page).

We saw how to add images to our web pages, and how to link one web page to another when our site has multiple pages. Furthermore, when multiple pages have content in common, we saw how Server Side Includes (SSI) can be used to avoid the maintenance nightmare of trying to keep duplicate code consistent when updating takes place.

Finally, we now know what a valid web page is, and how to determine if a given web page is in fact valid.

3.14 Quick Questions to Test Your Basic Knowledge

1. Who was Tim Berners-Lee and why is he noteworthy?

2. HTML was designed to describe web page structure. Some browser vendors tried to make it do more, but they should not have done so. Can you explain what we mean by these two statements?

3. What is the difference between an XHTML tag and an XHTML element, and how are they related?

4. What is an empty XHTML element, and what is its general syntax? Give an example.

5. Why is the current generally-accepted format of an empty HTML element likely to change in the foreseeable future?

6. What is, in your opinion, the best reason for keeping web page "structure" and web page "presentation" separate?

7. What does the high-level structure of every XHTML web page document look like?

8. What would you give for a short description of what it means for XHTML tags to be "properly nested"?

9. What is the main difference to remember between XHTML tags and HTML tags?

10. What have tables been used for in HTML and XHTML that they should no longer be used for?

11. What are the XHTML (and HTML) comment delimiters?

12. What is a pixel, and what is the abbreviation for it?

13. What is the syntax of an XHTML entity? Give an example.

14. Why do we need XHTML entities?

15. Aside from the lowercase requirement, what are two things you must remember about tag attributes and their values?

16. Why should every non-trivial website have a *site map*?

17. What does the acronym SSI stand for, and what is it used for?

18. What does it mean for an XHTML document to be valid?

19. How do you determine if an XHTML document is valid?

3.15 Short Exercises to Improve Your Basic Understanding

In these and subsequent exercises, we may sometimes explicitly ask you to make a copy of a file from the text and modify it in some way. However, it is worth pointing out that even in those cases when we do not explicitly ask you to make copies, whenever we ask you to make a change to a file from the text, it should be understood that we really mean for you to first make your own copy of that file and then do whatever is asked to the copy. That way, you can always go back to the original for a fresh copy if necessary.

1. Load the file `first.html` from Figure 3.1 into your browser. It will probably not look like the display we have shown in Figure 3.2. Try changing the size of the browser window to see if you can make it look more like that display. The main thing to note as you do this is how the text in both the heading and the following single paragraph "flows" to conform to the size of the display window.

2. Make a copy of the file `first.txt` from Chapter 2 and call it `first.html`.[9] In this case make no changes other than the file extension. Load both `first.txt` and `first.html` into your browser and see if there is any difference between how the two files are displayed. Explain any differences you see in terms of MIME types. Repeat the exercise with one or more additional browsers to see if they all exhibit similar behavior.

3. In the file `second.html` of Figure 3.3 make the line following the line break a separate paragraph, and to the <p> tag of that paragraph add the `align` attribute with a value of `"center"`. Load the revised file into your browser and note how the new paragraph is centered above the list. Then repeat the exercise, this time giving the `align` attribute the value `"right"`.

4. In the file `second.html` of Figure 3.3 change the `ul` tag to `ol`, so that you get a numbered list instead of a bulleted list. Note that by default your list items are numbered 1, 2, 3, ... and so on, just as the unnumbered list had a bullet marker as the default. These can both be changed, but that is best handled by CSS, the subject of the following chapter.

---

[9]Note that this `first.html` file will not be the same as the `first.html` file from the beginning of this chapter, since there will be no markup in it.

5. In the file of Figure 3.5 change the name of both image files so that the browser cannot find them, and then reload the page. You should see the text of the `alt` attribute value in the place where the image would otherwise appear. Try this in more than one browser as well.

6. In Figure 3.10 you see a border around the table of site map information. This is achieved by giving the `table` tag of the table containing the site map data a `border` attribute with a value of 1 pixel, as you can see in Figure 3.11. In Figure 3.8 (for example) we have used a table for the layout, but have not given the table a `border` attribute, since that would not be very visually appealing. Confirm this observation by giving that table a `border` attribute with a value of 1 pixel and reloading the page.

7. Construct a short test page that displays the characters corresponding to some (or all) of the symbols shown in Table 3.1.

8. Browse to the file `third.html` of Figure 3.14. Make a copy of its URL; then open up another window in your browser and go to `http://validator.w3.org`, paste in the URL, and click on the `Check` button. You should get a response highlighted in green saying the file validates. Make some changes in the file that will cause it *not* to validate (at least not according to the strict XHTML standard). For example, you could try capitalizing a tag, or leaving out a closing tag.

9. Do a web search and find the data necessary to make a table showing the history of HTML. That is, construct a table showing the sequential version numbers of HTML that were widely used (and any that weren't widely used), along with the dates they were approved as standards. Finally, design a web page containing a suitable table for the display of this data.

3.16   Exercises on the Parallel Project

In these exercises we ask you to replicate, for your previously chosen business, the kinds of web pages we have discussed in the text for our own sample health product business. Since the layout required is a table with two rows and two columns, you may use, as we have done in this chapter, the XHTML `table` tag for your page layout, but only because we do not yet have an alternate approach.

1. Before you begin, make sure you have thoroughly explored each of the three versions of our sample website: the single-file version, the version in which

each page document has the duplicate markup embedded within it, and the final version in which the common markup has been extracted into the three separate files.

2. Your first task is to produce a single-page website for your business that looks like the web page for our business shown in Figure 3.6, according to the following specifications for the content of each table cell:

   (a) The logo for your business goes in the top-left corner of the page. If you have a paint program,[10] you can produce your own logo for this purpose. Otherwise, at least for the moment, you can either search for a suitable logo on the Internet and hope you can find a free one to use, or simply place text in this cell for the time being. In any case, the name of your business must appear here.

   (b) Your business address and other contact information goes in the top-right corner.

   (c) Some general information about your business must appear in the bottom-left part of the page. This should be appropriate reading for someone coming to your site for the first time and should therefore be designed to catch the attention of visitors and make them want to explore the rest of your site as it develops.

   (d) Finally, a photographic image relevant to your business must go into the bottom-right corner of your page. You can take such a photo yourself and upload it, or download one from the Internet, provided you do not violate any copyright laws in so doing.

3. Your second task is to revise and extend the single-page website you created in the previous exercise. The goal is to have it "parallel" the site we have called our "nature3 website," which made use of SSI. With luck, you too will be able to make use of SSI; otherwise, you run the risk of getting into the kind of "maintenance nightmare" situation we described in this chapter.

   So, your home page should have an appearance analogous to the display in Figure 3.8. Recall that this display would be the same for both versions of our multi-file site. For simplicity and consistency, make your menu links the same as the ones we have used (at least for the time being), except that our link

---

[10] Once again, there are many good (and free) paint programs available for download. An excellent one that is available for several platforms is the **GIMP (Gnu Image Manipulation Program)**, from `http://www.gimp.org`.

called **Your Health** clearly must be replaced with a link more specific to, and appropriate for, your own business.

All links on your home page must be active, that is, link to an actual page, and some of those pages must also have their own links to other pages, in the manner or our sample site. You need not have exactly the same number of files as our sample site, and of course the content of these additional pages will depend on the nature of your chosen business. Many of these pages can contain a short "coming soon" message, similar to that found on some of the pages of our sample site.

3.17   What Else You May Want or Need to Know

1. In keeping with our need-to-know approach, in this chapter we have introduced you to only a very small selection of the XHTML tags that are available to you when you are constructing the XHTML document for one of your web pages. You are likely already curious to see what else is available, and to begin experimenting with various other tags and their attributes. There is no better place to do this than at the **W3 Schools** site. (See the link in the **References** section that follows.) This is a wonderful site to explore. You will find both reference material and tutorials, as well as examples that you can modify and experiment with right there on the site. However, we give here a summary list of some tags that includes all those we have discussed, as well as some that are closely related to those we discussed, and some new ones. You should explore all of these further on your own by going to the website mentioned above, because you will find them useful for constructing your own web pages.

> **html, head, title, body** The "infrastructure" elements used to set up any website.
>
> **link** The (empty) tag to place in the **head** element of your document if it needs to link to an external document (such as a CSS style sheet, discussed in the next chapter).
>
> **meta** The (empty) tag to place in the **head** element of your document if your document needs to make available to some external processing agent some high-level information about itself.
>
> **h1, h2, h3, h4, h5, h6** The heading tags that give progressively smaller text.
>
> **p** The ubiquitous paragraph tag, one of the most frequently used.

ul, ol, li The tags for bulleted (unnumbered) or numbered generic lists (which can be nested), and their items.

dl, dt, dd The tags for a special kind of list—a *definition list*—which is convenient when you are defining or explaining a sequence of terms.

table, tr, td, th The tags for tables, with rows and columns. The `th` is a new tag (for us) that is often used for the first table cell of a row or the top table cell of a column if the content of that cell is to be used as the label for the rest of the corresponding row or column. Use `th` instead of `td` if you want the text content to appear in bold and centered within the table cell.

br The (empty) line-break tag that moves the text following it in a paragraph to the next line, without adding any vertical space.

img The (empty) image tag that permits us to place images on our web pages.

hr The (empty) horizontal-line tag that creates a horizontal line on a web page, often used for separation purposes.

strong, em, tt Tags that emphasize text by making it (usually) bold, italic, or monospace, respectively. There are also `b` and `i` tags for bold and italic, but `strong` and `em` are preferred instead.

big, small Tags that make the enclosed text bigger or smaller. They are "cumulative," meaning (for example) that two nested `big` tag pairs make the enclosed text bigger than one `big` tag pair.

pre The tag to use if you want your text to retain the format you used when you typed it in.

blockquote, q The tags for two kinds of quotations: `blockquote` if you want your text to have extra space before and after it, and indented margins, and `q` if you just want quotation marks around it. Oddly, Internet Explorer does not support the `q` tag.

address, dfn, var, cite Tags to designate an address, a definition, a variable, or a citation, generally rendered in italics.

code, samp, kbd Tags to designate computer code, sample code, or data, or keyboard input, generally rendered in monospace.

div, span Tags for designating parts of a page for processing of some kind (such as CSS styling or responding to JavaScript events).

frame, frameset Tags for dividing your browser's window into several "frames" in which different pages may be displayed. Sounds like a good idea, but frames have had a bad reputation almost from their inception and new websites should avoid them.

applet, basefont, center, dir, font, isindex, menu, s, strike, u, xmp Tags that are *deprecated* (should no longer be used in new web pages), but are nevertheless still supported by many browsers.

2. As we have seen, XHTML tags can have attributes. These attributes fall into several categories:

   (a) Some attributes are *required* (the `src` attribute for the `img` tag, for example) and some are *optional* (the `border` attribute for the `table` tag, for example).

   (b) There are also very useful attributes called *core attributes* (or *standard attributes*) that are also optional and can be used with virtually any XHTML tag. These include the `id` and `class` attributes that we will meet in the next chapter in the context of CSS, as well as the `title` and `style` attributes.

   (c) Another kind of optional attribute is the *event attribute*, which can be used to fire up a JavaScript script under certain conditions. For example, the `onclick` attribute might have as its value a JavaScript script that would run when the element with that attribute was clicked on by the user. We will look at event attributes in a later chapter on JavaScript.

3. One of the reasons we often do not provide attributes for our tags when they are optional is because optional tags have default values that tend to be what we want most of the time. It is helpful to become familiar with the default values of commonly used tag attributes.

   For example, the `p` tag has an attribute called `align`, which may take any of the values `"left"`, `"right"`, `"center"`, or `"justify"`. Fortunately, the default value is `"left,"` since we want our paragraphs to be left-justified most of the time. Furthermore, this attribute is actually deprecated, so you should use CSS to get the effect you would like to achieve by using this attribute.

   Similarly, the `td` tag has an attribute called `valign`, which may take any of the values `"top"`, `"middle"`, `"bottom"`, or `"baseline"`. The default is `"middle"`, but when we used this attribute for the links in the first column of the main content area of a number of our "`nature3` website" pages, we found the value `"top"` more convenient.

4. Another important distinction to be aware of when you are placing XHTML elements into your web documents is the difference between the following two kinds of elements:

> **Block-level elements** These elements occupy their own "vertical space" on the page, and generally cause the browser to place extra space both before and after the element (how much space depends on the element and the browser). Examples include the heading elements (**h1**, etc.) and the paragraph element **p**.

> **Inline elements** These elements do *not* cause any additional space to appear either before or after them. Examples include the **img** element and any **strong** or **em** element.

Another aspect of nesting in XHTML is that some (but not all) block-level elements permit other block-level elements to be nested inside them, but you cannot nest a block-level element inside an inline element.

5. We know that clicking on a link will usually take us to the beginning of the page at the end of that link, but sometimes the **href** value of a link will look like

```
http://mysite.com/mypage.html#markedspot
```

and in this case clicking on the corresponding link will take you, as usual, to **mypage.html** on **mysite.com**, but rather than displaying that page from the beginning, the browser will start its display of the page at the place on the page identified by an **a** tag having a **name** attribute with a value of **"markedspot"**. For example, if you wanted to go to a certain heading on the page you could identify the heading like this:

```
<h1><a name="markedspot">This is the certain heading</a></h1>
```

6. HTML 5 was mentioned at the beginning of this chapter as the next iteration in the evolution of the standard markup language for the Web. We do not discuss it in detail because it is not yet widely, completely, or uniformly supported by the major browsers. This is changing rapidly, however, and every web developer should be keeping a finger on the pulse of associated events. HTML 5 is more like HTML than XHTML in that its specifications are less restrictive. For example, tags are again case-insensitive, and attribute values do not have to be enclosed in quotes. There are also many new tags, and some of the pre-existing tags have

new semantics. That having been said, if you have developed a good, consistent style for writing your XHTML markup, you will likely be able to continue using that style, with minimal disruption, since backward compatibility will be required if the majority of websites are to continue working. For example, you can still use lowercase tags and enclose your attribute values in quotation marks, as required by XHTML.

3.18   References

1. Many of our references here and in the rest of the text will refer you to particular pages on the W3 Schools site, since the site is very useful from both a tutorial and reference perspective, but you may want to start at the home page and explore, so here it is:

   `http://www.w3schools.com/`

2. Another tutorial site that you may find useful now and later is this one:

   `http://www.tizag.com/`

3. For further information on HTML and XHTML, including their history and the relationship between them, check the following Wikipedia links (the HTML page has a nice picture of Tim Berners-Lee):

   `http://en.wikipedia.org/wiki/HTML`
   `http://en.wikipedia.org/wiki/XHTML`

4. You will find a list of the available XHTML entities here:

   `http://www.w3schools.com/tags/ref_entities.asp`

5. Anytime you look up an XHTML tag on the W3 Schools site, you will also find information on its attributes and their values, but for a general overview of tag attributes see the following links:

   `http://www.w3schools.com/tags/ref_standardattributes.asp`
   `http://www.w3schools.com/tags/ref_eventattributes.asp`

6. For further information on the differences between HTML and XHTML, as well as the particulars of XHTML syntax, see the following links:

   http://www.w3schools.com/xhtml/xhtml_html.asp
   http://www.w3schools.com/xhtml/xhtml_syntax.asp

7. For further information on which elements can be nested inside other elements, see:

   http://www.cs.tut.fi/~jkorpela/html/nesting.html

8. To keep an eye on what's happening with HTML 5, you can check out the actual specification at

   http://www.w3.org/TR/html5/

   and a more web-author-friendly version of the specification here

   http://dev.w3.org/html5/spec-author-view/

   as well as a useful page summarizing all markup tags (with a clear indication of which tags are new and which have altered semantics) at this location:

   http://dev.w3.org/html5/markup/

   The W3C itself seems to be in a bit of a promotional mood with respect to HTML 5, and you too can get on board at this site:

   http://www.w3.org/html/logo/

   To read about the differences between HTML 5 and HTML 4 look here:

   http://www.w3.org/TR/html5-diff/

   The *Web Hypertext Application Technology Working Group (WHATWG)* is a community of folks interested in the "practical" evolution of the Web. It was this group whose work eventually convinced the W3C that continued development of the XHTML standard would not be a good idea, and work on XHTML 2 has now officially been abandoned, in favor of HTML 5. Both the W3C and the WHATWG are now fully behind the HTML 5 effort, though they remain separate entities. For more information, go to this site and check out the FAQ (Frequently Asked Questions) section in particular:

   http://www.whatwg.org/

CHAPTER 4

CSS for Content Presentation

CHAPTER CONTENTS

4.1   Overview and Objectives

In the previous chapter we introduced XHTML as the currently recommended markup language for describing the *structure* of a web page. Thus we use XHTML tags to mark the parts of our pages that are headings, paragraphs, list items, and so on.

Every browser will have its own default way of displaying each of these structures, and sometimes these defaults may be adequate for our purposes. On the other hand, there are many times when we wish to take control of how our pages look, and where on those pages our information is to be displayed. For example, we may want a different font size or text color, or we may want two columns of text rather than one, and that is where *Cascading Style Sheets* (*CSS*) come into play.

In this chapter we will discuss the following:

- Why CSS came into existence, and the problem they help to solve

- The syntax of a CSS style rule

- The placement of style sheets (or style rules) relative to the document (or element) being styled

- Some typical examples of style rules

- Some common types of CSS property values and their formats

- Structuring, commenting, and formatting CSS style sheets

- Using the CSS `class` and `id` selectors with the XHTML `div` and `span` attributes

- The "cascade" and inheritance

- The CSS box model

- Simple CSS page layout with "floating" `divs`

- CSS reset as a "best practice"

- Styling our Nature's Source website with CSS

- Validating our CSS style sheets

4.2   Why CSS?

In the early days of the Web there existed something of a wild west mindset, when browser developers were all doing their own thing. Before long there began to appear new HTML tags like the `font` tag which allowed a developer to specify the font size and color of paragraph text, for example. In other words, HTML was suddenly being used to describe certain presentational aspects of web pages, something that it was never designed to do. To make matters worse, because there were no standards for this sort of thing, different browsers did not always implement their rendering of these HTML "enhancements" in the same way.

By the mid-1990s it was recognized that this was not a good idea,[1] and *Cascading Style Sheets* (*CSS*) were developed—largely based on the work of Bert Bos and Håkon Wium Lie—to separate the description of how a page should look (its "presentation") from the description of the structural content of the page, which is the job of (X)HTML. We introduce some of the main features of CSS in this chapter.

4.3   Simple CSS Style Rules and Their Syntax

A CSS *style rule* is a rule that tells a browser how some part of a web page is to be displayed. For example, here are two simple style rules:

```
body {background-color: yellow;}
h1 {color: blue;}
```

These style rules can be used to tell a browser that the entire **body** of a web page is to have a background color of yellow, and the text of every **h1** element on that page is to be displayed in blue. A collection of style rules is called a *style sheet*, so these two rules could comprise a very simple style sheet for a web document, as prepared by a web developer. Everything else in this document would be displayed according to browser defaults, possibly modified by the user adjusting browser settings.

The syntax is typical of a simple style rule. In this case, **body** and **h1** are *selectors*. Think of a *selector* as the name of an XHTML element tag that has been "selected" to have elements of that kind styled in a certain way.

The other part of a rule, the part appearing within the braces, consists of one or more *declarations*. In this case, each rule has a single declaration. Multiple declara-

---

[1]So the `font` tag, among others, was deprecated, though it is still widely supported.

tions are separated by semicolons(;), and even if there is only a single declaration, placing a semicolon after it may be regarded as a "best practice." A declaration indicates just how its corresponding selector element is to be styled.

Thus each part of `background-color: yellow` and `color: blue` is a declaration. A declaration contains a *property* (such as `background-color` or `color`), followed by the *value* of that property (`yellow` or `blue` in this case), and separated from it by a colon (as well as a space, which is optional but enhances readability). Note that it might have been more helpful, and consistent, if the CSS folks had named the `color` property `text-color`, or perhaps `foreground-color`, but they didn't, and there's nothing we can do about it now.

4.4   Where Do You Place Your CSS Style Rules?

OK, once you have some style rules, how do you arrange to have them applied to one (or more) of your web pages? You have several options, and each one corresponds to a different style sheet "level," a concept we will explore further in section 4.10:

1. The *external level*, which permits you to place all of your styles in a separate file (which should have a `.css` extension) and link that file to the XHTML document to which you wish to have those styles applied (or to several different XHTML documents, for that matter). This is the recommended option and the one we will use. For added flexibility you can also bring one style file into another via the `@import` mechanism, but we will not use this technique.

2. The *document level*, which permits you to group all your styles, place them within an XHTML `style` element, and then place this `style` element and its contents within the `head` element of your document.

3. The *inline level*, which permits you to apply a given style directly to a single XHTML element by making the style rule the value of the `style` attribute of that XHTML element. Do not confuse the *style element* mentioned in the previous item with the *style attribute* mentioned here.

Styles at the document level apply only to the document in which they appear. A style at the inline level applies only to the XHTML element to which it is attached. These options do permit fine tuning of very specific presentational requirements, either for a single XHTML document or a single XHTML element, but our preferred first option permits the same collection of styles to be applied to as many documents as we like, and to whatever elements we choose within those documents. Among other things, this means that we could potentially change some aspect of the presentation of our entire website just by making one small change in one location (the style file). The advantages of this approach for site maintenance should be obvious.

We will explore the second and third options above in the exercises, but for now let's take a look at a simple example illustrating our preferred approach.

4.5 A Simple Example

To illustrate the application of CSS style rules stored in an external file we link the file `simple.css` shown in Figure 4.1 to the XHTML file `simple.html` shown in Figure 4.2. The CSS style sheet of Figure 4.1 contains (as its first line) a CSS-style comment giving the name of the file, and the two style rules discussed in section 4.3 above. The XHTML file `simple.html` of Figure 4.2 is the same one given as `second.html` in Figure 3.3 of the previous chapter, except that the **head** element now contains the additional line

```
<link rel="stylesheet" type="text/css" href="css/simple.css" />
```

shown as line 5, which serves to connect the file of CSS rules to the XHTML file where those rules are to be applied. Note that this line introduces the XHTML **link** tag (another empty XHTML tag that does not come in a tag pair), and three of its attributes:

- **rel**, which has the value **stylesheet** to indicate the "relationship" to the current file, of the file named in the **href** attribute

- **type**, which has the value **text/css** to indicate that this is a "text file containing CSS rules" (as opposed to some other kind of style file)

- **href**, whose value is the name of the file containing the style rules for this XHTML file (and can also be the full path to a file, as in this case, if the style file is not in the same directory as the XHTML file to which it is linked)[2]

The result of displaying the XHTML file shown in Figure 4.2, with the styles shown in the CSS file of Figure 4.1 applied to it, is shown in Figure 4.3. Our CSS rules for this web page affect only the color of two XHTML elements, **body** and **h1**,

---

[2]Note that our CSS file is in a subdirectory called **css**, a common convention that we will follow.

```
1   /* simple.css */
2   body {background-color: yellow;}
3   h1 {color: blue;}
```

FIGURE 4.1

cdrom/web04/css/simple.css
A very simple CSS style file containing a CSS comment indicating the name of the file and two style rules.

```
1   <!-- simple.html -->
2   <html>
3     <head>
4       <title>Nature's Source</title>
5       <link rel="stylesheet" type="text/css" href="css/simple.css" />
6     </head>
7     <body>
8       <h1>Welcome to the Website of Nature's Source!</h1>
9       <p>This is our first foray onto the World Wide Web. We are a small
10      company dedicated to the health of our customers through natural
11      remedies.
12      <br />
13      We have a wide range of products that include:</p>
14      <ul>
15        <li>books, and multimedia documents that help you get healthy and
16        stay healthy</li>
17        <li>herbal medicines</li>
18        <li>equipment for injury free body toning exercises</li>
19      </ul>
20    </body>
21  </html>
```

FIGURE 4.2

cdrom/web04/simple.html
A file with the same contents as second.html (from Figure 3.3), but this time linked to simple.css.

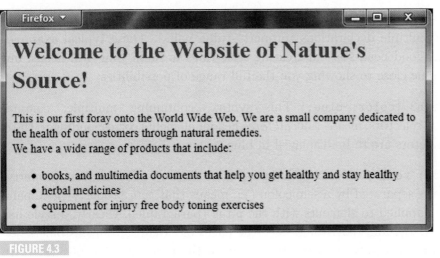

FIGURE 4.3
graphics/ch04/displaySimpleHtml.jpg
A Firefox browser display of `simple.html`, with CSS from `simple.css`.

but already you can probably get a sense of the possibilities. Not only the color of the text, and the page background color, but many other properties such as font size, font family, and other text properties, as well as higher-level features such as margin widths and page layout, may be controlled by CSS styles.

In this particular XHTML file, there was only one `h1` element, but in the absence of any further instructions, *every* `h1` element in this document would have been displayed in blue text, if there had been more. And, of course, the web page has only a single body, and its background is displayed in yellow. You may find these colors not to your taste. The point to be made here, however, is this: If you have, in one place, all of the style rules for all of the `h1` elements on this page (and possibly on many other pages, if those other pages are also linked to this CSS style document), you can change the color of *all* of those `h1` elements by making one small change to the appropriate style rule in the linked CSS document.

4.6 Some Basic CSS Markup: More on Selectors, Declarations, Properties, and Property Values

In the previous section we saw how a (simple) CSS style rule is comprised of a selector, followed by a declaration enclosed by braces, and how a (simple) declaration is in turn comprised of a property and its value, separated by a colon (`:`). In this section we will give a few examples of some more complex style rules involving multiple selectors and multiple declarations (property-value pairs). These typical examples will give you a good head start in creating style rules to fulfill your own needs, but they do not come close to showing you the full range of possibilities:

h1, h2, h3 {color: blue;} This syntax, containing multiple, comma-separated selectors, means that *all three* header elements corresponding to those three selectors are to be displayed in blue text.

p {color: red; font-size: large;} This syntax, with its two property-value pairs separated by a semicolon (;), means that *both* property-value pairs are to be applied to elements with the p tag (paragraphs). Clearly, a style like this one (large and red) would have the effect of catching your customers' attention and probably annoying them beyond the point of doing business with you.[3] As you might guess, you can have both multiple selectors, as in the preceding example, and multiple property-value pairs, as in the current example, within a single style rule.

body {font-family: Verdana, Arial, sans-serif;} This syntax, with a comma-separated list of property values for the font-family property, means that the browser should search for the Verdana font first, then Arial, and then whatever the system provides for a generic *sans-serif font* (a font *without* the little curlicues at the ends of its letters). If all these searches fail, the browser will simply use its default font, which may or may not be sans-serif. If a font-family name contains spaces, the name must be enclosed in quotes, as in "Courier New", for example.

ul li {font-style: italic;} The first thing to note about this syntax is that the list of (two) selectors is *not* comma-separated. This rule says that the text of a list element (li), when it appears in an unordered list (ul), should be italicized. In this situation li is called a *descendant selector*,[4] because the rule only applies to list items that appear within the context of an *unordered* list (a list with bulleted items, say, rather than numbered items). Thus if a list item appeared within the tags for an ordered list (ol), its text would *not* be italicized in that context (at least it wouldn't be because of *this* rule).

---

[3]The authors are more concerned with the technical aspects of web page development and do not consider themselves design experts. However, you may from time to time encounter a helpful reminder like this one.

[4]In the CSS level 1 specification such elements used to be called *contextual selectors*, but the terminology was changed to *descendant selector* in CSS 2. You will still encounter the earlier term here and there.

Some property categories	Names of some properties in each category
background	`background-color, background-image,` `background-position`
font	`font-size, font-style, font-weight, font-family`
text	`text-align, text-decoration, color`
border	`border-width, border-style, border-color`
margin	`margin-left, margin-right`

Table 4.1

Some CSS property categories and some properties from each category.

The point of these examples is to show you how several XHTML elements may be given the same style, how a single style may contain specifications for more than one property of an XHTML element, and how an XHTML element may be given a certain style only if it is found in a particular context. In the exercises of section 4.17 you will see these styles applied.

However, we have only shown a very limited number of properties that XHTML elements may have, as well as a limited number of their corresponding property values. Table 4.1 shows a few more property categories, in addition to the ones we've seen, along with some of the properties in each category. Neither the category column nor the property-name column contains a complete list, and no values are given for any of the properties. In the next section we provide some additional detail on how CSS specifies font size, lengths of various kinds, and color. See also the **References** section at the end of this chapter for further information.

4.7   Some Common Types of CSS Property Values and Their Formats

One of the best ways to learn CSS is to study some CSS style rules and try to reconcile their content with the display of whatever XHTML (or HTML) document employs those rules. However, when you begin to do this there is great potential for confusion, since the values of many CSS properties can be written in so many different ways. Thus if you look at CSS rules written by different authors it is quite likely you will notice inconsistencies that will raise some unsettling questions in your mind until you are able to recognize the equivalence of the various formats.

For example, if you look at Table 4.2 you will see how much variety is possible just with units of measurement (for a property like **font-size**) or color (for a property

Property value category	Possible units or formats for values in that category
measurement (absolute units)	in, cm, mm, pt (point) (72pt = 1in), pc (pica) (1pc = 12pt)
measurement (relative units)	px (pixel), em (width of M), ex (height of x), % (percentage)
measurement (absolute keywords)	xx-small, x-small, small, medium, large, x-large, xx-large
measurement (relative keywords)	larger, smaller
color (hex)	#0000FF, #008000, #708090
color (hex short)	#00F, N/A, N/A
color (rgb absolute)	rgb(0,0,255), rgb(0,128,0), rgb(70,80,90)
color (rgb relative)	rgb(0%,0%,100%), rgb(0%,50%,0%), rgb(27%,31%,35%)
color (keywords)	blue, green, slategrey

Table 4.2

Different formats for two kinds of CSS property values.

like `background-color`, or `color` itself). And again, this is just part of the story. For a more complete account, see the **References** section at the end of this chapter.

4.7.1   Specifying Font Sizes and Lengths

The information shown in Table 4.2 requires some comment. The first line of this table shows that a number of common units like inches (`in`), centimeters (`cm`), and millimeters (`mm`) can be used to specify properties like `font-size`. The point (`pt`) and pica (`pc`) units have been more commonly used by typesetters over the years, but find less use on the Web. These units allow the user to choose "absolute" sizes, in contrast to the "relative" units of the second line in the table. Relative units are generally preferred to absolute units on the Web because they "scale" up and down in size when the user adjusts the size of the browser window in a way that absolute units do not.

The first of the relative units is *pixel* (`px`), whose size depends on screen resolution. The size of the other units is relative to the current font size. An `em` is the width of a capital M in the current font, an `ex` is the height of a lowercase x in the current font, and one may also specify a percentage of the current `font-size` value.

Sizes may also be specified using keywords (`xx-large`, `x-large`, and so on). These keywords provide "absolute" measurements only in the sense that one can (usually) expect that `xx-large` will be the same size as the `font-size` of the XHTML h1 element, `x-large` the same as that used for the XHTML h2 element, and so on, with `xx-small` "something smaller than h6," since there is no XHTML h7 element. The "relative keywords" `smaller` and `larger` can also be used to specify a size smaller or larger than the current font size. A factor of 1.2 is generally used when scaling font sizes up or down. For example, the size of h2 text (`x-large`) is 1.2 times the size of h3 text (`large`), and so on.

Any of the following values may be regarded, most of the time, as representing the default font size in a browser: `12pt`, `16px`, `1em`, `100%`, `medium`.

4.7.2 Specifying Colors

The remaining lines of Table 4.2 show the many ways you can specify colors on your web page. If you use a "hex value" of six hexadecimal digits, preceded by a hash symbol (`#`),[5] you can choose any one of 16,777,216 colors. Your monitor may not be able to display all of these colors accurately, so you may be better off going with a color scheme that uses some of the more "standard" colors.

Note that if each group of two digits in a hexadecimal value contains two of the same digit, the value may be written in a shorthand form containing each digit once only. For example, `#22AA99` may be written as `#2A9`.

All colors are composed of various amounts of the three "primary" colors: red, green, and blue. In a six-digit hexadecimal value for color, the first two digits represent the amount of red, the next two the amount of green, and the last two the amount of blue. Thus any one of these colors can have a "hex value" in the range 00 to FF. This corresponds to the range 0 to 255 using decimal notation, or 0% to 100% if percentages are employed, either of which may be used if the user decides to go with the "rgb format" shown in the table.

Keywords like `blue` and `green` can also be used for common colors, as well as some less common ones like `slategrey`, but even here you need to be careful. For example, the color `blue` might be what you actually want when you choose that color, since it has the hex value `#0000FF` (the full amount of blue, and no red or

---

[5]The symbol # has various names. Its technical name is *octothorpe*, believe it or not, but it is more commonly called the "number sign," or, as we have done, the "hash symbol." You may even see it referred to, somewhat confusingly, as the "pound symbol."

green). But if you choose the keyword `green` for your color, you will get the color with hex value #008000, and not (as you might have expected) the color with hex value #00FF00. To get the latter color you must choose the keyword `lime`.[6]

Since CSS is case-insensitive, at least in this context, you can also write keyword colors `blue` and `slategrey` as `Blue` and `SlateGrey`. Using capital letters in this way enhances readability for multi-word names. You should decide which convention you wish to follow and stick with it. In other words, do not "mix and match." For reasons that we will discuss later, and just as a good general practice, it is always a good idea, and sometimes a critical requirement, for you to be completely consistent with the capitalization of names you use on your web pages.

The universal browser default color for text is `black` (#000).

Color Groupings

There are several "color groupings" you should be aware of as well. We will discuss this aspect of color very briefly here, explore the matter further in the exercises, and give you leads to further information in the end-of-chapter **References**.

The first and smallest of these color groupings consists of the 16 standard CSS colors. They all have keyword names (like `blue`, `green`, or `yellow`), and you can expect to see each of them displayed properly in all browsers on all color monitors, regardless of age or computing platform being used.

The next group consists of the 216 colors in the so-called *web palette* of *web-safe colors*, also called the *web-safe palette*.[7] These colors are web-safe in the sense that they will probably display consistently across any platform capable of displaying up to 256 colors. Any color in the web-safe palette must have a hex value composed by choosing three values, with repetition allowed, from the following: 00, 33, 66, 99, CC, and FF. For example, #3366CC (or #36C) and #99FF00 (or #9F0) are web-safe colors.

Another group of colors consists of all those colors that have recognized names, like the standard names `blue` and `yellow` that we have seen already, but many others we have not seen as well. Although many browsers recognize well over a hundred of these additional color names nowadays, there is still not as much conformity as we might like from one browser to another, so using a `hex` or `rgb` value for your desired color is usually a "safer" choice, and the one recommended.

---

[6]Surely this is one of those things that is true only "for historical reasons."

[7]This color grouping was developed by Lynda Weinman. If you're interested in online training, check out `http://lynda.com`.

4.7.3   The Important Takeaway from This Section

The thing to take away from this section is the desirability of choosing some conventions of your own to follow when you need to make use of a unit of measurement or a color or some other property whose values may be expressed in more than one way. Just as your web pages themselves should always have a consistent "look and feel," so should your behind-the-scenes XHTML and CSS markup. You can achieve this by always using the same type of representation for a given kind of data. At the same time, become familiar enough with the alternate representations to be able to read the source code of web pages written by other developers when you want to do so.

4.8   CSS Style Sheet Structure, Comments, and Formatting

Because a CSS style sheet file is just a text file with a `.css` extension, it can be created with any text editor. Good practice once again dictates that the file should have a comment containing at least the name of the file, and a brief description of the file's contents if required.

You should also give some thought to the organization of the rules within a style file. One way that lets you find the style of a particular element quickly is simply to order the XHTML element selectors alphabetically, but this may only be practical for a short and simple CSS style sheet. Once you have a header, footer, and content sections in your XHTML document, you will likely want to group your CSS styles according to these and perhaps other divisions. A preceding comment describing each grouping is always a good idea.

Figure 4.4 shows the contents of the file `mystyles.css`. First of all, the file shows a CSS comment[8] that begins with a forward slash and asterisk as the opening delimiter (`/*`), and ends with an asterisk and forward slash as the closing delimiter (`*/`) as we have already seen in an earlier example. This kind of comment can be used for either single-line comments, multi-line comments, or end-of-line comments, all of which are illustrated in this file.

We find it convenient to format our CSS style files as shown in this example, though you will certainly see other formatting used if you look at other such files. Note that if there is a single declaration, we put everything on one line. Otherwise, we place each declaration on a line of its own. In virtually every other context, the

---

[8]The style of comment used by CSS goes all the way back to the C programming language, and is also used in programming languages of more recent vintage, including C++, Java®, and JavaScript.

```
1    /* mystyles.css
2    A few styles to illustrate the structure and formatting of a
3    CSS style file
4    */
5
6    /* Styles that apply to every element in the body, unless overridden */
7    body {
8    font-family: Verdana, Arial, Helvetica, sans-serif;
9    font-size: large;
10   color: #000;
11   background-color: #FF0; /* yellow */
12   }
13
14   h1 {color: #00F;} /* Overrides body font color style above */
15
16   /* Styles any list item in an unordered list */
17   ul li {
18   font-size: medium; /* Overrides body font size above */
19   font-style: italic;
20   }
```

FIGURE 4.4

cdrom/web04/css/mystyles.css
A CSS style file illustrating a CSS comment and style rule formatting.

authors, who are big fans of readability, are inclined to use indentation and vertical alignment of braces as part of their formatting style. However, we find that with CSS, largely because there is no nesting of brace-enclosed blocks, the style illustrated here conserves some vertical space and is actually quite readable, as long as each rule is separated from the next by a blank line.

We apply the styles in this style file (or "style sheet") to an XHTML file called mystyles.html. We do not show this file because its contents are exactly the same as those of the file simple.html of Figure 4.2, except that mystyles.html is, of course, now linked to the new CSS style file mystyles.css. The resulting display is shown in Figure 4.5.

The style of the body tag for the web page of Figure 4.5 requires a background color of yellow, with black text in a large Verdana font, if available, unless some other style "overrides" these properties. The first override takes place with the style of an h1 element, which sets those elements to be displayed in blue. The h1 element also has a (much) larger font than the regular text, since this is part of the h1 element's (default, browser-determined) specification, which we have not altered. Finally, an italic style is added to any elements that appear in an unordered list, and in addition, those same list elements have a font of size medium, which is just the default size,

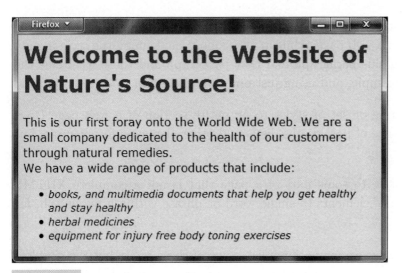

FIGURE 4.5

graphics/ch04/displayMystylesHtml.jpg
A Firefox browser display of `mystyles.html`, styled by the CSS from `mystyles.css`.

and which overrides the size `large` we specified earlier, and is used for the paragraph before the list.

See section 4.10 for more on how this "overriding" is handled in CSS by *inheritance* and *the cascade*.

4.9 The XHTML `class` and `id` Attributes and the XHTML `div` and `span` Elements

Whenever we have defined a CSS style, up to this point, that style was applied to one or more XHTML elements on a web page because we attached the style directly to one or more XHTML tags in the style rule definition. In the context of CSS, each such *XHTML element* became a *CSS selector*, and the given CSS style would apply to *each instance* of the XHTML element found in the styled document.

As we continue to develop our website, we will also find it convenient to do one or more of the following, which we cannot do with the kinds of style rules we have seen so far:

- Apply a given style to some, but not to all, of the XHTML elements of a particular type in a web page (to some of the paragraphs, but not to all of them, for example)

- Apply a given style to one or more XHTML elements of different types at different places in a web page, while at the same time defining the style in only one place (giving this paragraph and that paragraph and those list items the same style, for example, and using just one style definition to do it)

- Apply a given style or set of styles to an entire section of a web page (to a contiguous sequence of paragraphs, lists, and other elements, for example, but not to the whole page)

- Apply a given style to some part of a page that is not a complete XHTML element or group of elements (a single word or phrase within a paragraph, for example)

There are various ways we may accomplish some of these tasks, but the simplest approach to all of them involves the use of one or more of two XHTML attributes (`class` and `id`) and two XHTML elements (`div` and `span`) that we have not yet discussed.

4.9.1   The XHTML `class` and `id` Attributes (CSS `class` and `id` Selectors)

Let's begin by stating two important facts:

1. Virtually every XHTML element has both a `class` attribute and an `id` attribute.

2. Just as any XHTML element can become a CSS selector, so can either the `class` attribute or the `id` attribute, so we often refer to the CSS `class` selector or the CSS `id` selector.

Because of these two facts, we are able to use, in addition to element selectors, the `class` and `id` attribute selectors to help us style our web pages in the way that we shall now describe, with the help of the following example:

```
.BoldItalic {
font-weight: bold;
font-style: italic;
}
```

Here we have what we refer to as a CSS *class selector definition*, or just a *class definition* for short. We have chosen the name for our class to be `BoldItalic`, and we follow the name with the style declarations enclosed within braces, just as we would do for an element selector. Note, however, the period immediately preceding the class name. It is this period that identifies BoldItalic as the name of a class whose definition is contained within the following braces. The styles in the definition follow the declaration syntax with which we are already familiar.

Thus a CSS *class definition* is really just a mechanism for giving a name to a group of style declarations. The user-chosen name BoldItalic should, of course, be descriptive of the style(s) involved in a useful way.[9] Note the capitalization used, which is not required, but can serve to enhance readability and help distinguish class names from other entities in your file. This particular kind of CSS class definition is often called a "generic" class, since it can be applied to *any* XHTML element, as we will see.

On the other hand, if we knew that we only wanted to apply the styles in the class called Standout to certain paragraph elements, we could make this clear, and restrict the use of the class to paragraph elements, by defining the class like this:

```
p.Standout {
color: #FF0000; /* red */
background-color: #D3D3D3; /* lightgray */
}
```

The next question is this: Once we have defined a class, how do we use it to achieve the styling it was designed to accomplish? In the case of p.Standout we would do this:

```
<p class="Standout">
This paragraph will really stand out on your page ...
</p>
```

Note how we use the class attribute of the XHTML p tag and give it a value of Standout to indicate that this particular paragraph is to be displayed using the Standout style, and we could do this for however many paragraphs we wished to display in this way.[10] Other paragraphs, which have no class attribute, or whose

---

[9]But the name chosen here is not necessarily a good one, as one of the end-of-chapter quick questions tries to point out, and perhaps you can think of a criticism even now.

[10]A valid question at this point is, "How does this differ from using the style attribute, which is discouraged?" One answer is that if you were to use the style attribute in the same way, and wanted to change the style, you would have to change the value of the style attribute in every element that had been styled in that way. If you use the class attribute, you need only change the class definition.

`class` attributes do not have this value, are unaffected by the styles of the `Standout` class.

On the other hand, if we want to display a paragraph using our `BoldItalic` class, we simply do this:

```
<p class="BoldItalic">
This paragraph will appear in bold italic ...
</p>
```

The usage syntax here is exactly the same as it was when we invoked the `p.Standout` class. But here's the difference. If we have a list element that we want to display using `BoldItalic`, we can do it in a precisely analogous way:

```
<li class="BoldItalic">
This list item will appear in bold italic ...
</li>
```

This is OK, since the `BoldItalic` class is "generic" and hence can be used with *any* XHTML element tag that has a `class` attribute (most of them do). However, we *cannot* use the `Standout` class here with the list element because it has been restricted to paragraph elements (recall that we defined it as `p.Standout`).

The `id` selector is very much like the `class` selector, with respect to the way it is defined and used, but there are two major differences:

1. An `id` selector *must be unique within a web document*, unlike a `class` selector, which can appear many times in the same document.

2. The definition of an `id` selector is marked by an initial hash symbol (`#`), rather than the initial period (`.`) used in the definition of a `class` selector.

The uniqueness requirement allows an element with a particular `id` value to be distinguished from all other elements on the page. This will be very useful when we wish to access an element from within a JavaScript script, as we will do in later chapters. In our current context, it can be useful simply to identify uniquely a particular part of web page document for styling.

There is no need to discuss the `id` selector further here, because of its similarity to the `class` selector. However, note that you will see it employed when we use CSS to style our skeleton website for Nature's Source, and you will note as well that we use the same *camel capitalization*[11] for `id` selector names that we use for `class` selectors, except that we begin with a lowercase letter.

---

[11]The term "camel" as used here means that in multi-word names, the second and subsequent words begin with a capital letter (forming the camel's "humps," so to speak). The first word of the name may or may not be capitalized, depending on convention. For us, for example, `class` names are capitalized; `id` names are not.

4.9.2   The XHTML div and span Elements

Next, we introduce the XHTML div and span elements. Neither of these elements has any default layout of its own. However, since the span element is an inline-level element, we can use a span tag pair to enclose an "inline" portion of some element on our web page (a word or phrase in a paragraph, for example). Analogously, because the div element is a block-level element, we can use a div tag pair to enclose some "block level" portion of our web page (several contiguous paragraph elements, for example).

Since both the span tag and the div tag have a class attribute, we can apply any generic class or id selector to a span or div element with the same usage syntax we have seen above. For example, if there is a section of the web page in which we wish the text to be displayed using a bold, italic style, we could enclose that part of the web page like this:

```
<div class="BoldItalic">
The part of the web page to have the BoldItalic style goes here ...
</div>
```

Or, if we want a single word within an otherwise "normal" paragraph to have the BoldItalic style, we could do this:

```
<p>
Your users might think you a <span class="BoldItalic">nutcase</span>
if you did a great deal of this, but it really is quite handy at times.
</p>
```

Of course, for this particular style you could also achieve the same effect just by using (properly nested) XHTML tags, as in nutcase, but the CSS approach is much to be preferred, if only for the ease with which it allows you change the style: Make one change to the style itself, and see the effect of that change everywhere the style is used!

4.9.3   Using Our Class Definitions

Let's put at least some of this to work. To illustrate our class definitions in action, we add them to the file mystyles.css from Figure 4.4 and call the new file myclasses.css, which is shown in Figure 4.6. Note that we have also added a new style, BlackOnWhiteSerif, which will provide us with a serif font on a white background.

The XHTML file to which we apply the styles in myclasses.css is myclasses .html, which is shown in Figure 4.7. This file contains essentially the same content

```
1    /* myclasses.css */
2
3    /* Styles that apply to every element in the body, unless overridden */
4    body {
5    font-family: Verdana, Arial, Helvetica, sans-serif;
6    font-size: large;
7    color: #000;
8    background-color: #FF0; /* yellow */
9    }
10
11   h1 {color: #00F;} /* Overrides body font color style above */
12
13   /* Styles any list item in an unordered list */
14   ul li {
15   font-size: medium; /* Overrides body font size above */
16   font-style: italic;
17   }
18
19   /* A "generic" class whose styles can be applied to any element */
20   .BoldItalic {
21   font-weight: bold;
22   font-style: italic;
23   }
24
25   /* A "generic" class whose styles can be applied to any element */
26   .BlackOnWhiteSerif {
27   font-family: Georgia, "Times New Roman", Times, serif;
28   color: #000;
29   background-color: #FFF;
30   }
31
32   /* A class that can only be applied to paragraph elements */
33   p.Standout {
34   color: #F00; /* red */
35   background-color: #D3D3D3; /* lightgrey */
36   }
```

FIGURE 4.6

cdrom/web04/css/myclasses.css
A CSS style file containing the same styles as the previous style file mystyles.css, plus two generic classes and one class that applies only to paragraphs.

as the file simple.html from Figure 4.2 and mystyles.html, which was not shown in the text because it was the same as simple.html, except for the link. This version is sufficiently different that we show it again, so that you can see how the markup in the XHTML file accesses the CSS classes from the style file. The resulting display can be seen in Figure 4.8.

If we examine the XHTML markup in Figure 4.7, we see that everything in the body of the page *except* the h1 heading is now enclosed in a div element and that div element has the BlackOnWhiteSerif generic class style applied to it.

```
1   <!-- myclasses.html -->
2   <html>
3     <head>
4       <title>Nature's Source</title>
5       <link rel="stylesheet" type="text/css" href="css/myclasses.css" />
6     </head>
7     <body>
8       <h1>Welcome to the Website of Nature's Source!</h1>
9       <div class="BlackOnWhiteSerif">
10        <p>This is our first foray onto the World Wide Web. We are a small
11        company dedicated to the health of our customers through natural
12        remedies.</p>
13        <p class="Standout">We have a wide range of products that include:</p>
14        <ul>
15          <li>books, and multimedia documents that help you get healthy and
16          stay healthy</li>
17          <li class="BoldItalic">herbal medicines</li>
18          <li>equipment for injury free body toning exercises</li>
19        </ul>
20      </div>
21    </body>
22  </html>
```

FIGURE 4.7

`cdrom/web04/myclasses.html`
An XHTML document to illustrate the application of the CSS styles in `myclasses.css`.

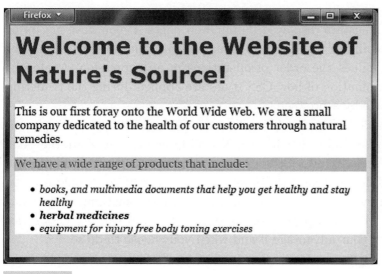

FIGURE 4.8

`graphics/ch04/displayMyclassesHtml.jpg`
A display of `cdrom/web04/myclasses.html` with styles from `cdrom/web04/css/`
`mystyles.css` in the Firefox browser.

To see how all of this comes together, and before continuing our discussion of this example, we need to say something about how a browser actually decides what style(s) to apply to a particular XHTML element as a web page is rendered on the screen, which we do in the following section.

4.10   What About the "Cascading" Part of Cascading Style Sheets?

We are well into a chapter on Cascading Style Sheets, but so far we have barely mentioned anything about the "Cascading" part of the title, so you may be starting to wonder why. The simple answer is that much of the time it is not something we need to worry too much about, since it often "takes care of itself." In fact, that is the general idea—it *should* take care of itself. This may well be all you ever need to know about such matters, but we also mention briefly in passing some of the details you may need to pursue if you have a mysterious problem of some kind and you need to track down its source, or you simply want to go beyond the basics.

As with many web technologies, the basic principles are quite straightforward, but the details can be quite complex. In this section we will just provide a brief overview of *inheritance* and the *cascade*, which control in a crucial and (normally) unobtrusive way how things are displayed on our web pages. If you have any prior experience with programming,[12] you will be familiar with the notion of *operator precedence*, which determines the order of operations in an expression. Analogous ideas apply in the determination of how CSS styles are applied during the rendering and display of a web page by a browser.

First of all, when we do not explicitly say how we want anything to be displayed, each browser has a set of defaults that it uses. Not all browsers may share the same set of defaults, so this is one cause for the differences we see when looking at the same web page using different browsers. However, it is unlikely you would ever be making use of all the browser defaults, and you need to know something about what actually happens when your web page is displayed, so that you can use CSS styles to modify the process to your advantage if and when you choose to do so.

4.10.1   Inheritance

Let's discuss the concept of *inheritance* first. To help you understand inheritance, first recall that a typical web page contains many instances of *nested elements*, that

---

[12]And though it may not be absolutely necessary, certainly at least a first programming course will make life much easier from Chapter 6 onward in this text.

is, elements inside one another. For example, the body will often contain several paragraphs (p elements) nested inside it. Any one of those paragraphs might contain a span element within it, and so on. This nesting structure creates a "parent-child relationship"[13] in which we might describe the body as the "parent" and each paragraph as a "child" of that parent, for example.

With this terminology, we can now describe *inheritance* by saying that many (but not all) properties of an element are "inherited" by default from its parent element. Another way of saying this is that if a parent has the property, and that property is one that *is* inherited, its children automatically have that property as well. Such properties include font-family, font-size, and color.

On the other hand, it would not be appropriate for some properties to be inherited, so they are not. The non-inherited properties include, for example, padding (the amount of space surrounding the content of an element, which we will say more about later in this chapter when we discuss the CSS "box model").

Thus, for example, if we specify that the body of a page is to have text in a font size of 20 pixels, so will all other elements that appear on that page, because font-size is an inherited property. Of course, such inherited properties can be "overridden" by other styles, according to the rules of the "cascade," and this is what we need to discuss next.

4.10.2   The "Cascade" and Resolution of Style Conflicts

You can easily imagine how a conflict might arise among styles. To take an extreme example, suppose for a given web page you gave a style in an external CSS style file that said all paragraph text should be blue. Then, in a document-level style sheet you gave another rule that said all paragraph text should be green. Furthermore, for the third paragraph on the page, you specified in a style attribute for that p element that its text should be yellow.

This situation represents a "cascading" of styles (three of them, in this case), all applying (potentially, at least) to that third paragraph. What color text do you suppose that third paragraph would actually have?

Well, you could argue that what happens makes intuitive sense, and that's what we meant when we said earlier that most of the time you don't need to concern yourself with "the cascade" and how such conflicts are resolved.

The general rule is that the "most specific" style applies. The full set of rules used to determine the *specificity*[14] of an element and how the cascade will unfold

---

[13]This parent-child relationship will be discussed further when we talk about the DOM (Document Object Model) in the context of the JavaScript language in later chapters.

[14]The specificity of an element is a numerical quantity that allows elements to be compared to

in any given scenario is actually quite complicated, but in this case it simply means that the third paragraph will have yellow text because the attribute style is the "most specific" style that applies to this particular paragraph. In the absence of any other relevant styles, other paragraphs on this web page would have blue or green text depending on which came first in the `head` element of the document, the `style` element containing the embedded rule that says the text should be green or the link to the external document, which contains the rule saying the text should be blue.

The operative rule here is that, *all other things being equal,* whichever style rule is the last one seen by the browser is the one that is applied. Thus, in our example, if the link follows the `style` element, the text will be blue, otherwise it will be green.

Because of this operative rule, you should proceed as follows when preparing styles for your website:

1. Begin by putting all your styles in an external style sheet, and linking that file to each of your pages. With luck you will be able to keep all your styles there, and if you can do this (which should be your initial design goal, at least) that's the end of the process.

2. If the styles in a particular document are modifications of the styles in the general document, you may wish to place the modifying styles in a `style` element in the `head` element of that document. If you do this, make sure that the `style` element comes after the `link` element that references the external style sheet, since both will appear in the same document `head` element.

3. Finally, if the style of a particular element needs to be tweaked, place the style in the value of the `style` attribute for the element itself. Try to avoid doing this if at all possible, since the practice is currently strongly discouraged, and may eventually be deprecated.

4.10.3   Applying the Theory to Our Example

Now let's go back to our example and explain why you see what you see in Figure 4.8. If you study the XHTML markup (Figure 4.7) and its CSS styles (Figure 4.6), you

---

see which has the greater value, a value that can be used to help decide how a certain style is to be applied. If you will permit a moment's editorializing, let us say this: If you find yourself needing to calculate specificity on a regular basis, it is probably time to re-evaluate your web development strategy.

will see that the body is to have a background color of yellow and you can see this behind the `h1` welcome header at the top and at the sides and bottom of the display window.

Everything in the `body` element except for the `h1` element is enclosed within a `div` element, to which the class `BlackOnWhiteSerif` has been applied. The white background defined in this class gives a white background to the `div` element. Otherwise, the `div` element would have the default value of `transparent` for its `background-color` property and the yellow background of the `body` element would then "show through." The *second* paragraph within the `div` has the `lightgrey` background for that paragraph mandated by its `Standout` class.

As for the fonts and font colors, note first of all that a large, black Verdana font is specified as the font for the `body` element, but this font never actually shows up as specified because:

- The `h1` header text is blue (according to our styling of that element) and much larger (according to the browser default font size for `h1`, which we have not altered). Note as well that, in terms of specificity, an `h1` within a `body` element is "more specific" than a `body` element alone.

- The two paragraphs (`p` elements) in the `body` element are both within the `div` element that is styled by the `class` selector named `BlackOnWhiteSerif`, so they both have the Georgia serif font, again because a `p` element within a `body` element is more specific than a `body` element alone. Moreover, the second paragraph has the `Standout` style applied to it, which is still more specific (to that paragraph), so it has the red text and light grey background of the `Standout` class, in addition to the Georgia serif font.

- Finally, in the unordered list within the `div` element, the text is also italic, because all unordered list items have been styled italic, and the font size is `medium` (in effect, set back to the browser default). The `middle list` element is given the specific style `BoldItalic`, which of course renders its text bold, but the italic part of that style is redundant, since the overall style of the list is already italic.

The cumulative effect of all these styles results in the rather garish page you see in Figure 4.8. The colors and the spacing are not particularly pleasing, and of course you would probably not want a page to look like this. Nevertheless, from the striking color contrasts and other features of this example you should be able to get a feel for how styles can be used to alter the presentation of your web pages and how potential conflicts among styles are resolved, at least in simple cases.

4.11 The CSS Box Model and Simple CSS Page Layout

We are working our way toward the point where we can cut to the chase and use CSS to style the shell website we have set up for our Nature's Source business. But before we do that we need to discuss the following additional concepts: the *CSS box model*, *CSS float positioning for simple page layout*, and *CSS reset*. It should help your understanding of these ideas to see each of them in isolation before encountering them in practice in the context of our sample website.

4.11.1 The CSS Box Model

The CSS box model is important because it underlies everything you see on a web page. Every element, whether it's an inline element or a block element, is treated as a "box," which has a content area at its center. This content area may (or may not) be surrounded by some "padding," which is usually just white space around the content. This padding, in turn, may (or may not) be enclosed by a "border," and finally, the whole thing may (or may not) be surrounded by a "margin," which again is usually just whitespace. These are often properties that we don't need to worry about because for many elements they may be absent altogether, or a browser may have default values for some of them if we do not specify them ourselves. This can also be a source of the differences one sees in displays of the same page in different browsers, since once again not all browsers will be using the same default values for these properties.

To make matters even more complicated, all three of these content-enclosing entities—padding, border, and margin—may appear on all four sides of the content box, or on just some of the sides. And even that is not the whole story.

Take a look at Figure 4.9, for which the corresponding XHTML is given in Figure 4.10 and the CSS is shown in Figure 4.11. This is once again a web page designed not to please the eye, but to illustrate some key points about the CSS box model. Begin by reading the text in Figure 4.9, which explains what you are seeing and encapsulates the essential features of the box model. Although you may be able to read it here in the text, we recommend that you browse to the file on your CD-ROM and display it in your browser of choice. It should look the same in any current browser.

If you resize the page in your browser several times, you will experience in real time some essential-to-know default behavior of the box model. In particular, you will note how the various "boxes" on this particular page always expand horizontally to fill the browser window, whatever its width. That is the default behavior when no width is specified for the page body or for an outer box in a page layout.

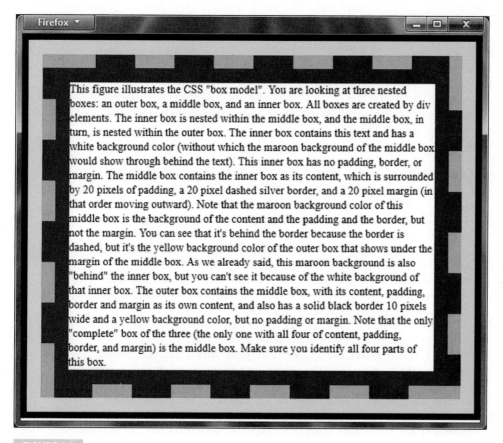

FIGURE 4.9

graphics/ch04/displayBoxmodelHtml.jpg
A Firefox browser display of `cdrom/web04/boxmodel.html`, illustrating the CSS box model.

Just as critical to observe is the fact that the behavior in the vertical direction is quite different. In this direction, only enough "expansion" takes place to accommodate the content, whatever the size of the browser window. Once again, this is best seen and appreciated by adjusting the size of your browser window while displaying the page, but even in Figure 4.9 you can see a white strip along the bottom, which confirms that the boxes have not expanded downward to fill the browser window. Note that throughout any resizing of the browser window, the 20px and 10px widths specified in the CSS style sheet of Figure 4.11 are retained.

Study this example carefully. We do not pretend that it shows you everything there is to know about the CSS box model. However, you can learn a great deal about that model by experimenting with this example, and in particular by changing the property values in the style sheet shown in Figure 4.11.

```
1   <!DOCTYPE html PUBLIC "-//W3C//DTD XHTML 1.0 Strict//EN"
2       "http://www.w3.org/TR/xhtml1/DTD/xhtml1-strict.dtd">
3   <!-- boxmodel.html -->
4   <html xmlns="http://www.w3.org/1999/xhtml">
5     <head>
6       <title>CSS Box Model</title>
7       <meta http-equiv="Content-Type" content="text/html;charset=utf-8" />
8       <link rel="stylesheet" type="text/css" href="css/boxmodel.css" />
9     </head>
10    <body>
11      <div id='outerBox'>
12        <div id='middleBox'>
13          <div id='innerBox'>
14            This figure illustrates the CSS "box model". You are looking at
15            three nested boxes: an outer box, a middle box, and an inner box.
16            All boxes are created by div elements. The inner box is nested
17            within the middle box, and the middle box, in turn, is nested
18            within the outer box. The inner box contains this text and has a
19            white background color (without which the maroon background of the
20            middle box would show through behind the text). This inner box has
21            no padding, border, or margin. The middle box contains the inner
22            box as its content, which is surrounded by 20 pixels of padding, a
23            20 pixel dashed silver border, and a 20 pixel margin (in that order
24            moving outward). Note that the maroon background color of this middle
25            box is the background of the content and the padding and the
26            border, but not the margin. You can see that it's behind the border
27            because the border is dashed, but it's the yellow background color of
28            the outer box that shows under the margin of the middle box. As we
29            already said, this maroon background is also "behind" the inner box,
30            but you can't see it because of the white background of that inner
31            box. The outer box contains the middle box, with its content,
32            padding, border and margin as its own content, and also has a solid
33            black border 10 pixels wide and a yellow background color, but no
34            padding or margin. Note that the only "complete" box of the three
35            (the only one with all four of content, padding, border, and margin)
36            is the middle box. Make sure you identify all four parts of this box.
37          </div>
38        </div>
39      </div>
40    </body>
41  </html>
```

FIGURE 4.10

cdrom/web04/boxmodel.html
An XHTML document illustrating the CSS box model.

```
/* boxmodel.css */

body {
padding: 0;
margin: 0;
}

div#outerBox {
border: 10px solid black; /* Shorthand for styling a border */
background-color: yellow;
}

div#middleBox {
padding: 20px;
border: 20px dashed silver;
margin: 20px;
background-color: maroon;
}

div#innerBox {background-color: #fff;}
```

FIGURE 4.11

cdrom/web04/css/boxmodel.css
The CSS for the box model XHTML example in `boxmodel.html`.

One final item of interest in this example is the "shorthand" form of the **border** style shown in Figure 4.11. This works as follows. Line 9 of the file, which is the single style rule

```
border: 10px solid black;
```

is actually a shorthand form for the following three style rules:

```
border-width: 10px;
border-style: solid;
border-color: black;
```

It should be clear that shorthand forms for CSS styles can be handy for reducing the size of your style sheets. For further information see the **References** section at the end of the chapter.

4.11.2 Simple CSS Page Layout with float and clear

We already know how the inline and block elements found on a web page are rendered by a browser and displayed on a user's screen. Often, especially with very simple web pages, it may be perfectly OK for a web developer to "go with the flow" and let some or all of the web pages on a site be displayed in the default manner.

On the other hand, users generally expect to see something a little more interesting, especially on a site's home page, with a menu of options leading to other parts of the site, and perhaps some animation or at least an image or two for some color. And nowadays users fully expect to encounter pages capable of user interaction, for feedback, for payment for goods, and so on, especially on sites that expect to do business with their visitors.

The design of such sites very quickly leads to the desire by developers to exercise control over where things appear on their web pages, and hence to the question of how one can control element positioning via CSS. This too is a complicated subject, so we will give only a brief introduction here, and once again refer you to the **References** section at the end of the chapter for further information.

Another simple example will be useful for illustrating what we want to say here about CSS positioning, and you will also need to study the re-design of our Nature's Source website, which we discuss in the following sections.

For our purposes, we only need to understand the use of the CSS `float` and `clear` properties, which are illustrated by the page shown in Figure 4.12, whose XHTML markup and CSS styles are given in Figure 4.13 and Figure 4.14, respectively.

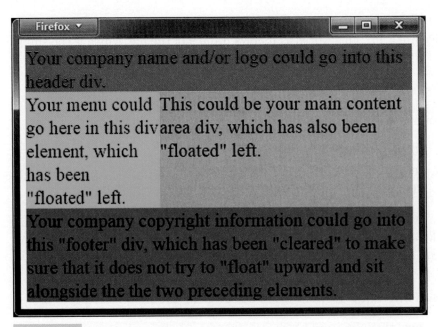

FIGURE 4.12

graphics/ch04/displayFloatHtml.jpg
A Firefox browser display of `cdrom/web04/float.html` illustrating CSS positioning using floats.

```
1    <!DOCTYPE html PUBLIC "-//W3C//DTD XHTML 1.0 Strict//EN"
2        "http://www.w3.org/TR/xhtml1/DTD/xhtml1-strict.dtd">
3    <!-- float.html -->
4    <html xmlns="http://www.w3.org/1999/xhtml">
5      <head>
6        <title>CSS Float Example</title>
7        <meta http-equiv="Content-Type" content="text/html;charset=utf-8" />
8        <link rel="stylesheet" type="text/css" href="css/float.css" />
9      </head>
10     <body>
11       <div id="page">
12         <div id="header">
13           Your company name and/or logo could go into this header div.
14         </div>
15         <div id="menu">
16           Your menu could go here in this div element, which has been
17           "floated" left.
18         </div>
19         <div id="content">
20           This could be your main content area div, which has also been
21           "floated" left.
22         </div>
23         <div id="footer">
24           Your company copyright information could go into this "footer" div,
25           which has been "cleared" to make sure that it does not try to
26           "float" upward and sit alongside the the two preceding elements.
27         </div>
28       </div>
29     </body>
30   </html>
```

FIGURE 4.13

cdrom/web04/float.html
An XHTML document illustrating simple CSS page layout using floats.

Note that the XHTML markup consists of four div elements nested inside a fifth "outer" div element, with each div element having an id attribute whose value is defined as an id selector in the CSS style sheet. Without the use of the CSS float property, all four of the inner div elements would display one after the other in a vertical sequence. The div identified as menu, however, has a float property with a value of left, which causes that div element to "float" up and to the left, with subsequent elements wrapping around it on the right if there is room for them to do so. Similarly, the same property and value for the div identified as content causes that div element also to float up and to the left and position itself to the right of the menu div.

Elements that are "floated" like this must have their widths specified, and the width of the containing element must be adequate to hold the two inner div elements side by side if that is how we wish them to appear. The "containing element" in

```
1    /* float.css */
2
3    body {
4    font-size: 1.5em;
5    }
6
7    div#page {
8    width: 500px;
9    background-color: silver;
10   }
11
12   div#header {
13   width: 100%;
14   background-color: red;
15   }
16
17   div#menu {
18   float: left;
19   width: 35%;
20   background-color: lime;
21   }
22
23   div#content {
24   float: left;
25   width: 65%;
26   background-color: lime;
27   }
28
29   div#footer {
30   clear: left;
31   width: 100%;
32   background-color: teal;
33   }
```

FIGURE 4.14

cdrom/web04/css/float.css
The CSS for the XHTML example in float.html illustrating CSS positioning with floats.

this case is the div identified as page. Since the menu div is 35% (of the enclosing page div) and the content div is 65% (of the enclosing page div), this criterion is satisfied.[15]

The clear property, with its value of left, will ensure that the div element identified as footer does *not* float up and to the left, even if there is room for it.

---

[15]A warning here is in order, however. If we use percentage widths in this way, browser rounding of calculated values *may* cause the total width of the enclosed elements to exceed the width of their container, leading to problems. For that reason, pixel widths *might* be safer.

Elements can also be floated to the right, with a value of `right` for the `float` property, in which case a following element will float upward and wrap itself around the right-floated element on the left, if there is room.

4.12   CSS Reset: A "Best Practice"

We should mention one other very useful concept that you may wish to explore before proceeding too far with the development of your website, the *CSS reset*. This notion relates to the fact that all browsers work with a number of default values for things like padding, margins, font size, and so on, but these defaults are not consistent across the various browsers.

Thus it makes sense for a web developer to reset certain values to a "baseline level," after which whatever values are desired can be set by the developer, using rules that are seen by the browser later than those that performed the CSS reset.

Some web developers have spent considerable time thinking about this and have recommendations of what to reset and how. Needless to say, they don't all agree. See the **References** section at the end of the chapter for further information.

For a very simple example, you might want to have the following rule as the very first one in your CSS style sheet:

```
* {
padding: 0;
margin: 0;
}
```

This rule uses the *universal selector* (*) to remove any browser-imposed margin and padding from *every* element on your web page, giving you free rein to establish your own margin and padding for individual elements. Note, however, that this depends on the above rule being properly implemented in the browser, which is unfortunately not guaranteed to be universally true either. However, we do use this rule ourselves in the re-styling of our Nature's Source website, as you will see.

You might find it "safer" to set the `margin` and `padding` properties to zero on all elements you intend to use individually. For example, note that in the CSS shown in Figure 4.11 we have used the style rule

```
body {
padding: 0;
margin: 0;
}
```

to remove any margin or padding that the browser would otherwise apply to any body element on our site. Because we have done this, we see no whitespace at the top or sides of our box model display in Figure 4.9. It is an interesting experiment to remove this style rule from the CSS file and re-display `boxmodel.html` in several different browsers to see what (default) spacing shows up in each browser. We have not done this for the CSS used for Figure 4.12, and you can see the surrounding default whitespace inserted by the browser.

4.13   Styling Our Nature's Source Website with CSS

The implementation of CSS in various browsers has been very uneven over the years, and the most widely used browser, Internet Explorer, has been particularly lax in standards compliance. With IE8, however, Microsoft has done a lot of catch-up, and some of what you read at the time of writing says that its browser now better supports the CSS page layout features that permit web developers to move away, finally, from using XHTML tables for this purpose.

Unfortunately, in the authors' experience this is not yet true to the extent one would hope. Nor do the other competing browsers exhibit consistent behavior when applying CSS rules to XHTML markup, sometimes even very simple rules.

We will show you in our examples what we believe to be "proper" behavior, given our markup and our styles, and based on current information at the time of writing. We will also continue to use Firefox as our browser of choice to display our pages the way we think they should look, and the way we hope they will look in all browsers at some future point. Your particular browser might not behave in quite the same way, but as time goes on all browsers should converge on the ideal and identical behavior as mandated by the evolving standards. Simply put, in a short text like this one we cannot delve into the intricacies of cross-browser support (making your pages look the same in a number of different browsers), and one hopes that such efforts will be needed less and less in the reasonably near future.

4.13.1   First, Our Simple Home Page

Recall that the display in Figure 3.6 was produced with XHTML table layout by the markup shown in Figure 3.5. In Figure 4.15 we show another version of this display,

FIGURE 4.15

graphics/ch04/nature1/displayIndexHtml.jpg
A Firefox browser display of cdrom/web04/nature1/index.html, our simple home page for Nature's
Source, with styles from cdrom/web04/nature1/css/default.css.

but this time it is produced by the XHTML markup shown in Figure 4.16, which is
linked to the CSS style file shown in Figure 4.17.

If you look at the XHTML markup in Figure 4.16, you see there is no longer any
sign of an XHTML table element. Instead, we have used XHTML div elements and
CSS id selectors to produce essentially the same display we had in Figure 3.6. This
is what we mean by a CSS layout, and nowadays you should be using CSS in this
way (or in some other way) for page layout, rather than XHTML tables, which were
so often employed for this purpose in the past.

This is a very simple page layout design that we are using here. You should be
prepared to leverage your knowledge of the CSS box model and floats from your
study of Figures 4.9 and 4.12 and their associated files to help you understand this
version of our Nature's Source website.

First, note that at the highest level, from the user's point of view, this page
contains four items: the company logo (upper left), the company address (upper
right), some text (lower left), and an image (lower right). As the XHTML markup
in Figure 4.16 shows, each of these is contained in its own div element. These div
elements are identified as logo, address, text, and image. Furthermore, the logo
and address divs are enclosed in a higher-level div (the header div), as are the
text and image divs (the content div). Finally, all of this is enclosed in the page

```
1    <!DOCTYPE html PUBLIC "-//W3C//DTD XHTML 1.0 Strict//EN"
2        "http://www.w3.org/TR/xhtml1/DTD/xhtml1-strict.dtd">
3    <!-- index.html for the simple one-page Nature's Sourece web site -->
4    <html xmlns="http://www.w3.org/1999/xhtml">
5      <head>
6        <title>Nature's Source - Canada's largest specialty vitamin store</title>
7        <meta http-equiv="Content-Type" content="text/html;charset=utf-8" />
8        <link rel="stylesheet" type="text/css" href="css/default.css" />
9      </head>
10     <body>
11       <div id="page">
12         <div id="header">
13           <div id="logo">
14             <img src="images/naturelogo.gif" alt="Nature's Source Logo"
15             width="608px" height="90px" />
16           </div>
17           <div id="address">
18             5029 Hurontario Street Unit 2<br />
19             Mississauga, ON L4Z 3X7<br />
20             Tel: 905.502.6789<br />
21             Fax: 905.890.8305
22           </div>
23         </div>
24         <div id="content">
25           <div id="text">
26             <h4>Welcome to Nature's Source - Protecting your health
27             naturally!</h4>
28             <p>Founded in 1998, Nature's Source was created to serve those who
29             use alternative healing methods. Offering only the highest quality
30             vitamins, minerals, supplements &amp; herbal remedies, Nature's
31             Source takes great pride in helping people live healthier, happier
32             lives.</p>
33             <p>Many Companies that talk about Customer Service fail to
34             deliver. Nature's Source exists to truly serve all the needs of
35             their customers. Each location features dedicated on-site
36             therapists along with knowledgeable staff who ensure that every
37             customer receives the best quality information available.
38             Continuing Education seminars are a regular event at Nature's
39             Source.</p>
40           </div>
41           <div id="image">
42             <img src="images/outdoor4.jpg" alt="Eternal peace"
43             width="272px" height="154px" />
44           </div>
45         </div>
46       </div>
47     </body>
48   </html>
```

FIGURE 4.16

cdrom/web04/nature1/index.html

The XHTML document showing the markup that uses CSS table layout rather than XHTML table layout to produce the simple home page for Nature's Source.

```
1    /* default.css for the simple one-page Nature's Source web site */
2
3    * {
4    padding: 0;
5    margin: 0;
6    }
7
8    body {
9    width: 900px;
10   font-family: Verdana, Arial, Helvetica, sans-serif;
11   font-size: 1em;
12   }
13
14   div#page {
15   margin: 10px;
16   width: 880px;
17   }
18
19   div#logo {
20   float: left;
21   padding: 10px 0;
22   }
23
24   div#address {
25   float: right;
26   padding: 20px 0 0 0;
27   text-align: right;
28   }
29
30   div#content {
31   clear: both;
32   }
33
34   div#text {
35   float: left;
36   width: 570px;
37   }
38
39   div#text p {
40   margin: 1em .2em .7em 0;
41   }
42
43   div#image {
44   float: left;
45   width: 310px;
46   padding-top: 40px;
47   text-align: right;
48   }
```

FIGURE 4.17

cdrom/web04/nature1/css/default.css

The CSS style file applied to the XHTML file index.html shown in Figure 4.16.

div, the highest-level div, which is the only element directly enclosed by the body element.

Let us now discuss the CSS in Figure 4.17, which consists mostly of style definitions for the id selectors seen in the XHTML markup of Figure 4.16. We make the following observations:

- The first style is a "mini-reset" that removes padding and margins from all elements by styling the universal selector (*) accordingly, and was discussed earlier.

- Next, we choose our own default font family and font size for the body element (recall that these will be inherited). We also do something else here for the first time: We choose a width for the body of 900 pixels. There is nothing special about the value 900; in fact, it might be a little high if you were expecting to have a lot of visitors using monitors with the 800 by 600 screen resolution, but it should not be a problem for most visitors these days.

- Note that our chosen width for the page div, plus its margin widths on the left and right, add up to the width of the body element.

- We do not provide any styles for the header id selector, since by default its width will be the same as its parent, the page div, and it needs no other styles. Thus, as far as the CSS is concerned, it was unnecessary to identify that particular div with an id attribute at all, but it's easy to argue that calling it header helps us understand the XHTML markup in Figure 4.16.

- The logo div and the address div, which form the content of the header div, are not given specific widths either. This is because the logo image has an intrinsic width of 608 pixels (see Figure 4.16, line 15), and the remaining horizontal space on the right is more than sufficient to hold the text of the company address. Furthermore, by floating the logo div left and the address div right, we ensure that any "leftover whitespace" will be in between the logo and the address.

- This style sheet provides a good opportunity to see some CSS "shorthand" style rules in action. Note that in the div#page style we have given the margin property a single value of 10px. This means there will be a 10-pixel margin on all four sides of the page div. The div#logo style gives the padding property a value of 10px 0. This means that the top and bottom of the logo div will have 10 pixels of padding, but there will be no padding on either side. Finally, the div#address style gives the padding property the value 20px 0 0 0, which puts

20 pixels of padding at the top of this `div`, and no padding on either the left, right, or bottom. Note that when four explicit values are given, the order must be for the top, right, bottom, and left sides. Note too that in this case, when a single non-zero value is required, and it applies to the top only, the entire rule could be replaced by `padding-top: 20px;`, and similar options apply to the other three sides if required.

- The `content div` has its `clear` property set to `both`, ensuring that the `content div` will sit below any previously occurring elements that were floated either left (the `logo div`) or right (the `address div`).

- The `text div` and the `image div` are both floated left, and to make them sit next to each other and take up the appropriate amount of horizontal space in each case, we give them specific widths that sum to the required total of 900 pixels.

- The `div#image` style also includes 40 pixels of padding at the top to push the image down a bit, and a `text-align` property with a value of `right`. This may seem a bit odd, since the `image div` contains no text. However, recall that the XHTML `img` element is an *inline* element that will show up in the middle of text just like a word, so the `text-align` property has the same effect on an image as it would have on some paragraph text.

- Since our "mini-reset" at the beginning of our style sheet removed all margins and padding, we have to restore either or both, even for paragraphs, if we want to have one or the other. Thus we restore just the margins we want for `p` elements within the `text div` with the `div#text p` style.

- Finally, with the `div#image img` style we add a narrow, ridge-style border of 5 pixels to the `img` element to help set off our image.

You should take some time to make sure you understand how each of the styles you see in this style sheet affects the relevant markup in the XHTML file. Experiment by changing some of the values to see the resulting effect on the page display.

4.13.2 Second, Our Expanded Site with its Home Page Menu and Footer and Additional Linked Pages

For our second example of using CSS to help us with the layout of web pages, we use the extended version of our Nature's Source website, the version with a menu of links and a footer on the home page and several additional pages that we could browse to from the home page via the menu links. Recall that the display in Figure 3.8 was produced with XHTML table layout by the markup shown in Figure 3.7. In Figure 4.18 we show the enhanced version of this home page display, this time produced by the XHTML markup shown in Figure 4.21, which again incorporates external XHTML markup files accessed via SSI.

There are many more pages on this version of the website, but we show only two others:

- First, the one obtained by clicking on the Buy Now link, and shown in Figure 4.19, which at the moment contains only a simple paragraph of text promising things to come.

- Second, the one obtained by clicking on the Products and Services link, and shown, in Figure 4.20, which contains what looks like a dropdown menu at the left. At the moment this menu is in a permanently dropped-down state, and you will see a similar thing on most other pages of the site in the current version. Later, we will see how to make this menu hidden until we place the mouse over it, at which point it will drop down and look like you see it here. We need to learn something about JavaScript before we do this.

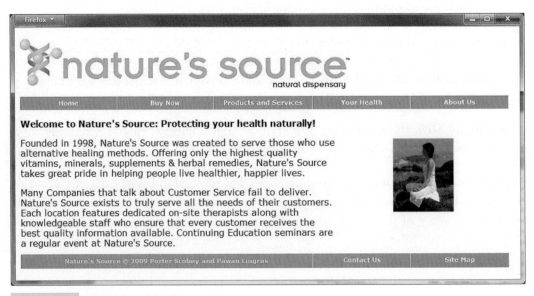

FIGURE 4.18
graphics/ch04/nature2/displayIndexHtml.jpg
A Firefox browser display of cdrom/web04/nature2/index.html, our expanded website for Nature's Source, with styles from cdrom/web04/nature2/css/default.css.

FIGURE 4.19

graphics/ch04/nature2/displayBuyHtml.jpg
A Firefox browser display of `cdrom/web04/nature2/buy.html`, our eventual e-store page, with styles
from `cdrom/web04/nature2/css/default.css`.

FIGURE 4.20

graphics/ch04/nature2/displayProductsHtml.jpg
A Firefox browser display of `cdrom/web04/nature2/products.html`, our eventual products database
connection page, with styles from `cdrom/web04/nature2/css/default.css`.

The XHTML files corresponding to these pages, as well as all other pages
for this version of the site, are linked to the CSS style file `web04/nature2/css/`
`default.css`, only the first few lines of which are shown in Figure 4.22 because the
file is too large for us to include in the text, but you should study the file as we
discuss it. Many of the styles are similar to those for the one-page version of our
site that you have already seen in Figure 4.17, but there are a number of new CSS
concepts in this style sheet, so we again make some general observations about the
style sheet, and in particular about these new features:

■ The first thing you should do is conduct your own "tour" of this version of
the website. Make sure that you click on all links to see what everything looks

```
1    <!DOCTYPE html PUBLIC "-//W3C//DTD XHTML 1.0 Strict//EN"
2        "http://www.w3.org/TR/xhtml1/DTD/xhtml1-strict.dtd">
3    <!-- index.html for the expanded Nature's Source web site -->
4    <html xmlns="http://www.w3.org/1999/xhtml">
5      <head>
6        <title>Nature's Source - Canada's largest specialty vitamin store</title>
7        <meta http-equiv="Content-Type" content="text/html;charset=utf-8" />
8        <link rel="stylesheet" type="text/css" href="css/default.css" />
9      </head>
10     <body>
11       <div id="page">
12         <!--#include virtual="common/logo.html"-->
13         <!--#include virtual="common/mainmenu.html"-->
14         <div id="content">
15           <div id="textLeft">
16             <h3>Welcome to Nature's Source: Protecting your health naturally!</h3>
17             <p>Founded in 1998, Nature's Source was created to serve those who
18             use alternative healing methods. Offering only the highest quality
19             vitamins, minerals, supplements &amp; herbal remedies, Nature's
20             Source takes great pride in helping people live healthier, happier
21             lives.</p>
22             <p>Many Companies that talk about Customer Service fail to deliver.
23             Nature's Source exists to truly serve all the needs of their
24             customers. Each location features dedicated on-site therapists
25             along with knowledgeable staff who ensure that every customer
26             receives the best quality information available. Continuing
27             Education seminars are a regular event at Nature's Source.</p>
28           </div>
29           <div id="image">
30             <img src="images/outdoor4.jpg" alt="Eternal peace"
31             width="272px" height="154px" />
32           </div>
33         </div>
34         <!--#include virtual="common/footer.html"-->
35       </div>
36     </body>
37   </html>
```

FIGURE 4.21

cdrom/web04/nature2/index.html
A first partial view of the XHTML document showing the markup that uses CSS table layout rather than XHTML table layout to produce the home page with links for Nature's Source.

like. The only link that does not currently respond to a click is the Give us feedback link that appears on the submenu you see when you go to the page under the Contact Us link. This will soon link to our feedback form.

■ This style sheet has some brief comments describing each of its sections, which you would do well to read before looking more closely at the file.

```
1    /* default.css for the expanded Nature's Source web site */
2
3    /* ===== global settings ===== */
4    * {
5    padding: 0;
6    margin: 0;
7    }
8
9    body {
10   width: 900px;
11   margin-top: 10px;
12   margin-left: 10px;
13   font-family: Verdana, Arial, Helvetica, sans-serif;
14   font-size: 1em;
15   }
16
17   /* top level container */
18   div#page {
19   width: 100%;
20   }
21
22   /* company logo appearing at top of each page */
23   div#logo {
24   padding: 10px 0;
25   }
26
27   /* ===== main menu appearing under logo on each page */
28   div#mainMenu {
29   width: 100%;
30   height: 20px;
31   }
```

FIGURE 4.22

cdrom/web04/nature2/css/default.css (partial)
The first few lines of the CSS style file that applies to the index file of our expanded Nature's Source website shown in Figure 4.21, and to all other pages of the site.

- Note that this one style sheet contains all the CSS for the site, and that not all pages have the same layout. So, of course, not all styles are used on every page. What is common to each page is the header containing the logo, the main menu under the header, and the copyright information and a couple of additional links (a mini-menu, if you like) in the footer. The markup for these items comes from three external files via SSI, just as it did previously, but that markup is now styled by CSS.

- The "content" area of the site pages, the part between the main menu and the footer, has three variations. The home page has some text at the left and an image on the right. It is the only page like this. Most other pages have some text at the right, and a permanently-dropped-down menu at the left. Finally, some pages have only text in the content area.

- We do not discuss margins, padding, fonts, text alignment, and the like again, since we hope these have been adequately covered in previous discussions, at least to the point where you should be able to figure out how those things work in this scenario.

- The first new feature that we do need to address is the menus, and how they are constructed. Believe it or not, our menus are really lists, but lists that have had their usual properties radically altered for the current purpose:

  - First, all the menus are *unordered* lists whose items have no list markers (bullets) because they all have been given property `list-style-type: none` (see line 151).
  - Second, note that the menu options in the main menu and in the footer menu are side by side, not one under the other as they are in the submenu that appears at the left on many of the pages. This side-by-side arrangement is achieved by giving the `float` property of the list items a value of `left`, so that each list item floats upward to the left and settles on the right of its predecessor. See lines 34 and 155.
  - Third, because list items are block-level, we can give them a specific width. See lines 35 and 156.
  - Fourth, our links are not underlined in the usual way, because we have said that for links we want `text-decoration: none` (see lines 92 and 166).

- A second new feature we need to mention is the use of a *CSS pseudo-class*. You can see one of these in action as you browse the `nature2` site, since every time your mouse hovers over a link, that link is highlighted by a change in the color of the link text as well as the background color of that text. There are four pseudo-classes that can be used with links, though we only use the `:hover` pseudo-class in our style sheet. Here is the syntax and how it works: A style like `a:hover {color: red;}` will cause the text of a link to turn red when the mouse hovers over it, and to turn back to its "normal" color (whatever that might be) when the mouse moves away. Note the colon between the `a` tag and the actual name (`hover`) of the pseudo-class. Make sure there is no space on either side of this colon. See lines 171-175 for our use of the `:hover` pseudo-class.

These are the highlights of the style sheet for the `nature2` version of our website in this chapter. Make sure you study the complete CSS file and reconcile the various styles with what is displayed in your browser.

4.14   Validating Our CSS Style Sheets

In the previous chapter (sections 3.11 and 3.12) we discussed what is meant for an XHTML file to be *valid*. For the same reasons we want our XHTML files to be valid (so they may be displayed correctly and consistently, we hope, by all browsers), we also want each of our XHTML pages to use a *valid CSS style sheet*. This in turn simply means that we must follow all the CSS syntax rules when composing styles for our style sheets. Thus, once again, a web developer needs to have at least some familiarity with what these rules are, and be able to follow them. For the most part this simply means following the syntax style for CSS style rules as we have discussed and illustrated them.

Also, as for XHTML pages, we can employ a `CSS validator` to check the validity of our CSS style sheets. Here is a link to the CSS validator on the W3C site:

`http://jigsaw.w3.org/css-validator/`

To use the validator, simply browse to this site, enter the URL of the CSS file you wish to validate, and click on the **Check** button. For example, Figure 4.23 shows the

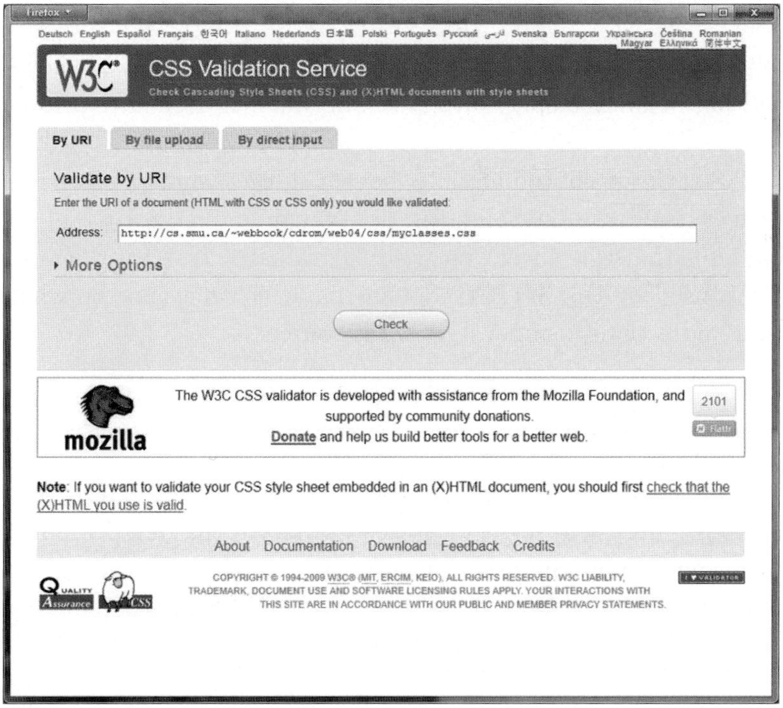

FIGURE 4.23

`graphics/ch04/displayMyclassesCssToValidate.jpg`
A Firefox browser display just before clicking the **Check** button to validate the `myclasses.css` file.

FIGURE 4.24

graphics/ch04/displayMyclassesCssValidated.jpg
A Firefox browser display showing a successful validation of the file myclasses.css.

validator page just before myclasses.css is to be validated, and Figure 4.24 shows the top part of the resulting browser display after the CSS file has been successfully validated.

When validating a CSS style sheet, you actually have a choice: you can enter the URL of the CSS style sheet itself into the validator, or you can enter the URL of an XHTML document that uses the style sheet you wish to evaluate. The latter choice will evaluate all the styles used by the XHTML document, which may not be what you want if you are using more than a single style sheet source.

4.15   Summary

Cascading Style Sheets were "invented" to help us keep separate the description of the structure of our web pages from the description of how those pages are to be displayed. Thus in this chapter we have learned how to use CSS styles to tell a browser how we wish to have the elements in our XHTML documents displayed.

A collection of one or more styles is called a style sheet, and a style sheet may be placed in a separate (external) file, in a `style` element within the `head` element of a document, or in the value of a `style` attribute of an XHTML element. The first of these three options is the recommended one, and the last should be avoided if at all possible.

A typical simple style rule consists of a selector and a brace-enclosed property-value pair called a declaration. There are many variations on this simple scheme that include multiple selectors, descendant selectors, and multiple declarations. Some property values such as units of measurement and color may be expressed using different formats, and a web developer needs to choose a consistent representation for the values of such properties. Consistency in formatting and commenting CSS style sheets is equally important.

CSS `class` and `id` selectors, combined with the XHTML `div` and `span` elements, provide a great deal of flexibility in laying out and formatting our web pages. Unfortunately, browser implementation and cross-browser consistency in the implementation of the relevant CSS standards still leaves much to be desired.

CSS uses the rules of inheritance, specificity, and "the cascade" to decide which style actually gets applied when there is a conflict. Fortunately, most of the time styles get applied as we would hope and expect, and we can often get by with placing all our styles in a single external style sheet file, with fine tuning for any particular document performed by placing modifying styles in a `style` element of that document.

The CSS box model underlies most of what appears on a web page, and it is important for a web developer to have at least a basic understanding of content, padding, border, and margin as they relate to this model.

CSS positioning for page layout is much to be preferred over the legacy approach that used XHTML tables. We discussed only CSS "floats," which were sufficient for our purposes.

The CSS reset is a useful concept that permits a web developer to establish a "baseline" set of values for such things as margins, padding, font size, and so on at the beginning of a style sheet and then reset them later on in the style sheet as required. What makes this so useful is that not all browsers use the same defaults for displaying the same elements, so setting a baseline and modifying it exactly as required gives a developer much more confidence that a page will be displayed in the way desired.

Just as XHTML documents can (and should) be validated, so can (and should) CSS style sheets. So, as a best practice, you should always validate your CSS style sheets along with your XHTML markup.

4.16   Quick Questions to Test Your Basic Knowledge

1. What was the reason for the introduction of Cascading Style Sheets, and who was responsible for their initial development?

2. How many "levels" of a CSS style sheet are there, what are their names, and what distinguishes one from the other?

3. Which one of the three style sheet levels of the previous question is the recommended one to use whenever possible, and which one are you advised to avoid if at all possible?

4. Using the generic terms "selector," "property," "property-value," "declaration," "declaration block," and "rule," how would you show the syntax of a simple CSS style rule using a diagram?

5. What are the CSS comment delimiters?

6. When you link an external style sheet to an XHTML document, what are the three attributes you need for the `link` element, and what are their values?

7. In this chapter we referred to the pixel as a "relative" measurement, as opposed to an "absolute" measurement. Suppose we decided to change our mind and call the pixel a "hybrid" measurement. Can you give a reason why this might make sense?

8. What are five different ways that color values can be specified in CSS?

9. In section 4.7.2 we mentioned that if you use a 6-digit hex number to specify a color value on your web page, you have a choice of 16,777,216 different colors. How is this number computed?

10. Without looking anything up, how would you describe two colors, and the relationship between them, if the two colors have the hex values #333333 and #999999?

11. How would you explain the (good) advice to "name CSS classes according to their meaning (also called *semantic naming*), and not according to their appearance"? Can you find an example from this chapter where that advice was not followed but should have been? Hint: Think about the `BoldItalic` class, and think about what it would mean if you wanted to change characteristics of this particular style (to light grey small caps, for example).

12. What is a CSS style rule that would cause the text in all h3, p, and li elements to be displayed with maroon text?

13. What is a CSS style rule that would cause the body of a web page to have a very dark gray background with very light gray text, and what would you say about such a style?

14. If every time you wanted to emphasize a word or phrase in a paragraph, you wanted its content to be displayed in bold italic red text, what style would you use to achieve this?

15. Here are the four major components of the CSS box model in alphabetical order: border, content, margin, padding. What is their order going from the inside out?

16. To which parts of the box model does the background color apply?

17. What happens if you give the float property for an XHTML element the value center?

18. What would be the purpose of the style float: right for an XHTML img element?

19. What is the purpose of the style rule clear: both?

20. What is a CSS reset, and how is it used?

21. What should you make a practice of doing with each of your CSS style sheets that you should also do with each of your XHTML documents?

4.17   Short Exercises to Improve Your Basic Understanding

Another reminder, probably for the last time: Be sure to work with *copies* of the sample files, so you always have the originals to go back to and start over.

1. It might be interesting to begin these exercises with a high-level "experiment" of sorts. Display the home page of each version of our website (nature1 and nature2) in every browser that you have available. Can you offer an explanation for any differences you see?

2. Validate each of the CSS files in this chapter to get a feel for the process.

3. Add the markup of the four examples at the beginning of section 4.6 to the markup in `simple.css` and then re-display `simple.html`. Be sure to reconcile what you see in the display with the new and revised styles in the style file. Then make a duplicate copy of the three-item list in `simple.html` and place it after the first list in that same file. Now change the `ul` tags of the duplicate list to `ol` tags and re-display to confirm our claim in section 4.6 that this list will *not* have the text of its items italicized.

4. Create a sample file called `style_levels.html` that illustrates how CSS recognizes and uses the three "style levels": external, embedded, and inline.

5. Make arguments for and against the following statement: "Permitting inline CSS styles defeats the whole purpose of CSS, and this practice should be deprecated."

6. List all of the CSS "generic" fonts and at least one specific font family in each category.

7. CSS can also use "system fonts." Find the names of these fonts, and explain why you might want to use them.

8. Find the names of all 16 standard CSS colors, along with their hex values.

9. Create a small example in a file called `standout.html` that shows you can have two classes with the same name but containing different styles, as long as you make them apply to different XHTML elements. For example, you could have both `p.Standout` and `li.Standout`.

10. We mentioned and used the CSS `:hover` pseudo-class. Find the names of the other CSS *pseudo-classes*, and explain how they are used.

11. CSS also has something called *pseudo-elements*. Explain the conceptual difference between a pseudo-class and a pseudo-element, and give at least one example of a pseudo-element. And note, by the way, that *pseudo-classes* and *pseudo-elements* are collectively called *pseudo-selectors*.

12. In our box model example (Figure 4.9 and associated files), remove the body style completely and re-display the page in all browsers at your disposal to see if there are any noticeable differences.

13. In our box model example (Figure 4.9 and associated files), change the various values for `padding`, `border`, `margin`, and `background-color` properties and re-display in your browser. Make sure you understand what you are seeing.

14. In our float example (Figure 4.12 and associated files), the `float` property appears twice and the `clear` property appears once. Experiment by removing all of these properties at once, then one at a time, then two at a time, and for each scenario explain what you see.

15. This exercise will lead you through most of the steps for turning an ordinary unordered list into a horizontally arranged menu of options, and also tell you something about browser differences. First, create a test file called `list_to_menu.html` with only the following in its body

```
<ul>
  <li>Go</li>
  <li>Stop</li>
  <li>Speed Up</li>
  <li>Slow Down</li>
</ul>
```

and an initially empty embedded style sheet. Then perform the following actions, in order:

- Add the style `* {padding: 0;}` to the style sheet and display in both Firefox and Internet Explorer.

- Remove the preceding style and then add the style `* {margin: 0;}` to the style sheet and display in both Firefox and Internet Explorer.

- Explain to yourself what the two preceding actions have told you about Firefox and Internet Explorer. Then proceed with the following actions, each time displaying the document in both browsers. From now on you may or may not see any differences in the display from one browser to another. If you do see any differences, that is always a good reason to check out what happens in one or more additional browsers.

- Remove the previous style and add the style `ul {list-style-type: none;}` as the only style in the file.

- Add the following style rule at the beginning of the style sheet:

```
* {
padding: 0;
margin: 0;
}
```

This time, and from now on, just add things; don't remove anything from the style sheet.

- Add the following style rule, but only one line at a time, in the order shown, and re-display after each entry:

```
ul li {
float: left;
width: 99px;
border-right: 1px solid black;
background-color: #0F0;
text-align: center;
font-family: Verdana;
}
```

- Finally, add the following style rule, and be sure to place the mouse over the various menu options after you re-display:

```
ul li:hover {background-color: #CCC;}
```

This menu does not contain any links, but you can extend the exercise by adding them and having the links change color during a "mouseover" (rather than the list element itself).

16. Experiment with the `padding` and `margin` values in the file `default.css` of Figure 4.17 to see what the effect is. Begin by commenting out lines 3–6 of the file to see what the browser default looks like; then try some values of your own.

17. Experiment with as many different property values in the file `default.css` of Figure 4.22 to see what the effect is, and in particular to see how changing a value causes the display to "come off the rails," if in fact that is what happens.

18. Find out what aspects of the presentation of a web page your browser will allow you (as the end-user) to modify and how you accomplish those modifications.

For example, how do you change the text size of your browser's display or disable its display of images? The fact that any user has the opportunity to make changes like this is of course a good thing, but also another thorn in the side of web developers.

4.18   Exercises on the Parallel Project

As we have pointed out in this chapter, best practice going forward demands that XHTML tables should no longer be used for web page layout unless what is being laid out is actually a table of data, and you should choose the CSS alternative.

1. From the Exercises on the Parallel Project of the previous chapter you should now have a home page for the website of your business that looks something like Figure 3.6. Your task in this exercise is to reproduce the same page, in appearance, for your business, but this time using a CSS style sheet for layout, in the same manner as we did for our business site in Figure 4.18. Experiment with padding, margin, and other settings to achieve a look that you feel works well for your site.

2. You should also now have, again from the Exercises on the Parallel Project of the previous chapter, a web page for your business that looks something like Figure 3.8. Your task in this exercise is analogous to that of the previous exercise. It is to produce a "better-looking" page, more like our Figure 4.18, for the home page of the website for your business. Also, this time you must use a CSS style sheet for layout, in the same manner as we did for our business site in Figure 4.18, and use SSI to load in the parts that will be common to all of your pages.

3. Complete all pages to which your main page links, as well as those additional pages to which *these* pages link. By "complete" in this context we mean there should at least *be* a page and that page should at least say what will eventually appear there. But of course you will not at this stage actually have any forms to be filled out by the user, or any capability for the user to browse a database containing your products and place an order. In other words, complete your website in the same sense that our `nature2` website is "complete."

4.19   What Else You May Want or Need to Know

1. We mentioned briefly, in section 4.4, the CSS `@import` mechanism, another way to gain access to an external style sheet. Recall that the XHTML `link` element associates an external CSS style sheet with the XHTML document in which that `link` element appears. On the other hand, the purpose of the `@import` *directive* (that's what it's called, and it's a part of the CSS language, *not* XHTML) is to bring an external style sheet into another style sheet. The receiving style sheet can itself be an external style sheet or an embedded style sheet. In any case, the `@import` directive must be the first item (except for comments) in whatever style sheet it is placed, though this requirement seems to be ignored by most browsers. Here is its syntax (note that it uses `url` rather than `href` and quotes around the `url` argument are optional):

```
@import url('[path]filename.ext')
```

One use for this functionality might be to keep either or both of your CSS reset values and global style values in one or two files and then `@import` those files (you can have more than one `@import` directive) at the beginning of the style sheet for your website.

2. In our examples we have only styled an XHTML element with a single class. However, CSS permits an element to be styled with two or more classes simultaneously. Here is the syntax (note the whitespace-separated class names):

```
<tagname class="FirstClassName SecondClassName">content</tagname>
```

3. If you are surfing the Web looking for CSS examples, you will quite often run into the "`Lorem ipsum ...`" text. This consists of several, perhaps many, paragraphs of Latin text that begin with these two words at the start of the first paragraph. This text is deemed to be useful for testing CSS styles and is widely used for that purpose.

4. CSS is case-insensitive, but if you read that statement quickly and don't stop to think about it, it can be quite misleading. Problems arise because although CSS itself is case-insensitive, when you are writing your CSS styles, you are often including other items that may or may not be case-insensitive, such as font family names and paths to image files. Further problems can be caused by the kind of DOCTYPE you are using, since HTML is case-insensitive as well, while

XHTML is case-sensitive, and whether or not you are using JavaScript, which is also case-sensitive. The bottom line here is that it is a best practice and, for that matter, just common sense, to be consistent with the capitalization you use when choosing and writing names, particularly when it comes to the names of your `class` and `id` selectors. You would be amazed to know the number of problems you *won't* have if you follow this simple advice.

5. When designing the CSS for your website, it is worthwhile to take some time to leverage as much as you can the inheritance of styles from the `body` element. By thinking about it and placing as many inheritable properties as you can in the style for the body element, you can ensure that those properties will be inherited and will therefore not have to be replicated elsewhere for individual elements.

6. Some font families are better than others when it comes to displaying web pages. For example, it is generally agreed that Verdana is an excellent sans-serif font, since it is very legible even at very small sizes. Similarly, Georgia is regarded as an excellent serif font for web design. As backup for the Verdana font if it is not available, you can request Arial (for Windows) and Helvetica (for Macintosh). For Georgia you can request "Times New Roman" (for Windows) or Times (for Macintosh), one of which should be available on virtually any platform. Note that multi-word font family names must be enclosed in quotes.

7. One advantage of having all your styles in a single external file linked to many documents is that when a visitor browses to one of these documents, the style file is downloaded and used to render the document (of course), but most browsers will also store the style sheet in the *cache* of the user's computer. Think of the cache simply as a storage area on the user's computer where things that might be used later are stored for quick access (memory access is much faster than disk access or download speed, so a cache is often a memory cache but could be a local file in some cases). Then, if the user browses to other documents that use the same style sheet, the browser can use the locally stored version from the cache and not have to download the style sheet again each time a file using it is displayed. This can help to make your site appear faster to your visitors.

However, this same feature can also be a pain in the wazoo for web developers. Let's say you are testing a web page by altering its associated CSS file and re-loading the XHTML file. But ... you are just not seeing the changes you *know* you should be seeing. The problem is that the browser is still using the "old" version of the style sheet from the cache and has not downloaded the new version of the file containing your carefully crafted revisions. Even XHTML may be stored in the cache and give rise to the same problem. There are ways to force most browsers to reload all required files from their original locations (and thus not use the cached versions). For example, pressing the `Ctrl` key while clicking the browser's `Reload` button will often do the trick. As for other options, `Ctrl+F5` works for Internet Explorer on Windows, as does `Ctrl+Shift+R` for Firefox on Windows.

8. When reading CSS styles containing margin and padding values, you need to be aware of some CSS "shortcut" methods of specifying these values. Fortunately, these shortcuts work the same way for both margins and padding, so we will discuss them in the context of margins alone.

Consider the following four CSS declarations:

```
margin: 10px;
margin: 10px 20px;
margin: 10px 30px 40px;
margin: 10px 20px 30px 40px;
```

The first of these indicates that there should be a 10-pixel margin on all four sides of the element box. The second declaration, which contains only two values, is interpreted to mean that the margin is to be 10 pixels for both top and bottom margins and 20 pixels for both left and right margins. The third declaration, containing three values, specifies a 10px margin for the top, a 30px margin for the left and right sides, and a 30px margin for the bottom. The last declaration specifies a specific and different value for the margin on each of the four sides, so here order is important, and that order is `top`, `right`, `bottom`, `left`.

9. The `font` shorthand styles

```
font: bold 11px Arial;
font: 11px Arial;
```

specify the `font-size` (11px) and `font-family` (Arial), as well as the font-weight (bold) if desired. Order is important here too. That is, if you want to specify the `font-weight` (bold), its value must come first among these three values.

4.20 References

1. For information on the history of CSS, including some of the adoption difficulties, the main features of the various specifications, and some information on browser support, see:

   ```
   http://en.wikipedia.org/wiki/Cascading_Style_Sheets#History
   ```

2. For more detailed information on browser support for CSS, check out this site:

   ```
   http://www.webdevout.net/browser-support-css
   ```

3. As was the case for XHTML, an excellent place to explore CSS further is, once again, the W3 Schools site. Both the tutorials and examples, as well as the reference material on properties and their values, color, positioning, and various other CSS topics, will help to consolidate your comfort level with CSS:

   ```
   http://www.w3schools.com/css/default.asp
   http://www.w3schools.com/css/css_reference.asp
   ```

4. For further information on the best fonts to use on your website, check out the following links:

   ```
   http://www.kathymarks.com/archives/2006/11/best_fonts_for_the
          _web_1.html
   http://www.hobo-web.co.uk/seo-blog/index.php/best-font-size/
   http://www.theinternetdigest.net/archive/websafefonts.html
   http://www.inspirationbit.com/16-best-loved-font-bits-in-web
          -design/
   http://dev.opera.com/articles/view/fonts-for-web-design-a
          -primer/
   ```

5. For further information on the use of absolute measurements vs. relative measurements, see:

   ```
   http://www.devarticles.com/c/a/Web-Style-Sheets/Learn-CSS-part
          -2-Units-of-Measurement/
   ```

6. To see all the web-safe colors, along with their hex and decimal values, follow this link:

   `http://www.web-source.net/216_color_chart.htm`

7. As CSS is updated, the list of colors recognized by most browsers will undoubtedly expand, but you can see the current list at this site:

   `http://www.w3schools.com/css/css_colornames.asp`

8. For further information on the CSS shorthand way of specifying multiple values of a single property, see:

   `http://www.dustindiaz.com/css-shorthand/`

9. For the definitive discussion of the exact rules governing inheritance and the cascade in CSS and for determining specificity, see:

   `http://www.w3.org/TR/CSS2/cascade.html`

10. For the definitive description of the CSS box model, see:

    `http://www.w3.org/TR/CSS2/box.html`

11. For additional information on the CSS box model, including some that offer user interactivity, check out these sites:

    `http://www.w3schools.com/css/css_boxmodel.asp`
    `http://redmelon.net/tstme/box_model/`
    `http://css-tricks.com/the-css-box-model/`

    Also, try Googling "CSS box model" and looking for a link called "Images for CSS box model." Clicking on this link will take you to a large collection of images from all over the Internet that depict various incarnations of the CSS box model.

12. You may be interested in going beyond the simple floats that we discussed in this chapter for page layout, so here are some sites that discuss both floats and additional CSS positioning techniques that give you some idea of the enormous possibilities open to you as you design your website (and be sure to check out other links provided by these sites):

```
http://css.maxdesign.com.au/floatutorial/
http://www.w3schools.com/css/css_positioning.asp
http://www.brainjar.com/css/positioning/default.asp
http://www.barelyfitz.com/screencast/html-training/css/
    positioning/
http://www.elated.com/articles/css-positioning/
http://www.alistapart.com/articles/flexiblelayouts/
http://www.vanseodesign.com/css/css-positioning/
http://www.tizag.com/cssT/position.php
```

13. Here are a few sites that will give you some ideas for your own CSS reset:

```
http://meyerweb.com/eric/tools/css/reset/
http://meyerweb.com/eric/thoughts/2007/05/01/reset-reloaded/
http://developer.yahoo.com/yui/reset/
http://sixrevisions.com/css/css-tips/css-tip-1-resetting-your
    -styles-with-css-reset/
```

14. As you know, you can and should validate your CSS style sheets, but you can also have them formatted and "optimized," which means, among other things, having styles consolidated and redundancies removed. Some sites that help you do this are these:

```
http://www.cleancss.com/
http://www.codebeautifier.com/
http://www.webdh.net/cssnet/css_optimiser.php?lang=en
http://www.nigraphic.com/tidycss/
```

CHAPTER 5

XHTML Forms for Data Collection and Submission

CHAPTER CONTENTS

5.1   Overview and Objectives

Up to this point we have seen only very limited interactivity between the user and any of our web pages. In fact, all a user could do was type in the URL of a page and press Enter to display that page, or click on a link on one page to browse to another page.

That is, there has so far been no way for the user to supply any additional information to a website, through one of its web pages, have the site process the information in some way, and then return some new information to the user based on the data supplied. This kind of two-way communication scenario is extremely useful in a business environment, since it permits a user to make product choices, pay for them online, and supply a shipping address, for example.

This chapter marks the beginning of our discussion of how such two-way communication is accomplished, and the first thing we need to study is how *web forms* can be placed on a web page in preparation for accepting information from the user on the client side. In subsequent chapters we will see how that information can be transmitted to the server and how our website can process, and respond to, the data received from its visitors.

In this chapter we will discuss the following:

- The general idea of a *web form*

- The `form` element (though we postpone a discussion of the `GET` and `POST` values of its `action` attribute, since these indicate how we wish to submit the form's data, and in this chapter we are only creating forms, not submitting their data to a server)

- The `input` element

- The `select` and `option` elements

- The `textarea` element

- The `submit` and `reset` button elements

- The `fieldset` and `legend` elements

- The `label` element and its `for` attribute

- Setting up a *Body Mass Index (BMI)* calculator form and a feedback form

- Getting ready to submit form data (but not actually submitting it)

Also in this chapter our examples will focus entirely on form design and we will not return to an update of our full website example until Chapter 7, after we have discussed forms (this chapter), form data validation via JavaScript (Chapter 6), and dropdown menus (also implemented using JavaScript) as an example of interaction with the *DOM (Document Object Model)* and interactively changing our document's CSS styles (Chapter 7).

5.2 Forms for Collecting User Input Data in the Browser and Sending It to the Server for Processing

We are all familiar, perhaps too familiar, with the forms we have to fill out in our everyday lives, such as employment applications, medical reports, student loan applications, income tax forms, and so on. Online forms contain the same kinds of blank lines or "textboxes" to be filled in, checkboxes to be checked, and so on, and we need to learn how to set these things up for data entry on our website. Even though a user can only communicate with a website in two basic ways—by clicking on various parts of a web page using a pointing device such as a mouse, or by typing text using a keyboard—such a *web form* allows the information supplied in this way to be quite sophisticated.

Once a web form is filled out, it "looks and feels" much like its paper counterpart. Submitting a web form, however, is accomplished in a different manner. Usually there is a button, often labeled `Submit`, that the user clicks, and there may also be one labeled `Reset`, to permit the user to start over and re-enter form data. It is what happens *after* the user clicks `Submit` that will be discussed in later chapters.

We are going to illustrate simple form design through two examples for our business:

1. The first one will be a web page containing a form that is essentially a tool to help users find out if their weight is reasonable by calculating a quantity known as the *Body Mass Index (BMI)*.

2. The second one will be a page containing a standard user-feedback form of the type used by many websites to gather user opinions on everything from the usability of the site to the overall customer experience if it is an e-commerce site.

5.3   The `form` Element

Placing a *form* on a web page is done using an XHTML `form` element. This `element` acts like a "container" for the usual kinds of things one sees on a form, in the sense that between the `<form>` and `</form>` tags we place the other XHTML tags that create the visual "widgets" that allow data entry by the user when the web page is displayed.

Let us begin with a web page that will eventually serve as our BMI calculator. Look at the XHTML markup from the file `bmi1.html` shown in Figure 5.1 to see

```
1   <!DOCTYPE html PUBLIC "-//W3C//DTD XHTML 1.0 Strict//EN"
2       "http://www.w3.org/TR/xhtml1/DTD/xhtml1-strict.dtd">
3   <!--bmi1.html-->
4   <html xmlns="http://www.w3.org/1999/xhtml">
5     <head>
6       <meta http-equiv="Content-Type" content="text/html;charset=utf-8" />
7       <title>Body Mass Index Calculator</title>
8     </head>
9     <body>
10      <center>
11        <h4>Body Mass Index Calculator</h4>
12      </center>
13      <p>Body Mass Index (BMI) is used as an indicator of total body fat.</p>
14      <form id="bmiForm" action="">
15      </form>
16      <p>Total body fat is correlated to the risk of certain diseases which can
17      be potentially fatal. BMI is valid for both men and women. However, it
18      should only be used as a guideline as it has some limitations. It may
19      overestimate the body fat in muscular persons and underestimate the body
20      fat in persons who have lost muscle mass.</p>
21      <p>More information can be found at the <a
22      href="http://www.nhlbisupport.com/bmi/bmicalc.htm">National Institute of
23      Health</a> website. This Calculator is based on the formula obtained from
24      the above site.</p>
25    </body>
26  </html>
```

FIGURE 5.1

cdrom/web05/bmi1.html
XHTML markup for our first web page containing a form that has no content.

how we introduce a form element into a web document. The relevant XHTML code is shown in lines 14 and 15 of that file:

```
<form id="bmiForm" action="">
</form>
```

The displayed web page itself does not look any different (see Figure 5.2) from any of the previous web pages we have seen so far. The page has no CSS styling and therefore uses the default browser fonts and font sizes and the page will grow and shrink according to any re-sizing of the browser window.

Note that mere introduction of the (empty) form element has no effect on the display. However, it helps us study the <form> tag and its attributes without worrying about the rest of the details.

We have identified our form element as bmiForm by giving this value to its id attribute. Every form tag must also have an attribute called action whose value tells the web server what to do when the user submits the data through the form. Generally this is the name of a program that the server should run, with the supplied data from the form as input. In our case, we have a null (empty) string for the value of the action attribute. That means no action is required when the user submits the data. In subsequent chapters, we will write programs in different languages (JavaScript and PHP) that will be used as form actions.

Obviously, having just an empty form element on a web page is not very interesting. The following sections will show how to put different *form elements*[1] on our BMI calculator page.

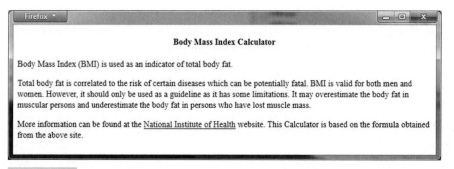

FIGURE 5.2
graphics/ch05/displayBmi1Html.jpg
A Firefox browser display of bmi1.html, showing that an empty form produces no visible output.

---

[1] These other XHTML elements that are placed within the form element itself and determine the interactive behavior of the form are also called *form controls*, or, more informally, just "widgets."

5.3.1   A Brief Aside, a Reminder, and Some Good Advice

Just before we move on, let's discuss a brief aside. Note that the XHTML file in Figure 5.1 contains an XHTML element you have not seen before, a `center` element. The effect of this element should be obvious ... it centers its content, in this case the `h1` element, and this is certainly a very easy way to achieve that effect.

Unfortunately, the XHTML `center` tag is now *deprecated*, and should no longer be used to do what it's doing here. Why not? Well, because "centering" something is a "presentational" aspect of that thing, and therefore rightly should be handled by CSS, and we will do this in our next example.

We use the `center` element here to remind you once again that you should try to avoid the easy way out when developing new web pages. One way of staying the course is to make sure you continually validate your web pages. If you attempt to validate the file `bmi1.html`, for example, you will find that in fact it does *not* validate as strict XHTML, precisely because of the presence of the `center` element.

5.3.2   How Will We Deal with CSS from Now On?

From now on, we will handle our CSS in the following way. We will have, for each chapter, a single CSS file called `default.css`, which will contain all the CSS styles for the general sample files in that chapter, and which we will place in a subdirectory called `css`. Not every style will necessarily be used for every sample file in the chapter, but that does not matter. In fact, that is the point. We can put all our styles in one place (one file) and link any XHTML document file that needs to use one or more styles in that style file. Of course, for a large and complex website you may well want to have more than one style file, but the point remains. Subsequent files in this chapter will be making use of the version of this file corresponding to this chapter. We will only discuss the `default.css` file if it contains something of particular interest or a new CSS feature of some kind.

If the chapter also contains an updated version of our complete website, we will put the corresponding files in a subdirectory called `nature` with its own `css` subdirectory containing its own `default.css`, as well as its own `images` subdirectory. We actually began this convention in the last chapter, where we had two such subdirectories, `nature1` and `nature2`, containing two different versions of our website, but we will not see a `nature` subdirectory again until Chapter 7.

5.4   The input Element

One of the most versatile XHTML form controls for collecting data from users is the
input element. It allows us to create *form fields* (places where the user can supply
data of some sort) of various types, including those in the following list:

- text creates a one-line text box whose length is determined by the value of the
  size attribute.

- radio creates a "radio button" that usually appears as a small circle in a group
  of small circles, only one of which may be selected.

- checkbox creates a small box, generally square, that may be "checked" or
  "unchecked."

- submit creates a button that is usually labeled with the word Submit and,
  when clicked on with the mouse, causes the data that has been entered in the
  form to be acted upon.

- reset creates a button that is usually labeled by the word Reset (or a similar
  term) and allows the values in the form to be cleared, or set to their default
  values, thus permitting the user to start over.

Any desired control is obtained by supplying the appropriate highlighted value
from the above list as the value of the type attribute of the input tag. For example,
in Figure 5.3 you see illustrated input controls of type text, radio, and checkbox.

Figure 5.4 displays our first "real" form, since it contains some actual "fields,"
form controls for entering or indicating data input. Each of the controls in the form
displayed in Figure 5.4 is created by using an input element. These controls include
textboxes, radio buttons, and a checkbox. Let us compare these controls with the
corresponding XHTML markup that produces them from the file bmi2.html that is
shown in Figure 5.3.

Note, first of all, as promised in the previous section, that we are no longer using
the XHTML center element for centering our page title, but instead a class called
Centered, which is defined in this chapter's default.css[2] file and used with the h4
element.

---

[2]As noted previously, unless there is some particular reason to examine the CSS for a particular
display, we will not show each and every variation of our default.css file as we go from chapter to
chapter. You should, however, continue to study the content of these files to answer any questions
you may have about any of the displays.

```
1    <!DOCTYPE html PUBLIC "-//W3C//DTD XHTML 1.0 Strict//EN"
2       "http://www.w3.org/TR/xhtml1/DTD/xhtml1-strict.dtd">
3    <!-- bmi2.html -->
4    <html xmlns="http://www.w3.org/1999/xhtml">
5      <head>
6        <meta http-equiv="Content-Type" content="text/html;charset=utf-8" />
7        <title>Body Mass Index Calculator</title>
8        <link rel="stylesheet" type="text/css" href="css/default.css" />
9      </head>
10     <body>
11       <h4 class="Centered">Body Mass Index Calculator</h4>
12       <p>Body Mass Index (BMI) is used as an indicator of total body fat. In
13       order to calculate your BMI, please input your height and weight.</p>
14       <form id="bmiForm" action="">
15         <table summary="BMI Calculator-Textbox, Radio Button, Checkbox">
16           <tr>
17             <td>Height:</td>
18             <td><input type="text" name="height" size="7" /></td>
19             <td>Units:</td>
20             <td><input type="radio" name="heightUnit" value="in" /> inches</td>
21             <td><input type="radio" name="heightUnit" value="cm" />
22             centimeters</td>
23           </tr>
24           <tr>
25             <td>Weight:</td>
26             <td><input type="text" name="weight" size="7" /></td>
27             <td>Units:</td>
28             <td><input type="radio" name="weightUnit" value="lb" /> pounds</td>
29             <td><input type="radio" name="weightUnit" value="kg" /> kilograms</td>
30           </tr>
31           <tr>
32             <td colspan="4">Please check here if you want a detailed analysis
33             of your BMI: <input type="checkbox" name="details"
34             value="yes" /></td>
35           </tr>
36         </table>
37       </form>
38       <p>Total body fat is correlated to the risk of certain diseases that can
39       be potentially fatal. BMI is valid for both men and women. However, it
40       should only be used as a guideline as it has some limitations. It may
41       overestimate the body fat in muscular persons and underestimate the body
42       fat in persons who have lost muscle mass.</p>
43       <p>More information can be found at the <a
44       href="http://www.nhlbisupport.com/bmi/bmicalc.htm">National Institute of
45       Health</a> website. This Calculator is based on the formula obtained from
46       the above site.</p>
47     </body>
48   </html>
```

FIGURE 5.3

cdrom/web05/bmi2.html

Our first XHTML document containing a `form` element, with several `input` elements.

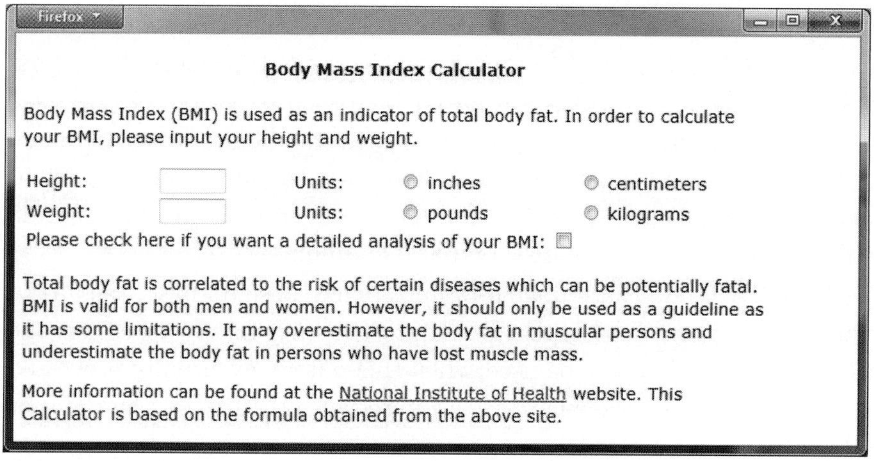

FIGURE 5.4
graphics/ch05/displayBmi2Html.jpg
A display of `bmi2.html` in the Firefox browser.

Second, note that for this form we are using a table layout with three rows and four columns to contain the controls used to collect information from the user. We can argue for a table layout here as the appropriate choice, since a table makes sense whether we are *displaying* data, or, as in the current case, *collecting* data. Note that although we are using a table, it is not immediately obvious since we do not display any table borders.

5.4.1 Textboxes (input Elements of Type text)

The empty textbox in the first row of the table allows a user to enter his or her height. The markup that creates this textbox is shown in line 18:

```
<input type="text" name="height" size="7" />
```

The **input** tag is an empty tag with three attributes. The **type** attribute tells the web browser what kind of **input** control this one is (textbox, checkbox, radio button, and so on). In this case, the value **text** indicates we have a textbox. The **name** attribute is used to identify this particular XHTML element and distinguish it from other elements of the same kind. This will be useful (necessary, in fact) when we write programs to process the information in this form control that will be "submitted" via the form, although we do not make use of it here.

The `size` attribute is used for textboxes to indicate how many characters will fit into the textbox "window" as displayed on the screen. Users can type more characters, but only the first `size` characters will be displayed (and seen by the user). We have chosen a value of 7 as a reasonable one for the size of this particular textbox. There is also an attribute called `maxlength` (not seen here) whose value can be used to restrict the maximum number of characters that may be entered. In other words, there are actually two sizes: a "visible size" and a "maximum size."

Although we have not used it here since it did not make sense to do so, the `value` attribute may be used to place a "default value" into the box. In any case, it is the value of the `value` attribute that will be used when this data is eventually processed as part of the form submission, since whatever is entered into the textbox by the user becomes the value of the `value` attribute.

It is important to note that just because we have given the name `"height"` to the form field that will receive the user's height does not make it obvious to users that they are supposed to enter their height into that particular textbox. That is why we have inserted the text `Height:` into the table column on the left. One can (and should) also use the `label` element to group the text that prompts the user for a height value, and the textbox that actually receives that height, into a logical unit. For simplicity we will omit this feature temporarily and come back to it at the end of the chapter in section 5.10.

5.4.2   Radio Buttons (input Elements of Type radio)

To the right of the height field we have two radio buttons, which are created by the markup in lines 20–21 of Figure 5.3. The user will click one of these to specify the unit for height as either inches or centimeters. We again use the `input` element to create each of these radio buttons, and this time we need the value `radio` for the `type` attribute.

When used for radio buttons, the behavior of the `input` element is a little more complicated, because radio buttons are normally used in a group. Radio buttons in the same group are identified by having the same value for the `name` attribute. We distinguish them based on the values of their `value` attributes. In our example, the first group of radio buttons contains two buttons and is found to the right of the height field. The common name for this group of radio buttons is `heightUnit`.

The value of the `value` attribute for the first radio button in the group is `in`, corresponding to "inches." The second radio button has the value `cm` for the `value` attribute, corresponding to "centimeters." Using the same name for both radio buttons ensures that only one of them can be selected at a time by the user. You may want to verify this fact by opening the file `bmi2.html` in a browser and clicking on each of these radio buttons in turn. The thing to note is that if one button is "selected," that is, has been clicked and shows a "bullet" in the center of its circle, and you click the other button, the first one is "deselected" as the second one becomes "selected."

The next row is essentially identical to the previous one in structure and format. It is used to obtain the user's weight and choice of weight unit. Again, we have three `input` elements. The first `input` element, of type `text`, is named `weight`. The next two `input` elements give us radio buttons grouped under the name `weightUnit`, with values `lb` (for pounds) and `kg` (for kilograms).

5.4.3   Checkboxes (input Elements of Type checkbox)

The third type of `input` element lets us create checkboxes. An example of a checkbox also appears in `bmi2.html`, just below the row for weight input. Checkboxes are similar to radio buttons in many ways. Multiple checkboxes can also be grouped together under the same name and distinguished by value just like radio buttons, even though our example only uses a single checkbox. Our checkbox has the name `details` and the value `yes`.

You will note that in the display of Figure 5.4 the checkbox is not checked by default. This is the typical case, and the user is asked to check the textbox if he or she wishes to take the option represented by that particular checkbox. There may, however, be times when you want the checkbox checked by default. To accomplish this the `input` element also has another attribute with the name `checked`. This attribute has only one possible value which, oddly enough, is the same as its name.[3] In other words, this attribute is either omitted, or always appears exactly like this: `checked="checked"` (at least if you expect your markup to validate). The point of including the attribute and its value is to have the checkbox checked by default when the page is displayed, should you wish to do that. The attribute `checked` can also be used (and is, in fact, more often used) for radio buttons, but in that case you should make sure that only one of the radio buttons in the group is checked (the one the user is most likely to choose, presumably).

It should be noted that data from `input` controls of type `radio` or `checkbox` is actually "submitted" by the submit button only if the corresponding `checked` attribute has the value `"checked"`.

---

[3]This rather odd situation comes about as a result of the fact that in XHTML every attribute must have a value. Since the checked attribute can only ever have one value, it is convenient, and easy to remember, to have its value the same as its name. In HTML it was only necessary to have the attribute present, without a value.

5.5   The `select` and `option` Elements for Dropdown List-boxes

In the previous section we illustrated how radio buttons can be used to allow a user to specify a choice of units for weight and height. Another method for letting the user pick an option is through a dropdown list-box (also called a dropdown menu, but we call this particular version a dropdown list-box to distinguish it from the dropdown menus we introduce in Chapter 7). Dropdown list-boxes are especially useful when the number of options is large, because they use much less display space on a web page.

The web page `bmi3.html` displayed in Figure 5.5 shows a dropdown list-box for units of height and weight. The corresponding `form` element markup is shown in Figure 5.6. We will only focus on the code between the `<select>...</select>` pairs of tags (the `select` elements) in `bmi3.html`. The rest of the file shows us nothing we have not already seen in `bmi2.html`.

Any `select` element used to create a web page dropdown list-box should be provided with a value for its `name` attribute for the same reasons we would give a name to an `input` element. Each text item corresponding to an option in the dropdown list-box is specified by the text content of an `<option>...</option>` tag pair. By default the option that appears first in the markup will appear in the little

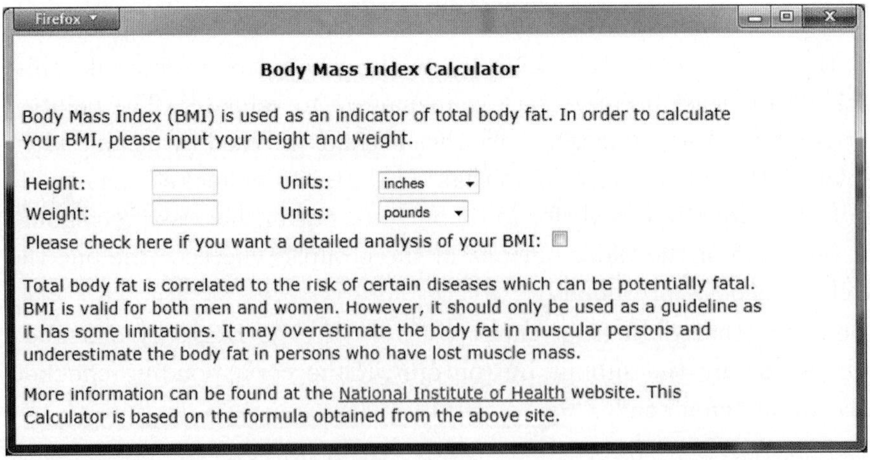

Body Mass Index Calculator

Body Mass Index (BMI) is used as an indicator of total body fat. In order to calculate your BMI, please input your height and weight.

Height: ☐   Units: inches ▾
Weight: ☐   Units: pounds ▾
Please check here if you want a detailed analysis of your BMI: ☐

Total body fat is correlated to the risk of certain diseases which can be potentially fatal. BMI is valid for both men and women. However, it should only be used as a guideline as it has some limitations. It may overestimate the body fat in muscular persons and underestimate the body fat in persons who have lost muscle mass.

More information can be found at the National Institute of Health website. This Calculator is based on the formula obtained from the above site.

FIGURE 5.5

`graphics/ch05/displayBmi3Html.jpg`
A Firefox browser display of `bmi3.html`, illustrating dropdown list-boxes.

```
 4     <form id="bmiForm" action="">
 5       <table summary="BMI Calculator-Textbox, Drop-Down Menu, Checkbox">
 6         <tr>
 7           <td>Height:</td>
 8           <td><input type="text" name="height" size="7" /></td>
 9           <td>Units:</td>
 0           <td><select name="heightUnit">
 1             <option>inches</option>
 2             <option>centimeters</option>
 3           </select></td>
 4         </tr>
 5         <tr>
 6           <td>Weight:</td>
 7           <td><input type="text" name="weight" size="7" /></td>
 8           <td>Units:</td>
 9           <td><select name="weightUnit">
 0             <option>pounds</option>
 1             <option>kilograms</option>
 2           </select></td>
 3         </tr>
 4         <tr>
 5           <td colspan="4">Please check here if you want a detailed analysis
 6           of your BMI: <input type="checkbox" name="details"
 7           value="yes" /></td>
 8         </tr>
 9       </table>
 0     </form>
```

FIGURE 5.6

cdrom/web05/bmi3.html (excerpt)
XHTML markup from bmi3.html, showing two select elements.

window of the dropdown list-box, so you should leave that option empty if you want the box to appear empty.

In our example, the **select** element for the weight unit has attribute **name= "weightUnit"** and the **select** element for the height has attribute unit **name= "heightUnit"**. Both of these dropdown list-boxes have only two options.

For simplicity we have not included **name** attributes for the **option** elements, but when we come to submit a form we will want to do this as well.

5.6 What Is Missing from the BMI Calculator Web Page?

If you look at Figure 5.5 for a moment, it should be clear that there is something missing. This web page allows the user to enter some information that will be needed to perform a certain kind of calculation, but does not provide any visible way to cause the calculation to take place. In other words, it is missing a "button" of some kind that the user can click on, and after which the BMI calculation will be performed and the results displayed to the user.

In this chapter we are concerned only with *displaying* the button, not *activating* it. As we have said earlier, we will deal with the calculations in the next chapter. But bear with us for a bit while we also postpone the introduction of buttons onto our BMI calculator page. In the next couple of sections we will start our second example, the feedback form, and use it to introduce both the `textarea` element (for extended text entry) and the `submit` and `reset` buttons for data submission and form reset. Then we will come back to our BMI calculator and extend it with buttons and some other enhancements.

5.7 The `textarea` Element

Providing a mechanism for getting feedback from its visitors should be one of the essential features of any e-commerce website. If the right kind of information is obtained and used properly, the user experience can be enhanced and sales increased.

Our second example illustrates just such a feedback form. The first version of the page containing this form is in the file `feedback1.html`, and the `form` element markup from that file is shown in Figure 5.7. The display of `feedback1.html` is shown in Figure 5.8.

Almost everything on this web page we have seen before. It has a dropdown list-box to let the user pick a title (or "salutation") such as `Ms.` or `Dr.` This is followed by standard text fields for the user's first name, last name, e-mail address, phone number, and the subject on which the user wishes to provide feedback.

It is a good idea to separate the name into two fields, one for the first name and one for the last name. This will help avoid any confusion between first and last names, and also allow us to personalize any response to the user using his or her first name, or a salutation followed by the last name, depending on the context. Note that the `textarea` element allows us to provide a large text area for the user to enter a message, since we can specify its size by supplying the desired number of rows and columns as values of its `rows` and `cols` attributes.

Some users may just want to have a one-way communication. Others may wish to receive a reply. Therefore, we give the user a choice of receiving a reply using a checkbox at the bottom.

```
2        <form id="contact" action="">
3          <table summary="Feedback Form Version 1">
4            <tr valign="top">
5              <td>Salutation:</td>
6              <td><select name="salute">
7                <option> </option>
8                <option>Mrs.</option>
9                <option>Ms.</option>
0                <option>Mr.</option>
1                <option>Dr.</option>
2              </select></td>
3            </tr>
4            <tr valign="top">
5              <td>First Name:</td>
6              <td><input type="text" name="firstName" size="40" /></td>
7            </tr>
8            <tr valign="top">
9              <td>Last Name:</td>
0              <td><input type="text" name="lastName" size="40" /></td>
1            </tr>
2            <tr valign="top">
3              <td>E-mail Address:</td>
4              <td><input type="text" name="email" size="40" /></td>
5            </tr>
6            <tr valign="top">
7              <td>Phone Number:</td>
8              <td><input type="text" name="phone" size="40" /></td>
9            </tr>
0            <tr valign="top">
1              <td>Subject:</td>
2              <td><input type="text" name="subject" size="40" /></td>
3            </tr>
4            <tr valign="top">
5              <td>Comments:</td>
6              <td><textarea name="message" rows="6" cols="30">
7              </textarea></td>
8            </tr>
9            <tr>
0              <td colspan="2">Please check here if you wish to receive a reply:
1              <input type="checkbox" name="reply" value="yes" /></td>
2            </tr>
3          </table>
4        </form>
5      </body>
6    </html>
```

FIGURE 5.7

cdrom/web05/feedback1.html (excerpt)

XHTML markup for a feedback form using a textarea element to receive user comments.

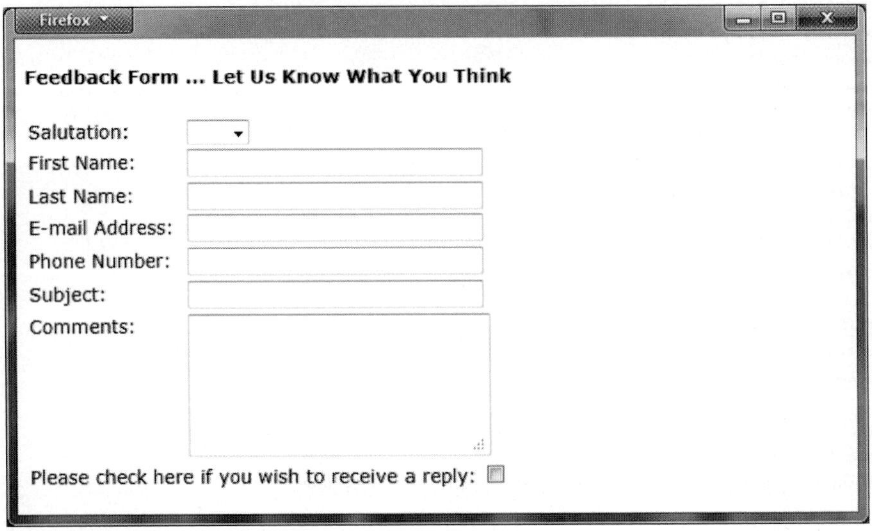

FIGURE 5.8
graphics/ch05/displayFeedback1Html.jpg
A Firefox browser display of `feedback1.html`.

We do need to point out a couple of things about the XHTML markup for the form in `feedback1.html`. First, since the salutation is obtained from a dropdown list-box, we have again used a `select` element to contain the options. However, since we did not want to presume any particular salutation, we have left the content of the first `option` element empty, causing the dropdown list-box to appear empty in Figure 5.8.

There is nothing unusual about the following five fields that are used to collect the first name, last name, e-mail address, phone number, and subject. They are all textboxes created by using `input` elements with their `type` attributes set to `text`.

The second new thing of interest in this form is the `textarea` element in lines 46 and 47. This particular `textarea` element has no content between its `<textarea>` and `</textarea>` tag pair, but if we wished to have some default text displayed when the page is rendered, we could supply that text as the element content. Just like other form fields, the `textarea` tag has an attribute called `name`, which we have set to the value `message`. Two additional attributes for the `textarea` tag are `rows` and `cols`, and they allow us to specify the height (number of rows) and width (number of columns, or characters) of the text area, respectively. We have chosen to have 6 lines (rows), each one allowing for 30 characters (columns). By default, a `textarea` element is "scrollable." That means a user can enter more than six lines of text, and the `textarea` control will then show a vertical scroll bar on the right.

The option that determines whether a user receives a reply uses an **input** element with the **type** attribute set to a value of **checkbox**. The name of the field is **reply**. We have set the value to be **yes**, in case the user does check the checkbox and data from this control is submitted. We have *not* set the attribute **checked** to the value **"checked"**, so the checkbox is unchecked by default when the page displays.

5.8 The submit and reset Button Elements

In general, every form needs to "submit" the data entered by the user. This capability is usually provided by a "submit button." Another useful button to have on a form is a "reset button," which can be used to clear any information that may have been entered and give the user a chance to start over.

Figure 5.9 shows the complete feedback form that includes submit and reset buttons. Since the rest of the form is exactly the same as the one in **feedback1.html**, we show only the XHTML markup that creates these buttons in Figure 5.10.

We use the versatile **input** element to create both the submit and reset buttons. The **type** attribute must be set to **submit** to get a submit button. The **value** attribute for our submit button is set to **"Submit Feedback"**, which is the text label that appears on the button in the display of the form.

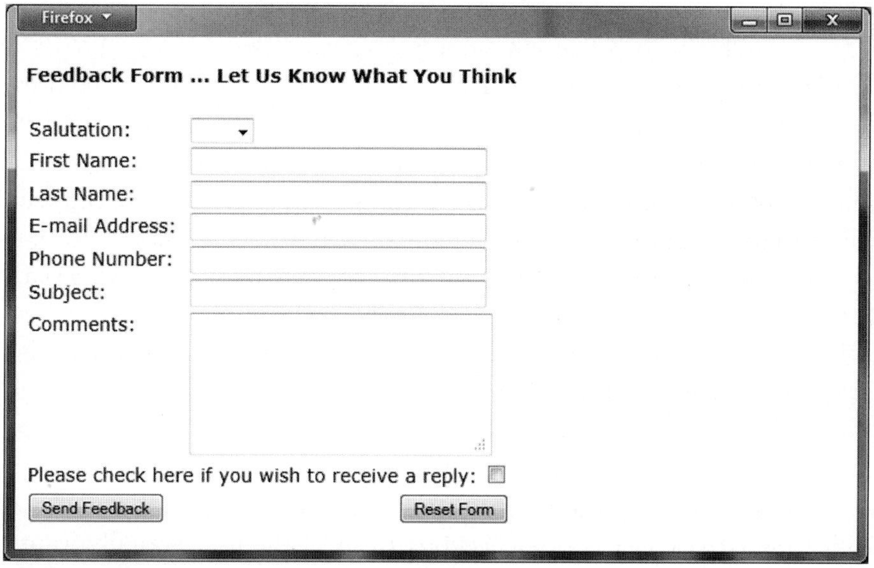

FIGURE 5.9

graphics/ch05/displayFeedback2Html.jpg
A Firefox browser display of **feedback2.html**.

```
53          <tr>
54            <td><input type="submit" value="Send Feedback" /></td>
55            <td align="right"><input type="reset" value="Reset Form" /></td>
56          </tr>
```

FIGURE 5.10

`cdrom/web05/feedback2.html` (excerpt)
Excerpt from this file to show the XHTML markup that produces the submit and reset buttons.

A value of `reset` for the `type` attribute of the `input` element creates a reset button. Its `value` attribute is set to the text `"Reset Form"`, which appears as the visible label on the reset button when the web page containing the form is displayed. The reset button is immediately active, in the sense that if you enter some data and click on the reset button, the data will disappear from the form. However, we have not yet activated the submit button in the sense of connecting it to a script (program) that will process the data, and will do so only in a later chapter when we have some programming code (a script) to respond when a user clicks on this button and data is submitted.

5.9   Organizing Form Controls with the `fieldset` and `legend` Elements

Usually, the high-level view of a web form consists of several logical parts—required input, optional input, processing buttons, and so on. Each logical part, in turn, consists of a group of fields to collect a particular category of information.

We have a more refined version of our BMI calculator in `bmi4.html`. Its browser display is shown in Figure 5.11, and we can see how the three logical data-collection parts of the BMI calculator have been labeled on the web page display: `Vital statistics`, `E-mail record?`, and `Processing`. We have the original fields related to BMI calculations, which make up the first logical part for getting the vital statistics from the user. This consists of the text fields for weight and height as well as dropdown list-boxes for their units and a checkbox to see if the user wants to see detailed calculations.

To this we have added a second logical part for e-mailing the BMI calculations to the user. This second part consists of a checkbox to see if the user actually wants an e-mail sent and, if so, a text field that collects the user's e-mail address.

The third part consists of submit and reset buttons that will process the information.

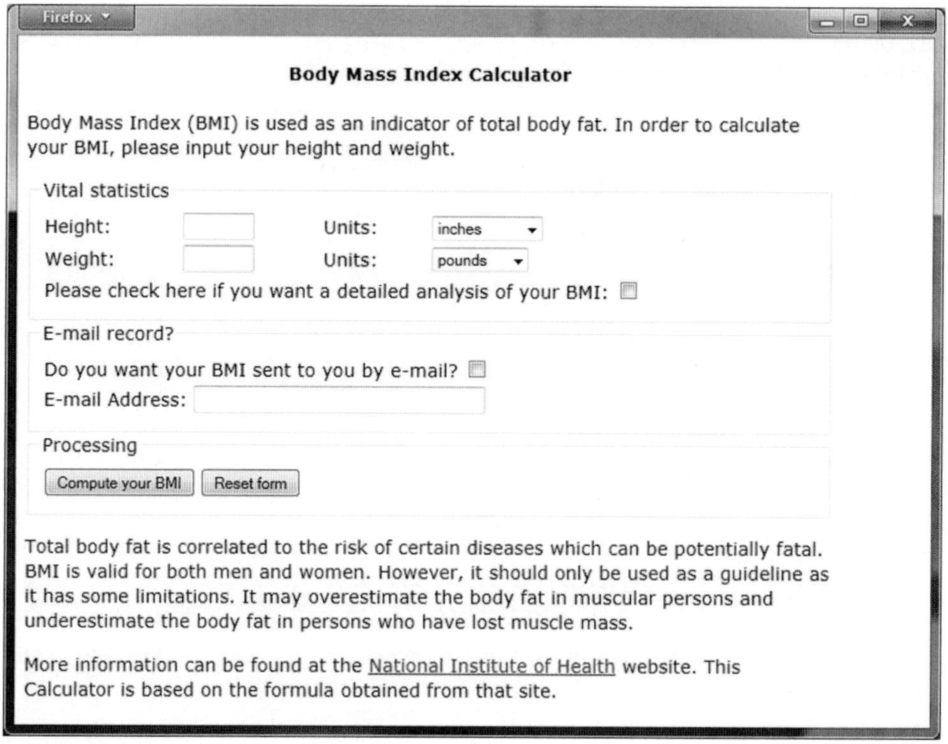

FIGURE 5.11

graphics/ch05/displayBmi4Html.jpg

A Firefox browser display of `bmi4.html`, illustrating the `fieldset` groupings.

To provide visual clues to the user when filling out the form there are boxes around these logical parts, and each box is supplied with an appropriate label, or, as it is called in this context, a *legend*.

Let us look at the relevant XHTML markup in the file `bmi4.html`, which is shown in Figure 5.12. The logical grouping of fields is accomplished with the help of the XHTML `fieldset` element, with the content of each particular logical grouping placed within its own pair of `<fieldset>...</fieldset>` tags. The legend for the box around each fieldset grouping is created by an aptly named XHTML `legend` element, with the text that appears between the `<legend>...</legend>` tag pair forming the legend itself.

The first `fieldset` element (lines 15–42) encompasses the `input` elements of type `text` for weight and height, the dropdown list-boxes for their units provided by the `select` and `option` elements, and a checkbox to indicate whether the user wants to see detailed calculations provided by an `input` tag of type `checkbox`. The `legend` element for this first `fieldset` element contains the text `Vital statistics`.

```
14    <form id="bmiForm" action="">
15      <fieldset>
16        <legend>Vital statistics</legend>
17        <table summary="Vital Statistics">
18          <tr>
19            <td>Height:</td>
20            <td><input type="text" name="height" size="7" /></td>
21            <td>Units:</td>
22            <td><select name="heightUnit">
23              <option>inches</option>
24              <option>centimeters</option>
25            </select></td>
26          </tr>
27          <tr>
28            <td>Weight:</td>
29            <td><input type="text" name="weight" size="7" /></td>
30            <td>Units:</td>
31            <td><select name="weightUnit">
32              <option>pounds</option>
33              <option>kilograms</option>
34            </select></td>
35          </tr>
36          <tr>
37            <td colspan="4">Please check here if you want a detailed
38            analysis of your BMI: <input type="checkbox" name="details"
39            value="yes" /></td>
40          </tr>
41        </table>
42      </fieldset>
43      <fieldset>
44        <legend>E-mail record?</legend>
45        <table summary="E-mail">
46          <tr>
47            <td colspan="2">Do you want your BMI sent to you by e-mail?
48            <input type="checkbox" name="want_mail" value="yes" /></td>
49          </tr>
50          <tr>
51            <td>E-mail Address:</td>
52            <td><input type="text" name="email" size="40" /></td>
53          </tr>
54        </table>
55      </fieldset>
56      <fieldset>
57        <legend>Processing</legend>
58        <table summary="Processing">
59          <tr>
60            <td><input type="submit" value="Compute your BMI" /></td>
61            <td><input type="reset" value="Reset form" /></td>
62          </tr>
63        </table>
64      </fieldset>
65    </form>
```

FIGURE 5.12

cdrom/web05/bmi4.html (excerpt)

The form element from bmi4.html, showing the three fieldset elements.

The second `fieldset` element (lines 43–55) uses the `legend` text E-mail record?, with the question mark suggesting the user may not wish to provide this information. It consists of two `input` elements. The first `input` element is of type `checkbox` and determines if the user wants to receive the e-mail. The second `input` element is of type `text` and collects the e-mail address of the user, if it is supplied.

The third `fieldset` element (lines 56–65) has the `legend` text Processing and two `input` elements, one of type `submit` that gives us the submit button and a second of type `reset` to provide a button for resetting the fields in the form. In the display of this form the two buttons are positioned side-by-side at the left.

Note that the content of each `fieldset` element is now a table. We cannot keep the single-table structure we had in `bmi3.html` and simply add more rows and columns to that table. The reason for this is that a `fieldset` element must be a "child" of the `form` element, and thus cannot be contained within a `table` element with the `table` element being the child of the `form` element.

5.10 Using the `label` Element for Behind-the-Scenes Logical Groupings

In the previous section we saw how the `fieldset` element could be used to group web page elements to provide visual clues to the viewer about the logical grouping of displayed items. It is also a good idea when designing web pages to provide some behind-the-scenes logical grouping as well. For this purpose the `label` element can be used to associate a label with form controls such as `input`, `textarea`, and `select`.

There are a number of good reasons for doing this. First of all, the association enhances the usability of forms. For example, when users of visual web browsers click on a label, the "focus" is automatically set in the associated form element. Thus, for users with visual disabilities who are making use of *assistive technologies*, establishing these associations between labels and controls helps clarify the spatial relationships found in forms and makes them easier to navigate.

In section 5.4 we mentioned that when designing forms, it is a good idea to group the text that prompts the user for a value with the component that actually receives that value so that they form a logical unit. In this context, a second reason for using a `label` element for logical grouping is that doing so can help to avoid the possibility that text describing a form field will get separated from that field in future changes to the page.

There are two ways to use the label element in this way. First, if the text describing an element and the element itself are immediately adjacent to one another, both may simply be included as the content of the `label` element, as in this example:

```
<td>
  <label>
    Height: <input type = "text" name = "height" size = "7" />
  </label>
</td>
```

This is referred to as an *implicit label.*

On the other hand, if the text description and the input element are separated (the text appears within one element, and the form control it describes appears within another element), then the `for` attribute of the `label` element may be used to bind the two elements together, as illustrated in the following example:

```
<td>
  <label for="heightValue">Height: </label>
</td>
<td>
  <input id="heightValue" type="text" name="height" size="7" />
</td>
```

This is referred to as an *explicit label,* and is preferred to the *implicit label* illustrated above, since it is more likely to be properly interpreted by the current crop of browsers.

Note that the value of the `for` attribute in the `label` element is the same as the value of the `id` attribute in the `input` element, which is what establishes the association between the two.

You might be inclined to try rewriting the above example as

```
<tr>
  <label>
    <td>Height: </td>
    <td><input type="text" name="height" size="7" /></td>
  </label>
</tr>
```

but this will not work. Or, to be more precise, it may work but it won't validate, since a `label` element is not permitted inside a `tr` element in this way because the label and the form control being labeled are in different table cells.[4]

---

[4]Why this should be so is not clear to either author, we might add.

```
4     <form id="bmiForm" action="">
5       <fieldset>
6         <legend>Vital statistics</legend>
7         <table summary="Vital Statistics">
8           <tr>
9             <td><label for="height">Height:</label></td>
0             <td><input id="height" type="text" name="height" size="7" /></td>
1             <td><label for="heightUnit">Units:</label></td>
2             <td><select id="heightUnit" name="heightUnit">
3               <option>inches</option>
4               <option>centimeters</option>
5             </select></td>
6           </tr>
```

FIGURE 5.13

cdrom/web05/bmi5.html (excerpt)
Part of the form markup from bmi5.html, showing a couple of label tags.

If you study Figure 5.13, which contains an excerpt from bmi5.html, the final
version of our BMI calculator, you will see that we have revised the XHTML form
markup from Figure 5.12 to include appropriate label tags. Figure 5.13 only shows
the first part of the form markup, and you should study the rest of the file as well,
looking for the remaining label tags to see where and how they are placed.

Note that placing other elements within a label element has absolutely no effect
on the display of those other elements. Doing this is simply a way of setting up a
logical grouping that can be used to bind elements together for manipulation purposes
and may even serve as documentation during future maintenance of the page. Thus,
the display of the form from bmi5.html is identical to that from bmi4.html shown
in Figure 5.11.

5.11   Getting Ready to Submit Your Form Data

We have gone as far as we can go without any programming. The purpose of the forms
that we have created in this chapter is to allow users to submit data to websites
for processing. However, in order to process the data, we need to write computer
programs.

Programming on the Web can be broadly placed into two categories: client-side
programming and server-side programming. On the client side, the programs run on
the user's computer through the web browser. Server-side programming involves the
running of programs on the computer that is hosting the web server.

Client-side computing can provide only limited features, as it cannot access any
databases, for example. It is also limited by security restrictions on the client's

computer. Server-side programming is essential for sophisticated e-commerce-related computing.

We will look at both client-side and server-side computing in the following chapters. We will begin with a study of JavaScript in the next chapter. This will allow us to perform client-side computing that accomplishes the following:

- Checking what the user has entered into either of our forms to make sure it is valid data before we try to do anything with it

- Using the data entered into our BMI form to compute and display the user's body mass index

In subsequent chapters we will use the PHP programming language and the MySQL database management software to do more sophisticated server-side computing.

5.12   Summary

In this chapter we discussed the web page form, which is used for collecting data input from site visitors. Such a form is created by placing an XHTML `form` element in the page document, and then placing within that element a number of *controls* or "widgets" that are able to receive data from the user in some form.

These controls include various forms of the `input` element (for textboxes, radio buttons, and checkboxes, for example). Radio buttons can be grouped and allow the user to choose only one option from the group. Checkboxes can also be grouped, but allow multiple choices.

Dropdown list-boxes provide a space-saving alternative to a group of radio buttons or checkboxes when the number of choices is large. A dropdown list-box is created by nesting `option` elements inside a `select` element.

If we want more text input than the single line of text allowed by the textbox variant of the input element, we can use a `textarea` element, and choose the number of rows and columns for its initial display, as well as any default text we want it to contain.

For enhanced usability, form controls that belong to the same logical grouping can be physically grouped as the content of a `fieldset` element, with an associated `legend` element. This has the effect of drawing a box around those controls in the display and labeling that box at the upper left with the text that formed the content of the legend element.

The label element can (and should) be used to provide a logical grouping of an input element and the text used to describe that element. This also has the effect of enhancing usability, since even clicking on the label of a labeled element will shift the focus to that element.

This chapter has taken us as far as we can go without programming, which we begin to discuss in the next chapter.

5.13 Quick Questions to Test Your Basic Knowledge

1. What is the purpose of having a form on one or more of your web pages?

2. If you place an empty form element on a web page, what do you see as a result when the page is displayed?

3. What are five different kinds of input elements, and what kind of input does each permit?

4. How much text can you put in a textbox created by an input element whose type attribute has a value of text?

5. Since all radio buttons in a group are given the same name, how is one distinguished from the others?

6. What is the purpose of the value attribute of an input element of type text?

7. Can you explain the purpose of the attribute-value pair checked="checked" for radio buttons and checkboxes, and also explain why it has this rather unusual form?

8. What must you do if you want the box display of a dropdown list-box to appear empty?

9. What kind of value does the action attribute of a form have, and what is its purpose?

10. What is the purpose of a fieldset element, and what other element is always associated with it?

11. How is a `label` element used to connect an `input` element and the text that labels that `input` element?

5.14   Short Exercises to Improve Your Basic Understanding

1. Try to validate the file `bmi1.html` to confirm that it will *not* validate, and explain *why* it will not validate.

2. Modify `feedback1.html` so that a first name and last name of your choosing show up in the corresponding text boxes when the form is displayed.

3. Modify `bmi2.html` so that the checkbox indicating that a detailed BMI analysis is desired is automatically checked when the form is displayed.

4. Modify `bmi3.html` so that `inches` and `pounds` do *not* show up in the `Units:` boxes when the form is displayed.

5. Experiment with `bmi4.html` and `bmi5.html` to convince yourself that label tags really do cause the two pages to exhibit the behavioral differences discussed in section 5.10.

5.15   Exercises on the Parallel Project

In these exercises you will create two forms for your own business, one that asks the user to make some choices from among your products or services and one that asks for some feedback on products or services previously purchased.

1. Design and develop a web page containing a form that allows the user to make a single choice from each of two different categories of product or service that your business provides, as well as multiple choices from a third category of product or service. The form must show the price per unit of each item and allow the user to enter the quantity required of each item, if appropriate. The tax on products and services must also be indicated (you may assume it is the same for both) and a checkbox provided for users to indicate if they have tax-exempt status. The form must have a button to submit the order and one

to reset the form if the user wishes to start over. To complete this web page, provide a suitable title and explanatory text and format it in such a way that, in your opinion at least, it is pleasing to view.

2. Design and develop a web page containing a form that queries the user on the level of satisfaction with previously purchased products or services from your business. Pick two categories from your business offerings. Within each category have a checkbox for each item to indicate whether the user has purchased that product or service, and a sequence of radio buttons to indicate the level of satisfaction. For each category, also have a box where the user can enter comments about that category. Provide as well boxes for the user to enter his or her first and last names, and another for e-mail. The form will also need the usual submit and reset buttons. Complete the web page by providing a suitable title and explanatory text and format it in such a way that it is pleasing to view.

5.16   What Else You May Want or Need to Know

Forms have long been the major tool in the web developer's toolkit for collecting information from users to be sent to the server for processing. As with many things in life and on the Web, simple is probably better, and appropriate variations of the simple web forms we have presented in this chapter may well be adequate for many data collection tasks on your website. Although we have not done so, you can of course use CSS to add all kinds of styles to your forms, and you will see some very fancy forms as you cruise around the Web. However, this is not necessarily a good idea, since many users will be expecting a more or less "standard" form and may not have the time or patience to deal with a form that appears to be too far from the norm. This can impact your business negatively if you are running an e-commerce website. The *KISS principle*[5] is alive and well in web development, and in the use of web forms in particular.

---

[5]This is a good one to Google if you've never encountered it before, or even if you have.

5.17   References

1. The W3 Schools site has a section on forms:

   http://www.w3schools.com/html/html_forms.asp

2. Wikipedia has something to say about almost everything, including web forms:

   http://en.wikipedia.org/wiki/Form_%28web%29

3. Here is another site that provides a tutorial on web form building:

   http://www.devarticles.com/c/a/Web-Design-Standards/Web-Forms/

4. With the coming of HTML 5 there will be some useful enhancements to forms as well as to many other features. You may be interested in getting a sneak preview by reading what is still a working draft of the section on forms in HTML 5, which you can find at this URL:

   http://www.w3.org/TR/html5/forms.html

5. There are websites that provide ready-to-use forms for various purposes, or even let you "roll your own":

   http://www.emailmeform.com/
   http://www.123contactform.com/

CHAPTER 6

JavaScript for Client-Side Computation and Data Validation

CHAPTER CONTENTS

6.1   Overview and Objectives

We have reached more or less the mid-point of our introduction to website development. From this point on in this text, all the web pages we create will exhibit some kind of dynamic behavior. Some will include two-way, client-server communication, but not until we have studied PHP in later chapters. Sometimes the "look and feel," as well as the content, of a web page may change, based on the current circumstances. The difference in those circumstances may be caused by input from the user, by the date and time of viewing, or by changes in the database of the business. All of this development will be controlled by programming.

We will begin our study of web programming with *JavaScript*, one of the most versatile and useful programming languages, yet one of the easiest to learn. In this chapter we will study some of the basic features of the language and use it to perform client-side computations such as the BMI calculations we postponed in the last chapter, and to check the data our users are entering into our web pages to ensure it is the kind of data we are expecting. This is an important aspect of creating a secure website.

So, in this chapter we will discuss the following:

■ The importance of keeping web page content behavior separate from content structure and content presentation, both conceptually and physically

■ An overview of JavaScript as a programming language, including a brief history, its limitations, and how we will use it

■ Writing to a web page for user notification via JavaScript

■ External and embedded JavaScript code

■ The Document Object Model (DOM) and JavaScript access to it

■ JavaScript data types and variables, functions (built-in and programmer-defined), expressions, control statements, arrays, and built-in objects

■ Website security and how JavaScript can help achieve it

■ Regular expressions and their use in JavaScript

■ Updates of our BMI calculator form and feedback form to incorporate validation of user input

This chapter, like the previous one, will not have a **nature** subdirectory containing an updated version of our complete sample website. The sample files of this chapter will focus directly on the chapter topics, namely the use of JavaScript for computation and data validation on the client side. In the next chapter we will present and updated version of our Nature's Source website illustrating all features discussed up to that point.

6.2 Another Important Distinction: Structure vs. Presentation vs. Behavior

In section 3.3 of Chapter 3 we drew your attention to the important notion of structure vs. presentation of a web page. Now we are about to make our web pages much more interactive by using JavaScript, and that introduces a whole new aspect of web pages: *web page behavior.*

We will follow the same approach we used in separating presentation from content. That is, although there is more than one way to make JavaScript code available to our XHTML pages, we will, for the most part, keep our JavaScript code in a separate file, and this is the recommended approach. The goal, then, is to keep the content of each XHTML page and its structure separate from the CSS file that determines its presentation style and also separate from the JavaScript code that determines its behavior.

All that having been said, it is nevertheless quite convenient for testing and illustrative purposes to place JavaScript code right in the XHTML file where it is to be used, just as it was for CSS.

6.3 What Is JavaScript? (It's *not* Java!)

First, a little bit of history. In the mid-1990s the folks who had developed the Netscape® browser began development of a new and appropriately named programming language called LiveScript for adding lively animations to web pages. Brendan Eich is credited with much of the early work. About the same time, Sun Microsystems®' Java programming language was fast gaining importance on the Internet due to its portability across different computing platforms, and its ability to provide users with interactivity on web pages via *Java applets*, small Java programs that could be downloaded from a web page and executed within a browser.

Before long, Netscape and Sun agreed that the name LiveScript would be changed to JavaScript, in an attempt to increase its appeal. Unfortunately, this name change has led to yet more confusion in the web community. Other than similarity in name, there is no obvious relationship between Java and JavaScript. Both languages share similar programming constructs, but the same commonalities are also shared with many other recent languages and can be traced back to the popular C programming language that was developed in the late 1960s.

6.3.1   JavaScript Is Interpreted, Not Compiled

JavaScript is a high-level programming language. Programs in high-level languages need to be translated into machine language prior to execution. There are two types of translators:

> **Compilers** translate an entire program into an executable machine language version that can be executed many times, after this one-time translation.

> **Interpreters** translate a program one statement at a time to its machine language equivalent, just prior to the execution of that statement, and do this every time the program is run. Interpreted languages are simpler and more portable to different hardware and software platforms, but result in much more translation overhead, since they are translated every time they are executed. This makes them generally less efficient than compiled languages.

JavaScript is an interpreted language that can be used to run programs for web computing on both the client side and the server side. Server-side web computing using JavaScript is less common. It can be used for retrieving and manipulating data from server-side databases as well as for communicating with other applications running on the server. However, most server-side computing is done using other options, including:

- Open-source programming languages such as PHP and Python

- CGI programming using Perl, also open source

- The open-source Java Server Pages™(JSP) technology from Sun Microsystems, a company which is now a part of Oracle®

- A proprietary (*not* open source) alternative such as the Active Server Pages (ASP) technology from Microsoft

We will use the very popular open-source PHP programming language for our server-side computing. Our treatment of JavaScript in this chapter and the next will focus on client-side computing, where it is most dominant.

6.3.2 Restrictions on What JavaScript Can Do

On the client side, JavaScript code is usually downloaded as part of, or in conjunction with, a web document, and runs in a web browser. By this we mean that the browser has built into it a JavaScript interpreter that is capable of executing any JavaScript code it encounters as the browser is downloading and rendering a web page.

JavaScript is somewhat limited in both the number of features and general abilities. However, the limited number of features makes it easy to learn, and the restrictions on its abilities are there for a very good reason, since they are based on security concerns. We do not want a JavaScript program from a website to come down to a client's computer and cause deliberate changes to its configuration or inflict other intended or unintended damage. Therefore, the actions that JavaScript can perform on your computer are typically restricted to these:

- Computations based on user input

- Validation of data entered by the user, before that data is sent to the server for processing

- Dynamically adding (X)HTML elements to a web page, or changing (X)HTML elements already on a web page

- Changing the look and feel of a web page as the user's mouse pointer interacts with the web page

6.3.3 How Will We Use JavaScript?

We will enhance our e-commerce website with the use of JavaScript and learn some essential features of the language in the process. We will be studying JavaScript in two chapters. This chapter describes the use of JavaScript for computation as well as validating data entered by the user (the first two items in the above list). The following chapter uses JavaScript for providing a dynamic look and feel to our web pages (the last two items in the above list).

The treatment of JavaScript provided in these two chapters barely scratches the surface of what is possible using the language. At the end of each chapter, we will again provide pointers to additional resources that users can go to for further information about JavaScript. While previous programming experience will be helpful from now on in this text, we attempt to make this and subsequent chapters self-contained for anyone with a reasonable aptitude for computer programming.

One other thing ... just as we have placed our `.css` files in a subdirectory called `css`, we will place our JavaScript files in a subdirectory called `scripts`. Although our JavaScript files have a file extension of `.js`, we give the directory containing them the more generic name **scripts** (rather than **js**, say), since directories with this name will later contain scripts written in languages other than JavaScript (PHP, for example).

6.4 A Simple JavaScript Example: User Notification with an Embedded Script

In order to be useful, every computer program must have some kind of output. In web programming, that output will often be some change in a visual or audio effect on a web page. However, the simplest output for most programs in any language is a textual display of some kind, and that is where we will start.

We see a working example of an "embedded" JavaScript script in Figure 6.1. This example shows that we can take an existing XHTML document for a web page and insert some JavaScript code directly into that document. The two lines of code in lines 13 and 14 are actual JavaScript "output statements" and form a simple JavaScript program, or *script*. Note that these two statements form the body of a **script** element, which itself is the content of an **h3** element. The complete document is entitled **buy2.html** and can be found on your CD-ROM in the **web06** directory.

```
1   <!DOCTYPE html PUBLIC "-//W3C//DTD XHTML 1.0 Strict//EN"
2       "http://www.w3.org/TR/xhtml1/DTD/xhtml1-strict.dtd">
3   <!-- buy2.html -->
4   <html xmlns="http://www.w3.org/1999/xhtml">
5     <head>
6       <title>Nature's Source - Canada's largest specialty vitamin store</title>
7       <meta http-equiv="Content-Type" content="text/html;charset=utf-8" />
8       <link rel="stylesheet" type="text/css" href="css/default.css" />
9     </head>
10    <body>
11      <p><img src="images/naturelogo.gif" alt="Nature's Source" /></p>
12      <h3><script type="text/javascript">
13        document.write("Watch this space for our e-store.<br/>");
14        document.write("Coming soon ...");
15      </script></h3>
16    </body>
17  </html>
```

FIGURE 6.1

cdrom/web06/buy2.html
A short XHTML markup file containing a simple "embedded" JavaScript script with two output statements.

A script of any kind that is inserted into an XHTML document (or "embedded" in the document, as we also say) will be the content of a `script` element. That is, the script will be placed between a `<script>...</script>` tag pair. The only attribute we see for the `script` tag in Figure 6.1 is `type`, with the value `text/javascript`. That means the script is in the form of simple text, and it is written in JavaScript (as opposed to some other scripting language).[1] The statements between the `<script>...</script>` pair (in other words, the content of the `script` element) is the actual JavaScript program.

So, the first JavaScript programming language statement in our first XHTML document containing a JavaScript script is this one:

```
document.write("Watch this space for our e-store.<br/>");
```

In this statement, it is most convenient to think of `document` as the name of a JavaScript *object* that represents the XHTML web page document in which the JavaScript is "embedded" within a `script` element.[2] The *Object-Oriented Programming (OOP)* way of doing things is to use a dot (or period) to connect an object with one of its *methods* for performing a task related to that object.

While *method* is the commonly used OOP terminology, programmers who started with the *procedural programming paradigm*, which does not use "objects," sometimes use other terms such as *function* or *procedure* to refer to a method. A JavaScript object generally provides a number of methods that help us achieve our goals with respect to that object. For example, in this case, to display text in a document, JavaScript provides the method called `write()`[3] that "belongs to" the `document` object.

We often describe what we are doing here by saying that we are "calling" the `document` object's `write()` method. When we call it, we supply the `write()` method

---

[1]Note that when talking about the language, we write "JavaScript," but in `type="text/javascript"` the language name is written completely in lowercase.

[2]`document` is actually a "property" of the browser `window` object, but since it is accessible to JavaScript in the way shown, we can think of it as a JavaScript object.

[3]When we use the name of a method to refer to that method, we include a set of parentheses following the method name to emphasize that it is in fact a method and not some other kind of JavaScript entity. In JavaScript code, in fact, a method name must always be followed by a set of parentheses, though there may or may not be anything between those parentheses.

with a string of characters as a *parameter* of the method. The parameter must be enclosed in a pair of parentheses that follow the method.[4] A string is a sequence of characters that is generally enclosed in double quotes, though JavaScript allows the use of single quotes to denote a string as well. In our statement the string is

```
"Watch this space for our e-store.<br />"
```

which is a *literal value* (or actual value) of a JavaScript *data type* named `String`. We will say more about data types and their values later.

This first output statement will output the above string to our document, just as if we had typed the string into the document directly. So what's the point, you might well ask, and why go to all this trouble? The point is that we are illustrating the `write()` method by getting it to write out a simple string, but we can use it to output lots of other things, such as the result of a calculation, for example.

Note that we have included a bit of XHTML code in our string, namely the line break tag `<br />`. This will ensure that any following text will be displayed on the subsequent line by the browser. Note in this context that it is the job of the JavaScript code to put content into our document, but it is the browser's job to display that content.

Note as well that our JavaScript statement ends with a semicolon. JavaScript is more forgiving than conventional languages such as Java and C++ in this regard. It will accept statements that are not terminated by a semicolon. However, it is regarded as good programming practice to use a semicolon to terminate a JavaScript statement.

Our first JavaScript program has another output statement that displays the string, `"Coming soon ..."`. If you open the file `buy2.html` in a web browser, you will see the display of the two lines that were output by the JavaScript `write()` method. You can also see the display in Figure 6.2. As we pointed out above, the XHTML code `<br />` in our first string is not displayed by the web browser. It simply ensures that the second string appears on the following line. Note as well that the text output by this short JavaScript script actually shows up in the XHTML document as the content of an XHTML `h3` element, which explains the formatting we see in Figure 6.2.

Finally, note that the display of Figure 6.2 is just a stripped-down version of the display in Figure 4.19, without the menu and footer and with a smaller amount of

---

[4]A method will often take one or more parameters, listed between its parentheses, to provide it with information it needs to perform its task.

FIGURE 6.2
graphics/ch06/displayBuy2Html.jpg
A Firefox browser display of buy2.html (and buy3.html as well).

text, this time produced by the JavaScript script. Remember that in this chapter we do not have a full version of our sample site and are concentrating on JavaScript alone.

6.5   Where Do You Place Your JavaScript Code?

In the previous section we saw how JavaScript code can be embedded in an XHTML document. However, cluttering up an XHTML document with JavaScript can make such a document very difficult to understand and maintain.

In previous chapters, we separated the presentation details from the XHTML document with the use of CSS files. Now we will do the same with JavaScript. All our JavaScript will be in separate files, except for some short illustrative examples of alternative scenarios. We will use the extension .js for these files and keep them in a subdirectory called scripts, which will be located off of the main directory where the XHTML files that use those scripts reside.

In fact, to avoid some possible confusion, now may be a good time to review the structure of our subdirectories to date. All the XHTML files for a given chapter are in a "main" directory corresponding to that chapter, or if there is a subgrouping required for a chapter, in an appropriate subdirectory of that "main" directory. Underneath any directory containing a group of XHTML files we are likely to have several subdirectories containing auxiliary files used by these XHTML files, and one or more subdirectories containing a complete version of our sample website, if these need to be separated from the sample files:

- A subdirectory called images containing any image files required by those XHTML files.

- A subdirectory called `css` containing any Cascading Style Sheet files that describe presentation details for those XHTML files. Often this will be a single file called `default.css`.

- A subdirectory called `scripts` containing any scripts (programs) used by those XHTML files.

- Subdirectories with names like `nature`, or `nature1` and `nature2`, for the version or versions of our website.

For example, the directory `web04` for Chapter 4 used essentially all of this structure except for the `scripts` subdirectory, while the directory `web06` (for this chapter) uses everything except there are no versions of the complete site here. These can all be found on your CD-ROM, of course, as well as on our text website.

6.5.1   The Simple Example Revisited: Linking to an External Script

Now let us see how we can use the JavaScript code that is kept in a separate file in our XHTML document.

Figure 6.3 shows the body of the XHTML document in `buy3.html`. In this case our JavaScript script is in another file, namely `scripts/buy3.js`. We specify the fact that the source of the JavaScript code is in a different file by using the `src`[5] attribute of the `script` tag with the value `scripts/buy3.js`. The file `buy3.js` from subdirectory `scripts` is shown in Figure 6.4.

The executable JavaScript code itself (from the external file `buy3.js`) is no different from the JavaScript code embedded in the XHTML of `buy2.html` shown in Figure 6.1 and the display is the same as that shown in Figure 6.2.

```
10    <body>
11      <p><img src="images/naturelogo.gif" alt="Nature's Source" /></p>
12      <h3><script type="text/javascript" src="scripts/buy3.js">
13      </script></h3>
14    </body>
```

FIGURE 6.3

`cdrom/web06/buy3.html` (excerpt)
The body of `buy3.html`, showing the script element that provides access to the JavaScript code stored in the external file `buy3.js`.

---

[5]Note that the XHTML `script` element is like the XHTML `img` element in that it has a `src` attribute for the required file, and is unlike the `link` element, which has an `href` attribute for that purpose.

```
1   //buy3.js
2   document.write("Watch this space for our e-store.<br/>");
3   document.write("Coming soon ...");
```

FIGURE 6.4

`cdrom/web06/scripts/buy3.js`
The content of the external JavaScript code file `buy3.js`.

Note that the closing `</script>` tag seen in Figure 6.3 is required, even though the `script` element has no content in this case.

6.5.2   User Notification Revisited: The `alert()` Method

Next, we look at a different way of notifying users, this time using another JavaScript method called `alert()`. The `alert()` method allows us to create a *pop-up window* that gives users whatever text message we choose to provide.

We use the files `buy4.html` and `buy4.js` to illustrate the use of the `alert()` method. The `body` element from `buy4.html` is shown in Figure 6.5, and is the same as the `body` element in `buy3.html`, except for the name of the associated JavaScript file `buy4.js,` which is shown in Figure 6.6. The executable script in this case consists of a single statement that calls the `alert()` method.

The `alert()` method, like the `document.write()` method, takes a single parameter of type `String`. However, this time the string we are sending to `alert()` is in fact a *concatenation* (a fancy term that means "putting together") of two strings using the plus operator (+). The first of these strings illustrates another technique that we have not seen before: the use of the special character `\n`.[6] The use of a `\n` in

```
10      <body>
11        <p><img src="images/naturelogo.gif" alt="Nature's Source" /></p>
12        <h3><script type="text/javascript" src="scripts/buy4.js">
13        </script></h3>
14      </body>
```

FIGURE 6.5

`cdrom/web06/buy4.html` (excerpt)
The body of `buy4.html`, showing the script element that provides access to the JavaScript code stored in the external file `buy4.js`.

---

[6]Don't be confused by the fact that `\n` looks like two characters. Actually, it really *is* two characters, physically, but in every other way it is treated as, and is considered to be, a single character. There are several other such characters, all called *escape characters*, as we will see shortly.

```
1   //buy4.js
2   alert("Watch this space for our e-store.\n" + "Coming soon ...");
```

FIGURE 6.6

cdrom/web06/scripts/buy4.js
The content of the external JavaScript code file buy4.js.

the first string has the effect of starting a new line at the point where it occurs, that is, the following part of the string will appear on the next line, as in:

```
Watch this space for our e-store.
Coming soon ...
```

Don't confuse the use of \n to move to the next line in this context (a pop-up window) with the use of the <br /> tag to accomplish the same task in an XHTML document. Each works well in its own context, but not in the other context.

Figure 6.7 shows the results of running the JavaScript from the file buy4.js. We get a pop-up window that gives us the familiar message:

```
Watch this space for our e-store.
Coming soon ...
```

The difference this time is that the message will not go away until the user clicks the OK button.

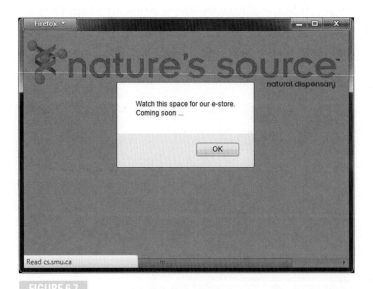

FIGURE 6.7

graphics/ch06/displayBuy4.jpg
A Firefox browser display of buy4.html.

Depending on what we want our scripts to do for us, the JavaScript code can become quite involved. For example, it may contain programmer-defined functions that can be called by other parts of the code. If you examine documents found on the Web, you will often see such complex code included within the **head** element of a web page.[7] We will be looking at more sophisticated JavaScript in the following sections, and in the next chapter.

6.5.3 JavaScript Escape Characters

Most modern programming languages that count the C programming language as one of their antecedents use essentially the same set of special characters to specify invisible *control characters*, such as the *newline* character (\n, as discussed above) and the *tab* character (\t), with the help of a backslash (\). Since the backslash is used to denote special characters, we also need a special character for the backslash itself. A complete list of special characters in JavaScript and their meanings is shown in Table 6.1.

Special Character	Description
\'	single quote
\"	double quote
\&	ampersand
\\	backslash
\n	new line
\r	carriage return
\t	tab
\b	backspace
\f	form feed

Table 6.1

List of special characters available for use in JavaScript strings.

---

[7]Thus, JavaScript code may be placed directly into an XHTML document, in either the **body** element or the **head** element, or it may be placed in a separate file that is associated with the XHTML document via the **src** attribute of a **script** tag. Where a particular piece of JavaScript code is placed depends on a number of things, such as whether the code is a function definition, when you want the code to be executed, and whether you are just testing or are in full "production mode."

6.6   What Is the *Document Object Model (DOM)*?

Every XHTML document consists of a number of "objects" that may be viewed as a tree-like structure. A simplified way to view this tree is to think of its "root" as being at the top instead of at the bottom where the root of a tree in the forest would be. Now think of the root as corresponding to the document itself. Immediately below this, at the next level, the first two "branches" are the `head` element and the `body` element of the document. At the next level down, in the `head` element, will be (among other things, perhaps) the `title` element, and at this same level, in the `body` element, will be (probably) some header elements, a `div` element or two, some paragraph elements, and so on.

The point of viewing an XHTML document in this way is that each of the various parts of the tree is in fact an "object" that can be accessed and manipulated by JavaScript, via the *Document Object Model*, which is usually referred to by its acronym *DOM*. The DOM is a W3C-defined standard that provides an *Application Programming Interface (API)* that is in fact language-independent, allowing many different programming languages, only one of which is JavaScript, to access a standard set of objects related to a web document, including the document itself, tables, rows and columns in the tables, images, headers, paragraphs, and various form elements such as textareas and buttons. A list of some of the most common and useful such DOM objects is given in Table 6.2. See the end-of-chapter **References** for more information.

The DOM also standardizes the ways in which web page elements are accessed and manipulated when XHTML documents are being processed. At the highest level, these processes include modification, deletion, and creation of new elements on the page. These standards are also platform and language independent. In the next chapter we will see how some of these processes can be performed using JavaScript. But they can also be carried out using many other programming languages as well.

As you may have guessed by now, we have already encountered the DOM when we used, via JavaScript, the `write()` method of the `document` property of the `window` object in section 6.4.

DOM Object	What It Represents
Document	The entire HTML document
DOM objects found within the **head** element	
Link	A `link` element
Meta	A `meta` element
DOM objects found within the **body** element	
Body	The `body` element itself
Anchor	An `a` element
Style	An individual style statement
DOM objects related to images	
Image	An `img` element
Area	An `area` element inside an image-map
DOM objects related to tables	
Table	A `table` element
TableCell	A `td` element
TableRow	A `tr` element
DOM objects related to forms	
Form	A `form` element
Event	The state of an event
Button	A `button` element, or an `input` element of type "button"
Checkbox	An `input` element of type "checkbox"
FileUpload	An `input` element of type "file"
Hidden	An `input` element of type "hidden"
Password	An `input` element of type "password"
Radio	An `input` element of type "radio"
Reset	An `input` element of type "reset"
Submit	An `input` element of type "submit"
Text	An `input` element of type "text"
Select	A `select` element
Option	An `option` element
Textarea	A `textarea` element

Table 6.2

Some HTML DOM elements (also accessible from an XHTML document).

6.7   How Do JavaScript and the DOM Interact?

We will use our Body Mass Index (BMI) calculator web page to study JavaScript's interaction with DOM elements, and also, in keeping with our need-to-know approach, to introduce JavaScript programmer-defined functions, JavaScript variables, and the JavaScript `if-else` decision-making construct.

The latest version of our BMI calculator is contained in the file `bmi6.html`, which can be found in the `web06` directory on our CD-ROM. The `head` element of that document includes a `script` element that tells the browser to get the JavaScript code from the file `bmi6.js`, which is located in the `scripts` subdirectory. Because this `script` element is in the `head` element and the JavaScript file contains only JavaScript function definitions, these function definitions are simply loaded in from the file and readied for future use, but no code is actually executed at this point.

Figure 6.8 shows just the form element from `bmi6.html`. The `form` tag in line 16 of Figure 6.8 now has a new attribute called `onsubmit`,[8] which has the value `processBMIform()`. When the submit button for this form is pressed, the function `processBMIform()` defined in the file `bmi6.js`, and previously loaded, will be invoked.

Usually data from a form is sent to the server for processing, but here we are dealing with client-side programming only, so we will not be sending our form data to a server in this chapter. All of our form data processing will be done on the client side using JavaScript. That is why the `action` attribute of the `form` tag still has an empty string as its value.

6.7.1   A First Programmer-Defined JavaScript Function

Figure 6.9 shows the definition of the function `processBMIform()` from the file `bmi6.js`. This is our first programmer-defined JavaScript function,[9] so let us spend a little time studying its structure. Here is the general format of a function definition:

```
function nameOfFunction(parameter_list)
{
    ... JavaScript code to perform whatever the function does ...
}
```

---

[8]This is an example of a new kind of tag attribute called an *event attribute* whose value is a function that is called when the event occurs.

[9]The terms "function" and "method" are often used interchangeably. This is generally not a problem, since they are essentially the same thing, though the term "method" is more often used when it belongs to an object, in an object-oriented context, and "function" when it is "stand-alone" and not associated with any object, as in this case.

```
     <form id="bmiForm" action="" onsubmit="processBMIform()">
       <fieldset>
         <legend>Vital statistics</legend>
         <table summary="Vital Statistics">
           <tr>
             <td><label for="height">Height:</label></td>
             <td><input id="height" type="text" name="height" size="7" /></td>
             <td><label for="heightUnit">Units:</label></td>
             <td><select id="heightUnit" name="heightUnit">
               <option>inches</option>
               <option>centimeters</option>
             </select></td>
           </tr>
           <tr>
             <td><label for="weight">Weight:</label></td>
             <td><input id="weight" type="text" name="weight" size="7" /></td>
             <td><label for="weightUnit">Units:</label></td>
             <td><select id="weightUnit" name="weightUnit">
               <option>pounds</option>
               <option>kilograms</option>
             </select></td>
           </tr>
           <tr>
             <td colspan="4"><label for="details">Please check here if you
             want a detailed analysis of your BMI:</label> <input id="details"
             type="checkbox" name="details" value="yes" /></td>
           </tr>
         </table>
       </fieldset>
       <fieldset>
         <legend>E-mail record?</legend>
         <table summary="E-mail">
           <tr>
             <td colspan="2"><label for="wantMail">Do you want your BMI sent
             to you by e-mail?</label> <input id="wantMail" type="checkbox"
             name="wantMail" value="yes" /></td>
           </tr>
           <tr>
             <td><label for="email">E-mail Address:</label></td>
             <td><input id="email" type="text" name="email" size="40" /></td>
           </tr>
         </table>
       </fieldset>
       <fieldset>
         <legend>Processing</legend>
         <table summary="Processing">
           <tr>
             <td><input type="submit" value="Compute your BMI" /></td>
             <td align="right"><input type="reset" value="Reset form" /></td>
           </tr>
         </table>
       </fieldset>
     </form>
```

FIGURE 6.8

cdrom/web06/bmi6.html (excerpt, part 1)

The form element from bmi6.html that will be processed by the programmer-defined JavaScript function processBMIform().

```
3    function processBMIform()
4    {
5        var bmiFormObj = document.getElementById("bmiForm");
6        if (validateInput(bmiFormObj))
7        {
8            var bmi = calculateBMI(bmiFormObj);
9            if (bmiFormObj.details.checked)
10               displayDetailed(bmiFormObj, bmi);
11           else
12               alert("Your BMI: " + precision(bmi));
13       }
14   }
```

FIGURE 6.9

cdrom/web06/scripts/bmi6.js (excerpt)
The JavaScript function processBMIform() from bmi6.js that processes the BMI form in bmi6.html.

The first line is the *header* for the function. It begins with the *keyword* function, which indicates the beginning of the definition of a function. This is followed by the name of the function, which should be chosen well so that it indicates the purpose of the function.[10] The function name, in turn, is followed by a comma-separated list of *parameters* the function should receive when it is called (if any), enclosed in parentheses. We call this its "parameter list."

The JavaScript code that actually performs the task of the function is called the *function body* and is enclosed by a pair of braces {··· } (also called *curly brackets*) immediately following the function header. The function in Figure 6.9 is processBMIform() and it does not take any parameters. That is why the parentheses following the name are empty, and you should note that the parentheses are required, even if the parameter list is empty. Note that when referring to functions in the text, we usually use the name of the function and an empty set of parentheses (whether or not the function has any parameters), just to emphasize that we are dealing with a function and not some other entity.

6.7.2   JavaScript Variables

Now let us examine the JavaScript code in the body of the function processBMI-form(). This statement declares a *variable* called bmiFormObj. Variables are used to store data in our programs. The word *variable* indicates that the stored data in the memory location named by the variable will vary, depending on the circumstances.

---

[10]A good rule of thumb to follow when naming functions is this: When the function computes a value, make the name of function a noun that reflects the kind of value computed, such as totalCost. When the function simply performs a task, but does not compute and return a value, give it a name that starts with a verb and indicates the nature of the task performed, such as displayResults.

Because this particular variable will contain a reference to the "object" that represents our `form` element, we attach the suffix `Obj` to the `id` of the form element (`bmiForm`) to get our variable name, `bmiFormObj`. This suffix helps to distinguish this variable from more "ordinary" variables (that do not represent objects) in our code.

In many languages, we need to specify the type of data that will be stored in a given variable. JavaScript uses a very flexible variable typing convention. Although it is not strictly necessary, all variables should be declared using the keyword `var`. The type of value a variable contains is determined by the assignment to that variable. The same variable can hold values of different types such as numbers, strings, and DOM elements. Of course, at any given time it can hold only a single value of one particular type. However, while this may seem like a handy feature, it can make debugging a real nightmare. Programmers should enforce a strong self-discipline to ensure that their programs are reasonably robust. The best attitude to have toward program bugs is to do your best to avoid them in the first place.

6.7.3 Accessing a DOM Element via Its `id` Attribute

The very first statement in the `processBMIform()` of Figure 6.9 shows the recommended way, among several ways, of accessing the DOM elements in an XHTML document. Our variable `bmiFormObj` is assigned the value returned by the `getElementById()` method call in the following statement:

```
bmiFormObj = document.getElementById("bmiForm");
```

The `getElementById()` method call retrieves the DOM element that has the `id` value specified by its parameter (`bmiForm` in this case). Figure 6.8 shows that the form in the file `bmi6.html` has an `id` value of `bmiForm`, which means that the variable `bmiFormObj` will represent this form in our JavaScript program.

The value of the `name` attribute for our `form` element is also `bmiForm` and, as we shall see shortly, a DOM object can also be accessed using the value of its `name` attribute. But before we do that let's take a look at a fundamental JavaScript control structure.

6.7.4 Making Decisions with the JavaScript `if-else` Statement

The second line in the function `processBMIform()` in Figure 6.9 begins an if-statement, which is also called a *conditional statement* because what the statement does is determined by whether the "condition" (the boolean expression) it contains is true or false. This particular if-statement contains as its "body" an example of the most general form of an if-statement in JavaScript, which is called an if-else-statement, and looks like this:

```
if (condition)
    statement1;
else
    statement2;
```

This works as follows. First, we need to know that a *boolean expression* is just an expression whose value may be `true` or `false` (both of which are JavaScript *keywords*). Now, if the boolean expression `condition` has the value `true`, then `statement1` is executed; otherwise, `statement2` is executed. The `else` part of this construct is optional.

Note that in the `processBMIform()` function both the `if` part and the `else` part contain only one JavaScript statement. If you want more than one JavaScript statement in either the `if` part or the `else` part, you have to enclose the `multiple-statement` part in braces $\{\cdots\}$. If you place even single statements in an `if-else` construct within braces, that makes it very easy to add further statements to either part of the construct at a later time without having to worry about introducing braces at that time. For this reason, doing so is often recommended as a good general programming practice.[11]

Look at the first if-statement in the function `processBMIform()` and you will see an example of this very useful control construct in action. We see that the condition, in this case, is actually a call to *another* programmer-defined function named `validateInput()`, which has as its input parameter our newly created variable `bmiFormObj`. The function itself is defined in the same file, `bmi6.html`, and is shown in Figure 6.10. We will examine this second function definition in more detail a little later on.

Let us focus on the if-statement for the moment. The call `validateInput(-bmiFormObj)` forms the condition, so the function must return either a `true` or a `false` value.[12] If the condition evaluates to `false`, the function `processBMIform()` does nothing, because there is no `else` part. The `if` part needs to have multiple JavaScript statements and those statements are therefore enclosed in braces. The first statement in the `if` part declares a variable called `bmi`. This variable is assigned

---

[11]On the other hand, it could be argued that *not* doing so can often make your code somewhat more concise and even enhance readability.

[12]Such a function is called a `boolean` function, since (like a boolean expression) it returns one of the two possible `boolean` values (`true` or `false`, both of which are JavaScript keywords).

```
6    function validateInput(bmiFormObj)
7    {
8        var hUnit = bmiFormObj.heightUnit.options[bmiFormObj.heightUnit.selectedIndex].text;
9        var wUnit = bmiFormObj.weightUnit.options[bmiFormObj.weightUnit.selectedIndex].text;
10       var height = bmiFormObj.height.value;
11       var weight = bmiFormObj.weight.value;
12       var email = bmiFormObj.email.value;
13       var heightOK, weightOK, emailOK;
14
15       if (hUnit == "inches")
16           heightOK = validateInches(height);
17       else
18           heightOK = validateCentimetres(height);
19
20       if (wUnit == "pounds")
21           weightOK = validatePounds(weight);
22       else
23           weightOK = validateKilograms(weight);
24
25       if (bmiFormObj.wantMail.checked)
26       {
27           emailOK = validateEmail(email);
28           alert("Warning: The e-mail feature is currently not supported.")
29       }
30       else
31           emailOK = true;
32
33       return heightOK && weightOK && emailOK;
34   }
```

FIGURE 6.10

cdrom/web06/scripts/bmi6.js (excerpt)
The validateInput() function called by the processBMIform() function in bmi6.html.

a value returned by a third programmer-defined function, calculateBMI(), which also receives the variable bmiFormObj as a parameter. The function calculateBMI() is also defined in bmi6.js and is shown in Figure 6.15. We will look at this function definition a little later on as well. In the meantime, let us continue our examination of the processBMIform() function.

6.7.5 Accessing a DOM Element via Its name Attribute

Once we have calculated the value of the BMI and stored it in our bmi variable, the next step is to display that value. We had decided earlier that the user should have a choice of receiving either a detailed report or just the BMI value. The user indicates that choice by checking, on the form, the checkbox whose name attribute is details.

The condition bmiFormObj.details.checked in line 9 of Figure 6.9 shows a different way of accessing a DOM object, as compared with the use of the getElementById() method that we saw in the first statement of the processBMI-form() function. The name attribute can be directly used without a method call as in the expression bmiFormObj.details.[13] The condition bmiFormObj.details.checked will have a value of true if the user has checked the checkbox named details on the form. If it is checked, we will call another programmer-defined function named displayDetailed(), with bmiFormObj and bmi as parameters. Once again, this function is defined in bmi6.js and shown in Figure 6.16, and we will discuss its details later on in this chapter.

On the other hand, if the checkbox named details is *not* checked, then the value of bmiFormObj.details.checked will be false and we will simply call the alert() method to display the computed value of the BMI. The alert() method receives a string that is a concatenation of the string "Your BMI: " and a string returned by the call to the programmer-defined function precision(). The function precision() takes the variable bmi and returns a string equivalent of the number with one decimal place. And, one more time, this function too is defined in bmi6.js, as shown in Figure 6.16, and will be discussed later on in this chapter.

6.8   The Importance of Website Security

Every time a user clicks on the submit button of a form, information of some kind that the user has entered into that form will either make its way to the server, for one purpose or another, or be processed on the client side, as we have just seen.

The Web is much like the rest of society, in that you will find good folks and bad folks roaming around there, and some of the bad ones might decide to visit your site. If they do, it is difficult to predict what they might attempt to do there. For example, a clever and malicious user might try to slip in some data, through one of your forms, that you were not expecting. That could lead to harmful effects, unless you take steps to prevent this from happening.

Therefore, it is a recommended *best practice* to verify all user-entered input on the client-side before it is sent to the server. This, of course, is only one of the ways you can try to make your website secure from attack, but it is a key one. Note that we say "try," which is a clue to the sad truth that no matter how much effort you put into making your website secure, hackers will probably always find new ways

---

[13]But, and this can be confusing and lead to hard-to-debug situations, the name attribute in the form tag itself, and in some other tags as well, has been deprecated! Here is a quote directly from the XHTML specification: "Finally, note that XHTML 1.0 has deprecated the name attribute of the a, applet, form, frame, iframe, img, and map elements, and it will be removed from XHTML in subsequent versions."

around your safeguards. Your initial goal, at least, should be to make life as difficult as possible for them.

Even with a web page as simple as the one that computes a BMI, we require the user to enter some data and click on a button to process that data. So, it makes sense that we should be satisfied that the user has entered only the kind of data that we were expecting.

6.9 How Can JavaScript Help Address the Security Issue?

Because JavaScript is the most popular programming language for client-side web computing, and because it can be used to help us make our websites more secure, we need to learn something about how to use it for that purpose. Indeed, we can use JavaScript to verify that all form input from any user is within acceptable ranges before processing it and possibly forwarding it to the web server.

We illustrate this principle in the context of our BMI calculator, for which we use the `validateInput()` function for validating all the input entered into the BMI form. The definition of the `validateInput()` function is a little more involved than that of the `processBMIform()` function, in that it accepts a parameter. In this case, we are sending (or passing) to the function the DOM `form` object, called `bmiFormObj`, as that parameter.

The first four JavaScript statements in the body of the function `validate-Input()` shown in Figure 6.10 collect the form input entered by the user for weight and height, and their corresponding units. Getting the information for the units is a little involved, due to the use of the `select` element. But this gives us a chance to introduce the notion of an *array*, since all the options specified in a `select` element are represented as an *array* in our JavaScript script.

6.9.1 A First Look at JavaScript Arrays (in the Context of the DOM)

An *array* is essentially a list of elements. Usually, arrays are stored in such a way that each element of the array can be efficiently accessed. The elements of an array are addressed using a *subscript* (or *index*) that appears in a pair of square brackets following the name of the array. In our case, the options for the DOM element `heightUnit` will be represented by an array called `bmiFormObj.heightUnit.options`.

The expression `bmiFormObj.heightUnit.options` requires some comment. Note that it starts with `bmiFormObj`, the variable that we are using to refer to the form element shown in Figure 6.8. At the next level down in the DOM hierarchy of this XHTML document is the `select` element whose `name` attribute has the value `heightUnit`. Thus, in good object-oriented fashion we can refer to this `select` element as `bmiFormObj.heightUnit`. Every select element will, of course, have some `option` elements associated with it that form its content. And, finally, these options are available to us in an array called, not surprisingly, `options`. Note that `bmiFormObj` and `heightUnit` are names that we have made up, but `options` is a built-in name. This kind of expression shows up all the time in JavaScript code, so you should make an effort to become familiar with the syntax. The first time you see it, it can be a little intimidating but a little usage goes a long way toward understanding.

OK, back to the main thread of our discussion.

Since there are only two elements in this array (two options in this select), the first element of the array is given by `bmiFormObj.heightUnit.options[0]` and the second element by `bmiFormObj.heightUnit.options[1]`. It is important to note in this context that, like other C-based languages, the subscripts of arrays in JavaScript start with 0. Since you will be using JavaScript arrays of various sizes, you will need to keep in mind what this means: If a JavaScript array has n elements, the subscripts used to access those elements will go from 0 to n-1 (and *not* from 1 to n).

Furthermore, each element of the `options` array has a field called `text` that gives us the text used to describe that particular option. So, in our case, `bmiFormObj.heightUnit.options[0].text` has a value that is the string `"inches"` and `bmiFormObj.heightUnit.options[1].text` has the value `"centimeters"`.

Similar expressions, with `heightUnit` replaced by `weightUnit`, will give you `"pounds"` and `"kilograms"` as the text values used to describe the weight unit options.

6.9.2   Accessing DOM Elements for the Purpose of Validating User Input

The question still remains as to which option the user has selected. Just as the DOM object `heightUnit` had a field containing an array called `options` that we could access, it has another field called `selectedIndex` that provides us with the answer we need this time around. If the user has chosen `inches`, then `bmiFormObj.heightUnit.selectedIndex` will be 0 (corresponding to the first item of the `options` array). If the user has chosen `centimeters`, the value of `bmiFormObj.heightUnit.selectedIndex` will be 1 (corresponding to the second item of the `options` array). Therefore, the expression

```
bmiFormObj.hUnit.options[bmiFormObj.hUnit.selectedIndex].text
```

from line 18 of Figure 6.10 will give us the option selected by the user for the height unit, which is then stored in the variable `hUnit`. Similarly, the expression

```
bmiFormObj.wUnit.options[bmiFormObj.wUnit.selectedIndex].text
```

from line 19 of the same figure will give us the option selected by the user for the weight unit, which is then stored in `wUnit`.

The next two JavaScript statements (lines 20 and 21 of Figure 6.10) retrieve the values of the user's height and weight as entered by the user. Both height and weight are specified using DOM elements with the same names that are of type `text`, and their values are given by a field called `value`. So `bmiFormObj.height` `.value` gives us the string entered by the user into the text field named `height` and `bmiFormObj.weight.value` gives us the string entered by the user into the text field named `weight`. We store them in variables called `height` and `weight`, respectively. Similarly, we also store the text entered by the user for the e-mail address into a variable called `email`. Note here that all user-entered values, whether they are ultimately to be interpreted as numbers or not, are received as text.

After retrieving the values entered by the user for weight, height, and e-mail address, the function declares three variables called `heightOK`, `weightOK`, and `emailOK`. These variables are expected to hold either a `true` or a `false` value, depending on whether the corresponding data entries are in fact OK, or not.

The following three conditional `if-else`-statements validate the values input by the user for these three quantities: weight, height, and e-mail address. The format and logic of each of the first two `if`-conditionals are essentially the same. The condition checks to see which unit is used for the height (or weight) and calls an appropriate function for validation. The value returned by the function is assigned to `heightOK` (or `weightOK`).

The conditional `if`-statement for the e-mail address is slightly different. We first check to see if the DOM object `bmiFormObj.want_mail` is checked. If it is checked then we validate the e-mail address using the function `validateEmail()`. The variable `emailOK` is set to the value returned by the call `validateEmail( bmiFormObj)`. Otherwise, we just set the value of the variable `emailOK` to `true`. We need this value to be `true` since it will be part of the overall evaluation of whether "everything is OK," even though no e-mail address has been entered.

Since we are only dealing with client-side computing using JavaScript, we have not implemented the e-mail facility. All that happens is a message using the `alert()` method will be displayed to the user. Allowing JavaScript programs to send e-mails from a client's computer would be a major breach of security since malicious JavaScript code could exploit the ability to send spam from client computers. We will implement the e-mail facility when we study server-side computing using PHP.

6.9.3   Evaluating Compound Boolean Expressions

Once we collect the individual validation flags for the three text fields, namely `heightOK`, `weightOK`, and `emailOK`, we need to check to see if all of them are `true` (that's why we wanted `emailOK` to be `true` even if no e-mail address was entered). If all of them are in fact `true`, then we should return a `true` value back from the `validateInput()` function. This is achieved with the help of the keyword `return`, which returns the value of the expression that follows it. In our case, the `return` statement will return the value of this expression:

```
heightOK && weightOK && emailOK
```

All three variables in the above expression—`heightOK`, `weightOK`, and `emailOK`—must be `true` for the entire expression to have the value `true`. This is because operator `&&` is the "logical and" operator. Only when all operands connected by the operator `&&` are `true` does the entire expression have the value `true`; otherwise, the expression has the value `false`.

Table 6.3 shows the typical logical operators available in JavaScript (and in many other programming languages) for combining simple boolean expressions to express more complex conditions and the results of operations involving these operators. The first two columns list the four possible values for the two logical expressions $expr_1$ and $expr_2$, considered as a pair. The third column gives the values for the "logical and" operation $expr_1$ `&&` $expr_2$. The fourth column shows the values of the "logical or" operation $expr_1$ `||` $expr_2$. The "logical not" operator is represented by the symbol `!` and the results of "logical not" applied to $expr_1$, that is, `!`$expr_1$, are given in the fifth column.

$expr_1$	$expr_2$	$expr_1$ && $expr_2$	$expr_1$ || $expr_2$	!$expr_1$
true	true	true	true	false
true	false	false	true	false
false	true	false	true	true
false	false	false	false	true

Table 6.3

Logical operators in JavaScript.

You should study Table 6.3 carefully. Its content is deceptively simple. Even though the bottom line is that these operators behave in more or less the same way that we English-speaking humans use the words "and," "or," and "not" in everyday language, many programming errors result from the improper use of these operators in code. Note in particular that the "logical or" operator is the so-called "inclusive or," which is true when *either* operand is true or *both* of the operands are true.

Here's a handy rule that summarizes the "and" and "or" columns of Table 6.3:

1. The only way $expr_1$ && $expr_2$ can be `true` is if both $expr_1$ and $expr_2$ are `true`.

2. The only way $expr_1$ || $expr_2$ can be `false` is if both $expr_1$ and $expr_2$ are `false`.

6.9.4 Functions for Validating Numerical Input

Figures 6.11 and 6.12 show the JavaScript code for validating the values of height and weight values entered by the user. There are a total of four functions. All of them use similar logic. For no particular reason we will study the last of the four, function `validateKilograms()`, in detail. You should browse through the other three functions to ensure that you understand them as well.

So, take a look at the function `validateKilograms()` from Figure 6.12. This function is called if the user has indicated that weight is specified in kilograms. It receives the parameter `weight`. The function body contains two conditional statements. The first one calls a very handy built-in JavaScript function `isNaN()` (think of this as `isNotANumber()`) with `weight` as its parameter. The function call `isNaN(weight)` returns a `true` value if `weight` is *not* a number. In that case, we alert the user with an appropriate message and return the value `false`. Note that after executing the `return` statement, we exit from the function, so the rest of the code will not be relevant in that case. If `isNaN(weight)` returns a `false` value, we continue through the rest of the function.

If the `weight` value passed to the function `isNaN(weight)` is indeed a number, the next conditional statement ensures that the value is reasonable.[14] If the weight in kilograms is less than or equal to zero or if it is greater than 500 kg, we will alert the

---

[14]For those who are familiar with other programming languages like C++ or Java, this is a scary juncture. We are now about to use an entry that has come in as text as a numerical value, and this is going to be alright because this is JavaScript. All we have done is use `isNaN()` to verify that the entry is in fact a number. Those other programmers will be squirming at this point, and rightly so. But that's life on the Web.

```
46    function validateInches(height)
47    {
48        if (isNaN(height))
49        {
50            alert("Error: Please input a number for height.")
51            return false;
52        }
53
54        if (height < 0 || height > 100)
55        {
56            alert("Error: Height must be in the range 0-100 inches.")
57            return false;
58        }
59
60        return true;
61    }
62
63    function validateCentimetres(height)
64    {
65        if (isNaN(height))
66        {
67            alert("Error: Please input a number for height.")
68            return false;
69        }
70
71        if (height < 0 || height > 300)
72        {
73            alert("Error: Height must be in the range 0-300 centimeters.")
74            return false;
75        }
76
77        return true;
78    }
```

FIGURE 6.11

cdrom/web06/scripts/bmi6.js (excerpt)
The height-validating functions from bmi6.js.

user that the input for weight is invalid and return a `false` value. The condition uses the "logical or" operator `||` that we saw in Table 6.3. It also uses two *comparison operators*, namely "less than or equal to" (`<=`) and "greater than" (`>`). A complete list of *comparison operators* (also called *relational operators*) that can be used to compare two values in various ways is given in Table 6.4.

If we did not execute the statement `return false;` in either of the two conditionals, we are still in the function `validateKilograms()`. That leaves us with the execution of the last statement in the function, that is, `return true;`. That means the function `validateKilograms()` will return true if `weight` is a number that is greater than zero and less than 500 (kilograms). The other three functions in Figures 6.11 and 6.12 follow similar logic.

```
function validatePounds(weight)
{
    if (isNaN(weight))
    {
        alert("Error: Please input a number for weight.")
        return false;
    }

    if (weight < 0 || weight > 1000)
    {
        alert("Error: Weight must be in the range 0-1000 pounds.")
        return false;
    }

    return true;
}

function validateKilograms(weight)
{
    if (isNaN(weight))
    {
        alert("Error: Please input a number for weight.")
        return false;
    }

    if (weight <= 0 || weight > 500)
    {
        alert("Error: Weight must be in the range 0-500 kilograms.")
        return false;
    }

    return true;
}
```

FIGURE 6.12

cdrom/web06/scripts/bmi6.js (excerpt)

The weight-validating functions from `bmi6.js`, which illustrate JavaScript logical and conditional expressions, as well as the `isNaN()` method, for validation of numerical values.

Operator	Description
==	Equal to
!=	Not equal to
<	Less than
<=	Less than or equal to
>	Greater than
>=	Greater than or equal to

Table 6.4

Comparison operators in JavaScript.

6.9.5 Functions for Validating String Input: A First Look at Regular Expressions in JavaScript

The four functions in Figures 6.11 and 6.12 validate numerical values. We need to be able to validate string input, such as e-mail addresses, as well. This is usually done using what are called *regular expressions*. We will study regular expressions in more detail in a later section when we validate data submitted via our feedback form. Here, we provide just a sneak preview of regular expressions by using a regular expression to validate a very simple e-mail address input as shown in Figure 6.13.

The function `validateEmail()` in Figure 6.13 accepts the e-mail address entered by the user as input and searches for a pattern that resembles an e-mail address using a JavaScript method called `search` that is available for JavaScript objects of type `String`. Since our string is called `address`, our method call will be `address.search()`. We pass a "pattern" that we hope to see in the e-mail value stored in `address` if it is in fact a valid e-mail address, and this "pattern" is described by a regular expression. A "real" e-mail address might, of course, be more complicated, but in our case we decide to search for a simple pattern that consists of one or more characters, followed by the specific character `@`, followed by one or more characters. We specify this pattern to the `search` method by using a *regular expression* that is enclosed in a pair of forward slash characters (`/`).

Regular expressions seem quite mysterious when you first encounter them, but if you stay the course you will find they are very powerful and versatile, and can even be fun to work with.

```
114   function validateEmail(address)
115   {
116       var p = address.search(/.+@.+/);
117       if (p == 0)
118           return true;
119       else
120       {
121           alert("Error: Invalid e-mail address.");
122           return false;
123       }
124   }
```

FIGURE 6.13

`cdrom/web06/scripts/bmi6.js` (excerpt)
The `validateEmail()` function from `bmi6.js` that uses a simple JavaScript regular expression to validate simple e-mail addresses.

For example, the pattern that we are interested in here can be specified by the following simple regular expression:[15]

```
.+@.+
```

In a regular expression, a period (`.`) stands for any character, and a trailing plus sign (`+`) indicates one or more repetitions. Note that this "repetition" does not mean that the same character has to be repeated, just that there be a "repetition of characters." In other words you *could* have `aaa`, let's say, but you could also have `abcde`, and either would qualify. Thus, the two characters `.+` together, as part of a regular expression, simply mean "one or more characters."

So, our pattern will match any string that has one or more characters, followed by a `@` character, followed by one or more characters. We are saying, in effect, that as long as we have some characters before and after the `@` character, we have an acceptable e-mail address. Clearly, this is not sufficient validation for an actual e-mail address. But this is just a preview of more sophisticated pattern matching that we will study later on in this chapter.

The `search()` function will return a 0 (zero) if the e-mail address matches such a pattern. We assign the value returned by the `search()` to a variable `p`. If `p` gets the value zero, then the address matches our simple expectations of an e-mail address. Hence, we return a `true` value. Otherwise, we return a `false` value. Figure 6.14 shows the error reported when we entered the string `"malicious code"` as input for the e-mail address. You should try different valid and invalid values of weight, height, and e-mail address to confirm that our input validation works.

6.10 Calculating the BMI: Numerical Calculations in JavaScript

Much of JavaScript programming deals with string manipulation. Of course, the language supports numerical computation as well. In this section, we will use the BMI computation as an example for studying basic numerical computations in JavaScript.

Figure 6.15 shows another excerpt from the file `bmi6.js` containing the three functions that perform numeric computations. The function `calculateBMI()` is called from the function `processBMIform()` and receives the completed `bmiFormObj` as its only parameter. Prior to calling the function `calculateBMI()`, the input data values

---

[15]Note that the two forward slashes in the input to the `search()` method, one at the beginning and one at the end, are *delimiters* of the regular expression, so technically only `.+@.+` comprises the regular expression.

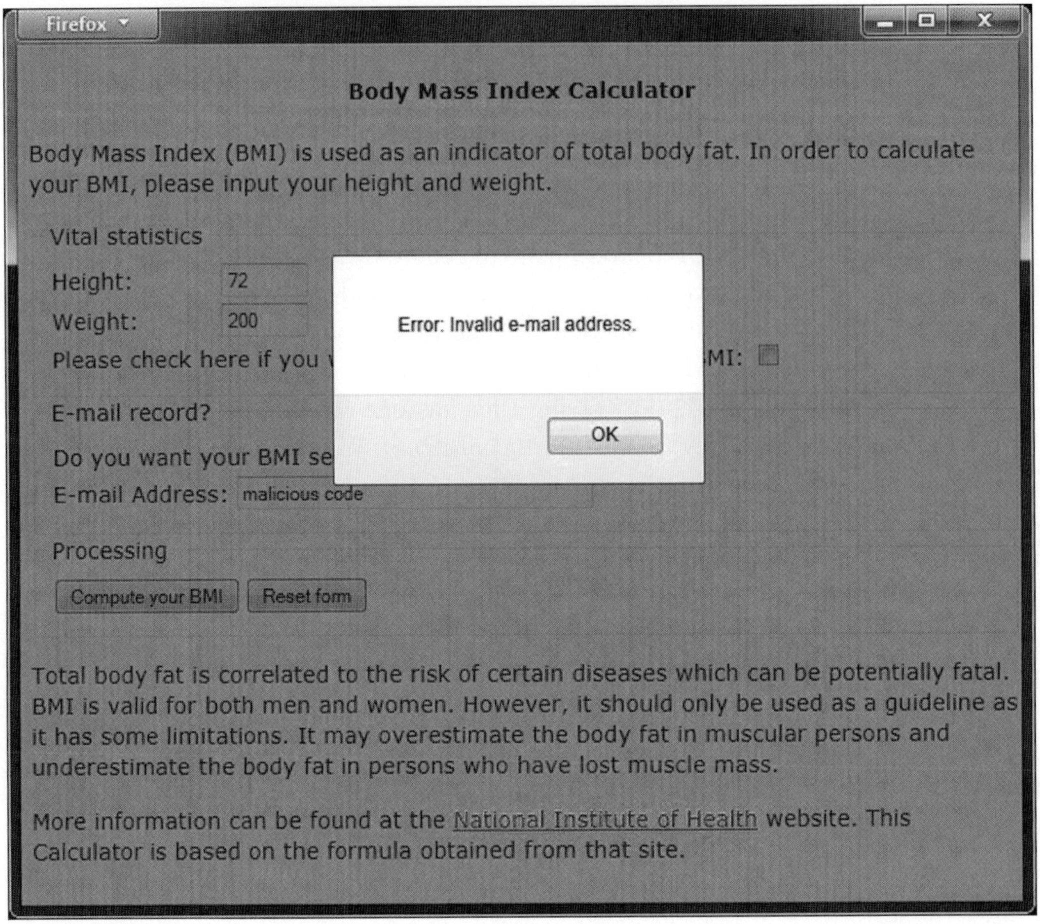

FIGURE 6.14

graphics/ch06/displayErrorBmi6.jpg
A Firefox browser display of an e-mail validation error generated from bmi6.html.

entered by the user have been validated, so we can assume that the fields **height** and **weight** of **bmiFormObj** contain numbers that lie within appropriate ranges.

The function first extracts the values of **height**, **heightUnit**, **weight**, and **weightUnit** from the **bmiFormObj** as we did in the function **validateInput()**. BMI calculations can be easily done with metric quantities. Hence, if the user has entered height in inches it is converted to centimeters using the function **inchesToCentimetres()** in the first conditional statement. Similarly, if the user has entered weight in pounds it is converted to kilograms using the function **poundsToKilograms()** in the second conditional statement. The function **calculateBMI()** then converts the centimeters to meters by dividing height (in centimeters) by 100. The BMI is then

```
function calculateBMI(bmiFormObj)
{
    var hUnit = bmiFormObj.heightUnit.options[bmiFormObj.heightUnit.selectedIndex].text;
    var wUnit = bmiFormObj.weightUnit.options[bmiFormObj.weightUnit.selectedIndex].text;
    var height = bmiFormObj.height.value;
    var weight = bmiFormObj.weight.value;

    if (hUnit == "inches")
        height = inchesToCentimetres(height);

    if (wUnit == "pounds")
        weight = poundsToKilograms(weight);

    height /= 100; //Convert height from centimeters to meters
    var bmi = weight/(height*height); //kilograms/(meters*meters)
    return bmi;
}

function inchesToCentimetres(height)
{
    var CENTIMETRES_PER_INCH = 2.54;
    return height * CENTIMETRES_PER_INCH;
}

function poundsToKilograms(weight)
{
    var POUNDS_PER_KILOGRAM = 2.2;
    return weight / POUNDS_PER_KILOGRAM;
}
```

FIGURE 6.15

cdrom/web06/scripts/bmi6.js (excerpt)
Some JavaScript code illustrating numeric calculations bmi6.js.

simply calculated as the ratio of the user's weight to the square of the user's height.

The functions inchesToCentimetres() and poundsToKilograms() return the centimeter or kilogram equivalents of inches or pounds using appropriate factors. JavaScript does not provide a mechanism for setting programmer-defined constants, which we would find convenient for setting the conversion factors in these two functions (CENTIMETRES_PER_INCH and POUNDS_PER_KILOGRAM), so we simply make them variables and use for their names an all-caps, word-underscore-separated style that is a typical convention for constants in many languages, such as C++ and Java.

In these functions we also get to see some typical JavaScript arithmetic using the arithmetic operators for multiplication (operator *) and division (operator /). Of course, JavaScript also provides the addition (+) and subtraction (-) operators. As usual, multiplication and division have a higher precedence than addition and subtraction. So, for example, the expression 4-3*8 has the value -20 because the multiplication takes place before subtraction. This operator-precedence behavior is typical of all programming languages.

JavaScript also provides a remainder (or modulus) operator, as do all the C-based programming languages. This remainder operator is % (the percent sign). It returns the remainder resulting from the division of its first operand by its second operand. For example, 47%5 has the value 2. The remainder operator has the same precedence as the multiplication and division operators. We will see the remainder operator in action a little later on in this section.

Our BMI form gives the user the option of displaying the BMI report in detail, or simply displaying just the value of the BMI. This decision is made in the function processBMIform() shown in Figure 6.9. Whether we simply print the BMI using a call to alert(), or create a more detailed format using the function displayDetailed(), we need to first format the numeric value so that it does not have a variable precision (number of places after the decimal) each time it is shown. That is, we do not want an answer like 20.3896543 one time, and 22.516 the next. We prefer to display it with a single digit after the decimal point every time. Oddly enough, this may be a little trickier to achieve in JavaScript than in some other programming languages.

The function precision() given in Figure 6.16 does the requisite formatting and returns the number as its string equivalent with a single digit after the decimal point. This is not necessarily the most elegant way to do it, but it gives us a chance to use two methods that are generally useful and that belong to the built-in JavaScript Math object: the floor() method and the round() method.

The Math object provides a number of other useful mathematical constants and methods. (See Tables 6.5 and 6.6, as well as the end-of-chapter **References** for more information.)

The function floor() essentially truncates (removes) the digits after the decimal point in a given number. For example, if our BMI calculations resulted in a value 20.589, Math.floor(20.589) would give the value 20. We save the value returned by the floor() method in a variable called intPortion, for obvious reasons.

Our next task is to get the first digit after the decimal place. In order to do this we employ a bit of clever numeric manipulation. We first multiply the number by 10. In our case, $20.589 * 10 = 205.89$. We then round off the resulting number to the nearest integer using the round() method as Math.round(205.89) = 206. Now we use the remainder of the division of the resulting number by 10, that is, 206%10, which has the value 6. This gives us 6 as the single digit after the decimal point for the number 20.589 using the JavaScript expression

```
Math.round(num*10) % 10
```

```
function precision(num)
{
    var intPortion = Math.floor(num);
    var decimalPortion = Math.round(num*10)%10;
    var text = intPortion + "." + decimalPortion;
    return text;
}

function displayDetailed(bmiFormObj, bmi)
{
    var hUnit = bmiFormObj.heightUnit.options[bmiFormObj.heightUnit.selectedIndex].text;
    var wUnit = bmiFormObj.weightUnit.options[bmiFormObj.weightUnit.selectedIndex].text;
    var height = bmiFormObj.height.value;
    var weight = bmiFormObj.weight.value;
    var text = "BMI Report\n" +
        "Your weight: " + weight + " " + wUnit + "\n" +
        "Your height: " + height + " " + hUnit + "\n" +
        "Your BMI: " + precision(bmi) + "\n";
    if (bmi < 18.5)
        text += "Your BMI suggests that you are underweight.\n";
    else if (bmi < 25)
        text += "Your BMI suggests that you have a reasonable weight.\n";
    else if (bmi < 29)
        text += "Your BMI suggests that you are overweight.\n";
    else
        text += "Your BMI suggests that you may be obese.\n";
    alert(text);
}
```

FIGURE 6.16

cdrom/web06/scripts/bmi6.js (excerpt)

Some JavaScript code from bmi6.js illustrating the building of a string message for output display.

Constants	Description
E	Euler's number $e \approx 2.71828$
PI	$\pi \approx 3.14159$
LN2	Natural logarithm of 2
LN10	Natural logarithm of 10
LOG2E	Base-2 logarithm of E
LOG10E	Base-10 logarithm of E
SQRT1_2	$\sqrt{0.5}$
SQRT2	$\sqrt{2}$

Table 6.5

Some constants from the JavaScript Math object.

Method	Return Value
abs(x)	Absolute value of x
ceil(x)	Integer greater than or equal to x
floor(x)	Integer less than or equal to x
round(x)	Nearest integer to x
max(x,y)	Maximum of x and y
min(x,y)	Minimum of x and y
random()	Random number between 0 and 1
exp(x)	$Math.E^x$
log(x)	Natural logarithm (base Math.E) of x
pow(x,y)	x^y
sqrt(x)	Square root of x

Table 6.6

Some methods of the JavaScript Math object that make available many of the common functions one expects to find in any programming language.

after which, finally, we concatenate this single digit after the decimal point to the variable intPortion to get the string equivalent of 20.589 to be "20.6". The details for all of this are a little involved, so if you have not seen calculations like this before you may want to sit back and study the logic for a few minutes.

The function displayDetailed(), also shown in Figure 6.16, is used for a detailed BMI report. The function receives two parameters: the bmiFormObj itself, as well as the computed BMI value given by the variable bmi. The function first extracts the values of height, heightUnit, weight, and weightUnit from bmiFormObj. A variable called text is formed by concatenating all the variables interspersed with appropriate text and line feed characters. Based on the interval within which the value of the BMI falls, a message about whether the BMI is low, high, or reasonable is further appended using a "nested" if-else-statement.[16] The message thus formed in the variable text is displayed to the user using the alert method. The display of results from such form processing can be seen in Figure 6.17.

---

[16]This works as follows: Each condition is tested, in turn, until a true condition is found, at which point the statement following that condition is executed and the program continues with the statement following the nested construct. If none of the conditions is true, the else part of the construct is executed, if there is one; otherwise, the nested construct causes no action. Once again, this is typical of virtually all programming languages.

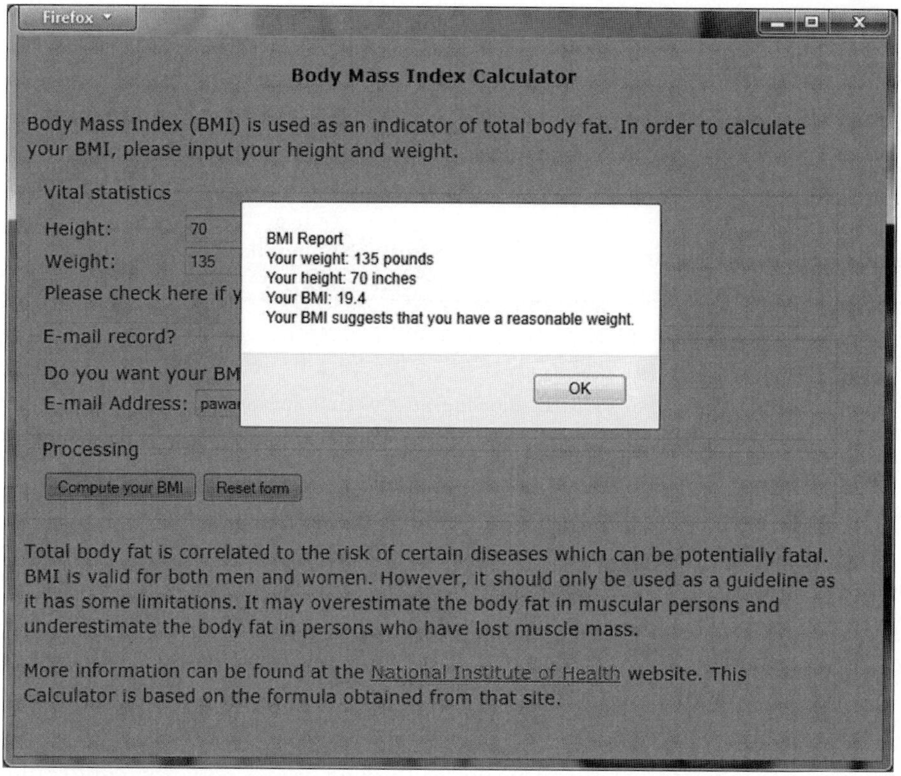

FIGURE 6.17

graphics/ch06/displayBmi6.jpg
A Firefox browser display of the result of a typical BMI calculation.

6.11 JavaScript and Regular Expressions

We saw a brief preview of regular expression usage earlier in the chapter when we performed a validation of a simple e-mail address entered into our BMI form. We simply looked to make sure that the e-mail address contained an @ sign and at least one character before and after that symbol.

In this section, we will look at more sophisticated validation using regular expressions. We will work with a revised version of the feedback form that was developed in the previous chapter. Figure 6.18 shows the relevant portion of the file feedback3.html from the web06 directory on our CD-ROM.

The **head** element of the modified file includes a **script** element that tells the browser to get the JavaScript code for validation from the file **feedback3.js**, which is located in the **scripts** subdirectory. The **form** tag is now modified with a new

```
4    <html xmlns="http://www.w3.org/1999/xhtml">
5      <head>
6        <title>Contact Us</title>
7        <meta http-equiv="Content-Type" content="text/html;charset=utf-8" />
8        <link rel="stylesheet" type="text/css" href="css/default.css" />
9        <script type="text/javascript" src="scripts/feedback3.js">
10       </script>
11     </head>
12     <body>
13       <h4>Feedback Form ... Let Us Know What You Think</h4>
14       <form id="contactForm" action="" onsubmit="validateContactForm()">
```

FIGURE 6.18

cdrom/web06/feedback3.html (excerpt)

Part of the feedback form from feedback3.html showing an external JavaScript file import and a form action that is a call to a function defined in that file.

attribute called onsubmit, which has the value validateContactForm(). When the submit button for the form is pressed, the function validateContactForm() defined in the file feedback3.js will be invoked. All of this is quite similar to what we did with our BMI form example.

The fields from the form that we will be validating are the first and last name, the telephone number, and the e-mail address. Figure 6.19 shows a couple of the errors we hope to trap through our data validation. Where this example departs from the previous BMI example is in its enhanced usage of regular expressions for validation purposes.

Figure 6.20 shows the function validateContactForm(), which is defined in the file feedback3.js. The function does not have any new features, but the logic for validation is slightly different. We use the value "contactForm" of the id attribute of the form to access the form and get a reference to the form object, which we assign to the variable contactFormObj. The values of firstName, lastName, phone, and email from the form are validated. We begin by taking the "optimistic approach" and assuming by default that all fields are OK and assign a value of true to a variable called everythingOK. Then, if any one of the fields that we validate has an invalid input value, we set the value of everythingOK to be false and ultimately return a value of false. Otherwise, everythingOK remains true, and in this case we use alert() to display the message

All the information looks good.
Thank you!

and return true. Otherwise, we return false. In fact, because we are using a sequence of if-statements, any and all fields containing invalid data will cause an appropriate error message to be displayed via a call to alert().

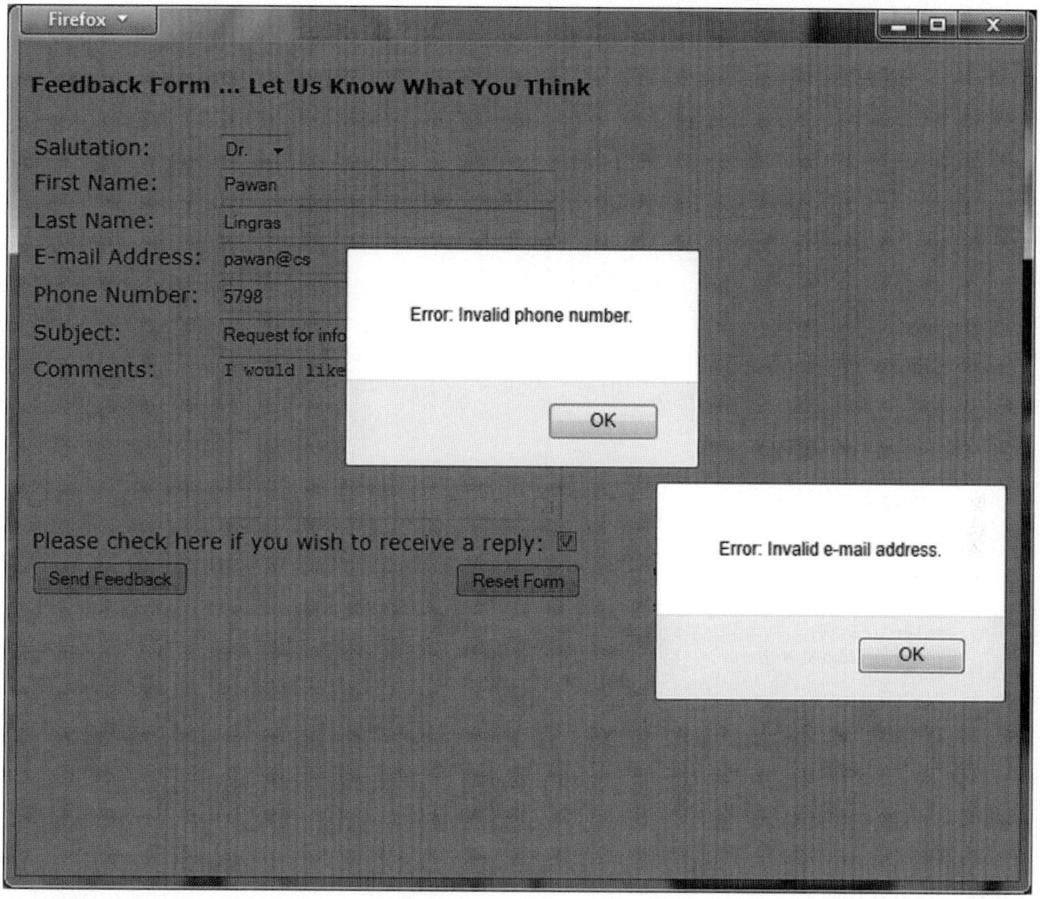

FIGURE 6.19

graphics/ch06/displayErroneousFeedback3.jpg
A Firefox browser display of two different feedback form errors generated from
feedback3.html.

Now that the fundamental logical structure of the function validateContact-
Form() is out of the way, we are ready to study the functions that actually validate
the data. These functions are shown in Figure 6.21. The basic structure of all of these
functions is the same. They search for an acceptable pattern that is specified using
a regular expression. If the text conforms to the acceptable pattern, search() will
return a 0. If the search returns 0, we return a true value. Otherwise, we return
a false value. The most interesting parts of these functions are the actual regular
expressions used in them.

```
3    function validateContactForm()
4    {
5        var contactFormObj = document.getElementById("contactForm");
6        var firstName = contactFormObj.firstName.value;
7        var lastName = contactFormObj.lastName.value;
8        var phone = contactFormObj.phone.value;
9        var email = contactFormObj.email.value;
10       var everythingOK = true;
11
12       if (!validateName(firstName))
13       {
14           alert("Error: Invalid first name.");
15           everythingOK = false;
16       }
17
18       if (!validateName(lastName))
19       {
20           alert("Error: Invalid last name.");
21           everythingOK = false;
22       }
23
24       if (!validatePhone(phone))
25       {
26           alert("Error: Invalid phone number.");
27           everythingOK = false;
28       }
29
30       if (!validateEmail(email))
31       {
32           alert("Error: Invalid e-mail address.");
33           everythingOK = false;
34       }
35
36       if (everythingOK)
37       {
38           alert("All the information looks good.\nThank you!");
39           return true;
40       }
41       else
42           return false;
43   }
```

FIGURE 6.20

cdrom/web06/scripts/feedback3.js (excerpt)

The "high-level" validateContactForm() function from feedback3.js that calls several other functions to validate the individual pieces of data entered into the form.

```
function validateName(name)
{
    var p = name.search(/^[-'\w\s]+$/);
    if (p == 0)
        return true;
    else
        return false;
}

function validatePhone(phone)
{
    var p1 = phone.search(/^\d{3}[-\s]{0,1}\d{3}[-\s]{0,1}\d{4}$/);
    var p2 = phone.search(/^\d{3}[-\s]{0,1}\d{4}$/);
    if (p1 == 0 || p2 == 0)
        return true;
    else
        return false;
}

function validateEmail(address)
{
    var p = address.search(/^\w+([\.-]?\w+)*@\w+([\.-]?\w+)*(\.\w{2,3})$/);
    if (p == 0)
        return true;
    else
        return false;
}
```

FIGURE 6.21

cdrom/web06/scripts/feedback3.js (excerpt)
The "lower-level" functions from feedback3.js that validate names, phone numbers, and e-mail addresses via JavaScript regular expressions.

In order to understand the more sophisticated regular expressions given in Figure 6.21, we need a little more information about regular expressions in general.[17] Tables 6.7–6.10 list some of the most frequently used (and useful) such features.

Table 6.7 describes some of the commonly used modifiers to indicate the position in a regular expression. A ^ matches the beginning of a string, while a $ matches the end of the string. These two modifiers appear in the regular expression

`^[-'\w\s]+$`

---

[17]Although there are some differences from one programming language to another, virtually all the most commonly used regular expression features in JavaScript are the same as those you will find elsewhere.

Character	Position
^	At the beginning of a string
$	At the end of a string
\b	At a word boundary
\B	Not at a word boundary

Table 6.7

Characters denoting positions in JavaScript regular expressions.

Special Character	Description
\0	The null character
\n	The newline character
\f	The form feed character
\r	The carriage return character
\t	The horizontal tab character
\v	The vertical tab character
\nnn	The character whose ASCII code is octal nnn
\xnn	The character whose ASCII code is hexadecimal nn
\unnnn	The character whose 4-digit Unicode representation is nnnn

Table 6.8

Special characters that can be used in JavaScript regular expressions.

from the function `validateName()` in Figure 6.21. This regular expression is saying, first of all, that the pattern specified starts at the beginning of a string (^) and ends at the end of the string ($). No other string can precede or follow the pattern. In fact, we use these two modifiers for every regular expression in the file `feedback3.js`.[18]

Let's look at the rest of the regular expression: `[-'\w\s]+`. The square brackets encloses a set of characters, any one of which may be repeated one or more times, because of the trailing + symbol. Other types of repetition in regular expressions are given in Table 6.10.

Now for the characters in the character set itself. The simplest ones are the hyphen or dash character (-), and the single quote or apostrophe character ('), which match themselves. (See Table 6.8 for some special characters that can be used in a regular

---

[18]Two other position modifiers that are useful from time to time, but that we do not illustrate here, are \b, which matches the beginning or end of a word (i.e., a word boundary), and \B, which matches any position that is not the end or beginning of a word (i.e., not a word boundary).

Character Class	Description
[xyz]	Any character from the list enclosed in square brackets
[^xyz]	Any character *not* in the list enclosed in square brackets
. (period)	Any character except the newline character
\d	Any single digit (same as [0-9] (A dash denotes a range of values)
\D	Any non-digit character (same as [^0-9])
\w	Any alphanumeric character, including the underscore (same as [A-Za-z_0-9])
\W	Any character that is not alphanumeric or an underscore (same as [^A-Za-z_0-9])
\s	A single whitespace character (same as [\r\t\n\f])
\S	A single non-whitespace character (same as [^ \r\t\n\f])

Table 6.9

Character classes that can be used in JavaScript regular expressions.

Modifier	Description
{x}	Exactly x repetitions
{x,}	x or more repetitions
{x,y}	Minimum x, maximum y repetitions
?	No more than 1 repetition
*	Zero or more repetitions
+	One or more repetitions

Table 6.10

Modifiers that can be placed after a pattern (a character or expression) within a JavaScript regular expression to indicate the permissable amount of repetition of that pattern.

expression.) We can always use ASCII code or Unicode to specify any of these special characters, as indicated in the table.

The remaining two characters in our set are \w and \s. These are shorthand notations for character classes themselves, so we have in effect two additional character classes within the initial character class. The character class \w represents a single alphanumeric character or underscore, while the character class \s corresponds to a single whitespace character. A more complete list of character classes is given in Table 6.9.

After dissecting the regular expression `^[-'\w\s]+$`, one can conclude that it will match a string with one or more repetitions of any combination of alphanumeric, whitespace, hyphen, and single-quote characters. If the string entered for first or last name matches this pattern, then `validateName()` will return a **true** value.

Now let us look at the other regular expressions from Figure 6.21, starting with the function `validatePhone()`. This function accepts phone numbers with or without an area code. We allow for the use of either a space or a hyphen as separator, but no separator at all is also permissible. Therefore, all of the following variations of a telephone number are acceptable:

- 902 420 5798

- 902 420-5798

- 902 4205798

- 902420 5798

- 902420-5798

- 9024205798

- 902-420 5798

- 902-420-5798

- 902-4205798

- 420 5798

- 420-5798

- 4205798

The regular expression that is used to validate a telephone number with area code is:

`^\d{3}[-\s]{0,1}\d{3}[-\s]{0,1}\d{4}$`

As we discussed in the case of regular expressions for first and last names, the use of `^` and `$` indicates that no other string is allowed to precede or follow the pattern. Here is our analysis of the pattern:

- The initial `\d{3}` means that a telephone number must begin with exactly three digits.

- The [-\s]{0,1} means that after those three digits the next character may be missing altogether, or it may be a hyphen or a whitespace character. It should be noted that we could have replaced {0,1} with ? to indicate that a hyphen or a space is optional.

- The \d{4} means that the number must terminate with exactly four digits.

The regular expression to validate a phone number without an area code essentially uses the same pieces as the previous expression, except for the absence of the area code portion:

^\d{3}[-\s]{0,1}\d{4}$

Finally, let us look at the regular expression for validating e-mail, which is more complicated than any we have seen previously:

^\w+([\.-]?\w+)*@\w+([\.-]?\w+)*(\.\w{2,3})$

Clearly this is the scariest regular expression you've seen yet. But let's not panic. Because you know more or less what an e-mail address looks like, and most of what you see here you've already seen in Tables 6.7–6.10, once we explain a couple of new things, everything should fall into place if you're prepared to study the expression for a few moments.

First, note the use of parentheses (round brackets, if you like). They are used to enclose several entities that we wish to consider as a group, often to be able to apply a repetition factor to the members of the group. Second, note that since the period is a character with a special meaning in regular expressions (i.e., a regular expression *metacharacter*), we have to escape it with a backslash if we want a period to be treated as a real period, as we would want in trying to match an e-mail address.

With these two facts in mind, then, we can see that the subexpression

([\.-]?\w+)*

which appears twice in the above regular expression means "zero or more instances of an expression that contains at least one alphanumeric character, and these one or more alphanumeric characters may or may not be preceded by a period or a hyphen."

To complete our analysis we note the following:

- The regular expression says that the e-mail must have an @ character "somewhere in the middle."

- It also says the e-mail address must "start with a word," that is, with one or more alphanumeric characters, which is then followed (prior to the @ character) by any number of the subexpressions discussed above.

- Then, following the @ character, we again have a "word" followed by any number of those same subexpressions. That is, we have the same sort of thing after the @ character that we had before the @ character.

- Finally, the e-mail address ends with a period followed by a two or three character "word."

You should spend a little time scanning through this regular expression and analyzing its individual parts. While this validation of e-mail is much more refined than what we saw earlier, we do not claim that this is the definitive regular expression for e-mail address validation. The actual validation of an e-mail address may indeed need to be even more involved. A useful exercise might be to look for one or more strings that are invalid e-mail addresses, but that are still acceptable to our JavaScript validation.

Figure 6.22 shows a validated input for the feedback form.

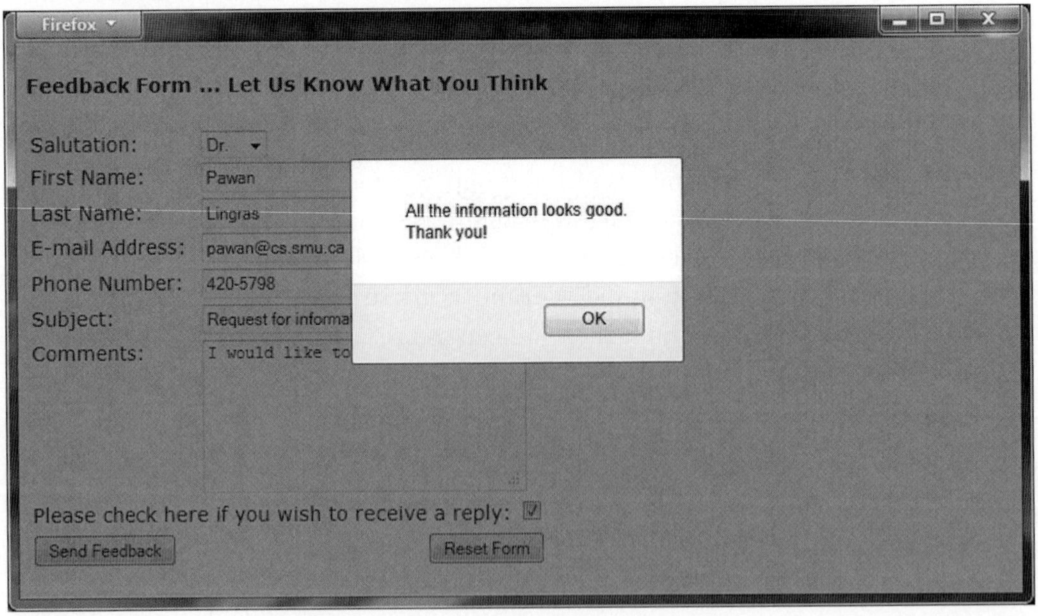

FIGURE 6.22

graphics/ch06/displayFeedback3.jpg
An Internet Explorer browser display of feedback from a successful form validation.

6.12 Summary

JavaScript is the premier programming language used for client-side programming on the Web at the present time. It is sufficiently powerful, flexible, and easy to learn that its popularity is justified. On the other hand, because it is not as strict with data typing and other features as some other programming languages, it can be harder to debug programs in the language. Be sure to investigate whatever may be available for your browser of choice to help you with JavaScript debugging.

Like CSS, JavaScript code should be kept in a separate file that can be accessed from the XHTML document where it is to be used via the `src` attribute of the opening `script` tag of an empty `script` element placed in the `head` of that document. That is, web page behavior should be separated from structure and presentation. However, if JavaScript code is to be executed immediately (as the document is loading) it may be inserted as the content of a `script` element within the body of an XHTML document.

JavaScript is an interpreted language that is restricted, for security reasons, in the actions it may perform on a user's computer. Its major uses on a client machine include computation, form data validation, and facilitating dynamic web page behavior via access to the Document Object Model (DOM), a language-independent Application Programming Interface (API) that allows JavaScript to perform many actions during and after the time when a web page is loaded.

The JavaScript `alert()` function is a convenient way to inform web page users of input errors when filling out forms.

DOM objects are treated as JavaScript objects, and the methods and fields of these objects can be accessed using the `object.methodName()` or `object.fieldName` syntax of the typical object-oriented environment. The preferred JavaScript way of getting access to the DOM object itself on a web page is to use the `getElementById()` method with an argument that is the value of the `id` attribute for that element (considered as a DOM object).

JavaScript data types include numbers (integer and real, with the usual arithmetic operators), strings (which may be concatenated with the + operator), booleans and zero-based arrays, and built-in objects such as the `Math` object. A usual function for determining whether a value is a number is `isNaN()`. Decisions can be made using `if`-statements or `if-else`-statements.

JavaScript can be used to verify that data entered into web page forms conforms to the expected input requirements for that form before the data is sent to a server. This is an important security feature that all web designers should take pains to implement. Regular expressions make this goal much easier to accomplish than other methods, so it is worthwhile for any web developer to have at least some knowledge of them.

6.13   Quick Questions to Test Your Basic Knowledge

1. What are the two major categories of "translation" of high-level programming code to something that an actual machine can run, and into which of these categories does JavaScript fall?

2. Can you think of at least one thing that a JavaScript program running in a web browser would *not* be allowed to do on the client machine?

3. If you want to embed some JavaScript code in your XHTML web page, what is the name of the element you use, and what attribute-value pair should you also supply?

4. If you want to place your JavaScript code in an external file, how do you do that?

5. What JavaScript method is used to create a pop-up window for displaying messages?

6. Even though you are not required to do so, how should you terminate each statement in a JavaScript script if you wish to follow "good programming practice"?

7. How would you describe the difference in the usage of \n and <br /> in the context of the current chapter?

8. What is the DOM?

9. What is the recommended way, in a JavaScript script, to get access to a DOM object on a web page?

10. What is the difference between an `if`-statement and an `if-else`-statement?

11. If a JavaScript array contains seven elements, what is the range of index (subscript) values you would use to access all the elements of that array?

12. What distinction is sometimes made between the use of the terms *method* and *function*?

13. What is the value of `Math.floor(7.28)`? Of `Math.floor(10.99)`? Of `Math.floor(-3.2)`?

14. What is the value of `Math.round(2.34)`? Of `Math.round(5.65)`? Of `Math.round(8.5)`? Of `Math.round(-3.99)`?

15. What is the value of `Math.ceil(7.28)`? Of `Math.ceil(10.99)`? Of `Math.ceil(-3.2)`?

16. What does it mean to validate an item of data entered into one of our forms?

17. Why should we validate the data that a user enters into one of our forms?

18. Why is there no validator that we can use to validate form data entry in the same way that we validate our XHTML and CSS?

19. What regular expression would you use if you wanted to validate a license plate number for a jurisdiction in which a valid license plate consists of three capital letters followed by a space and then three digits?

20. What regular expression would you use if you wanted to match a string containing a real number with up to three digits before the decimal point and up to five after it, if in addition the real number may or may not be preceded by a plus or minus sign?

21. What regular expression would you use if you wanted to match either a six-digit or a three-digit hexadecimal color value?

6.14   Short Exercises to Improve Your Basic Understanding

1. Rewrite the three `if-else`-statements in the program of Figure 6.10 as six `if`-statements. Give at least one argument for, and one argument against, this change.

2. Look up the `search()` method of the JavaScript `String` object under the JavaScript reference section of the `w3schools.com` site and determine why it is that we said, in subsection 6.9.5, that we expected the method to return a value of 0 if it found a match for the regular expression in its argument. When would it return a value other than 0 after a successful search?

3. In Figure 6.14 we see that a user has entered an invalid value for the e-mail address and our JavaScript script has responded by displaying a pop-up window with an appropriate message for the user. This is only one of several ways in which the user can go astray when trying to use this form. Our testing regime before "going live" on the Internet should always include as many tests as we can think of to make sure our form is going to behave gracefully in the face of bad data entry by users. In this particular case, you should study the JavaScript code in `bmi6.js` to confirm that you need to test this form to make sure the right message is displayed in each of the following cases:

- The user enters something other than a number for height.
- The user enters something other than a number for weight.
- The user enters a height value that is outside the allowable range. What *is* the allowable range? Is this reasonable?
- The user enters a weight value that is outside the allowable range. What *is* the allowable range? Is this reasonable?
- The user asks for an e-mail replay and supplies a valid e-mail address. (The e-mail reply feature is not implemented here.)
- The user asks for an e-mail reply and supplies an invalid e-mail address.

4. In Figure 6.19 we see the error-message windows that are popped up when a user enters invalid values for the phone number and for the e-mail address. There are other cases where invalid input will cause a similar pop-up window to appear. Study the JavaScript code in `feedback3.js` to confirm that you need, for your own testing of this form, to make sure the right message is displayed in each of the following cases:

- The user enters an invalid first name.
- The user enters an invalid last name.
- The user enters an invalid phone number.
- The user enters an invalid e-mail address.

Be particularly diligent in testing for invalid phone numbers and e-mail addresses.

6.15   Exercises on the Parallel Project

A main goal of this chapter was to show how JavaScript can be used on the client side to validate, using regular expressions, the data input by a user before sending that data to a server.

In this section of the last chapter you developed two forms, one for choosing products or services that your company offers, and one for getting feedback on customer satisfaction. Now you need to make those forms as secure as you can by checking as much of the input as you can to make sure it is nothing other than what you expect it to be. So, complete the following exercises:

1. Write a JavaScript script that validates all user entries for which it makes sense to do so in the form that permits your customers to choose a product or service. Be sure to inform the user if any data entry is invalid. Once all input has been validated, display to your customer some relevant output related to the data that has been entered. A typical display would be a summary of the items ordered, the numbers of each item, the cost of each item and the total cost.

2. Write a JavaScript script that validates all user entries for which it makes sense to do so in the form that permits your customers to give you feedback on their experience with your business. Report to the user if a particular entry is invalid, and be sure to tell the user that everything is OK if that is the case.

Some of your data validation and computation can be modeled on what you see in the text examples, but of course some will be peculiar to your particular business as well.

6.16   What Else You May Want or Need to Know

1. The official name of JavaScript is ECMAScript, although almost no one actually uses that name. See the **References** for further information.

2. When you view JavaScript code that is embedded in an XHTML document, especially code that you find out there on the Internet, you may see that code enclosed in a comment block. We could have done this with our embedded code shown in Figure 6.1, and if we had it would have looked like this:

```
<!--
document.write("Watch this space for our e-store.<br/>");
document.write("Coming soon ...");
// -->
```

This arrangement is designed to prevent browsers that cannot, or do not wish to, deal with JavaScript (for whatever reason) from simply displaying the JavaScript code in the browser window.[19]

The idea here is simply that both parties involved (namely, the browser and the JavaScript interpreter) know what they need to know to do the right thing. An older browser, or one ignoring JavaScript, will ignore the tag pair that denotes a `script` element, and the body of this element will be ignored as well, since it is just an (X)HTML comment.

A browser that wants to have the JavaScript code processed will, of course, pass the content of the `script` element to the JavaScript interpreter. JavaScript interpreters have been tweaked to recognize (actually, ignore) the first line, namely

```
<!--
```

and begin processing with the second line of the content (the first line of code). The character sequence used to indicate the end of the JavaScript must be on a new line and must be preceded by two slashes, which are actually the start of a single-line JavaScript comment. This is simply to prevent the JavaScript interpreter from trying to process the closing XHTML comment delimiter (`-->`) as JavaScript code.

When code is in an external file, you do not need to enclose the script in an XHTML comment in this way, since if JavaScript is not being processed, the `script` tag pair will be ignored, and in this case no JavaScript code actually appears anywhere within the XHTML markup.

---

[19]However, since virtually all current browsers support JavaScript, this preventive measure is not nearly as necessary as it used to be, and you will be seeing it less and less frequently as time goes on. For simplicity and to conserve space, we opt not to make use of this convention.

3. One of the things we did not discuss in this chapter is what to do when your JavaScript code does not seem to be working. This can be a very frustrating situation, since JavaScript is not like other programming languages such as C++ or Java. There is no compile stage at which you get compile-time errors that tell you that your syntax is incorrect. The first sign that something is amiss may be the disappearance of some or all of your web page, or the display of something very strange on the page.

However, some hope may be at hand. Many browsers are capable of providing some assistance with debugging when you are having trouble with your JavaScript scripts. Firefox is generally regarded as one of the better ones in this regard. Under its `Tools` menu you can choose `Error Console` to open a window that will show you warnings and errors that are generated when your script runs. Clear this window and then re-load the page and re-run your script to get a "clean" display of any reported problems. You may find this, or a similar facility in another browser, very helpful in your JavaScript debugging.

The Firefox browser also has an extension called Firebug that you may find useful for your web development. It allows the debugging, editing, and monitoring of any website's CSS, HTML, DOM, and JavaScript, and provides other web development tools as well. This tool, along with the Web Developer toolbar for Firefox, gives you considerable power for analyzing the structure and behavior of your web pages. See the **References** for the relevant links to these tools.

4. Although we can use JavaScript to check a user's input into our forms, we should not be overly confident that this will prevent a site visitor with evil intent from bypassing our validation code in some malicious way, which a clever hacker may be able to do. The Web can be a dangerous place, and when you are browsing it, one of the things you should be aware of is the difference between the `http` and `https` protocols. The first is, of course, the one we have been using all along. The second is a secure version of the HTTP protocol, and the one that should be used by any site that asks you for critical personal information, such as your bank account number and password. There is usually some visual sign that you are visiting a secure site. The `https` and/or a lock icon may appear in the address bar of your browser, for example. However, it is also important that you know you are visiting the site you think you are visiting, since it would defeat the purpose of such security to be visiting a secure but rogue site. One way of avoiding the kind of trap that many web users fall into is to enter the full web address of your intended destination yourself, rather than click on a

link that purports to take you to that site. The implementation of a secure website via `https` and encryption is, however, beyond the scope of this text.

6.17   References

1. You may be surprised to learn that the organization that counts JavaScript as home is the European Computer Manufacturers Association (ECMA), which at least explains why the formal name for JavaScript is ECMAScript. If you do want or need to visit the official home page of ECMAScript (much better known as JavaScript) here it is:

   ```
   http://www.ecma-international.org/
   ```

2. The W3 Schools site has both a JavaScript tutorial and a reference on both JavaScript and the DOM and its objects:

   ```
   http://www.w3schools.com/js/default.asp
   http://www.w3schools.com/jsref/default.asp
   ```

3. Here are links to two other JavaScript tutorials you may find useful:

   ```
   http://www.tizag.com/javascriptT/
   http://www.quackit.com/javascript/tutorial/
   ```

4. Here are two JavaScript language references, the second of which provides more detail:

   ```
   http://javascript-reference.info/
   http://www.devguru.com/Technologies/ecmascript/quickref/
        javascript_index.html
   ```

5. Here is a link to a JavaScript Quick Reference Card that you might want to print and keep handy:

   ```
   http://www.explainth.at/downloads/jsquick.pdf
   ```

6. Here are the links to the Firebug and Web Developer Firefox add-ons:

   ```
   http://getfirebug.com/
   https://addons.mozilla.org/en-US/firefox/addon/web-developer/
   ```

CHAPTER 7

JavaScript for Client-Side Content Behavior

CHAPTER CONTENTS

7.1   Overview and Objectives

We began our exploration of JavaScript in the previous chapter with a primary focus on data validation. Data validation on the client side is essential for ensuring that potentially malicious data is not sent to the web server. In this chapter, we will look at another aspect of JavaScript usage. JavaScript can also help us improve the functionality as well as the appearance of our web pages. In particular, we will enhance our home page by dynamically adjusting its content with a rotating sequence of business-related images, and also with dropdown menus. In fact, the dropdown menu feature will persist as we navigate to other pages on our website.

Thus, in this chapter we will discuss the following:

- How to create a rotating sequence of images (often called a "slide show"), along with the associated JavaScript

- The `onload` event attribute for the `body` element, whose value will be a JavaScript function that activates the slide show

- The JavaScript `switch`-statement for decision making

- More on JavaScript arrays

- The JavaScript `for`-loop for repetition

- How to create a dynamic dropdown menu, along with the associated CSS and JavaScript

- The `onmouseover` and `onmouseout` event attributes, whose values will be JavaScript functions that cause a dropdown menu to appear or disappear

Recall that in neither of the previous two chapters did we have a complete version of our Nature's Source website. However, in this chapter we will again have two versions of this sample site.

The first version, found in the **nature1** subdirectory of the **web07** directory on your CD-ROM or on the book's website, contains only enough files to display the revised home page and demonstrate both of the new features discussed in this chapter: the "slide show" of rotating images and the dropdown menus. In this version, none of the links on the home page are active.

In the second version, found in the **nature2** subdirectory, the home page is the same as in the first version, except that now *all* links on the home page are active. Most of these just take you to pages with minimal content that you have seen in previous versions of the site. However, we also have two important links that provide the features we discussed in the previous two chapters: one that takes a user to the BMI calculator and a second that goes to our feedback form.

7.2 A Revised Home Page with a "Slide Show" of Rotating Images and Dropdown Menu Options

Let's begin with a look at Figure 7.1, which illustrates the home page (either the `nature1` version or the `nature2` version[1]) for our sample Nature's Source website.

When compared with the last version of our home page, seen in Figure 4.18, the only visible difference you see is the list of dropdown menu[2] options under the `Products and Services` menu item of the main menu immediately under the company logo. However, there are actually two major enhancements in this version: in addition to the dropdown menus (also under the `Your Health`, and `About Us` items on the main menu and the `Contact Us` item on the footer menu), now the image shown in the figure is just one of a sequence of six images that continually rotate as long as the page is displayed. This chapter discusses the new CSS and JavaScript features that enable these enhancements.

The XHTML file producing the display in Figure 7.1 is `nature1/index.html`, shown in Figure 7.2. The only difference between this file and `nature2/index.html` is the opening comment. Note, first of all, the following features of this file:

1. As another version of our `index.html` document, it continues to make use of three external XHTML files included via SSI (lines 17, 18, and 39). Two of those files—`mainmenu.html` and `footer.html`—have been revised to accommodate the new dropdown menu feature that we discuss in detail later in this chapter.

2. As usual, it makes use of a `default.css` style file, found in the `nature1/css` subdirectory and accessed via a `link` element in the `head` element of the document (line 11).

3. The `head` element also contains two `script` elements (lines 12 and 13), which provide access to the JavaScript scripts `rotate.js` and `menu.js` from the

---

[1] Recall that although you have access to all of the files, you cannot view either of these home pages directly from the CD-ROM, since they make use of SSI. You must either go to the book's website, or set up your own SSI-aware server to serve the book's files.

[2] The dropdown menu we discuss here is based on ideas from the website `http://javascript-array.com/`.

FIGURE 7.1

graphics/ch07/nature1/displayIndexHtml.jpg
A Firefox browser display of nature1/index.html (or nature2/index.html), both of which illustrate
rotating images and dropdown menus.

scripts subdirectory. The script in rotate.js will handle the rotating images, and the script in menu.js will handle the dropdown menus.

7.3 Implementing Our "Slide Show" of Rotating Images: The onload Attribute, a Revised img Element, and the rotate.js Script

The replacement of a static image on our home page with a "slide show" that consists of a continuous, cyclic display of a sequence of various images related to our business might be regarded in some quarters as somewhat frivolous. On the other hand, it might also help to grab and keep a visitor's attention. It is worth keeping in mind that choosing how much activity to have on your home page (or any page) is both a key design decision and a bit of a balancing act. You can either attract and keep visitors or cause them to quickly abandon your site, depending on how much and what kind of dynamic activity they encounter when they first come to visit.

```
1   <!DOCTYPE html PUBLIC "-//W3C//DTD XHTML 1.0 Strict//EN"
2       "http://www.w3.org/TR/xhtml1/DTD/xhtml1-strict.dtd">
3   <!-- index.html for the simplified home page of Nature's Source web site
4   containing the drop-down menu and rotating images, but with no active
5   links from this home page -->
6   <html xmlns="http://www.w3.org/1999/xhtml">
7     <head>
8       <title>Nature's Source - Canada's largest specialty vitamin store</title>
9       <meta http-equiv="Content-Type" content="text/html;charset=utf-8" />
10      <link rel="stylesheet" type="text/css" href="css/default.css" />
11      <script type="text/javascript" src="scripts/rotate.js"></script>
12      <script type="text/javascript" src="scripts/menu.js"></script>
13    </head>
14    <body onload="startRotation()">
15      <div id="page">
16        <!--#include virtual="common/logo.html"-->
17        <!--#include virtual="common/mainmenu.html"-->
18        <div id="content">
19          <div id="textLeft">
20            <h3>Welcome to Nature's Source: Protecting your health naturally!</h3>
21            <p>Founded in 1998, Nature's Source was created to serve those who
22            use alternative healing methods. Offering only the highest quality
23            vitamins, minerals, supplements &amp; herbal remedies, Nature's
24            Source takes great pride in helping people live healthier, happier
25            lives.</p>
26            <p>Many Companies that talk about Customer Service fail to deliver.
27            Nature's Source exists to truly serve all the needs of their
28            customers. Each location features dedicated on-site therapists
29            along with knowledgeable staff who ensure that every customer
30            receives the best quality information available. Continuing
31            Education seminars are a regular event at Nature's Source.</p>
32          </div>
33          <div id="image">
34            <img id="placeholder" src="" alt="Healthy Lifestyle"
35            width="280px" height="160px" />
36          </div>
37        </div>
38        <!--#include virtual="common/footer.html"-->
39      </div>
40    </body>
41  </html>
```

FIGURE 7.2

cdrom/web07/nature1/index.html
The file index.html showing the XHTML code for the home page of our Nature's Source website
with dropdown menu options and rotating images.

The general idea of our "slide show" is this. When the script in rotate.js of
Figure 7.3 is run after the index.html page is loaded, the first thing that happens

```
1    //rotate.js
2
3    //Get all of today's information in a JavaScript Date object
4    var today = new Date();
5
6    //Build the appropriate prefix for filenames, depending on whether
7    //today is a weekday (indoor images) or the weekend (outdoor images).
8    var prefix = "images/";
9    switch (today.getDay())
10   {
11       case 0:
12       case 5:
13       case 6:
14           prefix += "outdoor";
15           break;
16       default:
17           prefix += "indoor";
18   }
19
20   //Use that prefix to put the proper sequence of image filenames into an array
21   var imageArray = new Array(6);
22   for (i=0; i<imageArray.length; i++)
23       imageArray[i] = prefix + (i+1) + ".jpg";
24
25   //Rotate the images in the array
26   var imageCounter = 0;
27   function rotate()
28   {
29       var imageObject = document.getElementById('placeholder');
30       imageObject.src = imageArray[imageCounter];
31       ++imageCounter;
32       if (imageCounter == 6) imageCounter = 0;
33   }
34
35   function startRotation()
36   {
37       document.getElementById('placeholder').src=imageArray[5];
38       setInterval('rotate()', 2000);
39   }
```

FIGURE 7.3

cdrom/web07/nature1/scripts/rotate.js

The JavaScript code for handling the rotating images on the home pages of our **nature1** and **nature2** websites.

is a determination of the current date. An appropriate collection of images is then assembled, depending on whether it's a weekday or a weekend. Then those images are displayed one after the other, with repetition when the end of the sequence is reached, until the user closes the page or clicks on a link to another page.

For this purpose, we have assembled, in the subdirectory **images** of the **nature1** directory (as well as the **nature2** subdirectory), two sets of images, one set showing indoor exercises and the other showing outdoor exercises. The images of outdoor exercises are named **outdoor1.jpg** to **outdoor6.jpg**. These outdoor images will be displayed on a weekend (Friday to Sunday). On the other hand, the images of indoor exercises will be displayed on weekdays. These image files are named **indoor1.jpg** to **indoor6.jpg**.

To understand how the slide show works, we need to examine both the **index.html** file of Figure 7.2, which contains the **onload** attribute and the revised **img** element, and the **rotate.js** script shown in Figure 7.3.

7.3.1   The onload Attribute of the body Element: Starting the Slide Show When the Home Page Loads

In line 15 of Figure 7.2 we see the following XHTML markup for the opening tag of the **body** element:

```
<body onload="startRotation()">
```

The **onload** attribute of the **body** tag is an *event attribute* whose value should be whatever action is to be taken[3] once the page with the given body has fully loaded. In this case, that value is a call to the JavaScript function **startRotation()**, which has been defined as part of the script in **rotate.js**, and it begins the image rotation that now features prominently on our home page. We will discuss this function shortly.

7.3.2   The Revised img Element for the Slide Show

Finally, in our overview of the current **index.html** in Figure 7.2, we should look at the **img** element in lines 35–36:

```
<img id="placeholder" src="" alt="Healthy Lifestyle"
width="280px" height="160px" />
```

---

[3]This action is often, as in this case, simply a function call, but it could also be several JavaScript statements, separated by semicolons.

The `img` tag now has an `id` attribute with the value `"placeholder"`, suggesting (correctly) that the `img` element is to "hold the place" for each successive image to be inserted into the image location during the rotation. Also, the value of the `src` attribute starts off as the empty string, but the script will change this value to the name of each successive image file as the rotation proceeds.

The value of the `alt` attribute is `"Healthy Lifestyle"`, a term that may reasonably be applied to all of our images, so it does not have to be changed.

The `width` and `height` attributes have fixed values. Recall that for the sake of efficiency all of the images we display should ideally have the same size to eliminate the need for any resizing effort by the browser (or any distortion in the image if the actual dimensions give a different *aspect ratio*).[4]

7.3.3   The `rotate.js` Script

In what follows, we use our discussion of the `rotate.js` script to introduce (or examine further) the following JavaScript topics:

- The `Date` object

- The `switch`-statement

- Creating and populating an array

- The `for`-loop

The JavaScript `Date` Object

The first of the new JavaScript features we encounter in the `rotate.js` file shown in Figure 7.3 is the JavaScript `Date` data type. The executable part of the script begins in line 4 by creating a new `Date` object (with the `Date()` method call[5]) and storing it in a variable called `today`:

```
var today = new Date();
```

---

[4]The *aspect ratio* of an image is defined as the ratio of its width to its height.

[5]A method call of this type is usually referred to as a *constructor*, since it "constructs" a new object of type `Date`. Those familiar with other languages such as C++ or Java will already be familiar with this terminology and syntax.

Method	Return Value
Date()	A Date object containing today's date and time
getDate()	day of the month (1-31)
getDay()	day of the week (0-6) (0 is Sunday)
getFullYear()	year (a four-digit number)
getHours()	hour (0-23)
getMilliseconds()	milliseconds (0-999)
getMinutes()	minutes (0-59)
getMonth()	month (0-11)
getSeconds()	seconds (0-59)

Table 7.1

Methods of the Date object in JavaScript.

We gave the variable this name because by default such a Date object contains all the information we might need to know that pertains to today's (i.e., the current) date.

There are many pieces of information we might want to know about today, or any other day, and an equal number of methods that we can call on the Date object referred to by the today variable to get that information. Table 7.1 shows some of those methods. See the **References** section at the end of this chapter for more information.

The particular method we will need is getDay(), which returns a value of 5, 6, or 0 if today is Friday, Saturday, or Sunday (respectively), or a value of 1 to 4 if today is a day from Monday to Thursday, inclusive.

The JavaScript switch-statement for Decision Making

We have already seen how the JavaScript if..else-statement can be used to choose between two alternatives. Sometimes, however, we need to choose one alternative from among many (one day from seven possible days of the week, for example). The JavaScript switch-statement is another form of conditional statement that is found in many other languages as well, including C, C++, and Java, which allows us to make this kind of choice.

Here is the general format of the `switch`-statement[6]:

```
switch (expression)
{
    case value_1:
        statements;
        break;
    case value_2:
        statements;
        break;

        . . .

    case value_n:
        statements;
        break;
    default:
        statements;
        break;
}
```

The execution of a `switch`-statement proceeds as follows. First, the `expression` in the parentheses following the keyword `switch` is evaluated. This value is then checked against the value in the first `case` (`value_1` above). If a match is obtained, the statement(s) following this `case` are executed and the `switch`-statement terminates because the `break;` statement at the end of this `case` will cause execution to "break out" of the `switch` and carry on with the statement immediately following the `switch`-statement.

If the value of `expression` does not match the value in the first `case`, the search continues with each of the subsequent `case` values (also called "case labels") in turn. Any match further along the way will result in behavior analogous to that we described when we had a match for the first case.

Each group of `case` statements in a `switch`-statement is almost always terminated by a `break;` statement to exit the `switch`, once the statements for that `case` have been executed. Sometimes, however, programmers will omit the `break;` in one or more cases to create a "drop through" effect. For example, if you delete the `break;` statement before the second case, and if the value of our `expression`

---

[6]Although we don't need to do so for our purposes here, those readers who are familiar with the `switch`-statement from C, C++, or Java may be surprised (and happy) to know that in addition to integers and characters we can also use string values for the expression and the case labels in a JavaScript `switch`. Of course, this convenience may come at a cost of reduced efficiency.

matched `value_1`, the statements in both the first and second case will be executed. In fact, we see one form of this usage in the `switch`-statement in our `rotate.js`.

If no `case` value is matched by the value of `expression`, the statements after `default:` will be executed. While it is not necessary for the `default:` option to be the last part of a `switch` statement, it is a good programming practice to always include it. Also, the `break;` statement at the end of the `default:` option is not strictly necessary, since the `switch`-statement ends at that point in any case.

Choosing the Appropriate Group of Images by Putting the `switch`-statement to Work

In order to handle the images for our slide show properly, the first thing we need to do is decide which group of images to use, the indoor ones or the outdoor ones. As we know, this depends on the day of the week.

We begin by setting a variable called `prefix` (the prefix to which a number will be added to get an actual file name) to an appropriate initial value. Since every file is located in the subdirectory `images`, we initialize this variable with the string `"images/"` (line 8 of the `rotate.js` script in Figure 7.3):

```
var prefix = "images/";
```

Next, depending on the day of the week, we want to append either `"indoor"` or `"outdoor"` to the value in the variable `prefix`. This is achieved using a `switch`-statement in which the expression to be evaluated is `today.getDay()` (lines 9–18 of the `rotate.js` script in Figure 7.3):

```
switch (today.getDay())
{
    case 0:
    case 5:
    case 6:
        prefix += "outdoor";
        break;
    default:
        prefix += "indoor";
}
```

The return value of the method call `today.getDay()` will be an integer in the range from 0 to 6. If it is either 0, 5, or 6 we have a weekend day, since these values correspond to Sunday, Friday, and Saturday, respectively. In these cases we want to append the string `"outdoor"` to our variable `prefix` so that the value of `prefix` becomes the string `"images/outdoor"`. On the other hand, if the value returned is 1, 2, 3, or 4 we have a weekday, and the value of `prefix` becomes `"images/indoor"`.

Note the use of the "extended + operator" to add either `"outdoor"` or `"indoor"` to the original value of `prefix`. Most operators in JavaScript can be extended in this way using the assignment operator. In our case, the statement

```
prefix += "outdoor";
```

has exactly the same effect as this statement:

```
prefix = prefix + "outdoor";
```

We have also chosen to not use a `break;` for the first two cases allowing for the fall through effect discussed earlier. In fact, those first two cases do not even have statements of their own in this particular `switch`-statement. Here we are using our `default:` option to deal with the remaining days of the week, and we will append the string `"indoor"` to our variable `prefix` in that case. Other alternatives to this code will be explored in the end-of-chapter exercises.

Creating Your Own JavaScript Array to Store the Image Filenames

In the previous chapter we had a very brief encounter with a built-in JavaScript array that was useful when accessing certain DOM elements. Here our goal is to have a easy way to access a sequence of image files, and the JavaScript array turns out to be the most convenient way to do that since arrays are generally used to store lists of values of any kind. In our case, therefore, we will store a list of the filenames of the images that will be displayed in our slide show.

Now, however, we have to create our own array. We do this by first declaring a variable called `imageArray` to hold a reference to an array object and then we call the constructor method of the `Array` data type with the operator `new` in much the same way as we did earlier when we created a `Date` object (line 21 of the `rotate.js` script shown in Figure 7.3) statement:

```
imageArray = new Array(6);
```

The constructor, as always, performs the necessary operations to set up our array. A significant difference this time around is that we provide the value 6 as a parameter to the constructor, which specifies that we want the array to have a size of six (be able to hold six values, i.e., six image filenames). The net effect is as though we now have six variables, named `imageArray[0]`, `imageArray[1]`, `imageArray[2]`, `imageArray[3]`, `imageArray[4]`, and `imageArray[5]`.[7] These are the *components* or *elements* of the array. Thus, the array gives us an easy way to handle several, or even a very large number, of variables of the same kind. In fact, we can easily automate the processing of all the array elements with the help of another JavaScript *control statement*, the `for`-loop, which we do next.

The JavaScript `for`-loop for Repetition

A JavaScript script will often require that one or more actions be repeated. For example, to build our array of images, we have to repeat the act of inserting the name of an image file into that array six times. Most C-based programming languages, including JavaScript, have three different kinds of *loop control statements* to handle repetition: the `for`-loop, the `while`-loop, and the `do..while`-loop. Because it is the most convenient choice for our immediate purpose, we examine the `for`-loop more closely here, and discuss the other two in the end-of-chapter exercises.

Here is the general format of a `for`-loop:

```
for (initialization; condition; update)
{
    statements;
}
```

The keyword `for` is followed by a required pair of parentheses containing three semicolon-separated parts: `initialization`, `condition`, and `update`. The statement(s) in the braces are called the *body* of the `for`-loop. If there is only a single statement in the body, the braces are optional.

This is how we execute a `for`-loop. The `initialization` is performed (once) before the loop begins. Then, if the `condition` is true, we execute the body. Next, the `update` is performed and the `condition` is re-checked. As long as the `condition` remains true, we continue to re-execute the loop body. When a check of the `condition` finds it to be false, the loop terminates and script execution continues with the first statement following the `for`-loop. Thus, perhaps at the risk of some redundancy, we may outline the order of execution of a `for`-loop as follows:

```
initialization;
Check condition and if false, exit the loop.
```

---

[7]Note again that arrays in JavaScript (your own as well as any that are built-in) are zero-based, that is, index numbering starts at 0.

```
statements;
update;
Check condition and if false, exit the loop.
statements;
update;
Check condition and if false, exit the loop.
statements;
update;
Check condition and if false, exit the loop.
statements;
update;
...
```

Of course, most of the time we want the loop to terminate eventually, so we must ensure that the `update` eventually causes the `condition` to become false.

Building Our Image Array by Putting the `for`-loop to Work

Once we have set up the "infrastructure" for our image array—the `imageArray` variable itself, and the correct prefix for our image filenames that will go into that array—we can populate the array with the required filenames with a simple `for`-loop (lines 23–24 of `rotate.js` in Figure 7.3):

```
for (i=0; i<imageArray.length; i++)
    imageArray[i] = prefix + (i+1) + ".jpg";
```

The execution of this `for`-loop proceeds as follows:

- The `initialization` sets the variable i to 0.

- The `condition` (i<imageArray.length) is then checked. Any JavaScript `Array` object has a `length` property that is accessed using the same dot-notation syntax that is used to access an object method. This condition uses that `length` property, which in this case has the value 6, and since the value of i is currently 0, the `condition` is true.

- Since the `condition` was true, we now execute the (`single`-statement) body of the `for`-loop. This statement creates the proper filename for the first image and inserts it into the array. The proper filename is created by appending the `prefix` variable with the value of (i+1), and then adding the string for the file extension, which is ".jpg". Note that we need i+1 here to avoid the classic "off-by-one" error, because i has started at 0, but the names of the image files start their numbering at 1. If the current day is a weekday (for example), the value of `prefix` to which we are adding this information will be "images/indoor", so that `imageArray[0]` will be assigned the value "images/indoor1.jpg".

- Next, we execute the `update` statement, i++, which increments i to 1.

- Now we check the variable i to see if it is still less than 6, which it is, so the `condition` is still true.

- Continue by executing the loop body again, which, this time around, assigns the value "images/indoor2.jpg" to `imageArray[1]`.

- This process continues until we have set the final value of our array, `imageArray[5]`, to be "images/indoor6.jpg".

- The following execution of the `update` statement, i++, sets i to 6, which is no longer less than `image.length`.

- At this point the loop terminates, and `imageArray` contains the names of all six image files.

Rotating Our Images: The `rotate()` and `startRotation()` Functions

We have now completed the setup of the array data structure that contains our "slides," and we are ready to define the functions that perform the slide show. It is important to note that the remainder of the script `rotate.js` in Figure 7.3 is in fact just setting up the functions to perform the slide show, but the show does not start as this script executes. It only starts when the page has loaded. This is a difference worth remembering.

To display our images we define two functions, one called `rotate()`, which performs the rotations, and a second one called `startRotation()`, which initializes the first image and then calls the first function to continue with the rotation. You will recall that it is the latter function, `startRotation()`, that was the value of the `onload` attribute in our `index.html` page. We could have used the `rotate()` function directly as the value of the `onload` attribute, but depending on the speed of things, a user might see the value of the `alt` attribute in the image location briefly before the rotation got under way. By initializing the first image directly and *then* starting the rotation we hope to avoid this possibility.

Here is the JavaScript code that sets up our two functions (lines 26–39 from rotate.js in Figure 7.3):

```javascript
var imageCounter = 0;
function rotate()
{
    var imageObject = document.getElementById('placeholder');
    imageObject.src = imageArray[imageCounter];
    ++imageCounter;
    if (imageCounter == 6) imageCounter = 0;
}


function startRotation()
{
    document.getElementById('placeholder').src=imageArray[5];
    setInterval('rotate()', 2000);
}
```

The function rotate() performs the actual image rotation. Each time it is called, it first creates a variable called imageObject and assigns it a reference to the DOM img element on our home page. Recall from the discussion of index.html that the img element had an id attribute with a value of "placeholder", so we get this reference with a call to the getElementById() method. Once we have this reference to the img element object, we can access the src attribute of the img element with the usual dot-notation syntax (imageObject.src) and assign to it the filename of the current image from our array of images (imageArray[imageCounter]). The browser then takes care of updating the home page display with that image.

Before leaving the rotate() function, we must increment imageCounter so that the next time rotate() is called the next image in the sequence will be displayed. And finally, note that when imageCounter reaches 6 we have to set it back to 0, for two reasons: first, to get our "rotational" effect and second, to prevent our array index from quickly getting out of bounds and trying to access images that don't exist.

Now that we know what rotate() does when called, the only remaining question is this: When, exactly, *is* it called? And that's the job of the startRotation() function, so let's look at it.

The startRotation() function does two things. First, it chooses an initial image for display, before rotate() is called to begin the rotation, for reasons we explained above. We opt to display the last image in the sequence first, as this initial image, so that the first image seen appears in its proper place in the rotation.

The second and last action of `startRotation()` is to call the `setInterval()` function. This is a built-in JavaScript function that takes two parameters. The first parameter is a string containing an action to be performed (often a function call, as in this case), and the second parameter is the length, in milliseconds, of a time interval. A call to `selectInterval()` with these two input values causes the action to occur after each time interval of the given length. Thus the call made by our `startRotation()` (namely, `setInterval("rotate()", 2000)`) causes our `rotate()` function to be called every 2 seconds (2000 milliseconds). This, in turn, causes the image on our home page to change every 2 seconds.

7.4 Implementing Our Dropdown Menus: Two New XHTML Attributes, Some New CSS, and the `menu.js` Script

In this section, we discuss the details of the second major new feature of our sample website, the dropdown menus. We are again dealing with the "stripped down" first version of the site found in the `nature1` subdirectory of the `web07` directory. In this version, none of the links on our home page are active, but the dropdown feature is fully functional in all cases, which is all we need for our discussion. Section 7.6 discusses the more complete `nature2` version of our site, in which all the links are active and lead to other pages, but there is no functionality to be seen there that we have not seen before.

To follow the discussion in this section, you will need to refer to four different files from the `web07` directory:

- `nature1/index.html` (see Figure 7.1)

- `nature1/common/mainmenu.html` (Figure 7.4)

- `nature1/css/default.css` (Figure 7.5)

- `nature1/scripts/menu.js` (Figure 7.6)

7.4.1   An Overview of How Our Dropdown Menus Work

Let's begin with a brief overview of how our dropdown menus work, and start by examining the XHTML markup structure that gives us those menus. This markup is in `mainmenu.html`, shown in Figure 7.4, and as you can see by looking at `index.html` in Figure 7.2, `mainmenu.html` is included, via SSI, right after the logo on our home page.

The main menu that sits below the logo on our home page now consists of two kinds of menu options, that is, two kinds of links to other pages. The first kind of "high level" option is illustrated by the five options that show up when the page displays. The second kind of option is illustrated by the dropdown list of options that appears ("drops down") when the mouse is placed over an option of the first kind. This only happens for the last three options on this main menu (`Products and Services`, `Your Health`, `About Us`). The first two main menu options (`Home`, `Buy Now`) do not have any suboptions.

Figure 7.4 shows that the entire main menu "strip" on our home page is enclosed in an outer `div` element with an `id` value of `"mainMenu"`. Within this `div` is an unordered list containing five list elements corresponding to the five menu options on the main menu. Finally, under each of these main menu options that has a dropdown submenu (only the last three) there is another `div` element containing a number of anchor elements corresponding to the number of dropdown options for that particular submenu. As you can see from the markup, that number of dropdown options happens to be three in each case.

Note that, for simplicity, we have followed the standard approach of making the hyperlinks "defunct" by using a value of '`#`', which simply means that the links will not actually take us anywhere. This is what we mean by saying that the links on this page are "inactive."

7.4.2 The `onmouseover` and `onmouseout` Attributes: Showing and Hiding Dropdown Menu Options

Continuing our examination of Figure 7.4, we note the appearance of two new *event attributes*: `onmouseover` (lines 5, 6, 8, 9, 17, 18, 25, and 26) and `onmouseout` (line 3). Each `onmouseover` attribute appears as the attribute of a list element containing one of the five main menu options, or as the attribute of a `div` element containing a group of dropdown options.

Because the value of each `onmouseover` attribute is a call to the `show()` function, when the mouse pointer is placed over any of the main menu options, a call to `show()` is made. Depending on which menu option the mouse pointer is over, that call is either `show(m1)`, `show(m2)`, `show(m3)`, `show(m4)`, or `show(m5)`. The parameter is the id

```
<!-- mainmenu.html -->

<div id="mainMenu" onmouseout="hide()">
  <ul class="Links">
    <li><a href="#" onmouseover="show('m1')">Home</a></li>
    <li><a href="#" onmouseover="show('m2')">Buy Now</a></li>
    <li>
      <a href="#" onmouseover="show('m3')">Products and Services</a>
      <div id="m3" onmouseover="show('m3')">
        <a href="#">Product Catalog</a>
        <a href="#">Featured Products</a>
        <a href="#">Services</a>
        <a href="#">Suppliers</a>
      </div>
    </li>
    <li>
      <a href="#" onmouseover="show('m4')">Your Health</a>
      <div id="m4" onmouseover="show('m4')">
        <a href="#">BMI Calculator</a>
        <a href="#">Ask an expert</a>
        <a href="#">Useful Links</a>
      </div>
    </li>
    <li>
      <a href="#" onmouseover="show('m5')">About Us</a>
      <div id="m5" onmouseover="show('m5')">
        <a href="#">Vision and Mission</a>
        <a href="#">Employment Opportunities</a>
        <a href="#">News Archive</a>
      </div>
    </li>
  </ul>
</div>
```

FIGURE 7.4

cdrom/web07/nature1/common/mainmenu.html
The included XHTML file containing the markup for our main menu and its dropdown menus on
all of our site's pages.

value of the corresponding `div` element containing the associated dropdown submenu
option group.[8]

---

[8]Except that there are only three groups of submenu options. In fact, there is no `div` with an `id`
of `m1` or `m2`, so the call to `show()` in either of these cases has no effect since there is no submenu
to drop down. We could explain this by saying we are "future proofing" our code: If we ever do
add submenu `div`s with these `id` values, they will drop down automatically without further code
modification.

The purpose of a function call like `show('m3')` (for example) is to make visible the dropdown menu contained within the `div` element whose `id` is `m3`, which is the one under the main menu item `Products and Services`. We shall look at the details of this function later in this chapter. As long as the mouse pointer is over the main menu option or the dropdown menu underneath it, that dropdown menu will remain visible.

The `onmouseout` attribute of the outermost `div` element with the `id` value of `"mainMenu"` (line 3) has as its value a call to the function `hide()`. The purpose of `hide()` is to make invisible any currently showing dropdown menu, which it does when the mouse pointer moves away from the `div` with `id` value `"mainMenu"`, that is, away from all of the main menu options and their dropdown submenus.

7.4.3   The CSS for Our Dropdown Menus

Much of the CSS for our home page in this chapter we have already discussed in Chapter 4. However, our dropdown menu setup makes use of some CSS features that we have not discussed previously, so we introduce them here. For purposes of the discussion, we include, in Figure 7.5, only the relevant portion of the current chapter's `default.css` file, in which we see, of course, familiar CSS along with the new features.

Here are the things to note about the CSS in Figure 7.5:

- We use a single class called `Links`, combined with various descendant selectors, to style both the main menu options, which are always visible, and the dropdown submenu options, which only appear when the mouse pointer hovers over one of the main menu options that actually *has* a dropdown menu. Comments indicate which styles apply to which menus.

- The style for the `Links` class itself in lines 100–103 simply sets padding and margins to a baseline value of zero.

- The `.Links li` style in lines 106–112 removes the markers from list elements and floats them left, setting up a horizontal main menu, just as we had in Chapter 4.

- In the style for `.Links li a` in lines 114–123 we see something we have not seen before: the style rule `display: block`. Turning these anchors (links) into block elements allows us to give them a width, padding, and margins, something we cannot do with inline elements. Thus we can give each of the main menu bar options a uniform width.

```
 8    .Links {
 9    padding: 0;
 0    margin: 0;
 1    }
 2
 3    /* for the always-visible menu options */
 4    .Links li {
 5    padding: 0;
 6    margin: 0;
 7    float: left;
 8    list-style: none;
 9    font: bold .7em Verdana;
 0    }
 1
 2    .Links li a {
 3    display: block;
 4    width: 159px;
 5    padding: 4px 10px;
 6    margin: 0 1px 0 0;;
 7    background-color: #048018;
 8    color: #FFF;
 9    text-align: center;
 0    text-decoration: none;
 1    }
 2
 3    .Links li a:hover {background-color: #5FB361;}
 4
 5    /* for the drop-down menu options */
 6    .Links div {
 7    position: absolute;
 8    background-color: #C5DCC9;
 9    border: 1px solid #048018;
 0    visibility: hidden;
 1    }
 2
 3    .Links div a {
 4    display: block;
 5    width: 156px;
 6    padding: 5px 10px;
 7    background-color: #C5DCC9;
 8    color: #048018;
 9    text-align: left;
 0    text-decoration: none;
 1    font: bold 90% Verdana;
 2    }
 3
 4    .Links div a:hover {
 5    background-color: #5FB361;
 6    color: #FFF;
 7    }
```

FIGURE 7.5

cdrom/web07/nature1/css/default.css (excerpt)
A portion of the CSS style file for this chapter, showing the styles for both the always-visible main menu options and for the dropdown submenu in nature1/index.html and its SSI-included files.

- The `.Links div` style in lines 128–133 contains three items of interest. First is the style rule `position: absolute`, which takes the menu strip out of the "normal flow" of the page and, in this case, allows the following blocks to rise up under the menu and close up the space that would otherwise be there to accommodate the dropdown submenus when they are activated. Second is the `border: 1px solid #048018` style rule, which gives us a 1-pixel, solid green border all around our dropdown submenu options. And finally, the `visibility` property is set to `hidden` to hide the submenu options when the page is first displayed.

- The `.Links div a` style in lines 135–144 styles the anchors (links) in our dropdown menus. The key thing to note here once again is the `display: block` style rule. As before, this allows us to give them all a uniform width. But this is needed here for an even more important reason. Normally an `a` element is inline, and without this rule the submenus would appear in a horizontal row across the page, instead of one under the other as we would like.

- The two pseudo-class styles, one in line 125 and the other in lines 146–149, provide different background colors for the main menu links and the submenu links, respectively, when the mouse pointer is hovering over those links. The style rule for the submenu links also alters the text color.

You may have to read through the above list several times while referring to Figure 7.5. An even better approach is to view the `nature1/index.html` file in a browser while you have the `nature1/css/default.css` file open in an editor. Then you can comment out or alter each style rule in some other way as that rule is mentioned, and then refresh the browser display to see the effect of your actions. There is no better way to learn quickly the real effects or purpose of a particular CSS style. One of the end-of-chapter exercises guides you through a number of such activities.

7.4.4   The JavaScript for Our Dropdown Menus: The `show()` and `hide()` Functions

Finally, we are now ready to look at the JavaScript code that causes the visibility state of the menu suboptions to alternate between visible and hidden. This code is found in the file `menu.js`, which is shown in Figure 7.6. It is a much-simplified version of the code from `http://javascript-array.com/`.

```
//menu.js

var isShowing = false; /* Flag to indicate if a drop-down menu is visible */
var menuItem = null;   /* Reference to a drop-down menu */

//Show the drop-down menu with the given id, if it exists, and set flag
function show(id)
{
    hide(); /* First hide any previously showing drop-down menu */
    menuItem = document.getElementById(id);
    if (menuItem != null)
    {
        menuItem.style.visibility = 'visible';
        isShowing = true;
    }
}

//Hide the currently visible drop-down menu and set flag
function hide()
{
    if (isShowing) menuItem.style.visibility = 'hidden';
    isShowing = false;
}
```

FIGURE 7.6

cdrom/web07/nature1/scripts/menu.js
The JavaScript show() and hide() functions for the dropdown menu in our nature1 and nature2
home pages.

This script consists of two global variables, one called isShowing and the other
called menuItem, and two short function definitions. One function is called show()
and the other hide(). The names of the variables and the functions have been chosen
to suggest their purpose, always a good programming practice.

When this script is run, the global variable isShowing is initialized to false
to indicate that none of the submenu options is showing, and the menuItem global
variable is initialized to null to indicate that no menu item has yet been chosen.
Remember that these global variables are accessible from any part of the script and
therefore, in particular, from each of the two functions.

If you now look again at the mainmenu.html file, you can see that the show()
function is called when the user places the mouse over one of the menu items in
the menu bar, and at that point the show() function is also passed the id value of
that menu item, as discussed earlier. This passed value will be one of 'm1', 'm2',

'm3', 'm4,' or 'm5', corresponding to the position of the menu item in the menu bar, although (as we pointed out earlier) there are currently no dropdown menus corresponding to either 'm1' or 'm2'.

The first action of the show() function is to hide any submenu that may be displayed by calling the hide() function. It then retrieves the DOM element whose id value it has been passed by calling the getElementById() method and passing along the same id that it received. The visibility property of that DOM element is then given the value visible and the global variable isShowing is set to true to indicate that this menu item now indeed "is showing."

The function hide() is even simpler. It checks to see if any DOM element is visible by looking at the variable isShowing, and if there is such a visible DOM element, it is made invisible by setting its visibility property to a value of hidden.

7.5   The Footer Menu

If you look at Figure 7.1 again, you will note that in addition to the main menu that lies immediately below the logo, there is a short, two-item menu in the right-hand part of the footer that is essentially part of the "main menu" as well. The first of these menu options (Contact Us) has a two-item dropdown submenu, while the second (Site Map) has no dropdown submenu. These menu items are constructed and styled in the same way as the main menu options and their dropdown submenus discussed earlier. You should confirm this by examining the footer.html file in either nature1/common or nature2/common.

7.6   Notes on the nature2 Version of Our Nature's Source Site

We pointed out at the beginning of the chapter that the nature1 version of our website in this chapter had no active links, since we were using it solely for demonstrating our slide show and dropdown menus. The nature2 version, on the other hand, is the most complete version of our site to date.

First, the home page looks the same as the home page for the nature1 version, except that all links are now active, so the nature2 directory includes an XHTML document file to be displayed whenever the user clicks on any of the now-active links. With two exceptions, these pages contain essentially the same content as they did in Chapter 4, except that all pages have been modified to show the same main menu and footer (but not the rotating images) of the home page. The two exceptions are the

`BMI Calculator` dropdown menu option found under the main menu `Your Health` menu option and the `Give us feedback` dropdown menu option found under the `Contact Us` menu option on the footer menu. This latter link brings up our feedback form.

The contents of the images and scripts subdirectories are the same for both `nature1` and `nature2`.

The `default.css` for `nature2` contains the full contents of that file for `nature1`, plus a few styles at the end to help with the styling of the BMI calculator form and feedback form pages.

It would be useful at this point for you to make yourself thoroughly familiar with this up-to-date version of our sample site before we enhance it further with server-side processing using PHP in the next chapter.

7.7 Summary

In this chapter we have seen how JavaScript could be used to provide a simple "slide show" of rotating images on our home page, and, in conjunction with CSS styles, to create a dropdown menu for navigation around our website.

In the case of the rotating images, we saw how the value of the `onload` attribute of the `body` element of a page could be set to a JavaScript function that is fired up when the page is loaded. In our case, this arrangement caused a sequence of images to be displayed in a rotational order that repeated until the page was closed.

In the case of the dropdown menu, we saw how the values of the `onmouseover` and `onmouseout` attributes of an element can be set to JavaScript functions that are triggered to execute and either show or hide menu options, depending on whether the user's mouse is hovering over an element or has moved away from it. The new CSS concepts we found useful in this context were the `display`, `visibility`, and `position` properties.

In the course of these discussions we also learned more about some basic JavaScript features, including the `Date` and `Array` data types, the `switch`-statement, the for-loop and `while`-loop, and the `setInterval()` function.

7.8 Quick Questions to Test Your Basic Knowledge

1. We have not actually used the term *dynamic XHTML document*, but what do you suppose we would mean by that term if we did use it?

2. What is different about the `switch`-statement in JavaScript, when compared with the same statement in languages like C, C++, or Java?

3. What is the name of the `element` attribute whose value you would set if you wanted something to happen when a web page is fully loaded?

4. What is the name of the `element` attribute whose value you would set if you wanted something to happen when the user moved the mouse over that element?

5. What is the name of the `element` attribute whose value you would set if you wanted something to happen when the user moved the mouse away from that element?

6. What is the recommended way of accessing the control elements inside an HTML form element via JavaScript?

7.9   Short Exercises to Improve Your Basic Understanding

1. The `switch`-statement that we used in our `rotate.js` script is certainly not the only way, and one could argue that it's not even the best way, to write this particular `switch`-statement. It does the job, but instead of using the `default:` option to handle the weekday cases, it might make the code a little clearer if we had one explicit case to handle the weekend days (which we do), another explicit case to handle the weekday cases (which we don't), and use the `default:` option for something that is extremely unlikely to happen, such as displaying for the user a message via the `alert()` function to inform the user that something strange has happened. Revise `rotate.js` to implement the `switch`-statement in this way, and test it to make sure the revision works.

2. Revise the script in `rotate.js` so that the images are shown in random order, rather than always repeating the sequence in the same order. Be sure to test to make sure the revision works.

3. The generic-`switch` statement discussed in this chapter is equivalent to the following generic nested `if`-statement:

```
if (expression == value_1)
{
    statements;
}
else if (expression == value_2)
{
    statements;
}
...
else if (expression == value_n)
{
    statements;
}
else
{
    statements;
}
```

Revise `rotate.js` by replacing its `switch`-statement with an equivalent nested if-statement of the above form, and test it to make sure it works.

4. The `switch`-statement in `rotate.js` can also be replaced by the following if..else-statement:

```
if (today.getDay()==0 || today.getDay()==5 || today.getDay()==6)
    prefix += "outdoor"
else
    prefix += "indoor"
```

Revise `rotate.js` by replacing its `switch`-statement with an equivalent if..else-statement of the above form, and test it to make sure it works. This exercise and the previous one should be a reminder that even for very short and simple code, it's often worthwhile to stop and think about the "best" way to write the code, rather that going with the first thing that comes to mind.

5. JavaScript provides two other loops in addition to the `for`-loop: the `while`-loop and the `do..while`-loop. Though you can use whatever loop you like in most situations, the kind of loop you actually choose in a particular situation will

often depend on the logic, since some loops can be more "readable" than others in certain cases.

Here, in generic form, are those other two loops:

```
initialization;              initialization;
while (condition)            do
{                            {
    statements;                  statements;
}                            }
                             while (condition);
```

The major difference between these two loops is that the body of the do..while-loop is guaranteed to execute at least once, since the condition is not checked until that has happened. The body of the while-loop, on the other hand, may never execute, since the check of the condition is made at the beginning.

In order for the body of either loop to execute properly, the initialization must be done correctly, and for either loop to terminate properly the body must contain an action that eventually causes the condition to become false. In the case of the for-loop, the initialization and update are handled by the loop structure itself. In the other two loops, it is the programmer's responsibility to ensure that proper initialization and updating is performed.

As a simple example, here is a version of each of the three loops that adds the positive integers from 1 to 10, inclusive:

```
var sum = 0;              var sum = 0;              var sum = 0;
var i;                    var i = 0;                var i = 0;
for (i=1; i<=10; i++)     while (i < 10)            do
{                         {                         {
    sum += i;                 ++i;                      ++i;
}                             sum += i;                 sum += i;
                          }                         }
                                                    while (i < 10);
```

We used the for-loop in this chapter to build our array of images. A for-loop was the appropriate choice in that case, because we knew exactly how many times we wanted the loop to execute (the number of images we had), and this is the kind of scenario for which the for-loop is well suited. However, either of the other loops could have been used.

Revise `rotate.js`, first of all, to replace the `for`-loop with an equivalent `while`-loop to build the image array. Then revise it a second time to use an equivalent `do..while`-loop. In each case, test to make sure everything still works.

6. In our `rotate.js` script we defined two separate functions, `rotate()` and `startRotation()`, to handle the slide show. We can also perform our image rotation with a single `rotate()` function if we implement it somewhat differently, making it a **recursive function**, which is a somewhat advanced concept. Here is that implementation:

```
var imageCounter = 0;
function rotate()
{
    document.getElementById('placeholder').src=imageArray[i];
    imageCounter++;
    if(imageCounter >= imageArray.length) imageCounter = 0;
    setTimeout("rotate()", 2000);
}
```

In this version of the image rotation, we begin by initializing a variable called `imageCounter` to 0, as before. This variable will again keep track of the subscript (or index) of the array element that provides the filename of the current image. This time around the function `rotate()` itself must be the value of the `onload` attribute of the `body` element in `index.html` and performs the image rotation starting when the page has loaded by proceeding as follows.

As before, we access the `img` tag as a DOM element by using the `id` ('placeholder') of the tag, and set its `src` attribute to the filename given by `imageArray[imageCounter]`. This makes sure that the image given by `imageArray[imageCounter]` is displayed in the web page.

We then increment `imageCounter` to prepare for loading the next image in the sequence when the time comes and, as before, we have to make sure the value "wraps to 0" when the time comes. Finally, we have to answer this question: When *does* the time come to load the next image? And this is where the major departure from the way we previously did things takes place. The last statement in our `rotate()` function is

```
setTimeout("rotate()", 2000);
```

which essentially says, "Wait 2000 milliseconds (2 seconds) and then call yourself again." Students coming from C, C++, or Java will immediately recognize this as a *recursive function* call (a function calling itself), but even they may be bothered by the fact that the function will continue to call itself forever. That is, there is no "stopping condition" for the function. But this is a case where that is not a major concern, since we do in fact want the images to keep rotating for as long as the user is viewing the page, which may be a long time. If the user displays our page and then goes home for the night, the images should still be rotating the next morning. Of course, if the user closes our page, or browses to another site, the function (and everything else associated with our page) goes away.

7. The markup file **nature1/index.html** is linked to the CSS style file **nature1/css/default.css**, and the part of this file dedicated to styling our menus is seen in Figure 7.5.

Make the following changes and perform the suggested actions to observe the changes in the display of **nature1/index.html** when you do so. This will give you a good sense of which style rules are affecting which parts of the display.

(a) There are a number of different colors, specified with hex values, in the CSS shown in Figure 7.5. Change each of these values, one at a time, to red. First predict what the effect will be, then reload the page to check your prediction.

(b) Comment out the style rule at the beginning (lines 100–103) that sets all margins and padding to 0, and then reload to see what effect, if any, this has had.

(c) Comment out the **float: left** style in line 109.

(d) Comment out the **list-style: none** style in line 110.

(e) Comment out the **display: block** style in line 115.

(f) Comment out the **width: 159px** style in line 116.

(g) Comment out the **visibility: hidden** style in line 132.

(h) Comment out the **width: 156px** style in line 137.

7.10   Exercises on the Parallel Project

The website for your business has now developed to the point where it has information about the business itself and some more detailed information about its products and/or services, as well as some data-validated forms for gathering requests and feedback from your users. Now it's time to improve the "look and feel" of your site by adding some additional images and some dropdown menus. Once again, of course, this "parallels" the look and feel of our own Nature's Source sample website.

1. Find some more images relating to your business that you can legally copy and use on your website (at least four, let's say) and replicate for your site the rotating image feature illustrated by our own example when you display the `index.html` file of this chapter.

2. Give the home page of your business a dropdown menu, similar to the one illustrated in Figure 7.1 of the text. Or, if you wish, give it a fancier dropdown menu. The one in the text can be regarded as a "minimal" dropdown menu whose functionality you should be able to replicate using the text code as a model and making appropriate changes for your particular situation. On the other hand, there are lots of dropdown menu options "out there" on the Internet, and you may find one more to your liking. If you do, and it's not illegal to do so, go ahead and use it instead. The menu options and suboptions will, of course, depend on the nature of your business, but at least some of them will be the same or similar to those in the text example.

3. Revise the pages of your site other than your home page so that the same kind of dropdown menu options that appear on your home page also appear on those other pages. This helps to give your visitors a feeling of consistency in the "look and feel" of your site as they browse from page to page.

4. The above three items are illustrated by the version of our second sample website in this chapter (in the `nature2` subdirectory), and you can use those ideas to replicate similar behavior for your own home page. There may be other features that you wish to implement that are peculiar to your business. If you wish to implement one or more of them, and have time to do so, feel free to add them to your site.

7.11   What Else You May Want or Need to Know

1. A significant difference between arrays in JavaScript and arrays in more "conventional" languages such as C, C++, and Java is that in JavaScript the size of an array is not fixed once the array is created. You can change the size of an array at any time. You can even assign a variable to an array location with a subscript that is beyond the current last element of the array. For example, if we only have a six-element array of images to begin with, we could nevertheless say

```
imageArray[20] = "pawan.jpg";
```

and the length of the array will be extended to 21 (remember that indices start at 0).[9]

2. The `img` tag also has a `name` attribute, and we could have used this attribute by giving it the same `"placeholder"` value that we gave to our `id` attribute. Then we could use this value in expressions like

```
document.placeholder.src = imageArray[imageCounter];
```

and you will see a lot of JavaScript code like this on the Web. Unfortunately, the name attribute of the `img` tag (and a number of other tags) has been deprecated in XHTML. In fact, here is a quote from `http://www.w3.org/TR/xhtml1/`:

> "Finally, note that XHTML 1.0 has deprecated the `name` attribute of the `a`, `applet`, `form`, `frame`, `iframe`, `img`, and `map` elements, and it will be removed from XHTML in subsequent versions."

3. You should be aware, particularly if you plan to do any extensive JavaScript programming for your webwsite, that there are many sources for JavaScript code on the Web, and it is always a good idea to avoid "re-inventing the wheel" if at all possible. First of all, if you see a site that exhibits some behavior that you admire and would like to use on your own site, that behavior may be produced by JavaScript and the code may (or may not, remember) be freely available for use by others. In the (reasonably frequent) cases where the code is available, often all the writer will ask is that acknowledgment be placed in

---

[9]That you can do this is not necessarily a good thing, and there are good reasons why those other languages won't let you do it, even though you may find it convenient from time to time.

the code wherever you use it. Also, there are many JavaScript code libraries (or "frameworks") that are also freely available and contain a great deal of ready-made functionality that you may find useful when designing your site. Examples include jQuery, YUI from Yahoo®, and Google's Closure™. See the **References** for a useful link.

7.12   References

1. The **W3 Schools** JavaScript tutorial start page is located here:

   `http://www.w3schools.com/js/default.asp`

2. The **W3 Schools** JavaScript reference site, which contains lots of examples on both JavaScript itself and the (X)HTML DOM, can be found here:

   `http://www.w3schools.com/jsref/default.asp`

3. In particular, for further information on the JavaScript `Date` and `Array` data types, see:

   `http://www.w3schools.com/jsref/jsref_obj_date.asp`
   `http://www.w3schools.com/jsref/jsref_obj_array.asp`

4. Here is another site you may find helpful when investigating JavaScript features:

   `http://www.javascriptkit.com/jsref/`

5. The following page contains a table showing many JavaScript frameworks and their features:

   `http://en.wikipedia.org/wiki/Comparison_of_JavaScript_frameworks`

CHAPTER 8

PHP for Server-Side Preprocessing

CHAPTER CONTENTS

8.1   Overview and Objectives

The client-side JavaScript programming that we looked at in the previous two chapters is limited to computing that can be safely executed within the confines of the browser. These limitations aside, client-side computing has certain advantages. For example, it limits the amount of data transfer by taking care of simple computing requests on the client computer, instead of transmitting those computational requests to the server, having the server perform them, and then sending the results back to the client. This relieves the server from servicing a large number of requests for minor computational tasks and cuts down on bandwidth consumption as well. Equally important is that client-side computing is very useful for filtering out potentially malicious data, or simply malformed data, on its way to the server.

However, client-side computing using JavaScript is not up to the task of performing much of the computation that is necessary on the contemporary Web. Our websites need to serve dynamically created web pages based on the data from users' input devices, files on both the client and server computers, and information contained in databases stored on servers. In general, for the sake of efficiency, it is better to have calculations on data performed wherever the data lives, so clearly we will want to do some serious computing on the server side as well.

Four of the most popular technologies for providing server-side computing are Active Server Pages (ASP), Java Server Pages (JSP), Perl, and PHP. The use of ASP requires a relatively intensive study of languages such as Visual Basic, C#, or C++ on Microsoft's .NET platform. A study of JSP requires a reasonable prior exposure to the Java programming language. On the other hand, Perl and PHP are both interpreted scripting languages that, by comparison, are much easier to learn, especially for those with no prior programming experience. These languages make it possible for us to get onto the server side of the web programming highway relatively quickly.

Of the two, PHP is our language of choice, so in this chapter we will discuss the following:

- A brief history of the PHP language, and why it is a reasonable choice for our server-side processing (or "preprocessing," as we often call it, since the PHP processing for a given page takes place *before* that page is sent to the browser for display)

- How PHP fits into the overall web picture as a scripting language, with the help of a simple initial example that introduces one of PHP's many useful built-in functions, the `date()` function

- PHP script development and testing

- Incorporating a PHP-generated welcome message, including the current date and time, on our home page

- How to cause our home page to be "refreshed" (reloaded) every so often so that the time is kept up to date if the page remains displayed

- Implementing the server-side functionality of our feedback form by first uploading the user's input data to the server and then performing the following actions on the server side: sending the user's feedback to the business via e-mail, sending a copy of the e-mail to the client, confirming the submission to the client via a browser display, and storing a copy of the feedback on the server

- Implementing an alternate version of our BMI calculator by shifting the computation from client-side JavaScript to server-side PHP, allowing us to e-mail the user a permanent record, if requested, in addition to providing the immediate browser display of the result

- How to send HTML-encoded e-mail, as we do when delivering our BMI report

- The `post` value of the `method` attribute of the `form` element, which we use to submit all of our form data to the server

- The features of the PHP language required for our purposes, which include comments, variables, and *superglobals* (a special kind of variable), numerical and string data types, expressions and operators, arrays, built-in and programmer-defined functions, file output, and using PHP to accomplish server-side inclusion of files

The updated version of our Nature's Source website for this chapter will require several new scripts written in PHP, which we will, of course, place in our `web08/nature/scripts` subdirectory, and discuss in detail as we encounter them. We will also have to modify the opening `form` tag attributes that appeared previously in `feedback.html` and `bmi.html` to make use of these new scripts.

To get the welcome message on our home page we will replace our `logo.html` include file with a file called `banner.php`, which is comprised of the content of `logo.html` plus another `div` element containing the PHP script that generates the welcome message.

Also, since we are now computing the BMI using PHP rather than JavaScript, we remove the BMI-computing code from `bmi.js`, leaving only the validation code, and rename the resulting JavaScript file `bmiValidate.js`.

Since SSI (as we have used it in previous chapters) and PHP do not always play well together without reconfiguring the server, which is beyond the scope of our discussion, we now use a simpler approach to get our server-side includes. The `include()` function of PHP can be used to include into our `index.php` (formerly `index.html`) our new `banner.php`, as well as the files `mainmenu.html` and `footer.html`, which are unchanged except for the `href` values which now contain links to files with a `.php` extension. Analogous changes need to be made to all of the other files to which we link from our home page, and to indicate this change we alter the extensions of these files from `.html` to `.php` to reflect the fact that each one now contains some PHP code.

A couple of minor changes to our `default.css` for this chapter complete the new setup. To our copy of the `default.css` for the `nature2` version of our site from Chapter 7 we add a `div#welcome` to style the `div` containing the welcome message. We also give this `div`, and the logo image `div`, the style rule `float: left`, which requires that we add a `clear: left` rule to `div#mainMenu` to keep the main menu from floating up to the right of the welcome message.

8.2   Some PHP History

In the early days of the Web, prior to the appearance of PHP, Perl was by far the most popular language of choice for server-side web programming. In recent years, PHP has gained immense popularity and has become a versatile and robust language with more than enough capability to meet the needs of any aspiring web developer.

PHP has its roots in the Perl programming language and many of its features reflect its origins. Many of its most commonly used features are also similar to those of JavaScript, which we have already seen, so our discussion of PHP will focus on pointing out those similarities and highlighting the differences.

Unlike Perl, which is a "standalone" programming language that can be used to write virtually any kind of software, PHP is designed specifically for web page development. In this chapter and the next two, we will gain enough experience with PHP and the MySQL database management system to create a prototype e-commerce system.

The acronym PHP originally stood for *Personal Home Page*, and the set of Perl scripts that comprised its original implementation was written by Rasmus Lerdorf in 1995. He used his PHP tools for tracking accesses to his online resumé. A revised version of the original product was called PHP/FI, where FI stood for "Forms Interpreter."

Lerdorf posted his work on the Web, where it very quickly caught the attention of other developers, and the system soon took on a life of its own. To support increased functionality, Rasmus then wrote a much larger C implementation. This major revision added abilities to communicate with databases, which led to even more interest in the software, and it eventually expanded to the point where it was no longer possible for a single individual to maintain it. Nowadays there is a worldwide community involved in PHP maintenance and development, and you can follow their progress on, and freely download the latest updates for many different platforms from, the home website for PHP, located at `http//www.php.net`. See the end-of-chapter **References** for further information.

Web developers owe a debt of gratitude to Rasmus Lerdorf for making the source code of PHP public, since the resulting vibrant online PHP community has produced many significant improvements in the language itself, as well as facilities that permit PHP to communicate with a wide variety of database implementations. The use of PHP has far outgrown its original motivation of creating Personal Home Pages. In fact, that original name has receded into obscurity, since more users now prefer to use the recursive name *PHP: Hypertext Preprocessor*. This definition describes the role of PHP more accurately, since PHP scripts are used for "preprocessing" a web page (on the server) to dynamically create a hypertext document (before it is sent to the browser). XHTML markup constructed via PHP, using data from server-side databases that is also obtained via PHP, allows programmers to develop very dynamic and timely web pages.

8.3   PHP as a Server-Side Scripting Language

All current major web server software packages are capable of providing access to a PHP interpreter on the server side of the client-server architecture. This does not mean that you, as a web developer, automatically have access to PHP, even if you have an Internet Service Provider. PHP has to be activated and configured on the server, so you need to check with your system administrator to make sure that PHP is enabled for your web server.

A web server may spawn a separate operating system "process" to handle PHP requests, or the server software itself may have an "internal" module that deals with PHP scripts. As long as PHP is available, which of these options is actually in use will generally be "transparent to the user."

Because of this PHP requirement, our PHP-related pages provided on the CD-ROM cannot be viewed directly from the CD-ROM. If you wish to test your PHP pages "locally," before uploading them to your server (always a good idea, of course), you can install a web server such as Apache, as well as PHP, on your personal computer, and place our files in a location accessible to the server. Failing that, you will still be able to test them from the website for this book. See the end-of-chapter **References** for further discussion.

A typical PHP web page will contain the usual XHTML markup we have seen, but this markup will also be interspersed with instructions in the PHP programming language. A PHP-enabled web server will "preprocess" a web page by running all the embedded PHP instructions on the page.[1] These PHP instructions will create additional XHTML markup. All of the XHTML—that generated by PHP, plus whatever other markup was present—is then sent to the client. This means that the client computer is not aware of any of the embedded PHP instructions, since they have "disappeared" by the time the client receives the page from the server. It also means that the use of PHP does not require any special plug-ins on the client side to work with PHP script output. Finally, all the PHP programming code is "hidden" from the client, which helps with the security issue since that code may contain additional information about data storage on the server or other sensitive information.

8.4   PHP Script Structure and General Syntax: A Simple Example

Before we start incorporating PHP into the pages of our Nature's Source website, it will be useful to examine a simple example in isolation. Moreover, we shall later incorporate the output of this example into our home page.

The example in question is found in the file `web08/welcome.php`, which is shown in Figure 8.1. The browser display can be seen in Figure 8.2.

From Figure 8.1 we see that the content of `welcome.php` is a normal XHTML document, except for the content of the `body` element, which contains some "ordinary" XHTML (an `h2` element), as well as a PHP script. This is typical, but there may also be JavaScript code and several additional PHP scripts embedded in a document body. Note that any XHTML document file that contains PHP code should be given a `.php` extension. This is a helpful visual aid to programmers and an essential indicator to the server that the file must be processed by the PHP interpreter before being sent to the browser.

---

[1]Note immediately this major difference between JavaScript and PHP: JavaScript code is downloaded from the server with the XHTML and run in the browser, while PHP code is run on the server and it is the output of this run, along with whatever other XHTML the document contains, that is downloaded to the browser.

```
1   <!DOCTYPE html PUBLIC "-//W3C//DTD XHTML 1.0 Strict//EN"
2       "http://www.w3.org/TR/xhtml1/DTD/xhtml1-strict.dtd">
3   <!-- welcome.php -->
4   <html xmlns="http://www.w3.org/1999/xhtml">
5     <head>
6       <title>Welcome Message with Output from the PHP date() Function</title>
7       <meta http-equiv="Content-Type" content="text/html;charset=utf-8" />
8     </head>
9     <body>
10      <h2>Welcome!</h2>
11      <?php
12      echo "<h3>It's ".date("l, F jS")."<br />";
13      echo "The time is ".date("g:ia").".</h3>";
14      ?>
15    </body>
16  </html>
```

FIGURE 8.1

cdrom/web08/welcome.php
A very short PHP script embedded in the body of an XHTML document.

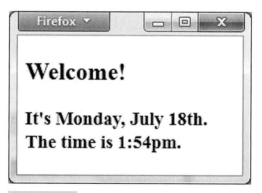

FIGURE 8.2

graphics/ch08/displayWelcomePhp.jpg
A Firefox browser display of welcome.php.

The first thing to note about the PHP script in Figure 8.1 is that the programming language statements in a PHP script are enclosed within a `<?php` delimiter at the beginning (line 11) and a `?>` delimiter at the end (line 15). For readability these are generally placed on lines by themselves. This particular script contains just two PHP `echo` statements. Note that PHP statements, like JavaScript statements, are terminated by a semicolon. The purpose of an `echo` statement is to "echo" (or print) some output that will become part of the final XHTML document that will be generated by the PHP processor and sent to the browser from the server.

In this case, the output in question consists of an XHTML h3 element. The content of this h3 element includes some ordinary text, an instance of the XHTML <br /> element, as well as the output from two calls to the PHP built-in date() function.

It is important to note here that the period (.) is the PHP concatenation operator for strings. This may take some getting used to, since many other languages, including JavaScript, use the + operator for this purpose. Study the code in Figure 8.1, compare it carefully with the corresponding display in Figure 8.2, and make sure you identify which periods in the code are concatenation operators used to join PHP strings (text enclosed in double quotes, as usual, and/or date() function return values, which are also strings), and which periods are simply part of the text output to be displayed.

The first call to the date() function returns the current day of the week and date, and its string input parameter indicates how we want this information formatted. Similarly, the second call to date() returns the time of day. Once we get the date and time information in our requested formats, and these strings have been combined with the rest of the XHTML markup, the final result becomes the body of the XHTML document sent to the browser.

8.4.1   The PHP date() Function

Since we have found it so useful, and you may too, let's take a moment to discuss the date() function. It is, of course, just one of many built-in functions provided by PHP, but a very handy one. The date() function can be quite complex, and you may wish to pursue further details about it and other frequently-used, predefined PHP functions that we will discuss later.

In the meantime, let's see what our calls to the date() function actually do. The function expects as input a string that specifies the format of the output string (i.e., the returned string value, since this is a value-returning function). The format string that we supplied in our first call to the function was "l, F jS". Unfortunately, the meaning of these symbols is not very mnemonic, and thus not easy to "guess," so let's explain what they mean.

First, the lowercase letter 'l' (not the digit 1, which is the first potential point of confusion) says that we want a full textual representation of the day of the week, such as Sunday, Monday, and so on. The next two characters (the comma and the blank space) are to be interpreted literally to give us a comma and a blank space following the day of the week in the output. Then the character F says we also want the full textual representation of the month, such as January, February, and so on. This is again followed by a literal blank space. Finally, the two-character sequence jS gives us the numerical date with an appropriate suffix appended, such as 1st, 2nd, 3rd, or 4th. The character j gives us the date, while the S character gives us the appropriate suffix (st, nd, rd, or th). As we said, somewhat demonic, rather than mnemonic.

Our second call to date() has as its input parameter the string "g:ia", which in fact gives us a time rather than a date, and things are no better here on the mnemonic front. The g gives us the current hour using a 12-hour format, *without* leading zeros, the i gives us the minutes in the current hour, *with* a leading zero if required, and the a appends a lowercase am or pm, as appropriate. The colon (:) is a literal value used to separate hours and minutes in the output.

See the end-of-chapter **References** for a link to a description of all the many ways you can describe the kind of output you want from the PHP date() function.

8.4.2   Generating and Displaying the Output from welcome.php

As we mentioned above, simply browsing to the welcome.php page on the CD-ROM will *not* allow you to view the PHP output in the resulting XHTML document. You have to serve it by a PHP-aware web server on your computer. However, you will be able to view this particular page from this link to the book's website:

http://cs.smu.ca/~webbook/cdrom/web08/welcome.php

If you view this page now, you should see something like what is shown in Figure 8.2. But, if you then choose the "view source" option of your browser, you will *not* see any PHP code. The XHTML markup resulting from the execution of the PHP code will appear as the source of the web page. As mentioned before, this ensures that clients cannot access the PHP code, which may reveal confidential information about the data stored on the server.

8.5   PHP Development and Testing

As with any programming language, writing PHP code will not always go smoothly. You will occasionally discover, sadly, that your code does not do what you wanted it to do. Or, even worse, it may cause your page to "crash" and not display properly or not display at all.

PHP does not as yet have a built-in debugger, so if there are semantic errors that simply cause your script to behave improperly you may find the old-fashioned debugging method of inserting output statements to display variable values at various execution points very helpful.

On the other hand, when you are beginning to program in PHP you may find that your problems tend to be syntax-related issues, and here PHP can be quite helpful by displaying an appropriate error message. For example, suppose that in line 12 of Figure 8.1 you change the name of the `date()` function to `datf()`. Then, instead of the complete page, including the welcome message and date shown in Figure 8.2, you will likely see only a partially displayed page, and then an error message something like the following:

```
Fatal error: Call to undefined function datf() in welcome.php on
line 12
```

This happens because you asked the PHP processor to call a function that it does not recognize, and the result is that the page rendering stops at that point. This can be frustrating, but you should regard it as a good thing, since you would not want your pages showing up on your users' screens with incorrect and potentially embarrassing information on them. It's much better to catch such problems at the development stage, and when PHP is set up to show us such errors we should take advantage of the assistance it provides. See the end-of-chapter **What Else ...** section for more on PHP error levels and error reporting.

8.6   Incorporating the Welcome Message into Our Home Page

We are now ready to incorporate our welcome message, along with the current date and time, into the home page for our Nature's Source website, as shown in Figure 8.3. As you can see from that figure, this information appears at the upper right of the page, next to the logo.

In order to see how this is accomplished, we need to look at the following two files:

- Our revised index file, now `index.php` rather than `index.html` (because of the embedded PHP code), which is shown in Figure 8.4

- The new file `banner.php`, which replaces the previous `logo.html`, and is shown in Figure 8.5

If we consider `index.php` from Figure 8.4 first, we note that the file contains two short PHP scripts, one in lines 15–18 and the other in lines 39–41. These scripts

FIGURE 8.3

`graphics/ch08/displayIndexPhp.jpg`
A Firefox browser display of `index.php` containing the welcome message, date, and time from the PHP script output.

contain only calls to the PHP `include()` function that is now being used to perform our "server-side includes," but the presence of these two PHP scripts is the reason we have changed the name of the file from `index.html` to `index.php`. Note that we can use the PHP `include()` function to include either strictly XHTML files, like `mainmenu.html` and `footer.html`, or an XHTML file which itself contains an "embedded" PHP script, like `banner.php`.

If we now look at `banner.php` in Figure 8.5, we see that it contains two `div` elements. The first is just the `div` with `id` value `"logo"` from our previous `logo.html` file. The second `div`, with `id` value `"welcome"`, has the same content we saw in the `body` element of `welcome.php`, except that we changed "The time" to a friendlier "Our time" and changed the header sizes to better accommodate the message location.

```
1    <!DOCTYPE html PUBLIC "-//W3C//DTD XHTML 1.0 Strict//EN"
2        "http://www.w3.org/TR/xhtml1/DTD/xhtml1-strict.dtd">
3    <!-- index.php for the home page of the current Nature's Source web site -->
4    <html xmlns="http://www.w3.org/1999/xhtml">
5      <head>
6        <title>Nature's Source - Canada's largest specialty vitamin store</title>
7        <meta http-equiv="Content-Type" content="text/html;charset=utf-8" />
8        <meta http-equiv="refresh" content="60" />
9        <link rel="stylesheet" type="text/css" href="css/default.css" />
10       <script type="text/javascript" src="scripts/rotate.js"></script>
11       <script type="text/javascript" src="scripts/menu.js"></script>
12     </head>
13     <body onload="startRotation()">
14       <div id="page">
15         <?php
16         include("common/banner.php");
17         include("common/mainmenu.html");
18         ?>
19         <div id="content">
20           <div id="textLeft">
21             <h3>Welcome to Nature's Source: Protecting your health naturally!</h3>
22             <p>Founded in 1998, Nature's Source was created to serve those who
23             use alternative healing methods. Offering only the highest quality
24             vitamins, minerals, supplements &amp; herbal remedies, Nature's
25             Source takes great pride in helping people live healthier, happier
26             lives.</p>
27             <p>Many Companies that talk about Customer Service fail to deliver.
28             Nature's Source exists to truly serve all the needs of their
29             customers. Each location features dedicated on-site therapists
30             along with knowledgeable staff who ensure that every customer
31             receives the best quality information available. Continuing
32             Education seminars are a regular event at Nature's Source.</p>
33           </div>
34           <div id="image">
35             <img id="placeholder" src="" alt="Healthy Lifestyle"
36             width="280px" height="160px" />
37           </div>
38         </div>
39         <?php
40         include("common/footer.html");
41         ?>
42       </div>
43     </body>
44   </html>
```

FIGURE 8.4

cdrom/web08/nature/index.php
Our new index file, index.php.

```
1   <!-- banner.php -->
2   <div id="logo">
3     <img src="images/naturelogo.gif" alt="Nature's Source"
4     width="608px" height="90px" />
5   </div>
6   <div id="welcome">
7     <h3>Welcome!</h3>
8     <?php
9     echo "<h5>It's ".date("l, F jS").".<br />";
10    echo "Our time is ".date('g:ia').".</h5>";
11    ?>
12  </div>
```

FIGURE 8.5

cdrom/web08/nature/common/banner.php
Our new banner file, which extends the previous `logo.html`.

We do not show it in the text, but we have slightly modified the `default.css` file for this version of the site to style the new contents of `banner.php`. These changes include adding a `float: left` rule to div#logo, adding a new style called div#welcome for that `div`, which also contains a `float: left` rule, and adding a `clear: left` rule to div#mainMenu. The net effect is the Welcome! greeting, with the date and time, that we see in Figure 8.3. Note that because `banner.php` is included in each page that is linked to from the home page, both the logo and the welcome appear on each of our site's pages.

8.6.1 Refreshing a Page to Keep the Time Current

There is one other aspect to our current home page that we need to point out, but which is not apparent from Figure 8.3. Each time a user browses to this page, or manually refreshes the page, the PHP script will run and the current time will be displayed as part of the welcome message.

However, unless the user refreshes the page every minute—something the average user is unlikely to do—the displayed time will very quickly no longer be the *current* time. This may or may not be a big deal on the home page, since one would expect that within a minute or so a typical user would probably click on one of our links and browse to another page on our site. However, there may well be one or more pages on which a user *would* linger, and it would be nice if the time could be kept current on that page while the user is still on it.

Fortunately there is a simple way to accomplish this.[2] Our `index.php` file, shown in Figure 8.4, contains a second `meta` element in line 8:

```
<meta http-equiv="refresh" content="60" />
```

This `meta` element instructs the browser to "refresh" (or "reload," if you like) the page every 60 seconds, thus accomplishing our goal of updating the time every minute and keeping it current.

Note that this `meta` element is not in any of the included files, so it will have to be inserted into any page that displays our welcome message, if we want that page to be refreshed in the same way.

8.7   Implementing the Server-Side Functionality of Our Feedback Form

Now we continue putting PHP to work in the ongoing development of our e-commerce website. We next implement the remaining part of our website's feedback facility. This will involve sending e-mails (to both the business and the client), preparing a browser display for immediate confirmation to the client, and storing information on disk (on the server) for future reference if required.

Recall that we created the feedback form itself in Chapter 5 and then, in Chapter 6, we provided data validation support for that form using JavaScript. However, when a user "submitted" the feedback form, all that happened was the data validation; there was no actual "submission" or any other communication between the customer and the business.

Client-side JavaScript programming does not allow us either to send e-mails or to upload information to the server, and there is good reason for such restrictions. If such activities were permitted, malicious web programmers could entice clients to their websites and when those users downloaded web pages from such sites, those pages could contain JavaScript that would use the client computer to send out spam, worms, viruses, or other kinds of malware. The origin of such e-mails could only lead forensic investigators back to the client's computer, and it might be very difficult to establish the true origin of such unwelcome software. Hence, any e-mails that are triggered by a user's interaction are best sent directly from the web server. This is

---

[2]And also more complicated, but more elegant, ways using something called *AJAX*, for example, but that is beyond the scope of our discussion.

achieved through server-side programming. So, we will now use our feedback form to demonstrate the following:

- How to upload to the web server the information that has been entered into a form

- How to send e-mail based on that information

- How to confirm the submission to the user with a browser display based on the submitted data

- How to store the uploaded information on the web server for future reference

8.7.1 What Happens When the User Clicks Send Feedback

Figure 8.6 shows a sample feedback form all filled out and ready to be submitted. When the user clicks the **Send Feedback** button, the first thing that happens is the

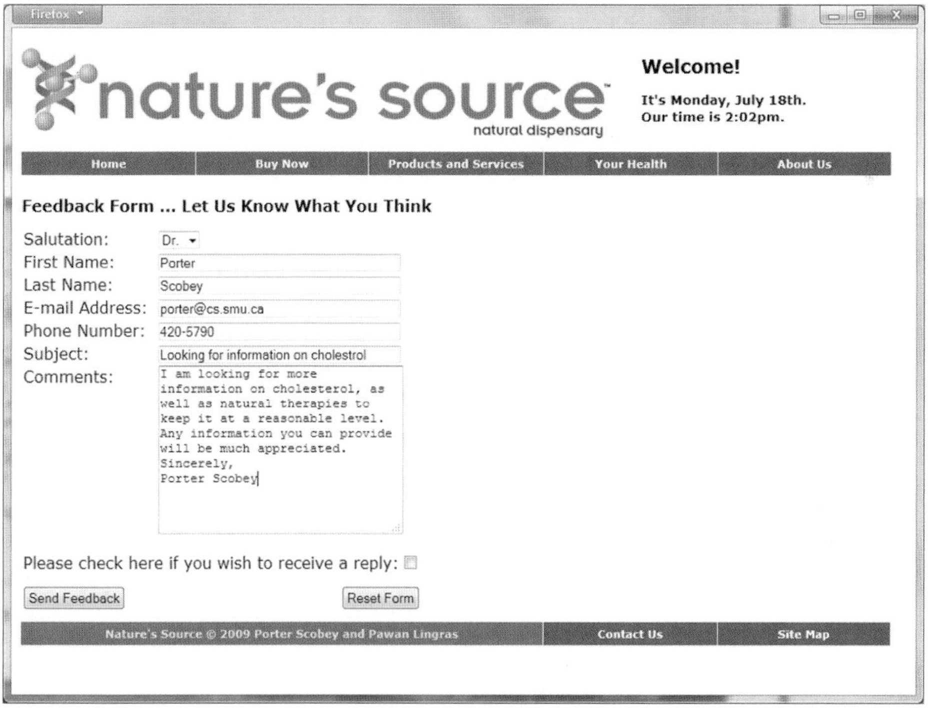

FIGURE 8.6

graphics/ch08/displayFeedbackHtml.jpg
A Firefox browser display of feedback.php.

validation of the form data via JavaScript. If there is a problem with any of the data items being validated by JavaScript, the form data will not be submitted. Instead, you will get a message of the type seen in Chapter 6 and you will have to correct the offending data item.

If all of the data is valid, the data from the form is then sent to the server for processing by PHP. Then the following four things happen:

- The PHP script sends an e-mail message to the business, like the one shown in Figure 8.9.

- The PHP script also sends a second e-mail message to the client as a permanent confirmation of the feedback submission. This consists of a message like the one shown in Figure 8.10.

- The user also gets an immediate browser-display confirmation that the feedback submission has been received, which is shown in Figure 8.11.

- Finally, a copy of the e-mail message shown in Figure 8.9 is appended to a textfile of all user feedback submissions from this form on the web server. Note that the date of submission has been prepended to the message stored on disk. This version of the message looks like the sample shown in Figure 8.12.

In the following sections we discuss in detail how each of these items is constructed and sent to its required destination. But first we need to talk about uploading the form data.

8.7.2 Uploading the Feedback Form Data from the Client to the Server

We need to revisit our feedback form from Chapter 6. Figure 8.7 shows the opening `form` tag in the file `feedback.php` from the `web08/nature` directory on your CD-ROM (the revised form of `feedback.html` from Chapter 6). Note carefully the form of the value of the `onsubmit` attribute. Even though `validateContactForm()` is a value-returning function that returns a boolean value, the keyword `return` is still required in this context. The `action` attribute of the `form` element no longer has an empty string as its value. This value is now a call to the PHP script `processFeedback.php`, which lives on the server (in `web08/nature/scripts`), and which will process the data that is sent to the server from our form.

The next (multi-part) question is this: How does the data get to the server, where does it show up on the server, and how do we access it there? There are actually several possible answers to these questions, but we have opted to use the

```
                <form id="contactForm" onsubmit="return validateContactForm()"
                action="scripts/processFeedback.php" method="post">
```

FIGURE 8.7

cdrom/web08/nature/feedback.php (excerpt)
The revised **form** tag in **feedback.html**, which invokes a PHP script for processing when the input data is valid.

recommended approach. See the What Else ... section at the end of this chapter for further details.

Note in Figure 8.7 the **method** attribute of the **form** tag, with its value of **"post"**. The **post** method is not the only one we could use to send data to the server, but it's the one generally recommended for submitting data from a form.

When we use the **post** method to send the data, the form data values appear on the server in an array variable named **$_POST**. We will discuss PHP variables and arrays in more detail later. For now, simply note that *all* PHP variable names, including array variable names, begin with a **$**, and for a special kind of variable called a *superglobal*, the **$** is followed by an underscore (**_**). **$_POST** is one of those PHP superglobals.

In this context we do not use an integer index to access a value in the **$_POST** array. Instead, we can think of the names that we gave the form controls in our XHTML document as index values that provide access to the data values input by the user and sent to the server from those form controls. For example, **$_POST['firstName']** would have the value **"Porter"** if the name **Porter**[3] had been entered into the input control (textbox) whose **name** attribute had the value **"firstName"**.

8.7.3 An Overview of the PHP Code that Processes the Feedback Form Data

It's now time to look at the PHP code that makes all of this possible: the two e-mails, the browser display confirming the submission, and the submission logging recorded on the server. The PHP script is in the file **processFeedback.php** from the **web08/nature/scripts** subdirectory on your CD-ROM, and is shown in Figure 8.8.

The script essentially consists of string manipulations to dynamically create the two e-mail messages, the web page reply, and the log message. The message is slightly

---

[3]Although "Porter" is usually a last name, it happens to be the first name of one of the authors. As if there wasn't already enough to confuse you ....

```php
1    <?php
2    //processFeedback.php
3
4    //Construct the message to be sent to the business
5    $messageToBusiness =
6        "From: ".$_POST['salute']." "
7            .$_POST['firstName']." "
8            .$_POST['lastName']."\r\n" .
9        "E-mail address: ".$_POST['email']."\r\n".
10       "Phone number: ".$_POST['phone']."\r\n".
11       "Subject: ".$_POST['subject']."\r\n".
12       $_POST['message']."\r\n";
13
14   //Send the e-mail feedback message to the business (but here, to the webbook site)
15   $headerToBusiness = "From: $_POST[email]\r\n";
16   mail("webbook@cs.smu.ca", $_POST['subject'], $messageToBusiness, $headerToBusiness);
17
18   //Construct the confirmation message to be e-mailed to the client
19   $messageToClient =
20       "Dear ".$_POST['salute']." ".$_POST['lastName'].":\r\n".
21       "The following message was received from you by Nature's Source:\r\n\r\n".
22       $messageToBusiness.
23       "-----------------------\r\nThank you for the feedback and your patronage.\r\n" .
24       "The Nature's Source Team\r\n-----------------------\r\n";
25   if ($_POST['reply'])
26       $messageToClient .= "P.S. We will contact you shortly with more information.";
27
28   //Send the confirmation message to the client
29   $headerToClient = "From: webbook@cs.smu.ca\r\n";
30   mail($_POST['email'], "Re: ".$_POST['subject'], $messageToClient, $headerToClient);
31
32   //Transform the confirmation message to the client into XHTML format and display it
33   $display = str_replace("\r\n", "<br />\r\n", $messageToClient);
34   $display =
35       "<html><head><title>Your Message</title></head><body><tt>".
36       $display.
37       "</tt></body></html>";
38   echo $display;
39
40   //Log the message in a file called feedback.txt on the web server
41   $fileVar = fopen("../data/feedback.txt", "a")
42       or die("Error: Could not open the log file.");
43   fwrite($fileVar, "\n----------------------------------------------------------\n")
44       or die("Error: Could not write to the log file.");
45   fwrite($fileVar, "Date received: ".date("jS \of F, Y \a\\t H:i:s\n"))
46       or die("Error: Could not write to the log file.");
47   fwrite($fileVar, $messageToBusiness)
48       or die("Error: Could not write to the log file.");
49   ?>
50
```

FIGURE 8.8

cdrom/web08/nature/scripts/processFeedback.php
PHP code to process feedback in processFeedback.php.

different in each case, depending on the recipient and where it is to be sent. Note that we have inserted comments to separate the various logical portions of the script. The two forward slashes (//) that we used in JavaScript to give us a single-line comment are available for the same purpose in PHP as well, as are the /* ... */ delimiters for multi-line comments.

8.7.4 Building the Feedback Message to the Business with PHP String Literals and the $_POST Array Values

In this section we discuss the code segment in lines 4–12 of Figure 8.8 and the content of the corresponding e-mail message of Figure 8.9.

from porter@cs.smu.ca

subject **Looking for information on cholesterol**   10:36 AM

to webbook@cs.smu.ca

```
From: Dr. Porter Scobey
E-mail address: porter@cs.smu.ca
Phone number: 420-5790
Subject: Looking for information on cholesterol
I am looking for more
information on cholesterol, as
well as natural therapies to
keep it at a reasonable level.
Any information you can provide
will be much appreciated.
Sincerely,
Porter Scobey
```

FIGURE 8.9

graphics/ch08/displayProcessFeedbackPhpEmailBusiness.jpg
A Thunderbird®e-mail display showing the e-mail received by the business as a result of the form being processed by processFeedback.php.

Our script in Figure 8.8 begins in lines 4–12 by constructing the basic message that is sent via e-mail to the business and that forms the basis of all the messages we will build:

```
4    $messageToBusiness =
5        "From: ".$_POST['salute']." "
6              .$_POST['firstName']." "
7              .$_POST['lastName']."\r\n" .
8        "E-mail address: ".$_POST['email']."\r\n".
9        "Phone number: ".$_POST['phone']."\r\n".
10       "Subject: ".$_POST['subject']."\r\n".
11       $_POST['message']."\r\n";
```

This message is constructed using the text values from the **input** controls of our XHTML feedback form, which are available as values of the **$_POST** array, as discussed earlier. This is where we see the importance of giving each input control in our form a **name** attribute with a meaningful value. For example, the input control with the **name** attribute value **"email"** received the e-mail address entered by the user and that address now shows up on the server as the value of **$_POST['email']**.[4]

The complete result that is assigned to **$messageToBusiness** is formed by joining the values from the **$_POST** array to the necessary "infrastructure" text items, such as **"From: "**, **"E-mail address: "**, and so on. We are, in effect, putting e-mail header information in front of the message text, because we are, after all, constructing a complete e-mail.

Once the message has been constructed by joining all the required text items with the period (.) concatenation operator, we then assign the completed result to the variable **$messageToBusiness**.

One other thing: Note that in constructing this variable's contents we have placed the string **"\r\n"** at the ends of lines to ensure that a proper line break will occur at the necessary places on most any platform where the message might have to be displayed.[5]

---

[4]This could also be **$_POST["email"]**, but using the two different kinds of quotes in the way we have done in this code makes the code much more readable.

[5]Some platforms may require *both* \r *and* \n, while others may require just one of the two. On any platform requiring only one of the two, the other of the two should simply be ignored.

8.7.5 Sending the Feedback Message to the Business with PHP's `mail()` Function

In this section we discuss the code segment

```
14  //Send the e-mail feedback message to the business (but here, to the webbook site)
15  $headerToBusiness = "From: $_POST[email]\r\n";
16  mail("webbook@cs.smu.ca", $_POST['subject'], $messageToBusiness, $headerToBusiness);
```

from lines 14–16 of Figure 8.8, which deal with the sending of the e-mail to the business seen in Figure 8.9.

We are now ready to send our message via e-mail. The e-mail is sent using the PHP built-in function `mail()`. The `mail()` function creates a message based on the *Simple Mail Transfer Protocol* (SMTP) specifications. SMTP is an Internet standard for sending e-mail. The `mail()` function creates an SMTP-conforming e-mail message using the following parameters:

- The e-mail address of the recipient

- The subject of the message

- The message itself

- Additional strings that you may want to be appended to the header, such as `From:`, `CC:` (Carbon Copy), or `BCC:` (Blind Carbon Copy) fields. These fields have to be separated from the other fields, and from each other, by the $\backslash r \backslash n$ sequence.

Under normal circumstances the business would be the recipient of this e-mail message, but here we are using the e-mail address of the book's website as a temporary placeholder, since our business does not yet have an actual e-mail address. The subject for the e-mail is whatever the client entered into that field of the form, so it is available from `$_POST['subject']`. The message we want to send is the one we constructed above and is now the content of the variable `$messageToBusiness`.

The only thing still missing is any additional header lines that we may wish to add. We choose to add just a `"From: "` field by supplying the variable defined in line 15 as the fourth (optional) parameter to the `mail()` function:

```
$headerToBusiness = "From: $_POST[email]\r\n";
```

Although this fourth parameter is optional, it is a good idea to include it with at least a `"From: "` field, because this will indicate, in the recipient's mail program, who *sent* the message. This information is in the body of the message as well, of course, but without this "header" information, the mail message may appear, in the recipient's mail program, to have been sent by a web server and may run the risk of being deleted or sent to a spam folder.

Also, there is quite a bit more going on in the code of line 15 shown above than first meets the eye. In particular, there is one new concept and one potential "gotcha."

The new concept is *variable interpolation*. What we mean by this is that in the string

```
"From: $_POST[email]\r\n"
```

the variable `$_POST[email]` is actually *replaced by its value*, so it's the value that shows up inside the double-quoted string, not the variable name. This is the process of *variable interpolation*, and though it happens inside double-quoted strings in PHP, it does *not* happen inside single-quoted strings.

The potential "gotcha" is this: Variable interpolation works for an ordinary variable as well as for an array variable, which is what we have in this situation. But because it *is* an array variable, PHP requires, in this context, that we omit the single quotes around `email` that we have used elsewhere in this script. You need to store this tidbit of information away for future reference!

Now that we have all four required parameters for the `mail()` function, we can issue the function call that sends the e-mail message to the business, which we do in line 16:

```
mail("webbook@cs.smu.ca", $_POST['subject'], $messageToBusiness,
$headerToBusiness);
```

This results in the "business" receiving the e-mail message shown in Figure 8.9.[6]

8.7.6   Modifying the Previous Message to the Business to Get One Suitable for the Client

In this section we discuss the code segment

```
18   //Construct the confirmation message to be e-mailed to the client
19   $messageToClient =
```

---

[6]Of course, PHP also has to be able to access the e-mail system on your server, which is another aspect of PHP configuration.

```
20        "Dear ".$_POST['salute']." ".$_POST['lastName'].":\r\n".
21        "The following message was received from you by Nature's Source:\r\n\r\n".
22        $messageToBusiness.
23        "----------------------\r\nThank you for the feedback and your patronage.\r\n" .
24        "The Nature's Source Team\r\n----------------------\r\n";
25    if ($_POST['reply'])
26        $messageToClient .= "P.S. We will contact you shortly with more information.";
```

from lines 18–26 of Figure 8.8, which deal with the construction of the e-mail to the
client seen in Figure 8.10.

This part of the script builds an additional e-mail message, based on the previous
one sent to the business. This time the message is a confirmation to the client. We
create this confirmation message by first *prepending* the message with additional

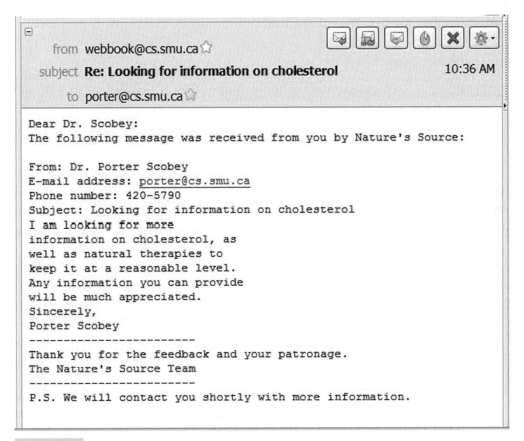

FIGURE 8.10

graphics/ch08/displayProcessFeedbackPhpEmailClient.jpg
A Thunderbird e-mail display showing the e-mail received by the client as a result of the form being
processed by processFeedback.php.

text that includes a greeting to the user using the salutation chosen by the user when filling out the form and the user's last name. We finish by *appending* a string containing a thank-you message and a company "signature."

Our feedback form has also given the user the option of asking for a reply by checking the appropriate form checkbox whose `name` attribute has the value `"reply"`. Thus in our PHP script we can treat the variable `$_POST['reply']` as a boolean variable and use its value to tell us whether the user wants a reply. This variable will have the value `yes` if the checkbox has been checked and will be empty (not present at all) if the user has not checked the box. We use an `if`-statement to make this test.[7] If it has indeed been checked, we append another string to our e-mail that informs the user that a reply will be forthcoming.

The appending is done with the special operator `.=` as follows:

```
$messageToClient .= "P.S. We will contact you shortly with more information.";
```

This is equivalent to the following:

```
$messageToClient = $messageToClient .
"P.S. We will contact you shortly with more information.";
```

Thus you can see that the operator `.=` is analogous to other similar operators like `+=`, `*=`, and so on, that appear in most of the C-based languages, such as JavaScript.

8.7.7   Sending the Confirmation Message to the Client with `mail()`

In the code segment

```
28   //Send the confirmation message to the client
29   $headerToClient = "From: webbook@cs.smu.ca\r\n";
30   mail($_POST['email'], "Re: ".$_POST['subject'], $messageToClient, $headerToClient);
```

from lines 28–30 of Figure 8.8 we create the header for sending to the client the e-mail message we constructed in the previous section, and then call `mail()` to actually send it.

There is nothing new going on here, but we should mention the following slight variation: For this version of the e-mail the subject is modified by preceding it with the string `"Re: "` just to help distinguish it more quickly if, during testing, you are sending both e-mails to the same address, as we were doing in our own testing.

---

[7]The syntax of the `if`-statement in PHP is the same as it is in any C-based programming language, and we have already seen that syntax in JavaScript.

8.7.8 Returning the Browser Display for Immediate Confirmation of Feedback Submission to the User

In this section we discuss the code segment

```
32  //Transform the confirmation message to the client into XHTML format and display it
33  $display = str_replace("\r\n", "<br />\r\n", $messageToClient);
34  $display =
35      "<html><head><title>Your Message</title></head><body><tt>".
36      $display.
37      "</tt></body></html>";
38  echo $display;
```

from lines 32–38 of Figure 8.8, which produces the browser display for immediate feedback to the client seen in Figure 8.11, and which contains exactly the same textual content as the e-mail message to the client.

However, to convert that plain text into XHTML markup appropriate for display in a browser there are at least two things we need to do.

```
Firefox ▼                                                    _ □ X

Dear Dr. Scobey:
The following message was received from you by Nature's Source:

From: Dr. Porter Scobey
E-mail address: porter@cs.smu.ca
Phone number: 420-5790
Subject: Looking for information on cholestrol
I am looking for more information on cholesterol, as well as natural
therapies to keep it at a reasonable level. Any information you can
provide will be much appreciated.
Sincerely,
Porter Scobey


-----------------------
Thank you for the feedback and your patronage.
The Nature's Source Team
-----------------------
```

FIGURE 8.11

graphics/ch08/displayProcessFeedbackPhpBrowser.jpg
A Firefox browser display of processing from `processFeedback.php` showing confirmation to the user that the feedback form input has in fact been received.

First of all, we need to add to each instance of $\backslash r \backslash n$ the XHTML tag `<br/>` to get line breaks in the right places when the page is displayed in the browser. This we accomplish with the PHP function `str_replace()` like this:

```
$display = str_replace("\r\n", "<br />\r\n", $messageToClient);
```

The `str_replace()` function takes three parameters. The first parameter is the "old" string that needs to be replaced; in this case that is (`"\r\n"`). The second parameter is the new string that will replace the old string; in this case that is `"<br />\r\n"`. Finally, the third parameter is the original containing string that is to be modified by the replacement; in this case that is the string contained in the variable `$messageToClient`. The string that is returned by the call to the function `str_replace()` is stored in a varible called `$display`.

Second, we add some XHTML markup to the contents of `$display` to turn it into an XHTML document:[8]

```
$display =
    "<html><head><title>Your Message</title></head><body><tt>" .
    $display.
    "</tt></body></html>";
```

The final value of `$display` is "echoed" back to the browser for display, resulting in the web page shown in Figure 8.11.

8.7.9   Saving the User's Feedback on the Server with PHP File Output

In this section we discuss the final code segment

```
40  //Log the message in a file called feedback.txt on the web server
41  $fileVar = fopen("../data/feedback.txt", "a")
42      or die("Error: Could not open the log file.");
43  fwrite($fileVar, "\n----------------------------------------------------------\n")
44      or die("Error: Could not write to the log file.");
45  fwrite($fileVar, "Date received: ".date("jS \of F, Y \a\\t H:i:s\n"))
46      or die("Error: Could not write to the log file.");
47  fwrite($fileVar, $messageToBusiness)
48      or die("Error: Could not write to the log file.");
```

of our `processFeedback.php` script, from lines 40–48. This final part of the script involves writing the user's feedback to a file on the server.

---

[8]We should note, however, that this is *not* a *valid* XHTML document because we have not taken the trouble in our script to insert the necessary additional "infrastructure" markup to make it so. Our only excuse is the transitory nature of the page.

```
1   From: Mr. Pawan Lingras
2   E-mail address: pawan@cs.smu.ca
3   Phone number: 5798
4   Subject: Hello
5   Thank you for providing me with an opportunity
6   to look at various health alternatives. I was
7   wondering if you had some products that will
8   help me reduce my cholesterol.
9
10  Thank you for the feedback and your patronage.
11  --
12  Naturally Yours! team
13  P.S. We will contact you shortly with more information.
```

FIGURE 8.12

cdrom/web08/nature/data/feedback.txt
The feedback message, with date of submission, as it is stored on the server in a log file called
feedback.txt in the subdirectory nature/data.

A distinguishing feature of server-side programming is its ability to store information obtained from the user on the server, something that cannot be done with client-side technology like JavaScript. This information storage can be achieved in at least two ways:

- By placing the information directly into a file on disk

- By setting up communication with some kind of database and storing the data in the form required by that database

We will be looking at the database option in the following two chapters. In this section, we will look at the simpler case of file storage.

The feedback submitted by the user has already been sent to our business via e-mail. However, it is also a good idea for our business to log all client feedback in a file on the server, so that we have it all in one place and can go through it at a later date to process it in some way, if we wish. We will store all user feedback in a file called feedback.txt in a subdirectory called data.

The first step in any input to, or output from, a file in a PHP script usually consists of opening the file. We accomplish this with a built-in function called fopen(). Typically this function takes two parameters:

- The name of a file or a URL containing the name of a file

- The mode in which the file is to be opened

and returns a file variable that can be used to work with the file once it has been opened.

The mode depends on the type of operation(s) we want to perform on the file once it has been opened. In our case, we are opening the file `data/feedback.txt` with the mode value `"a"` (line 41). This mode means that the file will be opened in "append mode," which in turn means that any new writing we do will take place *after* the existing last character of the file. In other words, we're adding to the end of the file. If the file does not exist, it will be created and then opened for writing. See Table 8.1 in the end-of-chapter **What Else ...** section for a list of other modes that can be used for opening a file, and further discussion of PHP I/O.

Let's get back to our usage of this function. The value returned by the function is stored in a variable called `$fileVar`. From this point on, we can refer to the file by using the variable name `$fileVar`, in a read or write operation for example.

We also have another interesting (and somewhat scary) appendage to the function call (line 42):

```
or die("Error: Could not open the log file.")
```

This is actually just a handy way of saying that if the function returns an error, terminate the script after displaying the message shown in the argument of the `die()` function.

Because we have opened the file for writing, we can use the function `fwrite()` to write to the file. The function `fwrite()` takes two parameters:

- The first parameter is the file variable returned by the call to `fopen()`. In our case, this is the variable `$fileVar`.

- The second parameter is the string that you want to write to the file.

Now, of course, we want to write to the log file the message string stored in the variable `$messageToClient`. However, before writing the message itself we want to write a line of dashes to signal the start of a new log entry and then the date of this entry, and only *then* the actual message. Thus we have three calls to `fwrite()` (lines 43–48), and, as before, we use the function `die()` to terminate the program with an error message if any one of the writing operations fails for any reason.

This completes our discussion of the server-side processing of our feedback form.

8.8   Revising the Implementation of Our BMI Calculator

In our discussions in the previous sections, all of our server-side processing was done by a PHP script contained in the single file `processFeedback.php`. In this and the following sections, we will learn how to write programmer-defined PHP functions that may be stored in a separate file and then included into our main "driver" script from that file. Breaking up even a relatively small script in this way makes it more modular and helps understand error tracking and updating if required. In other words, it makes "script maintenance" much easier.

So, let us revisit our BMI calculator from Chapter 6. That version of the calculator was implemented using JavaScript. It accepted the user's height and weight and displayed the user's body mass index after a short calculation. We gave the user the option of getting a detailed BMI report, and another option of receiving it by e-mail. Since we were working entirely within the limitations of JavaScript, we displayed the BMI information with the help of a JavaScript pop-up window and omitted the sending of any e-mails.

In this chapter, we will retain the JavaScript data validation, which is best done on the client side to avoid unnecessary and potentially harmful data being transferred to the server. However, once we are certain the data is valid we will transfer that data to the server and perform the BMI computations on the server side, with PHP functions that are stored in a file separate from our main script. Then we will send out an e-mail if requested, as well as return a browser display of the BMI calculation result. We will also implement the e-mail functionality this time by using XHTML encoded messages, rather than plain text.

Thus our remaining objectives of this exercise are:

- To learn how to write programmer-defined PHP functions, store them in a file of their own, and include that file into a main "driver" script where they can then be used

- To learn how to do numerical calculations in PHP

- To learn how to send XHTML-encoded e-mail messages

8.8.1 What Happens When the User Clicks Compute your BMI

A browser display of our BMI form is shown in Figure 8.13, where we have entered reasonable values for the form fields.[9] Note that we have chosen one unit from the metric system (kilograms, for weight) and one non-metric unit (inches, for height), just to show that it doesn't matter.

---

[9]Please note, once again, that you cannot proceed with the computations unless you have installed PHP on your computer and the form page is being served by a server on your computer that is PHP-aware. Failing this, you can try the form from the book's website.

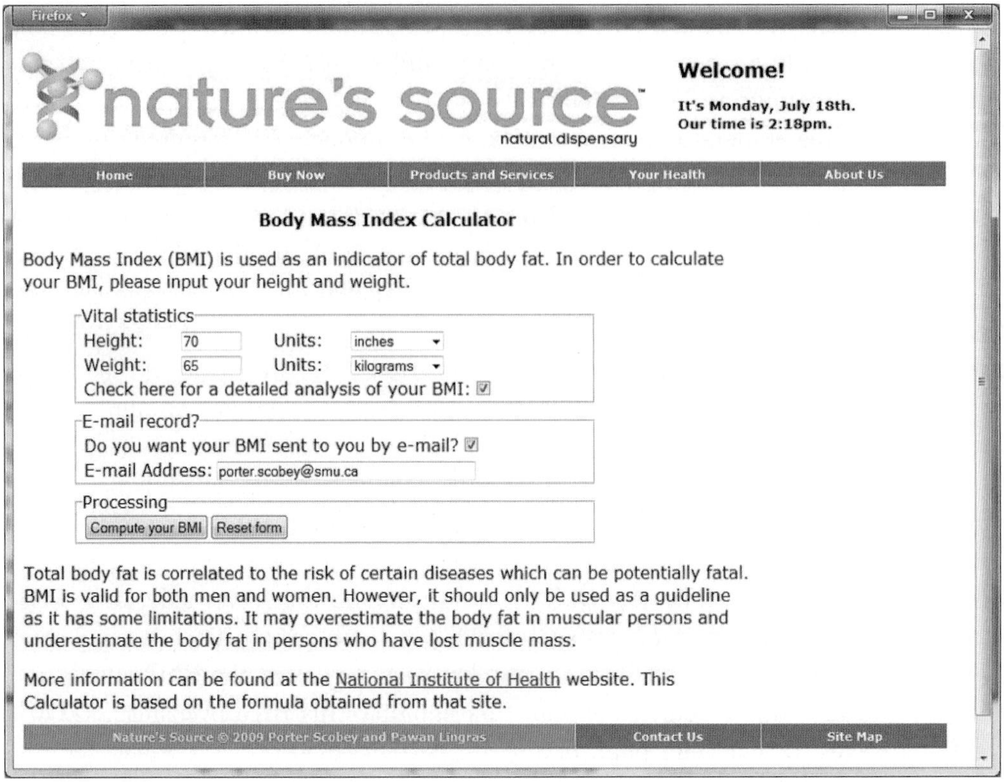

FIGURE 8.13
graphics/ch08/displayBmiHtml.jpg
A Firefox browser display of bmi.php.

As with our feedback form, when the user clicks the **Compute your BMI** button on the BMI calculator form, the first thing that happens is the validation of the form data. Once again, note the keyword **return** in front of the call to **validateInput()** in the value of the **onsubmit** attribute.

Only if all the input data is valid will the form data be uploaded to the server for processing. Otherwise a JavaScript-generated error will be displayed in a pop-up window, and the user will have to correct the invalid data and re-submit. Remember that in this version of our BMI calculator, all that JavaScript does is validate the data; all other processing is done by PHP on the server.

If all of the input data *is* valid, the data from the form is sent to the server. Then the following two actions are performed by our PHP script:

- Either a simple report, or a more detailed report, containing the user's BMI value is constructed and displayed in the browser. To get the more detailed report, the user must check the box indicating that choice on the form. An example of the detailed version is shown in Figure 8.14. In this case, the user has also checked the box requesting an e-mail report, as the last line of the display indicates.

■ If the user has requested it by checking the corresponding checkbox, an e-mail message containing the chosen BMI report is sent as well. An example of the e-mail version of the detailed report is shown in Figure 8.15. Note that this e-mail message is in HTML form, not just a plain text e-mail. We will discuss the creation of such messages shortly.[10]

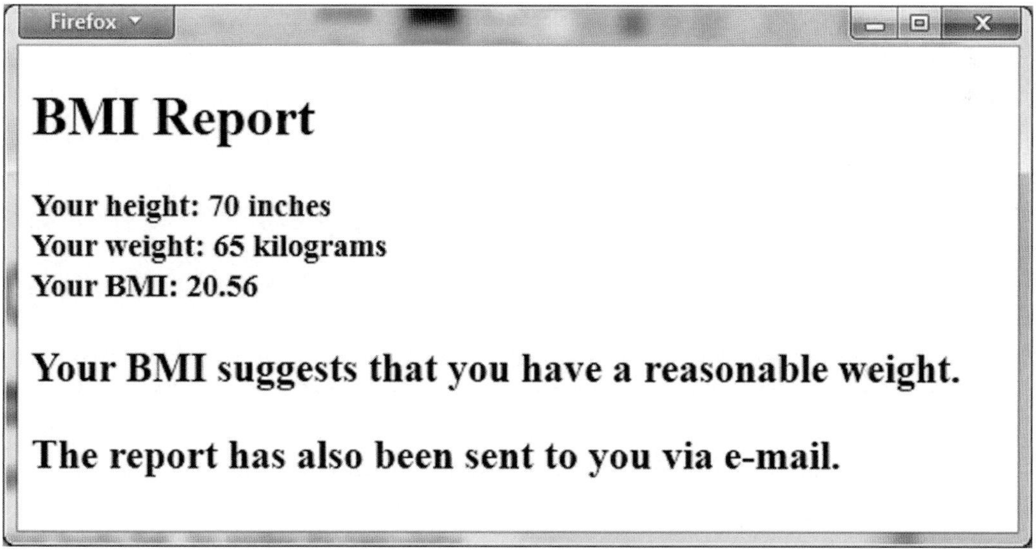

FIGURE 8.14

graphics/ch08/displayProcessBMIPhpBrowser.jpg
A Firefox browser display of processing from processBMI.php.

---

[10]If you try the form yourself from the book's website, for example, and cannot find the e-mail in your INBOX, you should check your SPAM box. E-mail messages that are coded using XHTML are subjected to stricter spam filtering scrutiny. The problem is further exacerbated by the fact that the sender address may not match the server that is sending the e-mail message, which is yet another reason for the spam filter to be suspicious. This is one of the curses of the proliferation of e-mail messages. You want to make sure that the e-mail is as user-specific as possible, so that the spam filter does not suspect a mass e-mailing. Also, if you experiment with the BMI form many times, a spam filter may suspect that an automatic mailer is trying to bombard you with multiple copies of the mail and start blocking the message.

FIGURE 8.15
graphics/ch08/displayProcessBMIPhpEmail.jpg
E-mail received by the client as a result of processing from processBMI.php.

In the following sections, we discuss in detail the script that makes the decisions described in the above list and performs the required actions. But first, for the sake of completeness, let's review the uploading of our BMI form data.

8.8.2   Uploading the BMI Form Data from the Client to the Server

Figure 8.16 shows the opening form tag of the BMI form in the file bmi.php from the web08/nature/scripts subdirectory on your CD-ROM (the revised version of bmi.html from Chapter 6). It has also been modified to include a value for the action

```
26          <form id="bmiForm" onsubmit="return validateInput()"
27          action="scripts/processBMI.php" method="post">
```

FIGURE 8.16
cdrom/web08/nature/bmi.php (excerpt)
The revised form tag form that invokes a PHP script for processing bmi.php.

attribute of the form, which is the PHP script stored in the file `processBMI.php` on the server.

Note that we are again using `method="post"`, the recommended form data upload method. So, once again, the form data will be available to our PHP script on the server as values of the PHP array `$_POST`.

As we will see shortly, our complete PHP script on this occasion is actually split over two files—`processBMI.php` and `bmiCalculate.php`—but only our higher-level "driver" script in `processBMI.php` appears as the value of the `action` attribute, since the driver script itself takes care of the necessary access to the other script file.

8.8.3 An Overview of the PHP Code that Processes the BMI Form Data

Let us begin by looking at our PHP "driver" script in the file `processBMI.php`, which is shown in Figure 8.17.

Practicing "Information Hiding" via Server-Side File Inclusion in PHP

Note first of all that in line 12 of Figure 8.17 we perform a PHP *server-side include*:

```
include 'bmiCalculate.php';
```

This single PHP statement allows us to include the PHP code contained in another file, namely `bmiCalculate.php`, which lives in the same directory (`web08/nature/scripts`). In this case, we are using this server-side include facility to practice "information hiding" and bury (or hide) some implementation details (some programmer-defined functions, in fact) in the included file.

Programmer-Defined Functions in PHP

The "higher-level" functions `detailedMessage()`, `simpleMessage()`, and `mailBMI()` that are called by the "driver" script in `processBMI.php` are defined in the file `bmiCalculate.php`, along with some auxiliary "lower-level" functions used by these higher-level functions but not called directly from our driver script. We will discuss all of these functions in detail in subsequent sections, but before doing that we need to make some general remarks about programmer-defined functions in PHP.

```
1    <!DOCTYPE html PUBLIC "-//W3C//DTD XHTML 1.0 Strict//EN"
2        "http://www.w3.org/TR/xhtml1/DTD/xhtml1-strict.dtd">
3    <!-- processBMI.php -->
4    <html xmlns="http://www.w3.org/1999/xhtml">
5      <head>
6        <title>Your BMI</title>
7        <meta http-equiv="Content-Type" content="text/html;charset=utf-8" />
8      </head>
9      <body>
10       <p>
11       <?php
12       include 'bmiCalculate.php';
13       if ($_POST['details'])
14           $message = detailedMessage($_POST['height'], $_POST['heightUnit'],
15                              $_POST['weight'], $_POST['weightUnit']);
16       else
17           $message = simpleMessage($_POST['height'], $_POST['heightUnit'],
18                              $_POST['weight'], $_POST['weightUnit']);
19       echo $message;
20       if ($_POST['wantMail'])
21       {
22           mailBMI($_POST['email'], $message);
23           echo "<h2>The report has also been sent to you via e-mail.</h2>";
24       }
25       ?>
26       </p>
27     </body>
28   </html>
```

FIGURE 8.17

cdrom/web08/nature/scripts/processBMI.php
PHP code to process BMI in processBMI.php.

The general format of a function definition in PHP is similar to what we saw in JavaScript:

```
function nameOfFunction(parameter_list)
{
    ... PHP code to perform whatever the function does ...
}
```

The first line is the header of the function. It begins with the *keyword* function, which indicates the beginning of the definition of a function. It is followed by the name of the function, which should be well chosen to indicate the purpose of the function.[11] This, in turn, is followed by a comma-separated list of parameters the function should receive when it is called, enclosed in parentheses.

The parameters listed in the parentheses differ from their JavaScript equivalents in that each name has to be preceded by a $ sign. In this respect PHP parameters are just like PHP variables. The PHP code that actually performs the task of the function is, as usual, called the *function body* and is enclosed in the usual pair of braces {···} immediately following the function header.

How the Driver Script Uses the Programmer-Defined Functions It Calls

The rest of the PHP script in `processBMI.php` is relatively simple. The variable `$message` is used to store the XHTML markup that will be used for browser display as well as for e-mailing. If the user has requested a detailed report, the variable `$_POST['details']` will have the value `yes`, and we will assign the value returned by the call to the function `detailedMessage()` to the variable `$message`. On the other hand, if the user did not check the checkbox named `details`, the value of the variable `$_POST['details']` will not exist, which is the same as being `false`. In that case, the variable `$message` will be assigned the value returned by the call to the function `simpleMessage()`. In either case, the variable `$message` is then echoed to a dynamically generated web page such as the one displayed in Figure 8.14, which shows a detailed report that was also sent by e-mail.

The next decision to be made in our `processBMI.php` script is whether to send an e-mail or not. This decision is based on whether the user has checked the checkbox named `wantMail`. If it *is* checked, then the corresponding variable `$_POST['wantMail']` in our PHP script will have the value `yes`. In that case, we call the function `mailBMI()` to build and send an XHTML-encoded e-mail report. The function takes two parameters:

- `$_POST['email']`, which contains the value from the textbox named `email` in the form

- `$message`, which contains the message we just generated by one or the other of the two message-generating function calls

---

[11] Remember that a good rule of thumb to follow when naming functions is this: When the function computes a value, make the name of the function a noun that reflects the kind of value computed, such as `totalCost`. When the function simply performs a task, but does not compute and return a value, give it a name that starts with a verb and indicates the nature of the task performed, such as `displayResults`.

In this case we also echo a message to the end of the dynamically created web page saying that the BMI report has also been sent via e-mail.

This completes our overview discussion of our driver script. In the following sections we proceed with a top-down discussion of the programmer-defined functions called by this driver script, namely `detailedMessage()`, `simpleMessage()`, and `mailBMI()`, as well as the lower-level programmer-defined functions that compute the BMI value.

8.8.4   Building the BMI Report Message with Programmer-Defined PHP Functions

We begin our study of the code from `bmiCalculate.php` by looking at the two functions `detailedMessage()` and `simpleMessage()`, shown in lines 4–32 of Figure 8.18:

```
4   function simpleMessage($height, $heightUnit, $weight, $weightUnit)
5   {
6       $bmi = sprintf("%.2lf", calculateBMI($height, $heightUnit, $weight, $weightUnit));
7       $text =
8           "<h1>BMI Report</h1>".
9           "<h3>Your BMI is ".$bmi.".</h3>";
10      return $text;
11  }
12
13  function detailedMessage($height, $heightUnit, $weight, $weightUnit)
14  {
15      $bmi = sprintf("%.2lf", calculateBMI($height, $heightUnit, $weight, $weightUnit));
16      $text = //"<p> "."<img src = ".
17              //" http://cs.smu.ca/~webbook/cdrom/web08/nature/images/naturelogo.gif ".
18              //" alt = 'Nature's Source Logo' />"."</p>".
19              "<h1>BMI Report</h1>".
20              "<h3>Your height: ".$height." ".$heightUnit."<br />".
21              "Your weight: ".$weight." ".$weightUnit."<br />".
22              "Your BMI: ".$bmi."</h3>";
23      if ($bmi < 18.5)
24          $text .= "<h2>Your BMI suggests that you are underweight.</h2>";
25      else if ($bmi < 25)
26          $text .= "<h2>Your BMI suggests that you have a reasonable weight.</h2>";
27      else if ($bmi < 29)
28          $text .= "<h2>Your BMI suggests that you are overweight.</h2>";
29      else
30          $text .= "<h2>Your BMI suggests that you may be obese.</h2>";
31      return $text;
32  }
```

```
1    <!-- bmiCalculate.php -->
2
3    <?php
4    function simpleMessage($height, $heightUnit, $weight, $weightUnit)
5    {
6       $bmi = sprintf("%.2lf", calculateBMI($height, $heightUnit, $weight, $weightUnit));
7       $text =
8          "<h1>BMI Report</h1>".
9          "<h3>Your BMI is ".$bmi.".</h3>";
10      return $text;
11   }
12
13   function detailedMessage($height, $heightUnit, $weight, $weightUnit)
14   {
15      $bmi = sprintf("%.2lf", calculateBMI($height, $heightUnit, $weight, $weightUnit));
16      $text = //"<p> "."<img src = ".
17              //" http://cs.smu.ca/~webbook/cdrom/web08/nature/images/naturelogo.gif ".
18              //" alt = 'Nature's Source Logo' />"."</p>".
19              "<h1>BMI Report</h1>".
20              "<h3>Your height: ".$height." ".$heightUnit."<br />".
21              "Your weight: ".$weight." ".$weightUnit."<br />".
22              "Your BMI: ".$bmi."</h3>";
23      if ($bmi < 18.5)
24         $text .= "<h2>Your BMI suggests that you are underweight.</h2>";
25      else if ($bmi < 25)
26         $text .= "<h2>Your BMI suggests that you have a reasonable weight.</h2>";
27      else if ($bmi < 29)
28         $text .= "<h2>Your BMI suggests that you are overweight.</h2>";
29      else
30         $text .= "<h2>Your BMI suggests that you may be obese.</h2>";
31      return $text;
32   }
33
34   function inchesToCentimetres($height) { return $height*2.54; }
35   function poundsToKilograms($weight) { return $weight/2.2; }
36
37   function calculateBMI($height, $heightUnit, $weight, $weightUnit)
38   {
39
40      if ($heightUnit == "inches") $height = inchesToCentimetres($height);
41      if ($weightUnit == "pounds") $weight = poundsToKilograms($weight);
42      $height /= 100; //Convert height from centimeters to meters
43      $bmi = $weight/($height*$height);
44      return $bmi;
45   }
46
47   function mailBMI($email, $message)
48   {
49      $header  = 'MIME-Version: 1.0' . "\r\n";
50      $header .= 'Content-type: text/html; charset=iso-8859-1' . "\r\n";
51      $header .= "From: webbook@cs.smu.ca\r\n";
52      mail($email, "BMI report from Nature's Source", $message, $header);
53   }
54   ?>
```

FIGURE 8.18

cdrom/web08/nature/scripts/bmiCalculate.php
PHP programmer-defined functions.

Let's consider the function `detailedMessage()` first. This function takes four parameters: `$height`, `$heightUnit`, `$weight`, and `$weightUnit`. In the body of the function, the very first statement is a call to the built-in function `sprintf()`. We use it here to format the numerical value and return the result as a string.[12] The function can take a variable number of parameters. In our case, we have two:

- The first parameter must be a string indicating a format specification for the number to be printed (the second parameter). We are using the string `"%.2lf"`, which means that the value given by the second parameter should be printed as a floating-point value (real number) with two places after the decimal. For more details on other formatting options, see the end-of-chapter **References**.

- The second argument in our case is the actual value that will be printed. It will be the value returned by a call to another programmer-defined function called `calculateBMI()`, which also takes four parameters, `$height`, `$heightUnit`, `$weight`, and `$weightUnit`, and returns the value of the BMI. We discuss this function in the following section.

The string returned by the call to the function `sprintf()` is stored in a variable called `$bmi` (line 15). The next statement in the function `detailedMessage()` (lines 16–22) builds the XHTML-encoded message (i.e., a message containing XHTML markup) using the four values that were passed to the function as well as the properly formatted value of the BMI given by the variable `$bmi`. The complete string thus formed is stored in a variable called `$text`.

Next, based on the range within which the BMI value lies, a message about whether the BMI is low, high, or reasonable is appended via a compound conditional statement. This conditional is really a sequence of nested `if`-statements of the kind also available in JavaScript.

The final message in the variable `$text` is returned to the calling function.

The function `simpleMessage()` returns a simpler report, but does similar computations. It contains nothing that requires further discussion, but you should confirm this by reading through its code in any case.

---

[12] We should mention that this function is similar to the function by the same name in the programming language C, on the off chance you may have seen it there. The existence of this function in PHP makes this particular task somewhat easier than it was in JavaScript, as you may recall.

8.8.5 Computing the BMI Value: Numerical Computations in PHP and More Programmer-Defined Functions

In previous sections, we dealt primarily with the string manipulations needed to create dynamic web pages and send e-mails. In this section, we will look more closely at numerical computations in PHP, which we choose to perform with programmer-defined functions in the same way we did in JavaScript. In fact, what we do here is remarkably similar to what we already did in JavaScript, and to further emphasize the similarity we use the same function names. Here, from Figure 8.18, are the relevant function definitions:

```
function inchesToCentimetres($height) { return $height*2.54; }
function poundsToKilograms($weight) { return $weight/2.2; }

function calculateBMI($height, $heightUnit, $weight, $weightUnit)
{

    if ($heightUnit == "inches") $height = inchesToCentimetres($height);
    if ($weightUnit == "pounds") $weight = poundsToKilograms($weight);
    $height /= 100; //Convert height from centimeters to meters
    $bmi = $weight/($height*$height);
    return $bmi;
}
```

The numerical computations used by the functions detailedMessage() and simpleMessage() are performed by the function calculateBMI(). The function calculateBMI() takes four parameters, $height, $heightUnit, $weight, and $weightUnit, and returns the BMI value. Note that prior to calling the function calculateBMI(), all input data entered by the user has been validated by JavaScript, so we can assume that the fields height and weight are numbers lying within a reasonable range.

The BMI calculation can be done in various ways, but before doing any calculations we choose to convert all values to the metric system, if they are not metric already. Hence, if the user has entered the height in inches, it is converted to centimeters using the function inchesToCentimetres() in the first conditional statement. Similarly, if the user has entered weight in pounds, it is converted to kilograms using the function poundsToKilograms() in the second conditional statement. The function calculateBMI() then converts the centimetres to meters by dividing the height by 100 and the BMI is simply calculated as the ratio of the weight to the square of the height.

The functions inchesToCentimetres() and poundsToKilograms() return the centimetre or kilogram equivalent of inches or pounds using appropriate factors.

In these functions you see the arithmetic operators for multiplication (∗) and division (/) in action, and you will be relieved to learn that the usual operators for addition (+), subtraction, (-) and modulus (%) are also available in PHP, all conforming to the usual precedence rules, again as in JavaScript.

8.8.6   Building and Sending an XHTML-Encoded E-Mail BMI Report to the User with Another Programmer-Defined Function

The e-mail messages that we sent to the business (Figure 8.9) and the client (Figure 8.10) from our feedback form were simple text messages. However, the e-mail message shown in Figure 8.15 is in XHTML format. The built-in PHP function `mail()` can actually be used to send any type of mail that is normally sent through most e-mail clients (including (X)HTML e-mail).

Our programmer-defined function `mailBMI()` to handle this is

```
47    function mailBMI($email, $message)
48    {
49        $header  = 'MIME-Version: 1.0' . "\r\n";
50        $header .= 'Content-type: text/html; charset=iso-8859-1' . "\r\n";
51        $header .= "From: webbook@cs.smu.ca\r\n";
52        mail($email, "BMI report from Nature's Source", $message, $header);
53    }
```

and is shown in lines 47–54 of Figure 8.18. This function does a little more work before it calls the built-in function `mail()` that sends the XHTML version of the BMI report. The function takes two parameters:

■ The e-mail address of the recipient

■ Our XHTML-encoded BMI report

To get the second parameter in the proper form so that the message is sent as XHTML rather than plain text by `mail()` we need to make that message conform to the requirements of the Simple Mail Transfer Protocol (SMTP) for such messages.

Here this means that we have to provide an appropriate header, which we do by adding these two lines at the top (note the MIME type `text/html`):

```
MIME-Version: 1.0
Content-type: text/html; charset=iso-8859-1
```

The rest of the header is the same as before, and again contains the `From:` address.

Finally, our programmer-defined function `mailBMI()` then calls the built-in PHP function `mail()` to send the message.[13]

This completes our discussion of the programmer-defined functions called either directly or indirectly from our driver script `processBMI.php`.

8.9   Summary

In this summary we state some things and assume you are familiar with JavaScript up to the level of the coverage in the earlier chapters of this text.

PHP is one of the most widely used non-proprietary server-side technologies in use on the Web today. It is an interpreted programming language designed specifically for preprocessing data on the server side and sending that data back to a browser on the client side as XHTML markup. As a programming language, it is another in the C-based category of languages, though it inherits much of its syntax more directly from Perl and has much in common with JavaScript as well.

One or more PHP scripts may be embedded within XHTML markup, as long as each one is enclosed in `<?php...?>` delimiters, in which case the script is executed on the server and its output is returned to the browser to be rendered for viewing by the user. Thus the user cannot see the PHP script code by choosing the "view source" option in the browser. Additional portions of a script may also be contained in one or more separate files and included into another script located within an XHTML page.

All of the standard decision making and looping control constructs from JavaScript are also available in PHP. PHP also has the usual arithmetic operators and the two scalar numerical types `integer` and `double`. The two other scalar types in PHP are `string` and `boolean`, and there are two compound types, `array` and `object`. Like JavaScript, PHP is dynamically typed, which means that a variable has the type of the value most recently assigned to it, and if a variable has no value at all its type is the special `NULL` type. The `NULL` type has only a single value, which is also `NULL`.

PHP also has functions, both built-in and programmer-defined, which are similar to those found in JavaScript and which can and should be used to modularize your code for enhanced readability.

---

[13]You should note that some recipients may not receive the message as (X)HTML, either because their e-mail program cannot handle it or because they have this feature turned off in that program. This is less of a problem nowadays but still one to consider.

Some differences in PHP, as compared with JavaScript, include the following:

1. A single-line comment introduced by the # character (in addition to the // and /*...*/ comments found in JavaScript).

2. All PHP variables begin with the dollar sign character ($).

3. PHP has case-sensitive variable names, but reserved words and function names that are case-insensitive.

4. The string concatenation operator is the period (.), not the + operator.

5. PHP arrays are unlike arrays in JavaScript or any other language. Among the differences are the fact that you can arrange to access elements of the same array with either a numerical or string index.

6. The contents of an external JavaScript file are *not* enclosed in a <script>... </script> tag pair, but the contents of an external PHP file *are* enclosed in <?php...?> delimiters.

The PHP script that will process the form data submitted from the browser on the client side must be supplied as the value of the `action` attribute of the XHTML `form` element. The `post` method is the recommended method for submitting form data.

It is a good idea to validate form data on the client side before submitting it to the server for processing. When doing this with a boolean validation function as the value of the `onsubmit` attribute of the `form` element, you must remember to include the keyword `return` in front of the function name. Without it, the data will not be uploaded even if the function returns `true`.

8.10   Quick Questions to Test Your Basic Knowledge

1. What is the major difference between how JavaScript is used and how PHP is used in web programming? Hint: Perhaps we should ask what the major difference is in *where* they are used.

2. What is the difference between the case-sensitivity of PHP and that of JavaScript?

3. What is the major difference between variable names in PHP and variable names in JavaScript?

4. What happens, or at least *should* happen, in a testing environment when your PHP script contains a syntax error?

5. What are the opening and closing delimiters for a PHP script?

6. We have seen that there is more than one way to make CSS styles available to our XHTML documents and more than one way to make JavaScript scripts available to our XHTML documents. How many ways can you think of to make a PHP script available to your XHTML documents, what are they, which is preferred, and why?

7. We could have used JavaScript to display the date and time on our pages so that the pages would look the same as they do using our PHP scripts. Why would this not be a good idea?

8.11 Short Exercises to Improve Your Basic Understanding

1. Confirm our claim in section 8.5 that a misspelling of the `date()` function will generate a PHP error similar to the one described. If this does not happen, your PHP installation may not be set up to display such errors, and you may want to speak to your administrator, or take steps yourself to make this happen. See the What Else ... section below for further information.

2. Revise `welcome.php` so that the script contains just a single `echo` statement.

3. Confirm that you need the `return` in `return validateContactForm()`.

4. Trace through all the decision paths in the filling out of both forms.

5. Remove the `<?php...?>` delimiters from the included file `bmiCalculate.php` to see if it makes any difference.

6. Remove the line containing the `include()` function call in `processBMI.php` from its current location and put it in a new one-line PHP script in the head of the file. Test the revised script to see if it works as before. If not, explain why not; if so, explain why we might want to do this.

8.12   Exercises on the Parallel Project

1. Modify your home page to include a simple PHP script that produces a welcome message for the user that is dynamically produced on the server for display in the user's browser. The message must include something that will be different each time a user accesses your home page, so obvious candidates for inclusion are the date and time at the location of your business. If you intend to have an international operation, you may want something as elaborate as a table showing the time of day at each of your locations.

2. Implement server-side PHP processing for your own feedback form that is analogous to what we described in this chapter. That is, when the user fills out and submits your feedback form, the following things should happen:

   - Your business receives an e-mail version of the feedback.

   - The user receives an e-mail confirmation of the feedback.

   - The user gets an immediate browser display confirming the feedback submission.

   - A dated copy of the feedback is stored on the server.

   Use a textfile called `feedback.txt` in a subdirectory called `data` to log your feedback messages. Also, since your business may not yet actually be up and running and have a bona fide e-mail address, the "business e-mail address" can be your own e-mail address. In fact, for testing purposes, you can be both customer and business, but the messages received should be at least slightly different in each case so that they may distinguished from one another. This too is what we did in the text.

3. In a similar manner, implement server-side PHP processing for your order form that provides the same four features described above for your feedback form. In this case, the output will include a summary of the input data (number of each item ordered, for example), as well the results of calculations involving the input data, such as subtotal cost of each item ordered, and grand total cost.

8.13   What Else You May Want or Need to Know

1. We have used the PHP script delimiters `<?php ... ?>` to separate PHP code from non-PHP code. We recommend consistent use of these delimiters, though you can also expect to see the short-form delimiters `<? ... ?>` used as well. However, these are less portable since their use can be disabled in the PHP configuration.

2. The use of `#` as a single-line comment delimiter and the use of the `$` to start a variable name are both features that are inherited directly from the Perl programming language, of which PHP may be regarded as a direct descendant.

3. When you are trying to understand how a PHP script works, be careful to distinguish between PHP's *read mode* and its *execution mode*. Only PHP code that is enclosed between proper PHP code delimiters will cause the PHP processor to be invoked to process that code. This is execution mode. Anything else is simply read and forwarded on to the browser (this is read mode).

4. The `post` method was our preferred method for uploading information to the server, and we have used it consistently. You should be aware, however, that there is another method called `get` that is also in frequent use. When the `post` method is used, the data being uploaded is "invisible" to the user. On the other hand, when `get` is used, the user can see the data at the end of the URL. For example, if `get` is being used to send data to a PHP script, the last part of the URL might have a format something like

   ```
   .../file.php?variable1=value1&variable2=value2
   ```

   in which the ? signals the start of a sequence of variable-value pairs, with the pairs being separated by an ampersand (&). If you have spent any time browsing the Web, you will likely have seen in your browser's address window URLs exhibiting this format.

5. We have used `$_POST`, which is called a *superglobal array* to access data uploaded from a form within our PHP scripts. There are a number of other such *superglobals*, as they are often called, including (as you might suspect) one called `$_GET` for accessing data uploaded via the `get` method. These superglobals have been available since PHP version 4.1 and should be used in the way we have illustrated in all new PHP code.

Before PHP 4.1, it was common (and perhaps still is) to make use of the fact that a value of a `name` attribute of a form element from a form on the client side will show up as a variable name (beginning with a $, of course) in your PHP script on the server side, and the value of that variable will be the data submitted by the user via that element. For example, if we were making use of this facility, instead of accessing `$_POST['firstName']` we would simply access `$firstName`.

This may seem to be very convenient, in fact more convenient than using a superglobal, but it also turns out to be less secure. For that reason, in order to make use of this feature, the `register_globals` directive must be turned on in the PHP configuration file, and starting with PHP 4.2, `register_globals` has been turned off by default. Moreover, by the time you read this, if PHP 6 is available and you are using it, you may find that this feature has simply gone away entirely.

6. Recall that JavaScript is not permitted to read from and write to files, for obvious security reasons, since it is downloaded from the Web and runs in the user's web browser. PHP, on the other hand, runs on the server and therefore is not subject to the same restrictions. We used PHP for very simple file output, appending each new feedback item to a file of text, but other file operations are possible, as indicated by various I/O modes shown in Table 8.1.

7. If your PHP script fails for any reason, it will (by default) send to the browser a message containing the name of the file in which the offending script is located, the line number where the error occurred, and a message that (one hopes) describes the problem. This is excellent default behavior to leave in place, but if you wish to do so there are ways to adjust the "level" of error reporting that PHP provides, and there may be some errors you wish to ignore from time to time. The `error_reporting()` function allows you to set the error level for a particular script. Follow the link given in the **References** for further information on this function.

8. Just as there are many JavaScript frameworks freely available for download, as we mentioned in the previous chapter, there are also numerous PHP frameworks available for download as well, such as CakePHP® and Zend™. On the other hand, one cannot obtain PHP code from sites on the Web in the same way one can find JavaScript code, because PHP code has "disappeared" from a web page by the time that page has reached the browser. Nevertheless, there are also

Mode	Description
"r"	Read from the beginning of the file
"r+"	Read and write from the beginning of the file
"w"	Write from the beginning of the file
	Previous contents are destroyed
	If the file does not exist, it is created
"w+"	Read and write from the beginning of the file
	Previous contents are destroyed
	If the file does not exist, it is created
"a"	Write from the end of the file
	If the file does not exist, it is created
"a+"	Read and write from the end of the file
	If the file does not exist, it is created
"x"	Create a file for writing from the beginning
	If the file already exists, return an error
"x+"	Create a file for reading and writing from the beginning
	If the file already exists, return an error

Table 8.1

Various modes for PHP file I/O.

many PHP scripts that you might find useful and which are freely available for download from various web repositories. See the **References** for some relevant links.

9. Under "normal" circumstances, when a browser sends information to a server and the server responds by sending a page back to the browser, the entire page must be re-displayed in the browser, even if only a small portion of that page has actually changed. This can cause browser response to slow down and generally appear to be much less satisfying to a user than a typical desktop application. A technology called AJAX (*Asynchronous JavaScript and XML*) can be used to help alleviate this situation. JavaScript (in conjunction with XML, which we will introduce briefly in a later chapter) can be used to communicate with the server and update only the changed part of a web page, thus speeding up the page-refresh process. Note that AJAX is not a distinct new technology,

but simply a way of combining a number of previously existing technologies. Your site may or may not benefit from the use of AJAX, and though we give some relevant links in the **References**, we do not discuss the implementation of AJAX on our sample website.

8.14   References

1. We refer you again to the website for this text, especially now that in this chapter for the first time you cannot get the full effect of the current version of the website simply by loading the home page from the CD-ROM into your browser and clicking on the various links. This is because the PHP of these pages contain will not be activated unless the pages are served from a PHP-aware web browser. If you have one of your own or your instructor has set one up and installed our files, fine. If not, you can go to our text website and load the index file for Chapter 8:

   `http://cs.smu.ca/~webbook/cdrom/web08`

2. The ultimate source of PHP information, including the latest downloads and up-to-date information on language and library developments is, of course, the "home" of PHP, which you can find here:

   `http://www.php.net`

   For example, a comprehensive listing of PHP functions—the `date()`, `include()`, `sprintf()`, `mail()`, `fopen()`, `fwrite()`, `die()`, `str_replace()`, and `error_reporting()` functions in particular—can be found at these locations:

   ```
   http://www.php.net/manual/en/language.functions.php
   http://ca.php.net/manual/en/function.date.php
   http://ca.php.net/manual/en/function.include.php
   http://ca.php.net/manual/en/function.sprintf.php
   http://ca.php.net/manual/en/function.mail.php
   http://ca.php.net/manual/en/function.fopen.php
   http://ca.php.net/manual/en/function.fwrite.php
   http://ca.php.net/manual/en/function.die.php
   http://ca.php.net/manual/en/function.str-replace.php
   http://ca.php.net/manual/en/function.error-reporting.php
   ```

From the form of these several links, if there is another PHP built-in function about which you need information, you can probably guess where to go for that information.

3. As they usually do for important web technologies, the **W3 Schools** folks provide a PHP tutorial with lots of useful examples and a PHP reference at their site:

   `http://www.w3schools.com`

4. Another PHP tutorial site, similar in approach to that of **W3 Schools** but perhaps with some additional detail, can be found here:

   `http://www.tizag.com/phpT/`

5. Here is a page containing a table showing a number of different PHP frameworks and their features:

   `http://www.phpframeworks.com/`

6. Here are some links to sites containing free PHP scripts that you might find useful:

   `http://gscripts.net/`
   `http://www.free-php.net/`
   `http://www.hotscripts.com/`

   A Google search will turn up many other similar sites.

CHAPTER 9

MySQL for Server-Side Data Storage

CHAPTER CONTENTS

9.1   Overview and Objectives

From the dawn of the computer age, computers have been required to deal with large amounts of data. In the beginning, much of that data was in the form of results from numerical calculations that scientists at universities and other research institutions wanted to perform. But it was not long before companies large and small doing business of all kinds, governments, and other organizations wanted to get in on the action. And all of them had data, lots and lots of data.

In the early years, data was simply stored in files, but that was soon recognized as an inadequate solution to the problem of organizing data and keeping it organized. Indeed, this problem was recognized early in the game as one that would be of long-term and great significance, and much effort has been devoted to the topic over the last half-century.

A major problem that needed to be solved was the duplication of data, which made it a nightmare to keep all versions of the data up to date. Moreover, duplication required additional storage, at a time when storage was relatively expensive. But the real problem was that humans had to be intimately involved in the various processes needed to maintain the data. And humans make mistakes.

In this chapter we will once again give just a brief introduction to a topic of enduring interest to both researchers in computing science and end-users of computers and the software that runs on them. That topic is the solution to many of those early problems that cropped up in the history of computing: the *database*. We begin by looking at the most widely used form of database, the *relational database*, and then move on to get some exposure to one of the major software packages for dealing with that kind of database, namely **MySQL**. This is a powerful, public-domain relational database management software system that can be used on a wide variety of computing platforms, and one that is freely available by download over the Internet. It is especially popular for website development using PHP. Databases like MySQL, as well as other (proprietary) systems from companies like Oracle® and IBM®, now play a major role in virtually all business applications that run on computers.

In particular, this chapter covers the following topics:

- A brief discussion of the history and a high-level view of the relational database model, including tables and their rows (*records* or *objects*) and their columns (*fields* or *attributes*)

- Some high-level goals to keep in mind when you are designing your own database

- A brief discussion of some important aspects of the "preferred" structure of a relational database, including *normalization*, table *keys*, the possible relationships between tables, and the *functional dependencies* between record attributes

- Making use of online resources to help you set up a suitable database for your needs

- The **phpMyAdmin** interface to a **MySQL** database system, and setting up a MySQL database for our Nature's Source website using this interface

- Using the *Structured Query Language (SQL)* to manipulate a database in various ways

- A brief look at the command-line interface of MySQL

- Importing and exporting tables and databases to and from MySQL

9.2 Relational Databases

At the highest level, a *database* is simply a place where you store data. And again, at the highest level, the first rule of databases is to think about what should go into one, and what you expect to get out of it, before you start putting one together. Most people are familiar with "tables" of data, and the first impulse might be to put all of your data into one giant table. You should resist this urge if you have it, since you might wind up with a *spreadsheet* (which is *not* a database) containing all of your data, and if you do you will likely eventually have a great deal of trouble getting the kind of access you want to the information you have stored.

So, one of the primary design issues in creating a database is deciding what representation model to use when doing so. Such a model must provide a theory or specification describing how the database is to be structured and used.

Early databases used somewhat unstructured hierarchical and network models. In 1970, E. F. Codd of IBM introduced the *relational database model*, which revolutionized the database world. Some of the newer models, such as the *object model* and the *object-relational model*, may be advantageous in some cases, but the relational database remains the most widely used model. It is the one we will use in all of our discussions in this book.

If you permit us a few words of formal-speak, we can say that data in the relational model is represented as *mathematical relations*. The data is manipulated using *relational calculus* (or *relational algebra*). The mathematical basis for the relational database model makes it possible to minimize data redundancy and verify data integrity. Although there are many subtleties involved, and non-obvious aspects to all of this, it is not quite as scary as it sounds.

In fact, we can say, somewhat more informally but still with complete accuracy, that data in a relational database is stored in tables, and a table is just what you thought it was. Each row of the table, called a *tuple* in relational algebra, corresponds to a *record* or an *object* (such as an item to be sold, or a service to be rendered). Each *field* in the record is called an *attribute* in database terminology and represents a property of an entity stored in a record (such as the color of an item to be sold or the price of a service to be rendered).

It is in making the decisions as to what goes into the various tables, and what the relationships between those tables should be, that we must be careful if we are to have a good *database design*.

9.3   Database Design Goals

Virtually every business needs to store its data in some form, and in deciding what that form should be certain goals must be kept in mind:

- All data necessary for the smooth operation of the business needs to be recorded with whatever frequency the business deems appropriate.

- Data integrity must be maintained as new information is added, information currently stored is updated, and (perhaps) some information is deleted.

- The data must be stored in such a way that the business can easily retrieve whatever information it needs, in whatever form it is needed, and whenever it is required. This process is referred to a "querying the database," or submitting "queries" to the database. We do this using a special language called *SQL* (*Structured Query Language*), which we discuss later in this chapter.

- And finally, in the best of all worlds, the database would also occupy minimal storage, have lightning-fast response times to all queries, and be easily modifiable and extensible when the needs of the business change and grow.

An obvious question, of course, is this: What exactly are we trying to achieve by working toward these goals? One answer is that we are trying to have a database that avoids certain kinds of "anomalies" that tend to crop up when we are working with a poorly-designed database. These include:

- The *insertion anomaly*, which occurs when we are entering a new record, but not all fields of that record can be filled in because some of the required data is missing.

- The *update anomaly*, which occurs when information is updated in one place in the database, but the same information is not updated in some other database location. Elimination or minimization of redundant data in the database can help alleviate this problem, and also help to ensure more logical and efficient storage.

- The *deletion anomaly*, which occurs when deletion of one piece of information from the database forces the deletion of something else that you perhaps would not want deleted.

Achieving all of the above goals is a tall order, seldom realized by any real world business, but if we are careful with our design, even to the point of just applying some common sense (that rare commodity) during setup, we may be able to avoid some major headaches down the road.

9.4 Some Architectural Aspects of a "Good" Database

We are all familiar with tables of data, and if we have some data to organize, one "quick and dirty" first-impulse solution might be to put it all into one large table, as we have already mentioned. The trouble with this approach is that the same data winds up being stored in several different places (data redundancy), we soon lose track of what we have stored, and it becomes more and more difficult over time to add new data.

9.4.1 Database Normalization

To deal with this problem, Codd did something more than simply invent the relational database. He also developed the concept of *normalization* for a relational database, a process that can help us to achieve at least some of the above goals.

A database is said to be in a particular *normal form* if the relationships between the attributes of the entities represented by the records in the tables of the database are rigorously defined in a certain way. Originally, in 1970, Codd specified three normal forms. These have the somewhat unimaginative, but easy-to-remember, names *First Normal Form*, *Second Normal Form*, and *Third Normal Form*, which are often abbreviated *1NF*, *2NF*, and *3NF*.

Since Codd's original proposal, several additional normal forms have been described, including the Boyce-Codd Normal Form (BCNF), as well as 4NF and 5NF, and a 6NF for "temporal" databases, for example. Clearly one can take the normalization process some distance, but going beyond the second or third normal form is often unnecessary, and may even, in some cases, be counterproductive. There are even "denormalization" procedures that can be applied if it is discovered that more normalization than is desirable has been performed and some needs to be "undone"! In any case, we will have no need to discuss any of these "higher-level" normal forms. For further information see the end-of-chapter **References**.

One important aspect of these normal forms to remember is that they are *cumulative* in the sense that to be in 2NF, a database must first be in 1NF, and to be in 3NF it must first be in 2NF, and so on. Also, a database is said to be in 1NF if each table in the database is in 1NF, and similarly for the higher normal forms.

The first normal form essentially deals with the "shape" of a record type. For a database to be in 1NF, each row of a table must have the same number of columns of information (i.e., each record must have the same number of attributes) and each attribute value must contain a single piece of information. A short way of describing the latter requirement is to say that each attribute value must be *atomic*.

You need to keep in mind, however, that just what *atomic* means in any given database can depend significantly on the nature of the data and the viewpoint of the database designer. For example, in one database the name of a customer might have the customer's first name, middle initial, and last name all together in one column and be regarded as being a single "atomic" value because there is no perceived need to have a name broken down into its constituent pieces. In another database, each of those three pieces of a name might be placed in its own column because there might well be a need for each part of the name to be accessible at one time or another, and having each name part in its own column makes that access much easier.

As a simple example, let us assume that we want to keep a list of products bought by a customer by using just two attributes (two fields per table row): `Customer` and `Product`. If a customer, say `Pawan`, buys two products, say `Vitamin B` and `Vitamin C`, the corresponding row of our table would look like the row shown in Table 9.1. The problem here is that the `Product` attribute value is not atomic (we cannot have

Customer	Product
Pawan	Vitamin B, Vitamin C

Table 9.1

A simple illustration of 1NF violated.

Customer	Product
Pawan	Vitamin B
Pawan	Vitamin C

Table 9.2

A simple illustration of 1NF satisfied.

a single record with `Customer = Pawan` and `Product = {Vitamin B, Vitamin C}`). Instead, we need two records with the same `Customer` value, but different `Product` values, as shown in Table 9.2. In other words, from the point of view of what's in a table, each column must contain a *single* value (whatever that means within the given context) in each row.

Before discussing 2NF we need to say something about *keys* for our tables, and the *functional dependency* that may or may not exist between key and non-key record attributes in our tables.

9.4.2 Database Keys: Primary and Foreign, Natural and Surrogate, Simple and Composite

Placing appropriate *keys* in our database tables is an important step in setting up our database. A table column in which the attribute value is used to uniquely identify the record in its row, and serve, in effect as a "lookup" value for that row, contains what we call the *primary key* for that table. Such a primary key must satisfy the following properties:

- It must be unique for every record in the table, and here it is important to remember that the uniqueness must apply to every *possible* entry that might be put into the table, *not* just the entries in the table at some particular time.

- It must always have a value and, moreover, a value that will never change.

A primary key column from Table A, say, may also appear in a second table, say Table B, and thus serve to "connect," or establish a "relationship" between those two tables. In this case, in Table B the primary key from Table A is called a *foreign key*.

Sometimes we have a "natural" choice for a primary key, such as the social security number, which will be unique for each person in a table, for example. Other times we may simply want to generate an artificial (or *surrogate*) identifier to use for the primary key. For example, we could use something as simple as a sequence of positive integers. This has the dual advantage of being totally under the control of the database designer, and many database management systems can generate such values automatically as data is entered into the database.

A simple key value that appears in a single column is perhaps the most frequent and convenient kind of primary key, but sometimes the concatenation of the attribute values in two (or more) columns can be also used as the primary key, in which case we refer to it as a *compound* (or *composite*) primary key.

9.4.3   Functional Dependencies and 2NF

The second and third normal forms (2NF and 3NF) deal with the relationship (or the *functional dependency*) between key and non-key attributes in a table.

In particular, 2NF is violated when a non-key attribute is a fact about a *subset* of the primary key (i.e., there is a functional dependency from an attribute that is only part of the primary key to the non-key attribute). Thus this is only relevant when the primary key is composite (consisting of more than one attribute). Another way of saying this is that for 2NF we want each non-key attribute in a table to be information "about the primary key, about the whole primary key, and about nothing but the primary key."

Let us illustrate what we mean by taking a simple example of a database that violates 2NF and converting it into one that satisfies 2NF.

Compare what you see in Table 9.3 with what you see in Table 9.4. Table 9.3 shows a single-table database with four attributes for purchases made in a store: `Customer`, `e-mail`, `Product`, and `Price`. Let us take the combination of the customer name attribute (the `Customer` field) and the product name attribute (the `Product` field) as the primary key. There are four records in the database. Clearly there is a functional relationship between the attribute `Customer`, which is part of the primary key, and the non-key attribute `E-mail`, since a customer's e-mail address provides a fact about

Customer	E-mail	Product	Price
Pawan	pawan@yahoo.ca	Vitamin B	$19.99
Pawan	pawan@yahoo.ca	Vitamin C	$24.99
Paul	paul@gmail.ca	Vitamin C	$24.99
Robert	robert@halifax.ca	Vitamin B	$19.99

Table 9.3

A simple illustration of 2NF violated.

Customer	E-mail
Pawan	pawan@yahoo.ca
Paul	paul@gmail.ca
Robert	robert@halifax.ca

Customer	Product
Pawan	Vitamin B
Pawan	Vitamin C
Paul	Vitamin C
Robert	Vitamin B

Product	Price
Vitamin B	$19.99
Vitamin C	$24.99

Table 9.4

A simple illustration of 2NF satisfied.

that customer. However, the `Customer` attribute is only part of the primary key and the customer's e-mail has nothing to do with any product the customer may be buying (the other part of the primary key).

A similar functional dependency also applies from the attribute `Product`, which is part of the primary key, to the non-key attribute `Price`.

Now suppose we split the single table of the original database of Table 9.3 into three tables, as shown in Table 9.4. The first thing we achieve by doing this is save some storage. This may not be obvious in this example, because we have so few records, but note, for instance, that in the single-table database Vitamin C and its price appeared twice, but in the new arrangement this pairing occurs only once, and think about the implications of this for a much larger data set.

We are also moved toward our goal of maintaining database integrity. For example, if we had to change the price of `VitaminC` to `$29.99`, then in the configuration of Table 9.4 we would need to make the change for only one record (the one in the table containing the record with the product Vitamin C and its price). That means we would not make the mistake of changing the price of Vitamin C in one place and not in the other (Vitamin C and its price appeared twice in the original table).

Note that these three tables can be "joined" together to recover the original table, and hence the decomposition shown in Table 9.4 is *lossless*. We will see how two or more tables can be joined in various ways using MySQL *queries* later on in this chapter.

Though we will not pursue the discussion any further, let us say here simply that 3NF is violated when a non-key attribute provides a fact about another non-key attribute. The creation of further tables from the existing ones may be necessary to achieve 3NF.

9.4.4   Table Relationships in a Database

Another important aspect of a database design to think about during setup is the nature of the relationships that the tables in the database will have to one another, as the above discussion suggests. There are essentially three possibilities:

- *one-to-one*: There is a one-to-one relationship between Table A and Table B if each record in Table A corresponds to one and only one record in Table B, and vice versa. For example, in your company there might be a one-to-one relationship between each employee and his or her desktop computer, if in fact each employee has a desktop computer.

- *one-to-many*: A one-to-many relationship from Table A to Table B means that each record in Table A will correspond (potentially at least) to several and perhaps many records in Table B, and several records in Table B can correspond to a single record in Table A. For example, a single customer may have placed several orders, so a perfectly "natural" relationship between a Customer table and an Order table might be one-to-one.

- *many-to-many*: A many-to-many relationship from Table A to Table B means that at least one record in Table A corresponds to several (or many) records in Table B and at least one record in Table B corresponds to several (or many) records in Table A. Without going into detail, we should say that such relationships often create redundant data in your database and lead to problems in other ways, and so are best avoided.

In all cases, the relationships between tables are established with the help of table keys, the primary key of one table becoming a foreign key in a second table, for example. Sometimes it may prove to be convenient to set up a table containing nothing but keys, just to help "connect" other tables, particulary when one is trying to simplify a many-to-many table relationship.

9.4.5   Some General Advice

So, the first step in creating a database application for a business, or for any other endeavor, is to create a data model that contains all relevant attributes that need to be stored. The next step is to use the functional dependencies among the attributes to create an appropriate set of tables, and then establish the relationships between these tables using keys. The resulting set of tables should minimize data redundancy and preserve data integrity as various operations are performed on the database.

As a best practice, one should ensure that the resulting database model is at least in second normal form. A normalized database tends to make general-purpose querying easier and faster, while a non-normalized database can favor some queries over others. However, keep in mind that normal forms represent only guidelines for the design of the records in the tables of your database. Though generally a good thing, they are just that—guidelines and *not* rules—and sometimes business requirements become the overriding factor in how a database is actually constructed. Nevertheless, some attempt at normalization is always a good starting point.

9.5   Make Use of Online Resources and Don't Reinvent the Wheel

The previous discussion was intended to give you a brief glimpse into some of the considerations that go into the setting up of a suitable database for any enterprise, but it did not provide enough detail to use as a guide for serious, hands-on database development. In fact, as a practical matter, many entrepreneurs simply do not have the time, energy, or expertise to make use of the theoretical underpinnings of database design when it comes to the actual real world task of doing so. Fortunately, help can be found online, and unless you have very special needs for your particular situation it may be a good idea to go looking for a database design that will serve your purposes. For example, the website **Database Answers** at `http://databaseanswers.org/` describes data models for a wide variety of applications, and readers may want to browse this website for a data model that might be suitable for their situation.

For our own e-commerce development, we have chosen a design that uses a combination of two of their data models, and we are actually using a subset of the combined data model. Furthermore, we have added and deleted attributes to suit our needs. Figure 9.1 shows the data model used in our database. The figure is drawn using the designer utility provided by phpMyAdmin, the GUI (Graphical User Interface) for the MySQL database management software.

9.6   The Data Model for Our Nature's Source Database

Let us take a few moments to examine our data model, which is illustrated in Figure 9.1. The figure shows that our database will consist of a total of 12 tables, with each box in the figure representing one of those tables. The rows in each box of the figure represent, in turn, the attributes of a record in the corresponding table. A common naming convention in the database world is to use multiple words to name an

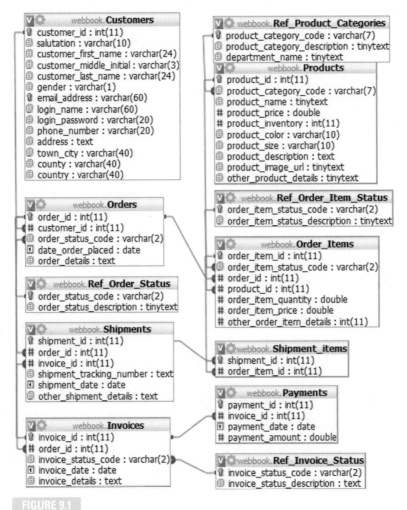

FIGURE 9.1

graphics/ch09/dbSchema.jpg

Data model for an e-commerce website based on models from DataBaseAnswers.com.

attribute, with the words joined by an underscore character (_), as in customer_id, for example.

On the left-hand side of each attribute you will see an icon that suggests the role and properties of that attribute. For example, an icon that looks like a key indicates that the corresponding attribute is a primary key for the table in which it appears. Recall that the primary key of a table uniquely identifies each record in that table, and it can be either of the following:

■ A single attribute that is guaranteed to be unique. For example, customer_id in the Customers table is unique in the sense that there is no more than one record in the table per value of `customer_id`. It is possible to generate these unique values automatically when inserting records into the table.

- A concatenation of multiple attributes. For example, in the `Shipment_Items` table the `shipment_id` and the `order_item_id` attributes are combined to form the primary key.

Other icons that we see on the left of an attribute include these:

- A # sign, indicating a type whose values are numeric

- A text page icon, indicating a type whose values are character strings

- A date icon, indicating a type whose values represent dates

These icons are actually redundant, because on the right of each attribute name, after the colon, we have text that describes the type of the attribute.

MySQL supports a wide range of data types. Like other keywords in MySQL, their names are case-insensitive. In Figure 9.1 we show them in lowercase, but in the text discussion we show them in uppercase to help them stand out. So, here are the ones we use in our data model shown in Figure 9.1:

- `INTEGER` (or its synonym INT, which can also be used), a numeric data type capable of storing 32-bit integer values

- `DOUBLE`, a numeric data type capable of storing 64-bit floating point values (values containing a decimal point, i.e., "real numbers")

- `VARCHAR(M)`, an efficient data type for storing variable-length strings (At the time of writing, the maximum size M of such a string is 65,535 characters, but the effective maximum length is also subject to the maximum row size—also 65,535 characters, and shared among all columns—and the character set in use.)

- `TINYTEXT`, another data type for storing strings of length not exceeding 255 characters

- `TEXT`, for storing large amounts of text (up to 65,535 characters)

- `DATE`, for storing date values

See the end-of-chapter **References** section for links to further information on these and other data types available in MySQL.

Let's dig a little deeper into the structure of our database by discussing some of the table relationships. Each table is connected to another table through a common attribute. Usually the common attribute is the primary key in one of the two connected tables, and that same key is therefore a *foreign key* in the other table.[1]

Figure 9.1 shows the connections from the primary key to the foreign keys. Lines with a small, filled-in semi-circle at one end and a larger, filled-in semi-circle at the other make these connections. The end with the smaller semi-circle points to the primary key, while the end with the larger semi-circle indicates the foreign key.

We have three main tables:

1. `Customers` This table contains all the relevant information for each customer. Note that it is linked to the `Orders` table through its `customer_id` primary key attribute. For every order, there will be a `customer_id` foreign key in the `Orders` table identifying the customer in the `Customers` table who placed that order. On the other hand, a particular customer may typically have placed multiple orders, so there is a one-to-many relationship from the `Customers` table to the `Orders` table.

2. `Products` This table contains all the relevant information for each product. Note that it is connected to the `Ref_Product_Categories`,[2] which provides information about the category of each product. Examples of product categories listed in `Ref_Product_Categories` include *exercise equipment, stomach remedies, vitamins*, and so on. Each category will contain many products that are listed in the `Products` table, so again we have a one-to-many relationship, this time from a product category to the products in that category.

3. `Orders` This table contains some basic information about each order but is also connected to a number of other tables that provide additional information about each order. In particular, through its `order_id` primary key, which appears as

---

[1]It is a good idea to make the foreign keys *indexed* in a table. Indexing an attribute allows for faster searching based on that attribute.

[2]We are using the convention from the **Database Answers** website under which tables that start with the prefix `Ref_` are essentially for reference. There is no physical object corresponding to one of the rows in such a table.

a foreign key in those other tables, the **Orders** table is connected to each of the following tables:

- **Shipments** This table keeps track of shipments. It is in turn connected to the **Shipment_Items** table to follow the details of the shipment of individual items.

- **Order_Items** This table contains information relating to the individual items in a particular order. The attributes for an "order item" include the **order_item_quantity** and the **order_item_price** for that item.

- **Invoices** This table contains invoice information and is connected to a number of other relevant tables, such as the **Payments** table.

Study Figure 9.1 until you have a reasonable sense of our data model. Once you have some understanding of the structure we are going to use for our database, we can proceed to implement that database using MySQL, and that is our next task.

Our choice of MySQL is based on the fact that it is the most popular open source database management software for web programming. We will begin by using the phpMyAdmin GUI for MySQL, but we will always provide corresponding commands in SQL that we would enter directly if we were using the command-line interface to MySQL. In fact, we shall also discuss that command-line interface and how to enter these commands later in the chapter.

And by the way, these SQL commands[3] tend to be the same for all the major database management systems. Using these commands is how you "talk to" a database system. There are various ways of doing this: using phpMyAdmin or the command-line interface, as we do in this chapter, or using an API (Application Programming Interface) provided by some programming languages such as Java or (in our case) PHP. We will make use of the PHP approach in the following chapter.

At this point we assume that you have the necessary access to both MySQL itself and the phpMyAdmin interface to MySQL. You may wish to install both of these software packages on your own computer, and there are some links to information that will prove helpful in doing so in the end-of-chapter **References** section.

More realistically, particularly if you are working in an academic environment, your instructor may have arranged for your system administrator to create an account and an empty database for you. Then, once you log in to the system and choose that database, you will be ready for the next step of creating and "populating" the

---

[3]SQL commands are very often called *queries*, whether or not they are actually asking a database for information, and we will use the terms interchangeably. So, a "query" might also be creating a table, putting some information into a table, or updating that information as well.

database tables based on the design from Figure 9.1, or based on a design of your own.

If you are working with some other database system, much of what we say will still be meaningful and useful, but the screenshots shown in the text will not be as relevant.

9.7   Using SQL and phpMyAdmin to Set Up the MySQL Database for Our Nature's Source Website

The phpMyAdmin software is a Web-based tool, so to use it for accessing your MySQL installation you will need a URL for phpMyAdmin on the server on which your MySQL and phpMyAdmin have been installed, and on which you have a MySQL account. For example, in our case that URL is

```
http://cs.smu.ca/phpmyadmin
```

and we simply browse to that web address and respond to the login window we get by entering our MySQL username and password. You would do the same, and you would then get the local "home page" of your phpMyAdmin and at that point you would have whatever access your system administrator has established for you. We assume you have progressed to this point, if you wish to follow along with the discussion that comes next in the text.

We also assume that you are starting with an empty database (ours is called webbook). Once again, that is a likely scenario in an academic environment, though if you don't have such a database but do have permission to create one, it is easy enough to do so, as we shall see shortly.

So, we want to start creating and populating tables within our webbook database, based on our design from Figure 9.1, and using phpMyAdmin. Figure 9.2 shows the dialog box that appears by default once you have logged in to phpMyAdmin and have chosen the database that you are building. We have filled in the necessary information to create a table called Customers, in which each row will have 13 fields. That is, each customer will have 13 attributes. The observant reader may notice that we actually have 14 attributes in the Customers table of our data model. An error like this during database construction is not uncommon, and we will see a bit later how we can fix such a mistake after the table has been created.

Once you click on the Go button shown in Figure 9.2, you will get a screen like the one shown in Figure 9.3. Here we enter the names of the customer attributes

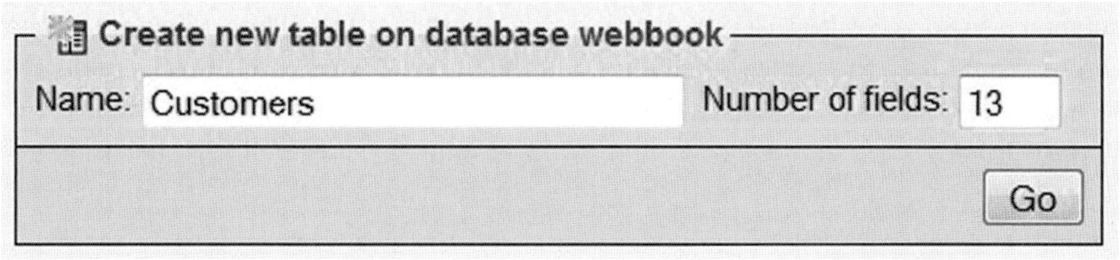

FIGURE 9.2

graphics/ch09/displayCreateTableCustomers.jpg
Specifying the name and size of the Customers table using phpMyAdmin.

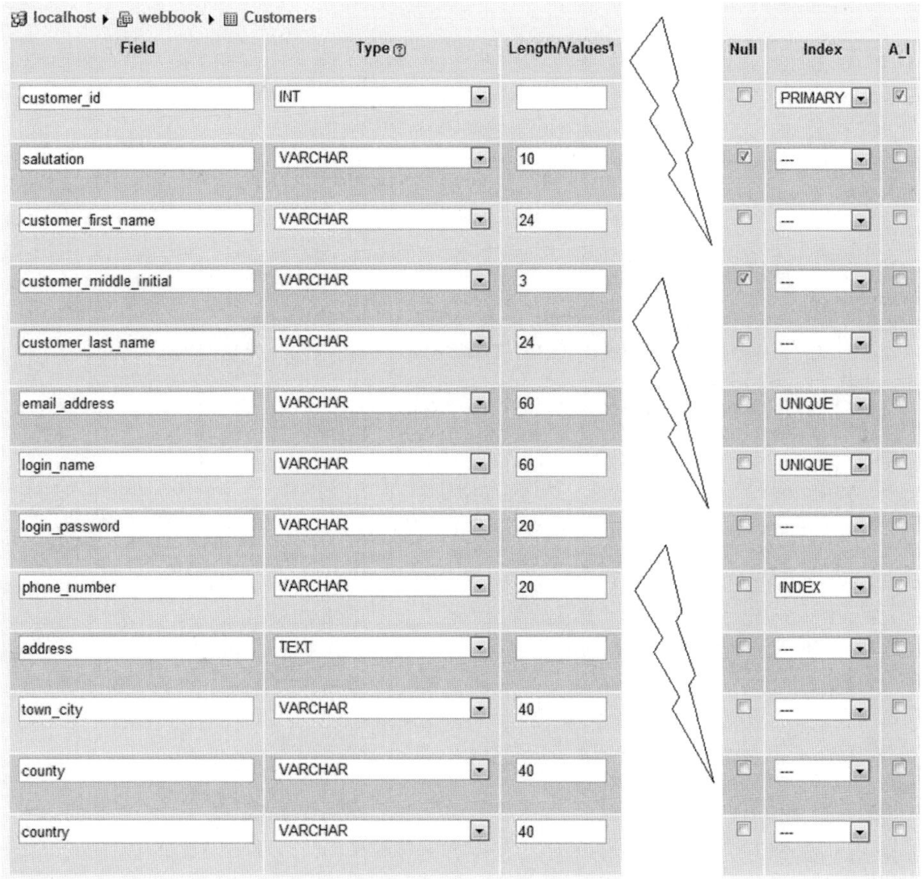

FIGURE 9.3

graphics/ch09/displaySpecifyAttributeCustomers.jpg
Specifying the attributes for the Customers table using phpMyAdmin.

and their types, according to our design shown in Figure 9.1. Then, clicking on the **Save** button causes the table to be created, as shown in Figure 9.4. This figure shows the complete structure of the table. Also, in the **Indexes:** part of the figure (at the bottom) we see a list of our primary and unique keys, as well as other indexed attributes. Finally, the figure also shows (partially) the actual SQL statement that was used to create the table.

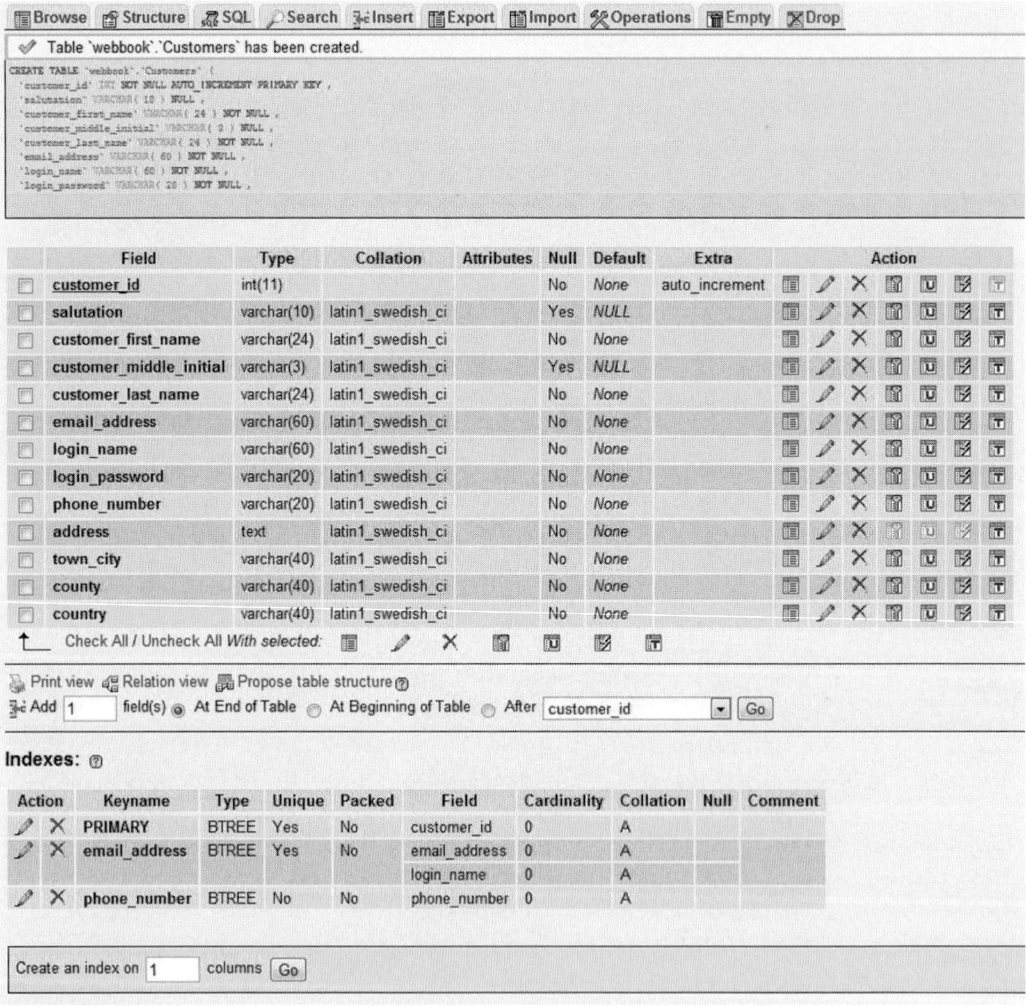

FIGURE 9.4

graphics/ch09/displayResultCreateTableCustomers.jpg
Result of creating the (empty) **Customers** table using phpMyAdmin.

```
1   CREATE TABLE 'webbook'.'Customers' (
2       'customer_id' INT NOT NULL AUTO_INCREMENT PRIMARY KEY,
3       'salutation' VARCHAR(10) NULL,
4       'customer_first_name' VARCHAR(24) NOT NULL,
5       'customer_middle_initial' VARCHAR(3) NULL,
6       'customer_last_name' VARCHAR(24) NOT NULL,
7       'email_address' VARCHAR(60) NOT NULL,
8       'login_name' VARCHAR(60) NOT NULL,
9       'login_password' VARCHAR(20) NOT NULL,
10      'phone_number' VARCHAR(20) NOT NULL,
11      'address' TEXT NOT NULL,
12      'town_city' VARCHAR(40) NOT NULL,
13      'county' VARCHAR(40) NOT NULL,
14      'country' VARCHAR(40) NOT NULL,
15      INDEX ('phone_number'),
16      UNIQUE (
17          'email_address',
18          'login_name')
19  ) ENGINE = MyISAM;
```

FIGURE 9.5

graphics/ch09/createCustomers.sql
The complete SQL command for creating our Customers table.

If you are using another database management software system, the same query should still be able to create this table for you. We have reproduced the query separately in Figure 9.5.

SQL commands, or queries, can be grouped into various categories. We give below a list of the major groupings, together with an indication of the category to which each command of interest to us belongs. In the text we introduce and discuss each command as and when we need it. There are, of course, many additional MySQL commands that we do not discuss, and many options for using the commands that we do discuss that we do not have the time or space to cover. See the end-of-chapter **References** section for links to the MySQL documentation.

- Commands for data definition (CREATE, ALTER, DROP) that are most frequently used to create, modify, and delete database tables

- Command for data retrieval (SELECT) used to query the database and retrieve useful information stored in it

- Commands for data manipulation (INSERT, LOAD, UPDATE, DELETE, TRUNCATE) that are used to enter data into tables, modify data that is already in those tables, and to remove data from tables

■ Commands for data transaction, and commands for data control, neither of which we will need to discuss

9.7.1   The CREATE Command

The **CREATE** command is most often used to create a table in a database, but can also be used to create the database itself. For example, the command

```
CREATE DATABASE webbook;
```

could be used to create our **webbook** database, provided we have the necessary MySQL permissions to do so. These permissions are under the control of the MySQL administrator, who will be you if you have installed MySQL on your home machine. However, many users in an academic environment may not have the authority to create their own databases. If this is the case for you, your system administrator would probably have created a database for you, based on information provided by a course instructor.

As for creating a table in an already existing database, the general syntax of the required command looks like this:

```
CREATE TABLE table_name (column_name column_type colum_constraints, ...);
```

Figure 9.5 shows the **CREATE** command[4] used to create our **Customers** table. This particular command illustrates almost all of the useful features of the **CREATE** command. In the first line, 'webbook'.'Customers' tells that we are creating a table called **Customers** in the database **webbook**. The use of single quotes is not always necessary, but phpMyAdmin has put them in for us. Within the parentheses we specify the list of attributes, along with their types, and their lengths and other constraints wherever appropriate (such as **NOT NULL**, which means that the attribute *must* have a value).

At the end of the list of attributes, we specify that **customer_id** is the primary key, that the table should be indexed based on **phone_number**, and that the attribute values of **email_address** and **login_name** should be unique. Outside the parentheses, the "storage engine" is specified to be **MYISAM**, a specification that was not really necessary since **MYISAM** is the default storage engine.

Now that we have created the **Customers** table using the **CREATE** command, let us move on to our next *data definition command* of interest, **ALTER**, and see how to make changes in the structure of our table.

---

[4]This command, as shown, could be typed in directly if we were using the command-line interface to MySQL, a topic for later discussion in this chapter. For the moment, we are happy to have phpMyAdmin "construct" this command for us "behind the scenes," based on information we enter into the form it displays for us.

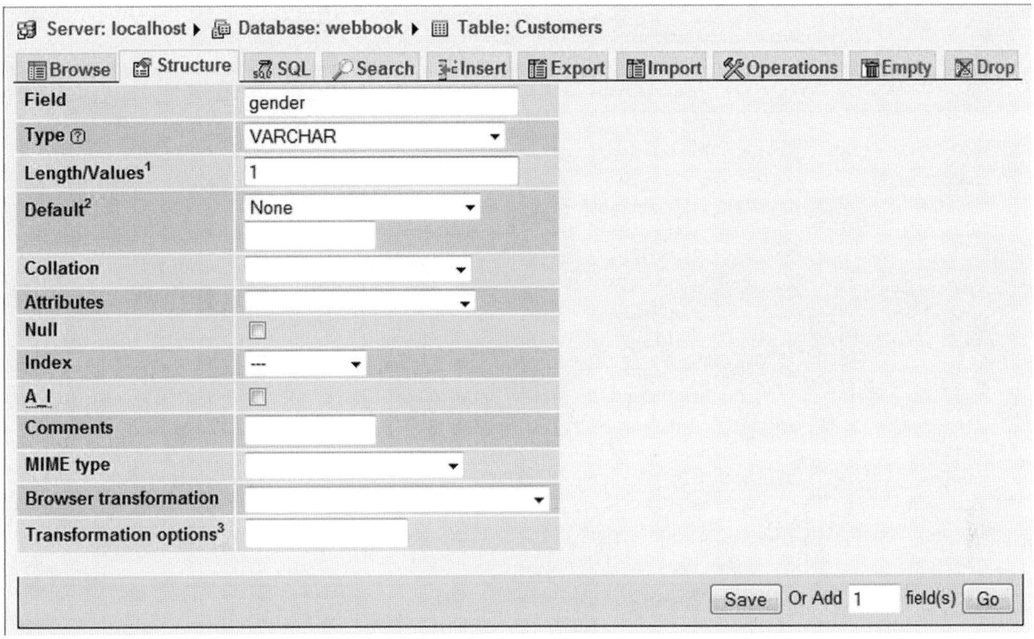

FIGURE 9.6

graphics/ch09/displayChangeAttributeProperty.jpg
Altering the Customers table using phpMyAdmin.

9.7.2   The ALTER Command

The **ALTER** command allows us to modify an existing object in our database. For example, we can use it to add a column to, or delete a column from, an existing table.

Recall that we had made a mistake in creating the Customers table by omitting the gender attribute. We will now add this attribute. Let us say that we realized our error as soon as we looked at the results returned by the CREATE command in Figure 9.4. Notice at the bottom of the figure that we have the option of adding an attribute. We can indicate that we want to add an attribute after customer_last_name and click on the Go button.

Figure 9.6 shows the page that will come up for specifying the properties of the new attribute. We indicate that the name of the attribute is gender, and it will be of type VARCHAR with a length of 1, and then click the Save button.

Figure 9.7 shows the structure of the altered Customers table, as well as the SQL ALTER command that was used to add the gender attribute. This command is also shown, more clearly, in Figure 9.8. ALTER is a very versatile command, which allows

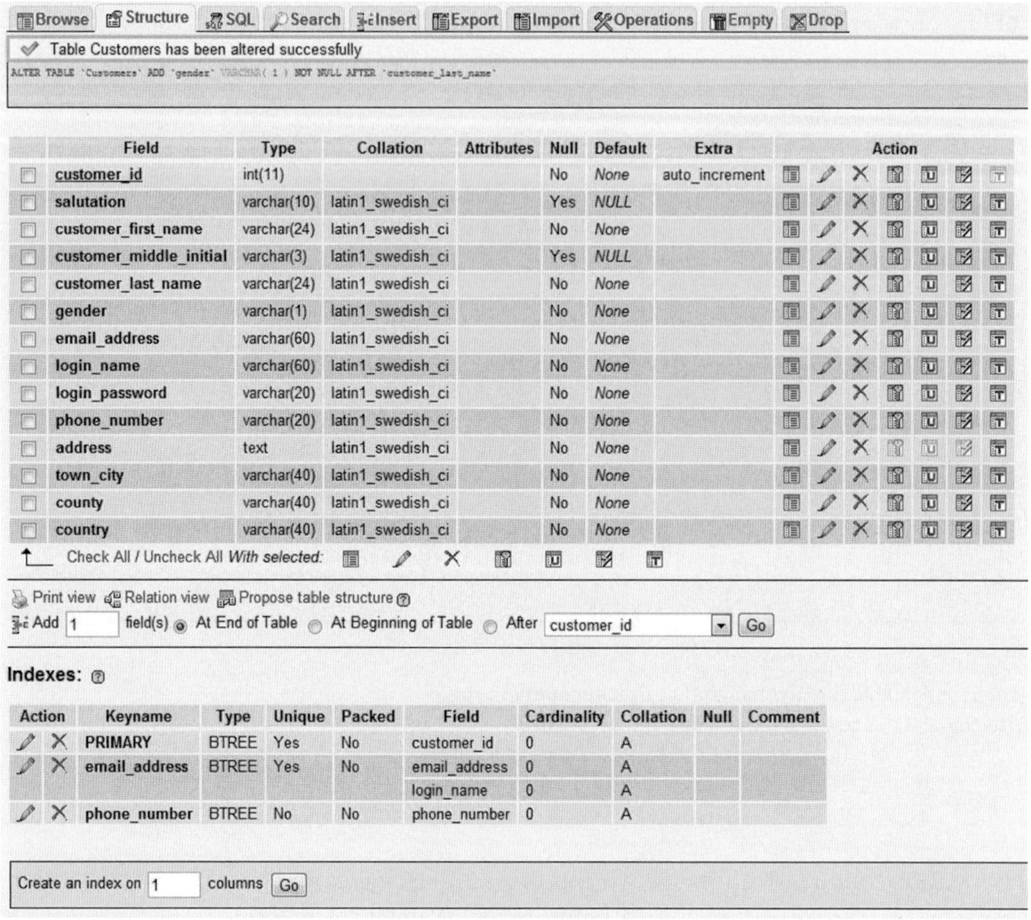

FIGURE 9.7

graphics/ch09/displayResultChangeAttributeProperty.jpg
Result of altering the Customers table using phpMyAdmin.

```
1   ALTER TABLE 'Customers'
2   ADD 'gender' VARCHAR( 1 )
3   NOT NULL AFTER 'customer_last_name'
```

FIGURE 9.8

graphics/ch09/changeAttributeProperty.sql
The SQL command for altering our Customers table by adding a new attribute.

us to add, change, or delete attributes. In our case, we have simply used the ADD "subcommand" to add gender after customer_last_name.

9.7.3 The DROP Command

The last SQL data definition command we want to look at is the DROP command. The DROP command can be used to remove an attribute from a table, a table from your database, or even to remove the complete database. Caution should be exercised when using this command, because the deletion is irreversible and the "dropped" data is therefore irretrievable.

We will study this command with the help of a table called TEMP. We have created such a table in our database with two attributes called dummy1 and dummy2, as shown in Figure 9.9. If you click on the red X icon in the row containing the dummy1 attribute, a dialog box will appear. This is also shown in Figure 9.9. The corresponding SQL query uses this ALTER command with a DROP subcommand:

```
ALTER TABLE 'temp' DROP 'dummy1';
```

As soon as you click on OK, the attribute dummy1 will disappear from the table. If we want to delete the entire table TEMP from the database, we can click on the database and then click on the red X icon in the row corresponding to that table, as shown in Figure 9.10. The required SQL query is:

```
DROP TABLE 'temp';
```

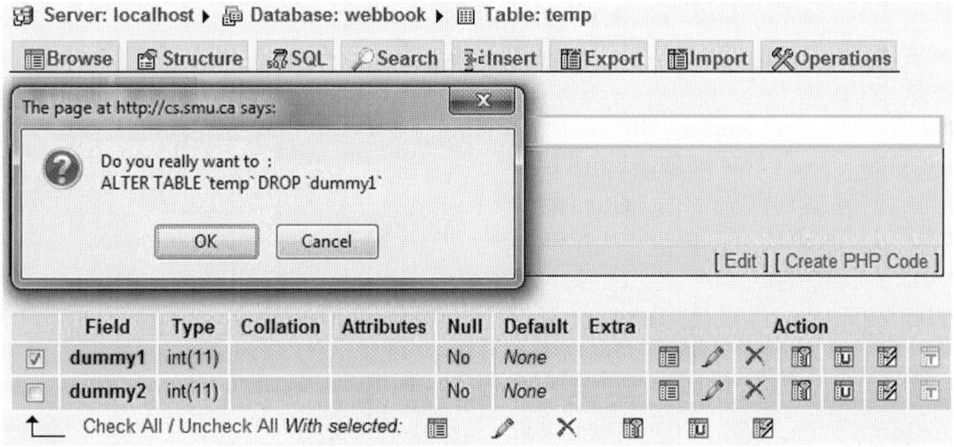

FIGURE 9.9
graphics/ch09/displayDropDummy1.jpg
Dropping an attribute from a table.

☐	**Products**					✕	0	MyISAM	latin1_swedish_ci

The page at http://cs.smu.ca says:

Do you really want to :
DROP TABLE `temp`

OK   Cancel

☐	**Shipments**						✕	0	MyISAM	latin1_swedish_ci
☐	**Shipment_items**						✕	0	MyISAM	latin1_swedish_ci
☑	**temp**						✕	0	MyISAM	latin1_swedish_ci
	13 table(s)			**Sum**			8	**MyISAM**	**latin1_swedish_ci**

FIGURE 9.10

graphics/ch09/displayDropTemp.jpg
Dropping a table from a database.

Clicking on the OK button will permanently delete the table TEMP from our database.

9.7.4   The INSERT Command

Now that we have dealt with the SQL *data definition commands* that are of interest to us, we turn our attention to *data manipulation commands*, beginning with the INSERT command. Suppose want to add two records to the table Ref_Invoice_Status. Clicking on that table in the database, and then clicking on the Insert link will bring up the web page shown in Figure 9.11. We then enter the values for the two records and click the Go button at the bottom right. The resulting web page, seen in Figure 9.12, shows the insertion as well as the corresponding SQL command. The SQL INSERT command is also reproduced in Figure 9.13.

Here is the general format of the INSERT command:

```
INSERT INTO table_name
( comma-separated list of attributes )
VALUES
( comma-separated list of values for attribute 1),
( comma-separated list of values for attribute 2),
( comma-separated list of values for attribute 3),
...
( comma-separated list of values for last attribute)
```

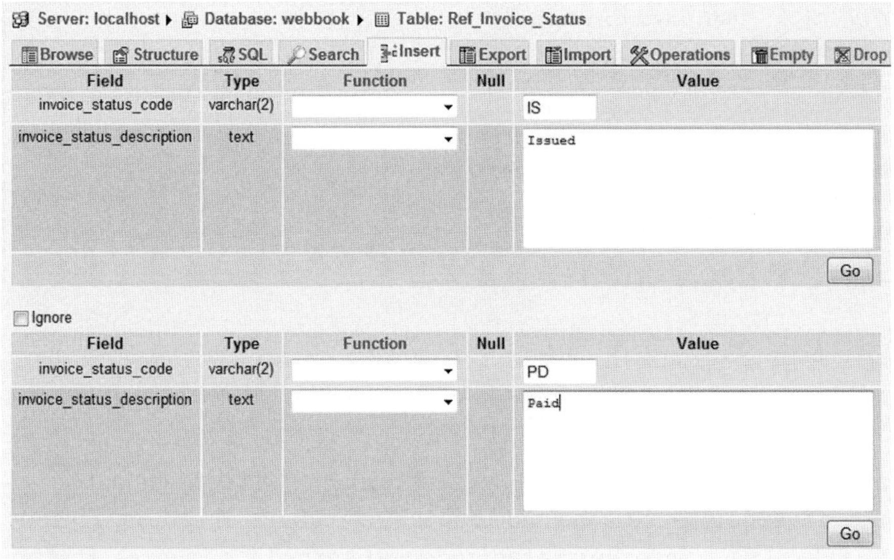

FIGURE 9.11

graphics/ch09/displayInsertRecords.jpg
Inserting records into the **Ref_Address_Types** table using phpMyAdmin.

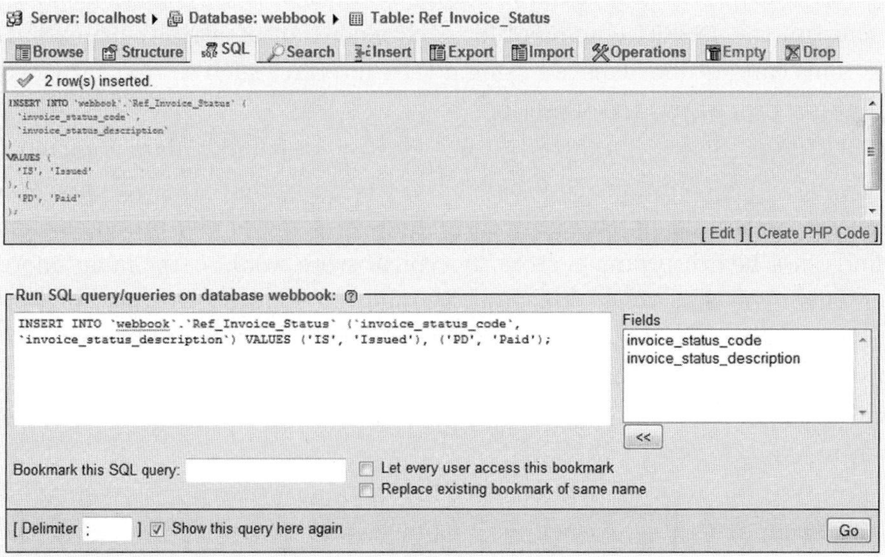

FIGURE 9.12

graphics/ch09/displayResultInsertRecords.jpg
Result of inserting records into the **Ref_Address_Types** table using phpMyAdmin.

```
1    INSERT INTO `webbook`.`Ref_Invoice_Status` (
2      `invoice_status_code` ,
3      `invoice_status_description`
4    )
5    VALUES (
6      'IS', 'Issued'
7    ), (
8      'PD', 'Paid'
9    );
```

FIGURE 9.13

graphics/ch09/insertRecords.sql
The SQL command for inserting two records into our Ref_Invoice_Status table.

In our command shown in Figure 9.13 we are indicating we want to enter the values of attributes invoice_status_code and invoice_status_description. The first record has the value IS for invoice_status_code and Issued for invoice_status_description. The second record has the value PD for invoice_status_code and Paid for invoice_status_description.

The INSERT command is quite useful for loading a small number of records into our database. But what if we want to insert a large number of records from a file? In this case we can run the INSERT command for each record automatically using SQL programming. This can also be achieved using a GUI interface such as that provided by phpMyAdmin, a process we now describe.

On your CD-ROM, under the directory web09, you will find a data file called products870.csv, which contains 870 product records. Note that these are not real products; they are generated by changing the names of some of the products that one usually finds in a health products store. A typical store would carry many more products than this. The first 20 records from the file are shown (partially) in Figure 9.14, with the lines truncated so the display will fit on the page. The value for each attribute is enclosed in a pair of single quotes and values are separated by commas. That is why we use the (conventional) file extension csv, which stands for "comma-separated values."

We can import these records into our Products table using phpMyAdmin. If we click on the Products table, we will see a link called Import. Clicking on the Import link brings up a web page similar to the one shown in Figure 9.15, where we have entered the name of our data file and clicked on the CSV radio button. We have also indicated that the fields are enclosed in single quotes and separated by commas.

```
1   '707689','ACID','HMF PRE+PROBIO 250G','39','28','','','HMF PRE+PROBIO 250G for Acidic suppleme
2   '707690','ACID','LACTOBACILLUS 60C','20','2','','','LACTOBACILLUS 60C for Acidic supplements',
3   '707691','ACID','100 ACIDOPHILUS WITH FOS','26.99','67','','','100 ACIDOPHILUS WITH FOS for Ac
4   '707692','ACID','S STRNGTH 5 LOZENGES 60T','16.99','14','','','S STRNGTH 5 LOZENGES 60T for Ac
5   '707693','ACID','PLUS ACID- BIFID-FOS 100VC','29.99','8','','','PLUS ACID- BIFID-FOS 100VC for
6   '707694','ACID','PLUS 100ML','55','46','','','PLUS 100ML for Acidic supplements','images/produ
7   '707695','ACID','HMF NATOGEN (NEOGEN)','29','74','','','HMF NATOGEN (NEOGEN) for Acidic supple
8   '707696','ACID','MEGA ACID 75GM','11.99','21','','','MEGA ACID 75GM for Acidic supplements','i
9   '707697','ACID','PCA-RX 30ML','199.99','26','','','PCA-RX 30ML for Acidic supplements','images
0   '707698','ACID','LACTOVIDEN ID 60C','40','16','','','LACTOVIDEN ID 60C for Acidic supplements'
1   '707699','ACID','S INFANTS BLEND 75G','24.99','16','','','S INFANTS BLEND 75G for Acidic suppl
2   '707700','ACID','LEAF ACIDOPHILUS 120C','44.99','7','','','LEAF ACIDOPHILUS 120C for Acidic su
3   '707701','ACID','ULTRA FLOR+ DF 50G','42','48','','','ULTRA FLOR+ DF 50G for Acidic supplement
4   '707702','ACID','FEM DOPHILUS 30CT','30','57','','','FEM DOPHILUS 30CT for Acidic supplements'
5   '707703','ACID','S STRNGTH 8 60C','36.99','3','','','S STRNGTH 8 60C for Acidic supplements','
6   '707704','ACID','YOGOURT STARTER 49GM','19','89','','','YOGOURT STARTER 49GM for Acidic supple
7   '707705','ACID','KAPS CAPS 30C','39.99','43','','','KAPS CAPS 30C for Acidic supplements','ima
8   '707706','ACID','S ADULT BLEND 60C','26.99','79','','','S ADULT BLEND 60C for Acidic supplemen
9   '707707','ACID','S CHILDRENS BLEND 60C','19.99','16','','','S CHILDRENS BLEND 60C for Acidic s
0   '707708','ACID','S DIGESTIVE ENZYME 120C','39.99','21','','','S DIGESTIVE ENZYME 120C for Acid
```

FIGURE 9.14

cdrom/web09/products870Truncated.csv
Partial view of a file of comma-separated values containing product records.

FIGURE 9.15

graphics/ch09/displayInsertManyRecords.jpg
Inserting multiple records in the **Products** table using phpMyAdmin.

Server: localhost ▶ Database: webbook ▶ Table: Products

Browse   Structure   SQL   Search   Insert   Export   Import   Operations   Empty   Drop

✓ Import has been successfully finished, 870 queries executed.

FIGURE 9.16

graphics/ch09/displayResultInsertManyRecords.jpg
Result of inserting multiple records in the Products table using phpMyAdmin.

Finally, we use the default value \ for the *escape character*. This means that any occurrences of tab, newline, or \ that are preceded by \ should be treated as literal characters. For example, \\ will be treated as a single \. Clicking on the Go button will add all 870 records to the table, using 870 INSERT queries, as confirmed by the message shown in Figure 9.16.

9.7.5   The LOAD Command

There is a more efficient way to import a large number of records, by using the LOAD command. Let us explore this option with the help of the same Import interface, but this time we will use the Customers table. The data file we will import contains 10000 customers, is called customers10000.csv, and a copy is also provided in the directory web09 on your CD-ROM. As with our products data file, a truncated version is shown in Figure 9.17.

```
1    '100005','Mr.','Michael','P.','McClune','M','Michael0@webbook.com','Michael0','Michael0','607-
2    '100007','Mr.','Michael','P.','Young','M','Michael1@webbook.com','Michael1','Michael1','470-64
3    '100009','Mr.','Jordan','I.','Ore','M','Jordan2@webbook.com','Jordan2','Jordan2','882-551-3892
4    '100011','Mr.','Bjorn','A.','Ditty','M','Bjorn3@webbook.com','Bjorn3','Bjorn3','846-305-8131',
5    '100013','Ms.','Riza','U.','Zalameda','F','Riza4@webbook.com','Riza4','Riza4','570-476-7282','
6    '100015','Ms.','Jacqueline','M.','Goldfeld','F','Jacqueline5@webbook.com','Jacqueline5','Jacqu
7    '100017','Mr.','Scoville','E.','Lepchenko','M','Scoville6@webbook.com','Scoville6','Scoville6'
8    '100019','Mr.','Nathan','T.','Blake','M','Nathan7@webbook.com','Nathan7','Nathan7','524-687-39
9    '100021','Mr.','Ryan','R.','Smyczek','M','Ryan8@webbook.com','Ryan8','Ryan8','576-452-5110','7
10   '100023','Ms.','Angela','C.','Nguyen','F','Angela9@webbook.com','Angela9','Angela9','474-367-1
11   '100025','Ms.','Ester','Z.','Muhammad','F','Ester10@webbook.com','Ester10','Ester10','511-803-
12   '100027','Ms.','Abigail','K.','Harrison','F','Abigail11@webbook.com','Abigail11','Abigail11','
13   '100029','Mr.','Mike','K.','DeHeart','M','Mike12@webbook.com','Mike12','Mike12','621-815-4208'
14   '100031','Mr.','Gonzalas','M.','Russell','M','Gonzalas13@webbook.com','Gonzalas13','Gonzalas13
15   '100033','Mr.','Alexander','T.','Buchanan','M','Alexander14@webbook.com','Alexander14','Alexan
16   '100035','Mr.','Michael','X.','Rolle','M','Michael15@webbook.com','Michael15','Michael15','782
17   '100037','Mr.','Junior','S.','Martin','M','Junior16@webbook.com','Junior16','Junior16','548-76
18   '100039','Ms.','Abigail','X.','Vandeweghe','F','Abigail17@webbook.com','Abigail17','Abigail17'
19   '100041','Mr.','Jordan','P.','Venus','M','Jordan18@webbook.com','Jordan18','Jordan18','786-454
20   '100043','Mr.','Johannes','K.','Kendrick','M','Johannes19@webbook.com','Johannes19','Johannes1
```

FIGURE 9.17

cdrom/web09/customers10000Truncated.csv
Partial view of a file of comma-separated values containing customer records.

Server: localhost ▸ Database: webbook ▸ Table: Customers

Browse | **Structure** | **SQL** | **Search** | **Insert** | **Export** | **Import** | **Operations** | **Empty** | **Drop**

File to import

Location of the text file | omers/customers10000.csv | Browse... | (Max: 2,048 KiB)

Character set of the file: utf8 ▾

Imported file compression will be automatically detected from: None, gzip, bzip2, zip

Partial import

☑ Allow the interruption of an import in case the script detects it is close to the PHP timeout limit. This might be good way to import large files, however it can break transactions.

Number of records (queries) to skip from start | 0

Format of imported file

○ CSV

Options

◉ CSV using LOAD DATA

○ SQL

☐ Replace table data with file
☐ Ignore duplicate rows
Fields terminated by | ,
Fields enclosed by | "
Fields escaped by | \
Lines terminated by | auto
Column names |
☑ Use LOCAL keyword

Go

FIGURE 9.18

`graphics/ch09/displayLoadFile.jpg`

Loading multiple customer records from a `csv` file into the `Customers` table using phpMyAdmin.

This time we choose the `CSV using the LOAD DATA` radio button, but the rest of the selections are the same as before. Clicking on the `Go` button will add all 10000 records using a single query based on the `LOAD` command in SQL, as shown in Figure 9.19. Caution should be exercised when loading large files through the phpMyAdmin interface. There is usually a limit of 2MB. Even if your file is smaller than 2MB, the `LOAD` command may not be successful. We recommend that you upload the file through other means to the server that hosts your MySQL server. Then execute the SQL query preferably through the command-line interface that we will look at in the next section.

In the meantime, let us look at the SQL query shown in Figure 9.20, which uses the SQL `LOAD` command. Here is the abbreviated (and generic) format of the `LOAD` command that we used for our example:

```
LOAD DATA LOCAL INFILE 'file_name'
    INTO TABLE tbl_name
    FIELDS TERMINATED BY 'string'
    ENCLOSED BY 'char'
    ESCAPED BY 'char'
    LINES TERMINATED BY 'string';
```

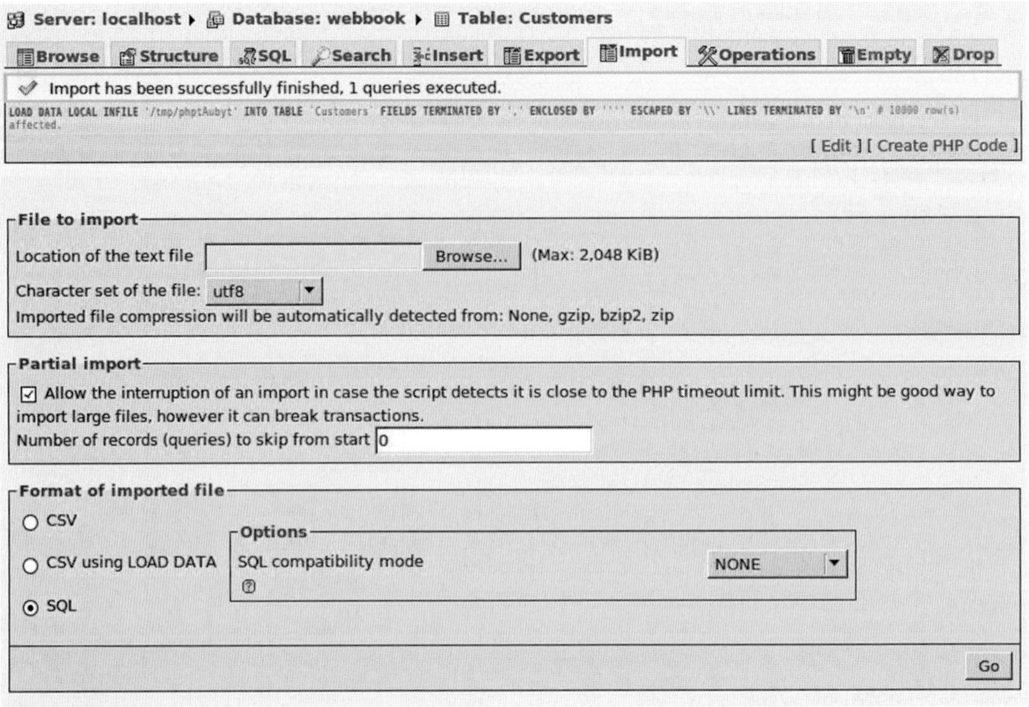

FIGURE 9.19

graphics/ch09/displayResultLoadFile.jpg
Result of loading multiple customer records from a `csv` file into the `Customers` table using php-MyAdmin.

```
1    LOAD DATA LOCAL INFILE '/tmp/phpvBgdxT'
2    INTO TABLE 'Customers'
3    FIELDS TERMINATED BY ','
4    ENCLOSED BY ''''
5    ESCAPED BY '\\'
6    LINES TERMINATED BY '\n';
```

FIGURE 9.20

graphics/ch09/loadFile.sql
The SQL command for loading multiple customer records from a `csv` file into the `Customers` table.

Here we see only the options that we actually used in loading our customer records. See the MySQL manual for details about many other options.

First, the keyword `LOCAL` means that the file needs to be copied to the server that hosts MySQL. That is why we have a funny file name in the command. Our file `customers10000.csv` was copied to a temporary file on the server, and the file name used in the command is that of the temporary file. We indicate that the fields

are enclosed in single quotes and separated by commas. We use the default value \
for the escape character. As before, that means all occurrences of `tab`, `newline`, or
\ that are preceded by \ should be treated as literal characters.

9.7.6 The UPDATE Command

We have now seen two commands (`INSERT` and `LOAD`) for getting data into our
database. But what if we inadvertently entered some wrong data, or some piece
of data already in the database has to be updated? Clearly we also need an `UPDATE`
command and, of course, there is one. We will not discuss it any further here, other
than to show you its syntax, which looks like this:

```
UPDATE 'table_name'
    SET column1_name=expression [column2_name=expression2, ...]
    [WHERE where_expression]
    [LIMIT n]
```

The command works as follows. The columns in the table that are modified are
those specified in the `WHERE` clause, and each of those rows has each column named in
the `SET` clause set to the value of the corresponding expression. If there is no `WHERE`
clause, *all* rows of the table are modified. If the `LIMIT` clause is given, the value `n`
specifies the maximum number of rows to be modified.

See the end-of-chapter **Short Exercises** section for an exercise giving you a
chance to get familiar with this command.

9.7.7 A First Look at the SELECT Command

We now know how to "populate" our database using two data manipulation commands, `INSERT` and `LOAD`. Two other commands, `DELETE` and `TRUNCATE`, will allow us
to "de-populate" our database. Before looking at these two destructive commands,
we will take a brief look at the most important data retrieval command, `SELECT`. It
will be discussed in more detail later in the chapter when we discuss the command-
line interface. However, in order to delete records, we will have to browse our tables
and find what to delete. So a simple introduction to data retrieval is in order.

The records we have in our database allow us to experiment with the `SELECT`
command. We can simply click on the `Browse` link when we are in the `Customers`
table, and we will get (by default) the first 30 records in the table, as shown in
Figure 9.21. The corresponding SQL query is shown in Figure 9.22 and you can see
that these records have been retrieved from the database using a `SELECT` command.

FIGURE 9.21

graphics/ch09/displaySelectAll.jpg
Selecting records from the Customers table using phpMyAdmin.

```
1    SELECT *
2    FROM 'Customers'
3    LIMIT 0 , 30
```

FIGURE 9.22

graphics/ch09/selectAll.sql
Selecting records from the Customers table using SQL.

In Figure 9.22 we show the use of the SELECT command in its simplest form to select the complete record by specifying '*' after the keyword SELECT. The word Customers after FROM indicates the table, and the range of 0 to 30 records appears after the keyword LIMIT. We will be experimenting with more sophisticated SELECT statements later on in this chapter, but for the moment let us just see how to delete a few, or all, of the records from a database.

9.7.8   The DELETE Command

The Customers table shown in Figure 9.21 has one of the records highlighted with a different color, because we are hovering our mouse over that record. We are going to pick the record for deletion by clicking on the red X icon that appears just before the beginning of the record. Figure 9.23 shows the window that will pop up. It also shows the corresponding SQL query. The query uses the DELETE command. Once again, there are more options than we show, but the typical (generic) syntax for deleting from a single table looks like this:

```
DELETE FROM table_name
    [WHERE where_condition]
    [ORDER BY ...]
    [LIMIT row_count]
```

The WHERE clause allows you to specify a condition that a record must satisfy for it to be deleted. In our case, we specified that the customer_id must match the specified value. The ORDER BY option allows us to specify the attributes that should be used to order the records for deletion. The ordering is especially relevant if we were going to limit the number of records that should be deleted using the option LIMIT. In our example query, we are limiting the number of deletions to a single record. This is redundant, since customer_id is unique, and there will be only one record that will match the WHERE clause in any case.

9.7.9   The TRUNCATE Command

Since we have started deleting records, why stop at one record? Let us delete all the records and then rebuild our data—we now have the power. The command TRUNCATE TABLE allows us to delete all the records in a table. We can invoke it from phpMy-Admin by clicking on the database and then clicking on the red X next to the table

FIGURE 9.23
graphics/ch09/displayDeleteRecord.jpg
Deleting a record from the Customers table using phpMyAdmin.

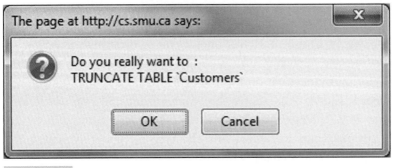

FIGURE 9.24

graphics/ch09/displayTruncateTable.jpg
Truncating the Customers table using phpMyAdmin.

name. A warning window including the SQL query will pop up as shown in Figure 9.24. Click the OK button and all the data in the table will be deleted. Most database engines implement the TRUNCATE TABLE command by dropping the table and recreating an empty table. It is much faster than deleting individual records when the tables are large. Should we spare you the obvious warning about exercising caution while using DELETE and TRUNCATE TABLE commands?

9.7.10   Inventory Management Systems

Most retail businesses will have some kind of *inventory management system* that will be part of the "back office" for the use of store management. It will handle the wholesale purchase of items from suppliers and maintain the data necessary to keep track of inventory.

Systems like this are not unique to e-commerce businesses. Our system can work with such an inventory management system simply by interacting with the product-related tables. We have chosen to limit the scope of our system, since the inclusion of many additional tables would not help us learn any new features of web programming. However, for the business you are working on in the "parallel project," you may find it convenient to add a number of additional tables to deal with the specific activities in which your business is involved. Be thinking about the possibilities as you work on the next iterations of the parallel project at the end of this chapter and the next.

In the absence of a complete inventory management system, we have filled as many tables as necessary for experimenting with the database. Readers are encouraged to browse through the populated tables from the book's website.

Later on in this chapter we will also describe how you can import our entire database into your own MySQL system so that you can experiment with it. In the next chapter, we will also see how to populate the rest of the tables using simulated e-commerce, when we process "purchases" of our products by our customers.

However, our limited discussion of database management is not yet complete. We need to look at the command-line interface to MySQL. The command-line interface is generally less user-friendly than phpMyAdmin, but much faster to use for those who know what they are doing, especially when queries are more complicated. It is also less forgiving than the GUI counterpart, and is therefore meant for more knowledgeable users. To become comfortable with database management, it is necessary for all web programmers to learn how SQL queries are executed via the command-line interface, since when such queries are sent through a programming language API the commands have essentially the same form as when they are entered directly by typing them in at a command-line prompt.

9.8 MySQL's Command-Line Interface

We will use the Linux command line to gain access to our MySQL command-line interface. You can also log in to MySQL from other operating systems such as Windows or the Mac OS. Once you have logged into MySQL from any operating system, you use essentially the same interface.

9.8.1 A First Session with the Command-Line Interface

Figure 9.25 shows our first command-line interaction with MySQL. In line 1 we use the Linux command

```
mysql -u webbook -p
```

to log in to the MySQL system.[5] The name following the -u option is the username by which MySQL identifies the user. The -p option indicates that the username requires a password, which is entered in response to the prompt from MySQL in line 2.

As is always the case in these situations, when the password is typed, it does not show up on the screen. Once the password is verified and accepted, the prompt

```
mysql>
```

appears, and we are then ready to enter our commands at the command-line interface.

---

[5]Note that the command to access the MySQL system under Linux is an all-lowercase `mysql`.

```
1   ok > mysql -u webbook -p
2   Enter password:
3   Welcome to the MySQL monitor.  Commands end with ; or \g.
4   Your MySQL connection id is 28603
5   Server version: 5.0.75-0ubuntu10.2 (Ubuntu)
6
7   Type 'help;' or '\h' for help. Type '\c' to clear the buffer.
8
9   mysql> use webbook;
10  Reading table information for completion of table and column names
11  You can turn off this feature to get a quicker startup with -A
12
13  Database changed
14  mysql> show tables;
15  +-----------------------+
16  | Tables_in_webbook     |
17  +-----------------------+
18  | Customers             |
19  | Invoices              |
20  | Order_Items           |
21  | Orders                |
22  | Payments              |
23  | Products              |
24  | Ref_Invoice_Status    |
25  | Ref_Order_Item_Status |
26  | Ref_Order_Status      |
27  | Ref_Product_Categories |
28  | Shipment_items        |
29  | Shipments             |
30  +-----------------------+
31  12 rows in set (0.00 sec)
32
33  mysql> select * from Ref_Invoice_Status;
34  +---------------------+----------------------------+
35  | invoice_status_code | invoice_status_description |
36  +---------------------+----------------------------+
37  | IS                  | Issued                     |
38  | PD                  | Paid                       |
39  +---------------------+----------------------------+
40  2 rows in set (0.01 sec)
41
42  mysql> quit
43  Bye
44  webbook >
```

FIGURE 9.25

graphics/ch09/mysqlSession1.txt
A first look at the command-line interface for MySQL.

The first thing we have to do is tell MySQL which database we would like to use. That is the purpose of the USE command in line 9:

```
USE webbook;
```

Note that most commands in MySQL have to be terminated with a semicolon (;). Some commands do not actually require the semicolon, but having a semicolon at the end of those commands does not cause an error, so it is much safer, and a recommended "best practice," simply to put a semicolon at the end of every command.

With the command

```
SHOW tables;
```

we can find out what tables are currently in the database we have said we want to use. In this case, we see the 12 tables of our own database that we have been discussing.

Next, we execute a simple SELECT command to retrieve all the records from the table Ref_Invoice_Status:

```
SELECT * FROM Ref_Invoice_Status;
```

There are only two such records, as the display shows. The use of ★ in this context means that we want to see all the fields from each record. This SELECT command is similar to the one we saw earlier. Note the format of the output for each of the queries we have seen here, which is typical.

In fact, all the SQL commands we saw in the previous section can be executed using the command-line interface, but in some cases—such as creating a table or adding one or two records—it may be easier to use the phpMyAdmin GUI.

9.8.2 A Closer Look at the SELECT Command

Unfortunately, the phpMyAdmin GUI may be of limited use when we are specifying more complex data retrieval queries using SELECT. Let's now investigate some more sophisticated retrievals using the command-line interface. In a SELECT query, the user describes only the desired *result set*. The following are keyword modifiers commonly used with a SELECT command:

- FROM, which is followed by a comma-separated list of the names of the tables from which the data is to be taken.

- WHERE, which is followed by a comma-separated list of the conditions that specify which rows are of interest for the retrieval.

- GROUP BY, which is followed by information indicating how the data in rows with related values is to be combined.

- ORDER BY, which is used to identify which columns are used to sort the retrieved data.

- LIMIT, which specifies a range of records for which the data is to be retrieved.

We will explore these keywords with the help of some queries. Note that in the text discussion we continue to use all uppercase for the names of MySQL commands and their modifiers to distinguish them from the (user-chosen) names of other entities. When typing them into the command-line interface, however, it is easier to take advantage of the case-insensitivity of MySQL and use all lowercase. Keep in mind, however, that the user-chosen names (for tables and attributes, for example) *will* be case-sensitive, at least on Linux and other Unix-based systems.

Calling Built-In MySQL Functions and Performing Simple Arithmetic During Data Retrieval

MySQL has some built-in functions that can be very useful in data retrieval. Let us begin by illustrating COUNT(), a function that retrieves just the total number of records, instead of the records themselves. So in Figure 9.26 our first query is

```
SELECT COUNT(*) from Customers;
```

```
1   mysql> select count(*) from Customers;
2   +----------+
3   | count(*) |
4   +----------+
5   |    10000 |
6   +----------+
7   1 row in set (0.00 sec)
8
9   mysql> select country,count(*) from Customers group by country;
10  +---------+----------+
11  | country | count(*) |
12  +---------+----------+
13  | Canada  |     1791 |
14  | USA     |     8209 |
15  +---------+----------+
16  2 rows in set (0.01 sec)
```

FIGURE 9.26

graphics/ch09/countSQL.txt
Use of the COUNT() function in SQL.

and the result shows the total number of records in the `Customers` table. You may recall that phpMyAdmin generated queries that used single quotes around table and attribute names. We are not using single quotes around the table names here, since they are unnecessary if the names do not contain any spaces. But if we had a table with a name like `Our Customers`, for example, we would have to enclose it in single quotes. However, best practice would dictate that we avoid such names.[6]

The second query in Figure 9.26 is

```
SELECT country, COUNT(*) FROM Customers GROUP BY country;
```

and uses the `GROUP BY` option, where the records are grouped by the values in the specified list of attributes. We are grouping by the country, so there will be a separate record for each country. That is why we get two records for two countries in our table, one for Canada and the other for the USA.

Another useful MySQL function is `SUM()`. Figure 9.27 shows its use with the following query:

```
SELECT SUM(product_inventory) FROM Products;
```

```
mysql> select sum(product_inventory) from Products;
+------------------------+
| sum(product_inventory) |
+------------------------+
|                  43097 |
+------------------------+
1 row in set (0.01 sec)

mysql> select sum(product_inventory)/count(*) from Products;
+---------------------------------+
| sum(product_inventory)/count(*) |
+---------------------------------+
|                         49.5368 |
+---------------------------------+
1 row in set (0.00 sec)
```

FIGURE 9.27
graphics/ch09/sumSQL.txt
Use of the `SUM()` function in SQL.

---

[6]In fact, Microsoft Windows notwithstanding, if you consistently avoid using names containing blank spaces when you are naming things on your computer, there will be several kinds of problems you will never have.

This query sums up the values of the attribute `product_inventory` for every record in the `Products` table. So we see that there 43,097 items in our inventory.

The second query in Figure 9.27 also shows that we can do simple arithmetic during data retrieval using SQL:

```
SELECT SUM(product_inventory)/COUNT(*) FROM Products;
```

This query gives us the average number of items per product.

9.8.3   Restricting the Set of Records from which We Retrieve Our Data

So far each of our queries has dealt with all of the records in a given table. We can restrict the scope of our retrieval by using a `WHERE` clause similar to the one we used for `DELETE`. Let us say we wanted to find out how many products in the `Products` table have less than 10 items in stock. We can use the query

```
SELECT COUNT(*) FROM Products WHERE product_inventory < 10;
```

the result of which is shown in Figure 9.28.

If we want to sort the records, we can use the `ORDER BY` option, as shown in Figure 9.29. In this case we want to retrieve a list of the products with inventory size greater than 90 and have it sorted based on the value of the attribute `product_inventory`. The `DESC` option indicates that we want the sorting performed in descending order. We also used the `LIMIT` option here so that we only see the top 10 records in the list. The LIMIT option has two (command-separated) values in this case, 0 and 10. The first indicates how many records to skip before starting the retrieval, and the second tells how many records to retrieve. Since the first value is 0, it is actually redundant in this case, and we could have used the single value 10.

```
1   mysql> select count(*) from Products where product_inventory < 10;
2   +----------+
3   | count(*) |
4   +----------+
5   |       96 |
6   +----------+
7   1 row in set (0.00 sec)
```

FIGURE 9.28

graphics/ch09/conditionSQL.txt
An SQL query illustrating "conditional retrieval."

```
mysql> select product_name, product_inventory
    -> from Products
    -> where product_inventory > 90
    -> order by product_inventory desc
    -> limit 0,10;
+-----------------------+-------------------+
| product_name          | product_inventory |
+-----------------------+-------------------+
| LACTOBACILLUS 30 C    |                99 |
| ALLERGY RELIEF 30C    |                99 |
| QUERCETIN 90C         |                99 |
| GOOD STRNGTH CARNOSINE |               99 |
| AS MEDICINE           |                99 |
| LINEN FOUNDATION      |                99 |
| CHAMMOMILE TEA        |                99 |
| D 400IU 100T          |                99 |
| VEGETARIAN BOOSTER 90C |               98 |
| STRNGTH AO FORMULA    |                98 |
+-----------------------+-------------------+
10 rows in set (0.00 sec)
```

FIGURE 9.29

graphics/ch09/orderSQL.txt
Ordering retrieved records using SQL.

Note that this (somewhat longer than usual) query is entered over several lines, and the prompt from MySQL changes to -> from the second line on, until we enter the terminating semicolon.

9.8.4 Retrieving Data from More than One Table

So far, in making our queries, we have only dealt with a single table. Our retrievals can also collect information from multiple tables at the same time, which is referred to as a *join*. We illustrate this in Figure 9.30. The query in this figure is our most complex query to date.

In this example, we want to list the number of products in each product category as well as the total number of items in each category. We want to use the category description as the first column in our retrieved data. The category description is in the table Ref_Product_Categories, while the rest of the information is in the Products table.

This query also employs another useful feature of SQL that allows us to assign temporary aliases to certain entities, which provide more meaningful or concise names to be used within the query itself. Here, for example, we are indicating that the

```
1    mysql> select product_category_description as category,
2        -> count(*) as products,
3        -> sum(product_inventory) as product_inventory
4        -> from Products as P, Ref_Product_Categories as R
5        -> where P.product_category_code = R.product_category_code
6        -> group by category
7        -> order by products desc
8        -> limit 0,10;
9    +----------------------+----------+-------------------+
10   | category             | products | product_inventory |
11   +----------------------+----------+-------------------+
12   | Adult multi-vitamins |    128   |              6063 |
13   | Nutritional bars     |     68   |              3311 |
14   | Body enhancement     |     64   |              3067 |
15   | Anti-oxidants        |     62   |              3431 |
16   | Acidic supplements   |     55   |              2295 |
17   | Application products |     34   |              1660 |
18   | Hair treatment       |     32   |              1741 |
19   | Aromatic therapy     |     28   |              1312 |
20   | Baby products        |     27   |              1414 |
21   | Relief from allergies|     26   |              1350 |
22   +----------------------+----------+-------------------+
23   10 rows in set (0.02 sec)
```

FIGURE 9.30

graphics/ch09/multiTableSQL.txt
Retrieving data from multiple tables using join in SQL.

product_category_description will also be known as category, using the keyword AS. Similarly, the count of products will also be known as products, and the sum of the product inventory will be known as product_inventory. We further abbreviate the Products table simply as P and the table Ref_Product_Categories as R.

These two tables are "joined" by requiring the following condition, which connects them via their common keys, to be satisfied:

P.product_category_code = R.product_category_code

The records are then grouped by category, and finally they are sorted in descending order based on the value of products, and we are also limiting ourselves to viewing the first 10 records. The *join* we have seen in this case is the simplest form of join. SQL allows for more sophisticated joining of tables. See the MySQL manual or the **References** section at the end of this chapter for more information.

The data from any of the SQL queries we might make can be stored in new tables. We will look into that facility in the next section, along with general importing and exporting of tables and databases.

9.9 Importing and Exporting Tables and Databases

In this section, we look at some of the SQL commands, as well as the GUI facilities, that we can use to copy, import, and export data in MySQL. You should know how to perform these tasks, since from time to time you may need to make a copy of one or more of tables, with or without modifications, or even make a copy of an entire database.

9.9.1 Copying a Table

Let us start by looking at how to copy a simple table. We can achieve this by combining the **CREATE** and **SELECT** commands. Let us add a little complexity to our task and say that we want to make a copy of just a portion of the Customers table. We will only copy the customer_id, customer_first_name, customer_last_name, and login_name to another table called Customers2. First, we have to retrieve the required information, and here is the **SELECT** command we need:

```
SELECT customer_id,customer_first_name,
       customer_last_name,login_name
       FROM Customers;
```

Now all we have to do is precede this command with

```
CREATE Customers2 AS
```

and the output from the **SELECT** statement will be stored in the table Customers2. Figure 9.31 shows the MySQL session that performs this copying. The show tables; command shows that the table Customers2 does not exist. We then create it using the above described combination of **CREATE** and **SELECT**. We then verify the creation of the table by looking at the first five records in the newly created Customers2 table.

Later, we delete the table with a

```
DROP TABLE Customers2;
```

command (not shown in the session), since we do not want it to be part of our database.

```
1    mysql> use webbook
2    Reading table information for completion of table and column names
3    You can turn off this feature to get a quicker startup with -A
4
5    Database changed
6    mysql> show tables;
7    +-----------------------+
8    | Tables_in_webbook     |
9    +-----------------------+
10   | Customers             |
11   | Invoices              |
12   | Order_Items           |
13   | Orders                |
14   | Payments              |
15   | Products              |
16   | Ref_Invoice_Status    |
17   | Ref_Order_Item_Status |
18   | Ref_Order_Status      |
19   | Ref_Product_Categories|
20   | Shipment_items        |
21   | Shipments             |
22   +-----------------------+
23   12 rows in set (0.00 sec)
24
25   mysql> create table Customers2 as
26       -> select customer_id,customer_first_name,customer_last_name,login_name
27       -> from Customers;
28   Query OK, 10000 rows affected (0.02 sec)
29   Records: 10000  Duplicates: 0  Warnings: 0
30
31   mysql> select * from Customers2 limit 0,5;
32   +-------------+---------------------+--------------------+------------+
33   | customer_id | customer_first_name | customer_last_name | login_name |
34   +-------------+---------------------+--------------------+------------+
35   |      100005 | Michael             | McClune            | Michael0   |
36   |      100007 | Michael             | Young              | Michael1   |
37   |      100009 | Jordan              | Ore                | Jordan2    |
38   |      100011 | Bjorn               | Ditty              | Bjorn3     |
39   |      100013 | Riza                | Zalameda           | Riza4      |
40   +-------------+---------------------+--------------------+------------+
41   5 rows in set (0.00 sec)
```

FIGURE 9.31

graphics/ch09/copyTableSQL.txt
Creating a copy of a portion of the Customers table using SQL.

9.9.2   Copying an Entire Database

Now let us see how we can create a copy of our entire database. First, we will use the phpMyAdmin interface, and then the command-line option.

In phpMyAdmin, you click on the database you want to "export" (`webbook` in our case) and then click on the `Export` link at the top. Figure 9.32 shows the web page that will pop up. You can select the tables you want to export, as well as the format of the exported file. We will use the default options of exporting all the files and exporting them as an SQL file. Clicking on the `Go` button will bring up the dialog

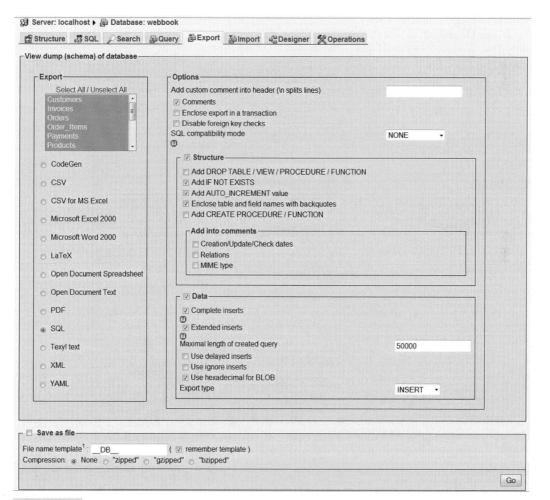

FIGURE 9.32

`graphics/ch09/displayExport.jpg`
Exporting a database using phpMyAdmin.

box that tells you that the file will be saved as `webbook.sql`. You can save the file in an appropriate location.

The exporting and importing of large databases using phpMyAdmin can be a problem, as it will result in a high volume of traffic over the Internet. For this reason, the command-line option is the preferred method for performing these tasks. You need a related command-line utility called `mysqldump` on your system, which should be available with any installation of MySQL.

Figure 9.34 illustrates how to export our entire database using a `mysqldump` command on a Linux system. The command works much like the `mysql` command. After the `-u` option, we specify that the user is `webbook`, and the `-p` option indicates that we will be entering a password. The name `webbook` after the `-p` option says that we want to dump the `webbook` database. The > sign redirects the output to a file called `backupbookSep09.sql`.

We confirm the existence of this file simply by doing a directory listing. The file is in place and has approximately 1.8MB worth of data. The format of the file created

FIGURE 9.33

`graphics/ch09/displayResultExport.jpg`
Result of exporting a database using phpMyAdmin.

```
1   webbook > mysqldump -u webbook -p webbook > backupbookSep09.sql
2   Enter password:
3   webbook > ls -l backupbookSep09.sql
4   -rw------- 1 pawan pawan 1751057 2009-09-20 07:01 backupbookSep09.sql
```

FIGURE 9.34

graphics/ch09/mysqldump.txt
Exporting a database using `mysqldump`.

by exporting from phpMyAdmin and mysqldump is identical. We can take a quick peek at the file created by mysqldump, as shown in Figure 9.35. The file is provided on your CD-ROM under the directory web09. As we can see, it is really just a file containing SQL commands that can be used to create a database.

You can run these SQL commands to recreate the database. In fact, you can import the entire webbook database to your own system using the commands in this file. First, you need to have an empty database with complete manipulation privileges. It can have any name. To illustrate, we will leave the webbook database unchanged and import its contents into another database called webbook1 using this file. Our system administrator has created this database for us and granted us all the necessary privileges. All we need to do is run the following command:

```
mysql -u webbook -p webbook1 < backupbookSep09.sql
```

After the -u option, we are specifying that the user is webbook. The -p option again indicates that we will be entering a password. The name webbook1 after the -p option tells us that we want to work with the webbook1 database. The < sign redirects the input from our previously created file backupbookSep09.sql, which contains all the commands necessary to replicate the original database.

All of this activity, including the results of the command-line import, is shown in Figure 9.36 and its continuation, Figure 9.37. We refer to the line numbers in those two figures to help you follow the action. First, we verify that we do in fact have a database called webbook1 (lines 9–10). There are no tables in the database, since the command show tables; comes up empty (lines 11–12). Now we exit from MySQL and run the mysql import command from the Linux command-line interface (lines 14–17). Going back into the database, we can see that all the tables are in place. We also perform two SELECT queries to do a "spot check" to convince ourselves that the records have been imported and we have the right number of customers. All of this takes place in lines 18–72.

```
 1   -- phpMyAdmin SQL Dump
 2   -- version 3.1.2deb1ubuntu0.1
 3   -- http://www.phpmyadmin.net
 4   --
 5   -- Host: localhost
 6   -- Generation Time: Jan 11, 2010 at 05:19 PM
 7   -- Server version: 5.0.75
 8   -- PHP Version: 5.2.6-3ubuntu4.4
 9
10   SET SQL_MODE="NO_AUTO_VALUE_ON_ZERO";
11
12
13   /*!40101 SET @OLD_CHARACTER_SET_CLIENT=@@CHARACTER_SET_CLIENT */;
14   /*!40101 SET @OLD_CHARACTER_SET_RESULTS=@@CHARACTER_SET_RESULTS */;
15   /*!40101 SET @OLD_COLLATION_CONNECTION=@@COLLATION_CONNECTION */;
16   /*!40101 SET NAMES utf8 */;
17
18   --
19   -- Database: `webbook1`
20   --
21
22   -- --------------------------------------------------------
23
24   --
25   -- Table structure for table `Customers`
26   --
27
28   CREATE TABLE IF NOT EXISTS `Customers` (
29     `customer_id` int(11) NOT NULL,
30     `salutation` varchar(10) default NULL,
31     `customer_first_name` varchar(24) NOT NULL,
32     `customer_middle_initial` varchar(3) default NULL,
33     `customer_last_name` varchar(24) NOT NULL,
34     `gender` varchar(1) NOT NULL,
35     `email_address` varchar(60) NOT NULL,
36     `login_name` varchar(60) NOT NULL,
37     `login_password` varchar(20) NOT NULL,
38     `phone_number` varchar(20) NOT NULL,
39     `address` text NOT NULL,
40     `town_city` varchar(40) NOT NULL,
41     `county` varchar(40) NOT NULL,
42     `country` varchar(40) NOT NULL,
43     PRIMARY KEY (`customer_id`),
44     UNIQUE KEY `email_address` (`email_address`,`login_name`),
45     KEY `phone_number` (`phone_number`)
46   ) ENGINE=MyISAM DEFAULT CHARSET=latin1;
47
```

FIGURE 9.35

cdrom/web09/backupbookSep09.sql (excerpt)
Exported database in an SQL file.

```
 1  webbook > mysql -u webbook -p
 2  Enter password:
 3  Welcome to the MySQL monitor.  Commands end with ; or \g.
 4  Your MySQL connection id is 37531
 5  Server version: 5.0.75-0ubuntu10.2 (Ubuntu)
 6
 7  Type 'help;' or '\h' for help. Type '\c' to clear the buffer.
 8
 9  mysql> use webbook1;
10  Database changed
11  mysql> show tables;
12  Empty set (0.00 sec)
13
14  mysql> quit
15  Bye
16  webbook > mysql -u webbook -p webbook1 < backupbookSep09.sql
17  Enter password:
```

FIGURE 9.36

graphics/ch09/importSQL.txt (Part 1)
Importing a database using the command-line interface to MySQL (up to the actual import).

9.9.3   Potential Problem with Importing via phpMyAdmin

As we cautioned before, using phpMyAdmin over the Internet can be problematic for importing large databases. Our database is of moderate size—less than 2MB. Let us see what happens if we try to import it using phpMyAdmin. Figure 9.38 shows what will happen if we click on a database such as webbook3, which is currently empty. We indicate that we want to import from the file webbook.sql that we had saved earlier by exporting through phpMyAdmin. Clicking on the Go button starts the importing process.

Unfortunately, as shown in Figure 9.39, phpMyAdmin returns an error saying that it does not have the resources to carry out the importing task. Given what we have said, this is not entirely surprising. It follows that your best option may well be to work at the command line when you are importing a database, as shown in Figure 9.34.

```
18    webbook > mysql -u webbook -p
19    Enter password:
20    Welcome to the MySQL monitor.  Commands end with ; or \g.
21    Your MySQL connection id is 37533
22    Server version: 5.0.75-0ubuntu10.2 (Ubuntu)
23
24    Type 'help;' or '\h' for help. Type '\c' to clear the buffer.
25
26    mysql> use webbook1;
27    Reading table information for completion of table and column names
28    You can turn off this feature to get a quicker startup with -A
29
30    Database changed
31    mysql> show tables;
32    +-----------------------+
33    | Tables_in_webbook1    |
34    +-----------------------+
35    | Customers             |
36    | Invoices              |
37    | Order_Items           |
38    | Orders                |
39    | Payments              |
40    | Products              |
41    | Ref_Invoice_Status    |
42    | Ref_Order_Item_Status |
43    | Ref_Order_Status      |
44    | Ref_Product_Categories|
45    | Shipment_items        |
46    | Shipments             |
47    +-----------------------+
48    12 rows in set (0.00 sec)
49
50    mysql> select customer_first_name,customer_last_name from Customers limit 0,5;
51    +---------------------+--------------------+
52    | customer_first_name | customer_last_name |
53    +---------------------+--------------------+
54    | Michael             | McClune            |
55    | Michael             | Young              |
56    | Jordan              | Ore                |
57    | Bjorn               | Ditty              |
58    | Riza                | Zalameda           |
59    +---------------------+--------------------+
60    5 rows in set (0.00 sec)
61
62    mysql> select count(*) from Customers;
63    +----------+
64    | count(*) |
65    +----------+
66    |    10000 |
67    +----------+
68    1 row in set (0.01 sec)
69
70    mysql> quit
71    Bye
72    webbook >
```

FIGURE 9.37

graphics/ch09/importSQL.txt (Part 2)
Importing a database using the command-line interface to MySQL (confirming the import).

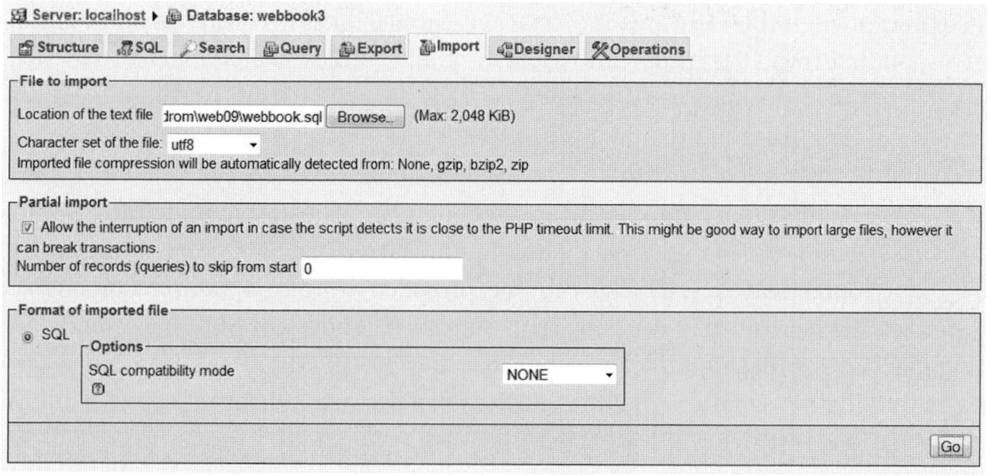

FIGURE 9.38

graphics/ch09/displayImport.jpg
Importing a database using phpMyAdmin.

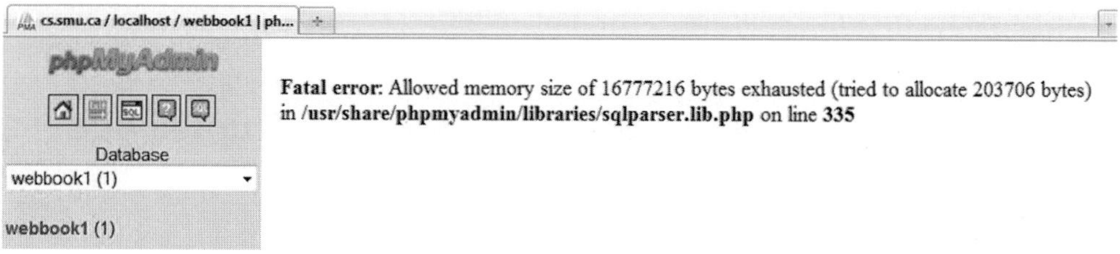

FIGURE 9.39

graphics/ch09/displayResultImport.jpg
Result of importing a database using phpMyAdmin.

9.10   Summary

All businesses need to keep track of their data and the most convenient and efficient way to do this is to keep that data in a well-designed database. Generally, a well-designed database will often have been *normalized* up to third normal form and will allow for scaling upward as the business grows.

MySQL is (currently, at least) an open-source database management system that is both simple enough for the home business owner to use and powerful enough for major corporations like Google and YouTube to employ as well.

A database comprises a number of tables in which each row (or record) contains related information about some aspect of a business, such as a customer or a product.

Each column of the table contains information (an attribute) relating to the item in its corresponding row. It is important to have "good" tables, which means that each table will contain information concerning a single aspect of the business, such as customers, invoices, or products for sale, and each table has a key column that can be used if we wish to refer to rows in that table from another table.

SQL (Structured Query Language) is the language we use to communicate with our database, and we can perform such communication using a command-line interface, or a sophisticated GUI like the one provided by phpMyAdmin, or one or more simple PHP scripts that we can write ourselves. There are SQL commands for creating databases, creating tables within those databases, adding information to the tables, modifying information that has already been stored, deleting some or all of that information, retrieving information and displaying it in various ways, and so on. We can also use SQL to perform numerical calculations on our data during the retrieval process.

Data can be imported to a database from external files, and exported to external files from a database. Even the entire database may be exported and used to replicate itself elsewhere.

9.11   Quick Questions to Test Your Basic Knowledge

1. Can you think of at least three reasons why storing large amounts of data in "ordinary" files turned out not to be a good idea? Here are some keywords to guide your thinking: duplication, maintenance, excessive human involvement.

2. What would you say to a business owner who had decided to keep all of the data for his business in one large table?

3. How would you describe what it means for a database to be in *first normal form*?

4. How would you describe what it means for a database to be in *second normal form*?

5. How would you describe what it means for a database to be in *third normal form*?

6. What has happened to MySQL that may (or may not) affect its future as a freely available, open-source database management system?

7. What is the MySQL command for creating a database? Can you always expect this command to work on any system?

8. What is the MySQL command that says you are going to use a database called `my_business`?

9. What MySQL command would you use to create a table called `Customers` with the following five fields: a unique identification number, first name, last name, telephone number, and e-mail address? Choose good names for the columns in your table.

10. Give a typical command for inserting a record in the table created in the previous exercise.

11. If you wanted to import a lot of data into this table from an external file, what would a typical line in that file look like?

12. What is the MySQL command for displaying all the information in this table?

13. What is the command for displaying just the names of the customers in the table?

9.12 Short Exercises to Improve Your Basic Understanding

The following exercises assume you have access to an installation of MySQL and that installation either has at least one database to which you also have access, or you have permission to create databases on the system. These are just a few suggestions to get you started on the road to becoming comfortable working with a database. Some of the exercises will take more time and effort than others, but all are well worth the effort. In fact, we do not specify whether to use the command-line interface or the GUI interface to perform any particular activity, and you should use both, preferably, to do the same exercise.

1. Log in to your MySQL and give the command that shows you all of the databases you are allowed to "see."

2. Decide whether you will work with an already existing database, or create a new one. If you are going to create a new one, first do that. Then, in either case, give the command that sets you up for using whatever database you plan to use.

3. Create a table called `Customers` that will hold, for each customer, that customer's first and last name, telephone number, e-mail address, and a unique identification number.

4. Modify your `Customers` table using the `ALTER` command to add a `city` attribute for each customer.

5. Enter some imaginary customers into your `Customers` table. First, use the `INSERT` command to enter just a couple of customers. Then create a file of customers and use the `LOAD` command to enter them.

6. Create a second table called either `Products` or `Services` that contains products or services that might be purchased by one or more of these customers. Enter some imaginary products or services into the table, based on the kind of business you are working on in your "parallel project."

7. Create a third table called `Invoices` that "connects" the customers and the products that they have purchased. Enter some imaginary invoices into the table.

8. Practice some SQL retrieval commands to display information from one or more of these tables in various forms.

9. Experiment with the `UPDATE` command by changing some attribute values. Then confirm the changes using a `SELECT` query. Finally, use `UPDATE` again to change the values back to what they were.

10. When you have finished the above experimentation, continue by experimenting with the `DELETE`, `DROP`, and `TRUNCATE` commands until all of your sample tables have been removed from your database.

9.13   Exercises on the Parallel Project

1. Re-think the objective(s) of your business, from the point of view of the kind of data that you will need to handle, and the kind of information you will need to store and later retrieve. Virtually every business has products and/or services to sell and needs to have some kind of inventory management system to deal with all aspects of information relating to those products and services. Time constraints may limit the scope of your effort, but give some thought to what is both reasonable and feasible to implement, given your particular situation.

2. Decide what tables you will need for your data, and the relationships between them.

3. Decide what attributes should go into each table, what data type each attribute should have, and what keys should be used to identify the rows in individual tables and connect the tables.

4. Think about any "business rules" that may be peculiar to your business and make sure they do not "break" your design. If you discover a business rule that is inconsistent with your database design, revise your design accordingly.

5. Implement your design in MySQL, using any combination of phpMyAdmin and the command-line interface, but try to use both enough to develop some familiarity with each.

6. Add enough data to each table so that you can perform some meaningful queries, and test your database until you are satisfied it is going to help you perform the necessary tasks your business requires.

9.14 What Else You May Want or Need to Know

1. MySQL started life as an open-source, freely available, database system. As of this writing, that is still true. However, MySQL was taken over by Sun Microsystems which, in turn, has been acquired by Oracle, who owns one of the largest proprietary database systems. Some believe that this does not bode well for the future of MySQL as a freely available system, and some of the MySQL websites are taking on a decidedly commercial look and feel. Nevertheless, until you hear differently, you should assume you will be able to download and install a free version of MySQL.

2. When you first begin to work with an *RDBMS* (*Relational Database Management System*) it can be an intimidating experience. Even the installation of such a system on your home computer can seem like a daunting undertaking, especially since to get the full advantage of the installation you will want to have a web server, the PHP programming language, and phpMyAdmin all installed as well. Fortunately, some very clever and helpful people have worked long and hard to make all this "easy" for you and you should know that it's not as bad as it may seem. This is not to say you will not encounter the odd bump in the road during the setup, but it should be nothing you cannot overcome

with a quick search on the Web or a question to a more knowledgable friend. See the following **References** section for some relevant links.

9.15   References

1. Whatever information and software you need to get started with MySQL should be available at one or both of the following links:

   ```
   http://www.mysql.com/
   http://dev.mysql.com/
   ```

2. The home page for phpMyAdmin can be found here:

   ```
   http://www.phpmyadmin.net/home_page/index.php
   ```

3. You can download MySQL, PHP, phpMyAdmin, and the Apache web server software in a single package as well. Such a package may also include other useful pieces of software. If you wish to pursue this option, check out one or both of the following sites:

   ```
   http://www.apachefriends.org/en/xampp.html
   http://www.wampserver.com/en/
   ```

4. The W3Schools tutorial on SQL starts here:

   ```
   http://www.w3schools.com/sql/default.asp
   ```

5. Wikipedia has articles on database normalization, functional dependency, and SQL:

   ```
   http://en.wikipedia.org/wiki/Database_normalization
   http://en.wikipedia.org/wiki/Functional_dependency
   http://en.wikipedia.org/wiki/SQL
   ```

6. All of the following links will take you to articles that discuss the database normalization process:

```
http://dev.mysql.com/tech-resources/articles/intro-to-normalization.html
http://databases.about.com/od/administration/u/database_basics.htm
http://www.bkent.net/Doc/simple5.htm
http://www.phlonx.com/resources/nf3/nf3_tutorial.pdf
```

7. Here is a link to a tutorial article on the **Database Answers** site entitled *How to Understand a Database Schema*:

```
http://www.databaseanswers.org/tutorial4_db_schema/index.htm
```

8. For a tutorial on joins in MySQL see:

```
http://www.tizag.com/mysqlTutorial/mysqljoins.php
```

CHAPTER 10

PHP and MySQL for Client-Server Database Interaction

10.1   Overview and Objectives

We have now arrived at the pinnacle of our e-commerce website development. In this chapter we combine all the knowledge we have learned so far to create a "complete" e-commerce solution for our business that will allow a user to visit our online e-store and perform each of the following tasks:

- Browse through our product catalog "anonymously" (as a casual web surfer, without registering) [Recall that a casual visitor can also perform a BMI calculation or send feedback to the company.]

- Open an account by registering with our website

- Log in to our website as a registered user, and later (after browsing and shopping, we hope) log out

- Browse through our product catalog as a registered user who can now "order" various items online and manage a "shopping cart"

- Purchase[1] the shopping cart items and then "check out"

We can customize the PHP scripts that allow users to connect to our MySQL database and perform the various new tasks that require such a connection. Note that phpMyAdmin and the command-line interface that we examined in the last chapter are tools to be used by a business owner or designated administrator to maintain the database for the business. These are not tools we want our site visitors to be using for access to our database. Instead, it is more appropriate (and safer) to provide our own specialized PHP scripts to control user interaction with our site and its database in very specific ways.

In the previous two chapters we laid the groundwork for what we are about to do now by introducing the PHP programming language and the MySQL database system. In this chapter we need to expand that discussion by covering the following topics:

- How a PHP script connects to a MySQL database

---

[1] Actually, our system stops short of accepting payment and shipping items, since in reality it has no items to ship and besides, that would involve connecting to other businesses under false pretenses....

- How a PHP script issues queries about customers or products to a MySQL database and then receives and processes the replies

- More about PHP arrays, which must be well understood and used properly if we expect our scripts to function as intended

- How to use a PHP *session* to keep track of a user's activity during a visit to our website

Figure 10.1 shows our revised home page, with the former `Buy Now` menu option now replaced with a dropdown menu. The options on that dropdown menu are also shown, are all e-store related, are essentially self-explanatory, and summarize the new functionality that we intend to implement in this chapter.

A user who clicks on the first option in the dropdown menu shown in Figure 10.1 is taken to the starting page for our e-store shown in Figure 10.2, which provides a little more information about the e-store links. The user may also click directly on the links in the dropdown menu, if appropriate.

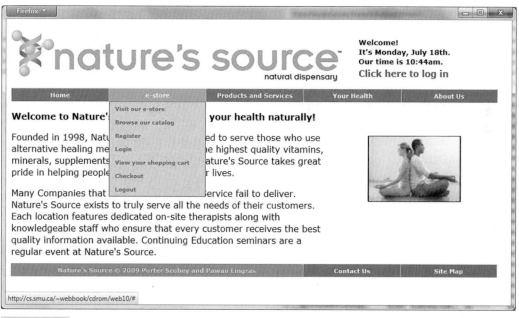

FIGURE 10.1

`graphics/ch10/displayIndexPhp.jpg`

The latest version of our home page, showing our e-store dropdown menu options and a handy login link at the upper right.

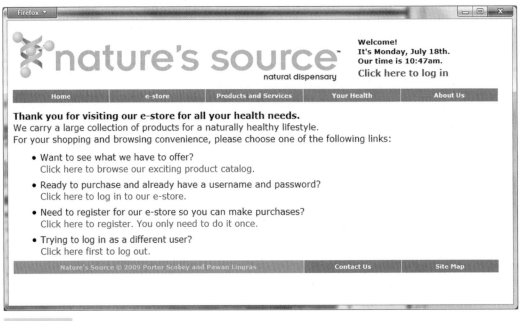

FIGURE 10.2

`graphics/ch10/displayEstorePhp.jpg`
Our e-store page, giving a bird's eye view of our e-store functionality.

10.2   PHP and MySQL

It is interesting to note how, in the history of computing, certain programming languages and other products have evolved together and give the impression that they were made for each other. In early business computing, you could see such symbiotic relationships illustrated by the association between COBOL and IBM's System/360 and its successor MVS. Computing enthusiasts reveled in the compatibility between Unix™ and C in the 1970s and 1980s. While the pairing of PHP and MySQL may not yet have attained the status of some of these earlier "marriages made in heaven," in this chapter we should come to appreciate the ease with which programming MySQL database management for the Web can be achieved using PHP.

We begin by assuming that you have access to a computing platform with both PHP and MySQL installed. Furthermore, the system must be able to establish a connection between the two. Usually, such installation and configuration tasks are left to more sophisticated users or system administrators, but they may also be performed on a PC by any dedicated and reasonably competent user who refuses to be intimidated, as we have pointed out in the previous chapter.

```php
1   <?php
2       //db.php
3       $db_location = "localhost";
4       $db_username = "webbook";
5       $db_password = "secret";
6       $db_database = "webbook";
7       $db_connection = mysql_connect("$db_location","$db_username","$db_password")
8           or die ("Error - Could not connect to MySQL Server");
9       $db = mysql_select_db($db_database,$db_connection)
0           or die ("Error - Could not open database");
1   ?>
```

FIGURE 10.3

cdrom/web10/scripts/db.php
Typical PHP code for connecting to MySQL.

As we know, connecting to a MySQL system as an authorized user and selecting an appropriate database can be done using phpMyAdmin or the command-line interface, but we are now interested in more direct control of our web pages using our own PHP scripts as the interface. This gives us business-specific solutions that allow our users access to our database in a more controlled fashion.

The first thing we need to know, as web programmers, is how to use PHP to connect to the MySQL system as an authorized user and select an appropriate database. Figure 10.3 shows the necessary PHP code, which is stored in a file called db.php. We can use this or similar code in any of our scripts that needs to make such a connection.

The script begins by creating some variables for convenience. The first one is $db_location, which is the name or the IP address of the computer that hosts the MySQL system we wish to access. It can be the same as, or different from, the computer that hosts our web server. In our case, both are the same so we use the value localhost for this variable. Next, the variable $db_username has the value webbook, which is our username for our MySQL system. A dummy password is assigned to the variable $db_password, and our database name (also webbook) is stored in the variable $db_database.

The connection to the MySQL server is established from PHP by calling the built-in function mysql_connect(), which takes as its three parameters the values from the first three variables above:

- The location of the MySQL server ($db_location)
- The user's MySQL username ($db_username)
- The user's password ($db_password)

If the connection does not succeed, we terminate the PHP program by calling the function `die()` with an appropriate error message. If the connection succeeds, we save the result returned by `mysql_connect()` in a variable called `$db_connection`. This variable, along with the name of the database, is then passed to another built-in function `mysql_select_db()` to select the database on which subsequent actions are to be performed. If the database cannot be selected for any reason, we again call the function `die()` with an appropriate error message. If the database selection was successful, we are ready to run almost any SQL query that we saw in the previous chapter from our PHP programs.

When writing PHP scripts that deal with MySQL, you can leverage your knowledge of SQL queries, since this is the form in which PHP delivers these queries to MySQL. The following sections look at how PHP performs database retrieval and manipulation operations to help us carry out the e-commerce tasks required by our business. And, of course, we shall be using several additional built-in PHP functions, like the two above, in dealing with our MySQL database.

10.3   Registration

While casual visitors to our site can browse through our catalog anonymously, actual e-commerce transactions will not be possible until the user has been authorized. The first step in establishing a user's identity for an e-commerce site is to have the user fill out a registration form such as the one shown in Figure 10.4.

The script that conducts the user registration can be found in the directory `web10` on your CD-ROM, and is called `register.php`. Unless you have installed PHP on your computer, you will have to view the resulting web page on the book's website. Even on the book's website, we will have certain restrictions. Any manipulations to the database will be difficult to manage on our server. We strongly recommend that readers import the database provided in the previous chapter on their own server. As is our practice, however, we will continue to provide detailed screenshots of various web interactions to ensure that the reader can follow the exposition in the text without having to access a computer.

During the registration process we must be prepared to deal with at least the following possible scenarios:

- The typical case where the user enters data that causes no problem and simply completes a successful registration

- The case where the user enters something on the form that does not pass JavaScript validation on the client side

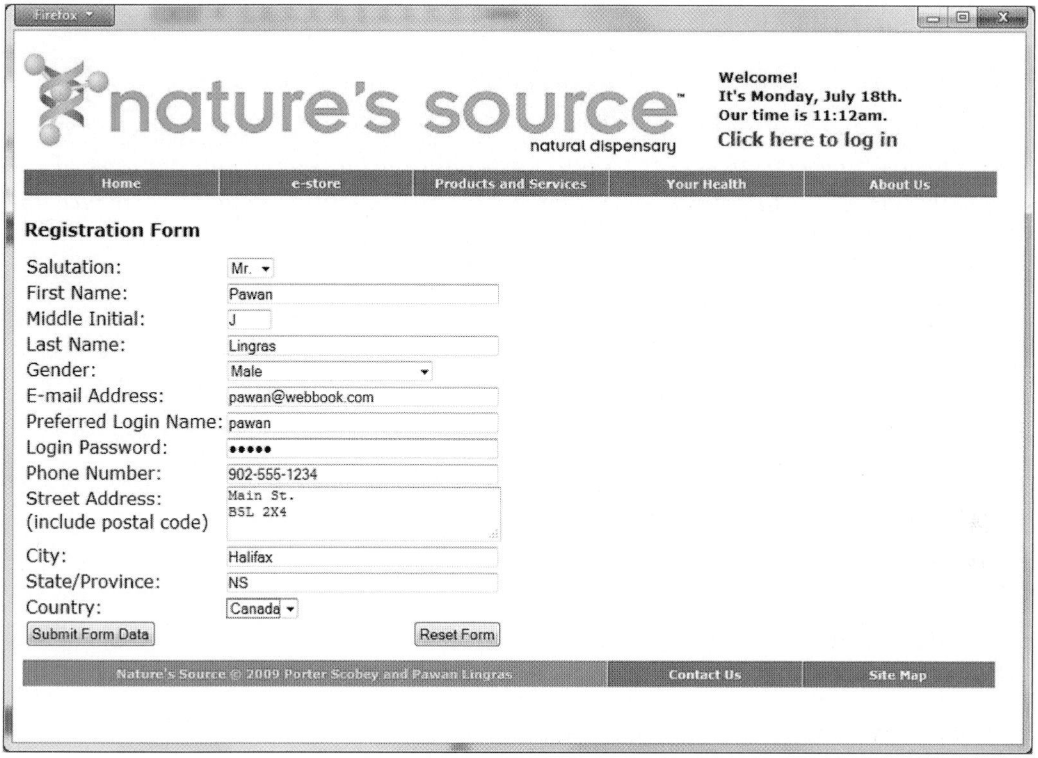

FIGURE 10.4

graphics/ch10/displayRegisterPhp1.jpg
Registering for our website.

- The case where a user has already registered and has perhaps forgotten they have done so, which will be recognized when the user is discovered to be in the database already

- The case where the user attempts to choose a login name that is already in use by a previously-registered customer

As we did with our previous forms, we also validate the user's data entries on the registration form using client-side JavaScript. However, in the following discussion it will be useful to keep in mind the following distinction: Data that is OK on the client side may turn out to be not OK on the server side. For example, a perfectly valid login name (as far as the client-side JavaScript validation is concerned) may turn out to be invalid upon being sent to the server and checked against the MySQL database, because it is already in use.

10.3.1   Getting Valid Data from the User via the Registration Form

First of all, let's admit right here that we are not going to follow two of our "best practice" recommendations in this chapter. We know we should be using label elements in our forms, and getting access to our form data on the server side via one of the superglobal arrays $_GET or $_POST, but in the files of this chapter we reduce the amount of XHTML markup by eliminating labels, and the amount of code in our PHP scripts by using global variables directly to access our form data.

The registration form itself is not very different from other XHTML forms we have seen in previous chapters, such as our feedback form. However, let us take a look at part of the document that gives us the registration form, so we can note any differences. We have reproduced some of the relevant code in Figure 10.5.

The first part of Figure 10.5 contains the **head** element of the file, which shows the inclusion of two JavaScript files: **menu.js**, and **register.js**. We have already studied the first of those JavaScript files, which relates to the display of our dropdown

```
5    <html xmlns="http://www.w3.org/1999/xhtml">
6      <head>
7        <title>Registration Form</title>
8        <meta http-equiv="Content-Type" content="text/html;charset=utf-8" />
9        <link rel="stylesheet" type="text/css" href="css/default.css" />
10       <script type="text/javascript" src="scripts/menu.js"></script>
11       <script type="text/javascript" src="scripts/register.js"></script>
```

. . .

```
21         <h4>Registration Form</h4>
22         <form id="register" name="register" action="registration.php"
23           method="post" onsubmit="return validateRegistrationForm();">
24           <table summary="Registration Form">
25             <tr valign="top">
26               <td>Salutation:</td>
27               <td><select id="salute" name="salute">
28                 <option></option>
29                 <option>Mrs.</option>
30                 <option>Ms.</option>
31                 <option>Mr.</option>
32                 <option>Dr.</option>
33               </select></td>
```

FIGURE 10.5

`cdrom/web10/register.php` (excerpts)
XHTML and PHP code for the registration form.

menus. The second file, `register.js`, provides the JavaScript code for validating the form fields in the form displayed by `register.php`.

Figure 10.6 shows the function `validateRegistrationForm()` from `register.js`, which goes through the validation, in order, of each of the fields that requires validation. The function uses four other helper functions, `validateName()`, `validateWord()`, `validatePhone()`, and `validateEmail()`, which are shown in Figure 10.7 for the sake of completeness. We discussed these functions earlier in Chapter 6, but we have also reproduced their code from the file `register.js` for completeness. Since we have already discussed and tested these or very similar for validation functions earlier, in Chapter 6, we will not go through the exercise of entering invalid data here.

10.3.2 Submitting the Form Data: Possible Outcomes

Let us take a quick look at the form itself from the second half of Figure 10.5. This part shows just the first few lines of the `form` element, which includes familiar fields such as the one for `Salutation`. Readers may want to look at the complete list of form fields in the file `register.php` on the CD-ROM. Of more interest at this point are the following two items:

- The value of the `onsubmit` event attribute of the form element, which is the following expression: `return validateRegistrationForm().`[2]

- The value of the `action` attribute of the form element is the (server-side) PHP script file `registration.php`, and we will be examining it in detail very shortly.

The sequence of events related to the filling out and submission of this form goes something like this. First, the user fills in the form and clicks on the `Submit` button. If the form data validates, according to `validateRegistrationForm()`, that function returns `true` and the form data is sent to the server. If the form data does not validate, the function returns `false` and the data is not forwarded to the server. If the form data makes it to the server, it is processed by the script in `registration.php`, and the outcome of that processing will depend on the data submitted, as we describe in what follows.

At the highest level, then, any one of the following scenarios may occur.

---

[2]Note the presence of return, which is necessary even though the function itself "returns" a boolean value.

```
1   //register.js
2   function validateRegistrationForm()
3   {
4       var firstName = register.firstName.value;
5       var lastName = register.lastName.value;
6       var phone = register.phone.value;
7       var email = register.email.value;
8       var check = true;
9       if (!validateName(firstName))
10      {
11          alert("Invalid first name");
12          check = false;
13      }
14      if (!validateName(lastName))
15      {
16          alert("Invalid last name");
17          check = false;
18      }
19      if (!validateName(middleInitial))
20      {
21          alert("Invalid middle initial");
22          check = false;
23      }
24      if (!validateWord(login_name))
25      {
26          alert("Invalid login name");
27          check = false;
28      }
29      if (!validateWord(login_password))
30      {
31          alert("Invalid login password");
32          check = false;
33      }
34      if (!validateName(city))
35      {
36          alert("Invalid city");
37          check = false;
38      }
39      if (!validateName(state))
40      {
41          alert("Invalid state");
42          check = false;
43      }
44      if (!validatePhone(phone))
45      {
46          alert("Invalid phone number");
47          check = false;
48      }
49      if (!validateEmail(email))
50      {
51          alert("Invalid e-mail address");
52          check = false;
53      }
54      return check;
55  }
```

. . .

FIGURE 10.6

cdrom/web10/scripts/register.js (Part 1)

The main JavaScript function for validating the form data collected by register.php.

```
57    function validateName(name)
58    {
59        var p1 = name.search(/^[-'\w\s]+$/);
60        return (p1 == 0) ? true : false;
61    }
62
63    function validateWord(name)
64    {
65        var p1 = name.search(/^\w+$/);
66        return (p1 == 0) ? true : false;
67    }
68
69    function validatePhone(phone)
70    {
71        var p1 = phone.search(/^\d{3}[-\s]{0,1}\d{3}[-\s]{0,1}\d{4}$/);
72        var p2 = phone.search(/^\d{3}[-\s]{0,1}\d{4}$/);
73        return (p1 == 0 || p2 == 0) ? true : false;
74    }
75
76    function validateEmail(address)
77    {
78        var p1 = address.search(/^\w+([\.-]?\w+)*@\w+([\.-]?\w+)*(\.\w{2,3})$/);
79        return (p1 == 0) ? true : false;
80    }
```

FIGURE 10.7

cdrom/web10/scripts/register.js (Part 2)
The supporting JavaScript functions for validating registration data.

Scenario 1: A Typical Problem-Free Registration

If all the data entered into our registration form as shown in Figure 10.4 is validated by the client-side JavaScript and the user clicks the **Submit** button, the form data is sent to the server and processed there by the PHP script registration.php. In this case we get a display like the one shown in Figure 10.8.

Scenario 2: A Problem with the Data Entered into the Form by the User

If one or more of the form data entries does not validate on the client side, the user will see a JavaScript-generated popup message of the kind discussed in Chapter 6, but which we do not illustrate any further here.

FIGURE 10.8

graphics/ch10/displayRegistrationPhp1.jpg
The resulting display when a new user registers successfully for our site.

Scenario 3: A Problem with Duplicate Registrations (User is Already in the Server-Side Database)

We have indicated in Chapter 9 that the e-mail address in our **Customers** table must be unique. If you try to enter the same information again, you should get an error because you are trying to duplicate the e-mail address. Figure 10.9 shows the reaction from the PHP script **registration.php** to such an attempt. This page can be easily obtained by clicking on the refresh button in your browser, immediately

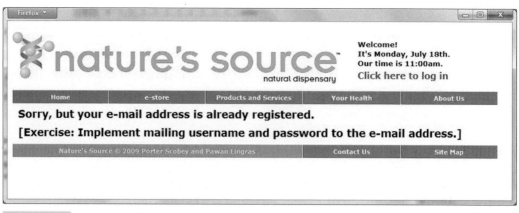

FIGURE 10.9

graphics/ch10/displayRegistrationPhp2.jpg
Unsuccessful registration for our site using an e-mail address already in our database.

after a successful registration. In that case, the browser attempts to send the same form information again, which is not permitted.

Scenario 4: A Problem with Duplicate Usernames (Username has Already Been Chosen by Another User)

Our Customers table also requires that the username be unique. However, it might be quite natural for another user named pawan, with a different e-mail address, to ask for pawan as a username. What should our PHP script do in such a case? A reasonable course of action might be to create a new username by simply appending a digit to the preferred username. If we do, in fact, attempt to specify a username of pawan from a different e-mail address, as shown in Figure 10.10, the PHP script registration.php gives us the output shown in Figure 10.11. The registration was accepted, but the username was changed to pawan0.

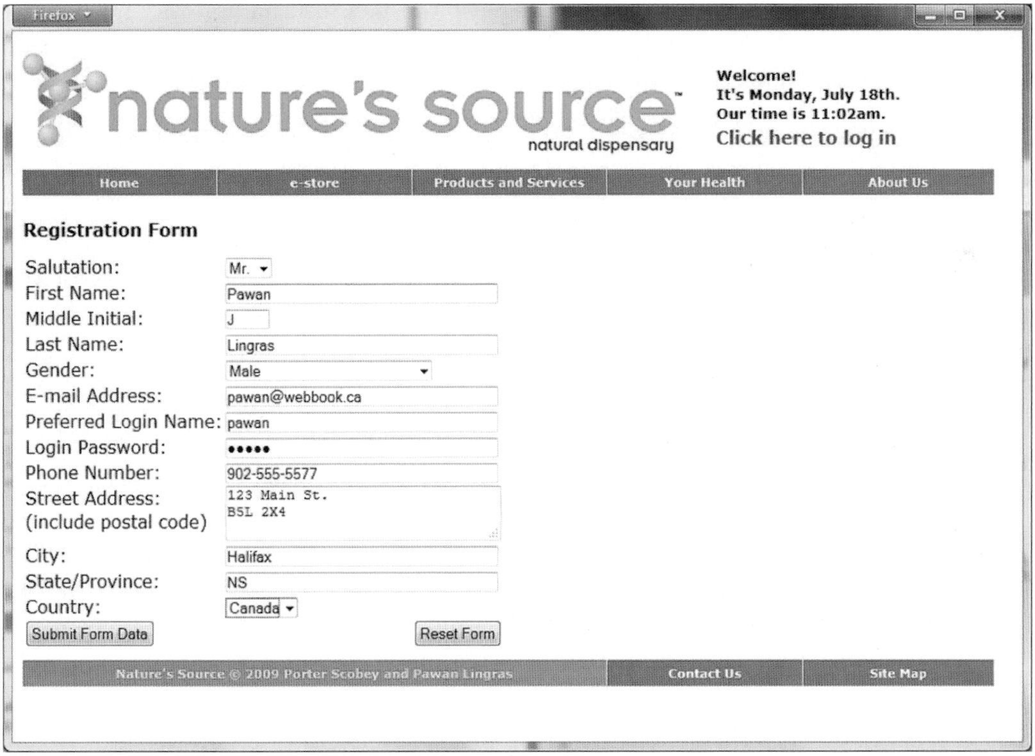

FIGURE 10.10

graphics/ch10/displayRegisterPhp2.jpg
Re-registering for the site with different e-mail but same username.

FIGURE 10.11

graphics/ch10/displayRegistrationPhp3.jpg
Successful registration for the site—username duplication avoided.

An alternate approach might be to suggest the new username, ask the user to re-register, and use the new (suggested) username. The logic for either of these two approaches is essentially the same.

10.3.3   Actual Processing of the Registration, with Valid Form Data

We are now ready to look at the PHP script that actually processes the registration, given that valid form data has been uploaded to the server. Most of the XHTML markup used to display our web pages remains the same. The script is in the file `registration.php`, which is shown in Figure 10.12, and we now discuss what is new here.

A First Look at PHP *Sessions*

So far our programs have not tracked the web browsing activities of our users, since there has been no need to do so. Now, however, we do have a need since, for example, we will have to keep track of who the user is and monitor that user's choices when products are placed into a shopping cart during online shopping.

PHP provides this appropriately named concept called a *session* to accomplish this. A session provides the means to store information in variables on the server, and those variables can be accessed and their values used across multiple pages. These variables are different from *cookies*, which are stored on the user's computer. They also differ from the variables that we have been passing from browser to server in form processing. The session variables are retrieved from the session that is opened at the beginning of each page.

We must call the PHP function `session_start()` at the very beginning of each page that participates in session tracking, as illustrated by the script in `registration.php`. A call to this function either creates a new session or resumes the currently running session. The real session tracking activity begins once a user logs into our website, so we will postpone our detailed discussion on session tracking until that time.

Including the "Connection Code" from `db.php`

Remember our PHP code for connecting to our MySQL database from Figure 10.3? It's now time to put that code to work, which we do at line 11 of the script in Figure 10.12:

```
include "scripts/db.php";
```

Including and running this external script will connect us to our database and allow us to enter the user's information.

The Script that Does the Processing: `processRegistration.php`

In line 21 of Figure 10.12 we have the following PHP `include` statement:

```
include "scripts/processRegistration.php";
```

This script is the one that actually processes the submitted registration data and produces one of the user-notification displays seen earlier, depending on the results of its analysis.

Figure 10.13 shows what could be called the "main program" for the registration task, from the file `processRegistration.php`, while the supporting "helper functions" are shown in Figure 10.14. Let us now discuss the actions taken by this script.

The first nested `if`-statement in our "main program" assigns an appropriate letter for the gender, since we shall store only a single letter in our database.

The next item on the agenda is to see if a user using the same e-mail address is already registered. This check is done using the function `emailExists()` (to be studied in detail shortly). If the function `emailExists()` returns `true`, we echo an appropriate error message, which can be seen in Figure 10.9. It is a relatively simple task to e-mail the login name and password to the user, and we have left this as an exercise for the reader.

```
1    <?php session_start() ?>
2    <!DOCTYPE html PUBLIC "-//W3C//DTD XHTML 1.0 Strict//EN"
3        "http://www.w3.org/TR/xhtml1/DTD/xhtml1-strict.dtd">
4    <!-- registration.php -->
5    <html xmlns="http://www.w3.org/1999/xhtml">
6      <head>
7        <title>Nature's Source - Registration</title>
8        <meta http-equiv="Content-Type" content="text/html;charset=utf-8" />
9        <link rel="stylesheet" type="text/css" href="css/default.css" />
10       <script type="text/javascript" src="scripts/menu.js"></script>
11       <?php include "scripts/db.php"; ?>
12     </head>
13     <body>
14       <div id="page">
15         <?php
16         include("common/banner.php");
17         include("common/mainmenu.html");
18         ?>
19         <div id="content">
20           <div id="textOnly" class="FeedbackForm">
21           <?php include "scripts/processRegistration.php"; ?>
22           </div>
23         </div>
24         <?php include("common/footer.html"); ?>
25       </div>
26     </body>
27   </html>
```

FIGURE 10.12

cdrom/web10/registration.php
The XHTML and PHP code for processing the registration data submitted from `register.php`.

On the other hand, if the e-mail address does not exist in the Customers table, we continue with the process of trying to add a new user to the table. The first step in recording a new user is to select a login name. The user specifies a preferred name. However, there is a possibility that this name may already exist in the Customers table, and we do not permit duplicate login names. Hence, line 16 calls a function getUniqueID(), which takes the $login_name preferred by the user and returns a unique name, which may in fact be the name requested by the user, or it may be a variation of that name. In any case, the value of the variable $unique_login will not exist in the Customers table at this point. Before we go ahead and add the new record into the table, we let the user know if the preferred name had to be changed. This is achieved by an if-statement that compares $login_name with $unique_login. If

```
1   <?php
2   //processRegistration.php
3   ///////////////////// main begins //////////////////////
4   if ($gender == "Female") $gender = "F";
5   else if ($gender == "Male") $gender = "M";
6   else $gender = "O";
7   if (emailExists($email))
8   {
9       echo "<h3 class=\"margin10\">Sorry, but your e-mail address is already
10          registered.</h3>";
11      echo "<h3 class=\"margin10\">[Exercise: Implement mailing
12          username and password to the e-mail address.]</h3>";
13  }
14  else
15  {
16      $unique_login = getUniqueID($loginName);
17      if ($unique_login != $loginName)
18      {
19          echo "<h3 class=\"margin10\">Your preferred login name exists.<br />
20              So ... we have assigned $unique_login as your login name.</h3>";
21      }
22
23      $query = "INSERT INTO Customers (
24          customer_id, salutation, customer_first_name, customer_middle_initial,
25          customer_last_name, gender, email_address, login_name,
26          login_password, phone_number, address, town_city, county, country
27      )
28      VALUES (
29          NULL, '$salute', '$firstName', '$middleInitial', '$lastName', '$gender',
30          '$email', '$unique_login', '$loginPassword', '$phone', '$address',
31          '$city', '$state', '$country'
32      );";
33      $customers = mysql_query($query)
34          or die(mysql_error());
35      echo "<h3 class=\"margin10\">Thank you for registering with our e-store.</h3>";
36      echo "<h3 class=\"margin10\"><a class=\"noDecoration\" href = \"login.php\">
37          Please click here to login and start shopping.</a></h3>";
38  }
39  ///////////////////// main ends functions begin //////////////////////
```

. . .

FIGURE 10.13

cdrom/web10/scripts/processRegistration.php (Part 1)
The "main program" from processRegistration.php.

. . .

```
39   ///////////////////// main ends functions begin /////////////////////////
40   function emailExists($email)
41   {
42       $query = "SELECT * FROM Customers WHERE email_address = '$email'";
43       $customers = mysql_query($query)
44           or die(mysql_error());
45       $numRecords = mysql_num_rows($customers);
46       if ($numRecords > 0)
47           return true;
48       else
49           return false;
50   }
51
52   function getUniqueID($loginName)
53   {
54       $unique_login = $loginName;
55       $query = "SELECT * FROM Customers WHERE login_name = '$unique_login'";
56       $customers = mysql_query($query)
57           or die(mysql_error());
58       $numRecords = mysql_num_rows($customers);
59       for ($i = 0; $numRecords > 0; $i++)
60       {
61           $unique_login = $loginName.$i;
62           $query = "SELECT * FROM Customers WHERE login_name = '$unique_login'";
63           $customers = mysql_query($query)
64               or die(mysql_error());
65           $numRecords = mysql_num_rows($customers);
66       }
67       return $unique_login;
68   }
69   ?>
```

FIGURE 10.14

cdrom/web10/scripts/processRegistration.php (Part 2)
The helper functions from processRegistration.php.

these two names do not match, we echo an appropriate message and also display the login name the user should use from this point on.

The Final Step: Entering the User into the Database

Having checked for all potential errors, we now add the user's record to the Customers database. The execution of an SQL query from a PHP script is achieved in two steps. First, we build the query as a string. In our case, we use a variable called $query and assign it a string that is constructed using data taken directly from the various form elements, except that we modified the value of $gender and are now using the variable $unique_login instead of $login_name.

The INSERT query string shown in Figure 10.13 is similar to the INSERT queries we studied in Chapter 9. The second step in executing an SQL query via a PHP script is to send the query string to the function mysql_query(). In our case, this is done by the statement

```
$customers = mysql_query($query)
    or die(mysql_error());
```

The result of the call to this function is stored in the variable $customers. On this occasion we have no use for this return value from the INSERT query. We are only interested in whether or not the query was successful. However, such return values from queries are useful for SELECT queries, as we will see later on.

If the function mysql_query() failed for any reason, we will terminate the program with the help of the die() function, as we have done in the past. However, there is a new twist in the call to the die() function. We want to display a helpful error message, and we get that error message via a call to the built-in function mysql_error(), which returns a textual description of what went wrong with the previous call to mysql_query(). The remaining part of the "main program" in processRegistration.php is simple echoing of XHTML markup, including a link to the login.php script, which will allow the user to log in to our site after successfully registering.

The Helper Functions emailExists() and getUniqueID()

Figure 10.14 shows the two functions used by the main program to ensure that the e-mail and login names are unique:

emailExists() This function accepts an e-mail address and returns **true** if it already exists in the database. It begins by creating a SELECT query that attempts to retrieve a record with the specified e-mail address, and then run the query with mysql_query(), as before. The result of the query is stored in the variable $customers.

This time we are trying to retrieve records matching a given e-mail address, but we do not really want to look at the records. We only want to know if there *are* any records with the given e-mail address. The function mysql_num_rows() takes the result from the query execution ($customers in our case) and returns the number of rows retrieved. We store this number of rows in a variable called `$numRecords`.

Our function `emailExists()` returns a value of `true` if `$numRecords` is greater than 0, `false` otherwise.

`getUniqueID()` This function interacts with the database in a manner similar to the one above, but requires a loop. It tries to retrieve a record with the user's preferred login name by setting `$unique_login` to `$login_name`, and then SELECTing the records from the `Customers` table with `login_name` matching the `$unique_login`.

As before, we store the number of records retrieved in `$numRecords`. The function then uses a `for`-loop that continues as long as `$numRecords` is greater than 0. The loop is never entered if the user's preferred login name did not exist in the `Customers` table, since the first `SELECT` statement will result in `$numRecords` being equal to 0. If we have to enter the loop, that means there was a record corresponding to the preferred login name. So, we create a new `$unique_login` by appending the value of the loop control variable `$i` to the user's preferred login name and then check to see if *it* exists in the database.

If the preferred login name were `pawan`, the loop would try names such as `pawan0`, `pawan1`, `pawan2`, and so on. The process continues until the login name given by `$unique_login` does not exist in the `Customers` table. In that case, the variable `$numRecords` will have the value 0, and we will come out of the loop.

In any case, the value of the variable `$unique_login` is returned to the main function.

10.4   Logging In and Logging Out

Registering for our website provides the user with a login name and password, which can then be used to log in to the site via the form shown in Figure 10.15. This is a standard XHTML form, with two text fields as well as submit and reset buttons. The PHP code is a little complicated, since we need to take care of a variety of conditions. The PHP scripts that we are going to use from this point on make critical use of arrays, so it is only appropriate that we should have a closer look at PHP arrays before moving forward.

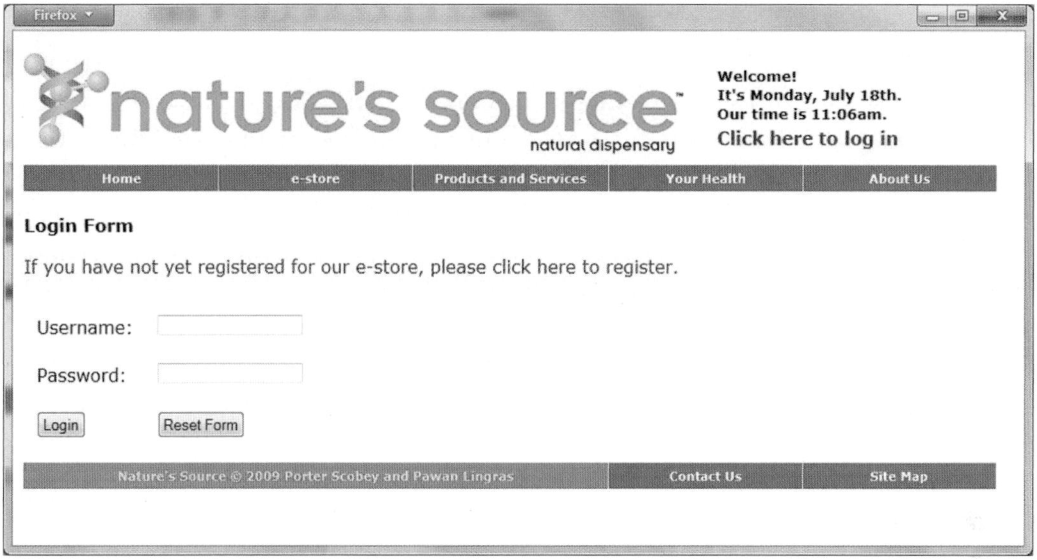

FIGURE 10.15

graphics/ch10/displayLoginPhp.jpg
Logging in to the e-store.

10.4.1 PHP Arrays: We Need to Know More about Them

We have already discussed arrays in JavaScript in Chapter 6, and you may have encountered them in another programming language such as Java or C++. PHP arrays are quite different from any other arrays you may have used, including those in JavaScript, which were already quite different from those of Java or C++. For the sake of completeness, in this section we reproduce some of the basic information about arrays in the context of PHP, just to set the stage. We will study some of the PHP enhancements to arrays later on in this section.

A PHP *array*, like other arrays, is essentially a list of elements. Usually, arrays are stored in such a way that each element of the array can be efficiently accessed. The elements of an array are addressed using a *subscript* (or *index*) that appears in a pair of square brackets following the name of the array, and this is true of PHP arrays as well. For example, if we have an array called $test, the first element of the array is given by $test[0], the second element by $test[1], and so on. Note that, just as in other C-based languages, the subscripts of arrays in PHP start with 0. You will need to keep in mind what this means: If a PHP array has n elements, the subscripts used to access those elements will go from 0 to n–1 (and *not* from 1 to n).

Now comes one of the interesting things about PHP arrays. The elements of a PHP array can be accessed not only by using integer indices, but also by using "string indices." Some readers may have encountered such string-indexable containers elsewhere and referred to them by such terms as *associative arrays* or *hash tables* or *maps* or even *dictionaries*. Oddly enough, in PHP the types of array indices are interchangeable. That is, some of the elements could be accessed using integers and others could be addressed using strings. If you do not specify an index, an "appropriate" numeric index will be assumed.

The following interactive PHP session should help to give you a reasonable idea of how arrays work in PHP. We are using the interactive PHP interpreter available on our Linux system to test our PHP code. On our system we start the interpreter with the command:

```
$ php -a
```

At the end of the session we use the command **exit** to stop the interpreter when we are finished. We have added some comments that will help you follow the session:

```
php > //The following command creates an array:
php > $a[] = "Hello";
php > //We ommitted the subscript so the next available
php > //subscript is used, which is 0 in this case.

php > //Cannot use the echo command to print an array.
php > echo $a;
Array

php > //But ... the echo command can print elements of an array.
php > echo $a[0];
Hello

php > //Let us now add a number of elements to our array.
php > $a[] = "World";
php > $a[-90] = "This is wild";
php > $a[90] = "This is wild";
php > $a[70] = "This is wild";
php > $a[name] = "Pawan";
```

```
php > //You can use the print_r() function to print an entire array.
php > print_r($a);
Array
(
    [0] => Hello
    [1] => World
    [-90] => This is wild
    [90] => This is wild
    [70] => This is wild
    [name] => Pawan
)
php > //As we can see, the indexes are not ordered as you would have
php > //expected, since -90 comes after 1, and 70 comes after 90.

php > //Note that "name" and name are the same index,
php > //as illustrated by the following statement.
php > $a["name"] = "Lingras";
php > print_r($a);
Array
(
    [0] => Hello
    [1] => World
    [-90] => This is wild
    [90] => This is wild
    [70] => This is wild
    [name] => Lingras
)

php > //If we do not specify the index, it will be one
php > //more than the highest current index, i.e. 90+1 = 91.
php > $a[] = "What is the index?";
php > print_r($a);
Array
(
    [0] => Hello
    [1] => World
    [-90] => This is wild
    [90] => This is wild
    [70] => This is wild
```

```
    [name] => Lingras
    [91] => What is the index?
)

php > //You can get numeric indices properly ordered
php > //by using the function array_values().
php > $b = array_values($a);
php > print_r($b);
Array
(
    [0] => Hello
    [1] => World
    [2] => This is wild
    [3] => This is wild
    [4] => This is wild
    [5] => Lingras
)

php > //You can delete an element using the function unset
php > unset($a[-90]);
php > print_r($a);
Array
(
    [0] => Hello
    [1] => World
    [90] => This is wild
    [70] => This is wild
    [name] => Lingras
)

php > //The count() gives you the size of an array.
php > echo count($a);
7

php > //The "construct"  array() (not a function) can be used
        //to create an entire array.
php > $a = array("This", "is", "different", 5, 6, 7);
php > print_r($a);
Array
```

```
(
    [0] => This
    [1] => is
    [2] => different
    [3] => 5
    [4] => 6
    [5] => 7
)
```

```
php > //The construct array() also allows you to specify the indices
php > $a = array(7=>"This", 0=>"is", "different", five=>5, 6=>6, eight=>7);
php > print_r($a);
Array
(
    [7] => This
    [0] => is
    [8] => different
    [five] => 5
    [6] => 6
    [eight] => 7
)
```

In summary, then, here are the essential array features illustrated by the above session:

- A PHP array index is really just a means of accessing a particular element in an array. It does not necessarily suggest an ordering. That is why we can use -90 as an index, which is stored in the array after the index 1.

- If we do not use an index to place a value in an array, the first numeric index greater than the last-used numeric index is used.

- Array elements can be displayed using echo, but you need to use the built-in function print_r() to print an entire array.

- A function called count() gives us the size of an array.

- An entire array can be created by using the array() construct.

- If we want conventionally ordered numeric indices from an associative array, we can use the function array_values().

- A variety of PHP functions also return arrays. For example, we will be working with functions that return database records as arrays.

The above introduction should be more than sufficient for our treatment of arrays in this chapter. See the end-of-chapter **References** section for more information.

10.4.2 Logging In: The Logic of `login.php`

One of the design decisions we have made for our e-store is that if a user is logged in, that user cannot log in again using the same identity or, for that matter, any other identity. In other words, the user will have to explicitly log out and then log back in. A currently logged-in user who tries to log in again will simply be directed to our `estore.php` page. This logic is implemented at the beginning of the file `login.php`, which is available on the CD-ROM under the `web10` directory. Figure 10.16 shows the first part of this file.

The short PHP script at the beginning of the file starts, or resumes, a session with a call to the function `session_start()` that we have discussed previously. When we have started or are continuing a session with the function `session_start()`, we can use the `$_SESSION` array to store information that can be shared by all the PHP scripts that will be run during that session.[3] In line 4 of Figure 10.16, we are checking

```
1    <?php
2    //login.php
3    session_start();
4    if ($_SESSION["customer_id"] != "") header('Location: estore.php');
5    ?>
6    <!DOCTYPE html PUBLIC "-//W3C//DTD XHTML 1.0 Transitional//EN"
7        "http://www.w3.org/TR/xhtml1/DTD/xhtml1-transitional.dtd">
8    <html xmlns="http://www.w3.org/1999/xhtml">
9      <head>
10       <title>Nature's Source - Logging In</title>
11       <meta http-equiv="Content-Type" content="text/html;charset=utf-8" />
12       <link rel="stylesheet" type="text/css" href="css/default.css" />
13       <script type="text/javascript" src="scripts/menu.js"></script>
14       <script type="text/javascript" src="scripts/login.js"></script>
15     </head>
```

FIGURE 10.16

`cdrom/web10/login.php` (Part 1)
The opening lines of PHP code and XHTML markup for the login form page.

---

[3]Note that it is our responsibility to populate the array `$_SESSION` with appropriate and useful key/value pairs. We will see how to do that when a user is successfully logged in a little later on.

to see if there is a non-null element in the array with index (or key) customer_id. If customer_id is not null, then we assume that the user is already logged in. In that case, we simply redirect the user to our estore.php web page.

The redirection is achieved using a built-in PHP function called header(). The header() function is used to send a "raw" HTTP header to the browser. Here we are using a special case of the header() function, where the parameter string begins with Location: and is followed by the URL of the web page to which we are redirecting the user. Thus our function call

```
header('Location: estore.php');
```

will redirect the browser to the file estore.php, which is located in the same directory as login.php, so we need only the file name and no additional path information.

The rest of the header section of the file login.php shows the JavaScript scripts that are included in the file: menu.js for the menu displays, which we have seen already, and login.js for validating field data entered into our new login form.

Figure 10.17 shows the file login.js, which contains the JavaScript validation functions validateLoginForm() and its helper validateWord(). These functions contain nothing we have not seen already in Chapter 6. Two fields are validated, customer_nm and customer_pw, and both are expected to contain words with no spaces.

The rest of the file login.php, shown in Figure 10.18, consists mostly of the login form itself, preceded by a reminder link (lines 25–26) if the user has not yet registered, and followed by a PHP script (lines 44–50) that we discuss at the end of this section. The form contains one field for the username (called customer_nm) and one for the password (called customer_pw), as well as the usual submit and reset buttons.

We now look at the actual processing of the login form. When a user fills out the form and clicks the Submit button, the form data will be validated and then control will be transferred to processLogin.php, which is the value of the form's action attribute in line 27 of Figure 10.18. Figure 10.19 shows this file, which is included on the CD-ROM in the script subdirectory web10.

As usual, we start the new session with session_start(), and then include the script db.php to establish a connection to our database. Next, we attempt to retrieve records from the Customers table for which the login_name attribute matches the name entered in the customer_nm field of our login form (lines 5–8). The variable $numRecords is assigned the number of records retrieved from the database by this query (line 9). Since login_name is unique, the only possible values for $numRecords are 0 and 1.

```
1    //login.js
2    function validateLoginForm()
3    {
4        var customer_nm = loginForm.customer_nm.value;
5        var customer_pw = loginForm.customer_pw.value;
6        var check = true;
7        if (!validateWord(customer_nm))
8        {
9            alert("Error: Invalid username!");
10           check = false;
11       }
12       if (!validateWord(customer_pw))
13       {
14           alert("Error: Invalid password!");
15           check = false;
16       }
17       return check;
18   }
19
20   function validateWord(name)
21   {
22       var p1 = name.search(/^\w+$/);
23       return (p1 == 0) ? true : false;
24   }
```

FIGURE 10.17

cdrom/web10/scripts/login.js
The JavaScript code for validating the login form data entries.

So, assume that we managed to find a record from the Customers table for which the login_name matches the customer_nm field in our login form. The next step is to see if the corresponding password is correct. In order to check the password, we must first fetch the appropriate row from the results retrieved by the statement

$rowsWithNumbersMatchingLoginName = mysql_query($query)}

in line 7. These results can be viewed as a table with a "current pointer" pointing to the first row. We then count the number of rows in this table of query results by passing it to mysql_num_rows() (line 9). The result had better be 1 or 0, since the username is either in the database once (we have unique usernames), or it is not there at all. In the case of a typical login, the value will be 1, which means that we will enter the following if-statement and proceed with the somewhat elaborate login processing described next.

The function call to mysql_fetch_array() in line 12 returns the row pointed to by the current point in the retrieved results as an associative array.[4] We store the

---

[4] Note that this function also advances the "current pointer" to the next row, if there is one, which would not be the case here.

returned array in an appropriately named variable called $row, and since values in associative arrays can be accessed by the names of their keys, we can retrieve the element corresponding to the key (or "index") login_password and check to see if it matches the value in the form variable $customer_pw.

If there is a match, we proceed to wrap up the login process. This involves setting up four elements in the $_SESSION array so that they will be available for all other PHP scripts that run during the life of this session. The keys for these elements are:

- customer_id

- salutation

- customer_middle_initial

- customer_first_name

- customer_last_name

Once these variables are set, we only need to decide where to redirect the user. The redirection location is stored in a variable called $goto. We have not studied the purchase-processing script yet, but when we look at that script we will see that if a user decides to purchase a product without having logged in, we perform the following steps:

- First, we set the element of $_SESSION with index purchasePending to the product_id of the product that the customer was trying to buy.

- Then we redirect the user to the login page.

In such a case, we take the user to the web page purchase.php after login to provide the opportunity to buy the product. This is done by setting a variable called $prod to $_SESSION["purchasePending"]. Once we have retrieved the value, we apply the unset() function to $_SESSION["purchasePending"] to delete the element from the $_SESSION array. The $goto is then set to the following value:

"Location: ../purchase.php?prod=$prod"

If there was no purchase pending, we simply redirect the user back to whichever page was being displayed prior to the login. This page is obtained by retrieving the value of the referer page as follows.

Whenever we are browsing, our browser keeps track of a set of *environment variables*. We can get a list of these environment variables for our particular environment by making a call to the function `phpinfo()`. We need the value of the variable called `HTTP_REFERER`, which is the web page our browser was at before accessing the current page. The value of this environmental variable can be retrieved using the function `getenv()`, like so:

```
$ref = getenv("HTTP_REFERER");
```

We then prepend the variable `$ref` with the string `"Location: "` to create the `$goto` variable. Finally, we redirect the user to the desired page using this statement:

```
header($goto);
```

Note that the above logging-in process only works if the `customer_nm` from the login form matched a `login_name` in the `Customers` table, and the `login_password` in the retrieved record matched the `customer_pw` from the login form. This is the case where the value of `$numRecords` was in fact 1, and the code in the `if`-statement was executed.

Otherwise (when `$numRecords == 0`), the execution falls through to the very last statement in the `processLogin.php` file. This statement redirects the user back to the login form with the URL

```
login.php?retry=true
```

which indicates that this is a retry for the login process by creating a global variable called `$retry` and setting its value to `true`.

Now the PHP script at the bottom of the login form kicks in (lines 44–50 of Figure 10.18). This script is used to check if this is a repeated attempt at logging in. If `$retry` is `true` (and it is at this point), then the XHTML markup between

```
<?php if ($retry == true) { ?>
```

and

```
<?php } ?>
```

is activated and adds a row of output to the display that will inform the user that the login attempt has failed, and ask for another try at logging in, as shown in Figure 10.20.

```
<body>
  <div id="page">
    <?php
    include("common/banner.php");
    include("common/mainmenu.html");
    ?>
    <div id="content">
      <div id="textOnly" class="FeedbackForm">
        <h4>Login Form</h4>
        <p><a href="register.php" class="noDecoration">If you have not yet
          registered for our e-store, please click here to register.</a></p>
        <form id="loginForm" name="loginForm" action="scripts/processLogin.php"
              onsubmit="return validateLoginForm();">
          <table summary="Login Form">
            <tr>
              <td>Username:</td>
              <td valign="top"><input name="customer_nm" type="text"
              id="customer_nm" size="20" /></td>
            </tr>
            <tr>
              <td>Password:</td>
              <td valign="top"><input name="customer_pw" type="password"
              id="customer_pw" size="20" /></td>
            </tr>
            <tr>
              <td><input type="submit" value="Login" /></td>
              <td><input type="reset" value="Reset Form" /></td>
            </tr>
            <?php if ($retry == true) { ?>
            <tr>
              <td valign="top" colspan="2">There was an error in the login.<br />
                Either username or password was incorrect.<br />
                Please re-enter the correct login information.</td>
            </tr>
            <?php } ?>
          </table>
        </form>
      </div>
    </div>
    <?php include("common/footer.html"); ?>
  </div>
</body>
</html>
```

FIGURE 10.18
cdrom/web10/login.php (Part 2)
The rest of the XHTML markup and PHP code for the login form page.

```php
1   <?php
2   //processLogin.php
3   session_start();
4   include "db.php";
5   $query = "SELECT * FROM Customers WHERE
6       login_name = \"".$customer_nm."\";";
7   $rowsWithMatchingLoginName = mysql_query($query)
8       or die(mysql_error());
9   $numRecords = mysql_num_rows($rowsWithMatchingLoginName);
10  if ($numRecords == 1)
11  {
12      $row = mysql_fetch_array($rowsWithMatchingLoginName);
13      if ($customer_pw == $row["login_password"])
14      {
15          $_SESSION["customer_id"] = $row["customer_id"];
16          $_SESSION["salutation"] = $row["salutation"];
17          $_SESSION["customer_first_name"] = $row["customer_first_name"];
18          $_SESSION["customer_middle_initial"] = $row["customer_middle_initial"];
19          $_SESSION["customer_last_name"] = $row["customer_last_name"];
20          $prod = $_SESSION["purchasePending"] ;
21          if ($prod != "")
22          {
23              unset($_SESSION["purchasePending"]);
24              $goto = "Location: ../purchase.php?prod=$prod";
25          }
26          else
27          {
28              $ref = getenv("HTTP_REFERER");
29              $goto = 'Location: ' . $ref;
30          }
31          header($goto);
32      }
33  }
34  //Either no records were received or the password did not match
35  header('Location: ../login.php?retry=true');
36  ?>
```

FIGURE 10.19

cdrom/web10/scripts/processLogin.php
PHP code for processing the login form.

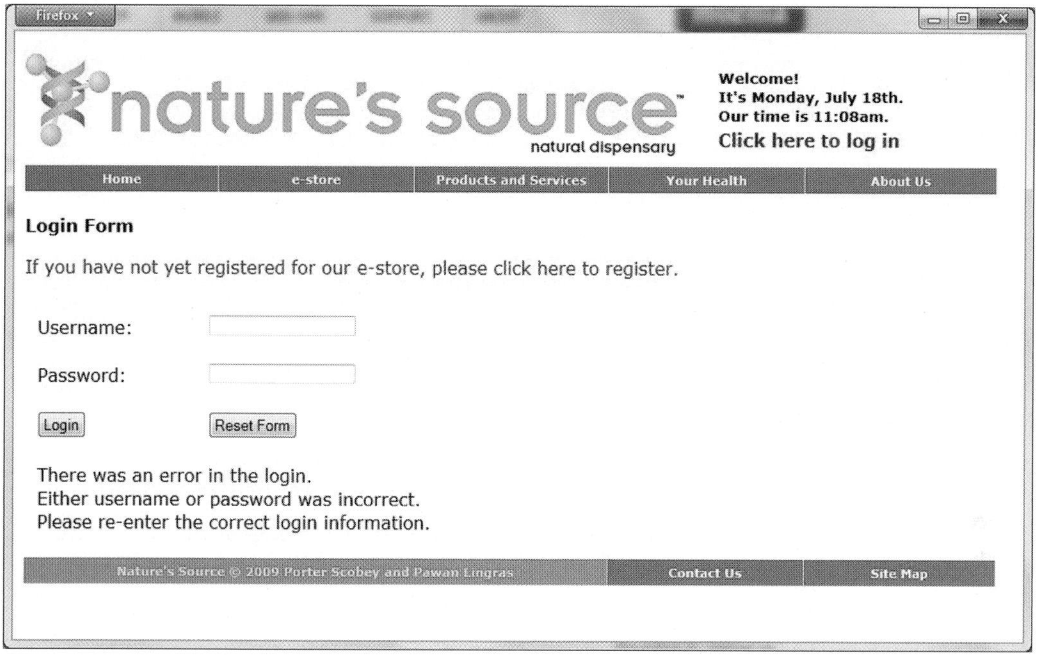

FIGURE 10.20
graphics/ch10/displayLoginRetry.jpg
Request for the user to try again after a failed login.

Passing Key/Value Pairs in a URL

Sometimes when we are browsing to a page, or when (as web programmers) we are redirecting a user from one page to another, we want to pass some information along to the new page. One way of doing this is illustrated in lines 24 and 35 of Figure 10.19:

```
24 $goto  = "Location: ../purchase.php?prod=$prod";
35 header('Location: ../login.php?retry=true');
```

At the end of each of these lines we see a ? separating a key/value pair in which the key and value are themselves separated by an equals sign. Note that the value half of the pair can be provided as a literal value (**true**) or as a variable (**$prod**). Note as well that more than one key/value pair can be passed along in this way, in which case an & separates the key/value pairs, like this:

```
login.php?retry=true&otherKey=otherValue
```

On the server side these key/value pairs become available in the superglobal array **$_GET**. That is, for example, the value of **$_GLOBAL["retry"]** will be **true**. Recall, however, as we pointed out earlier in this chapter, we are simply using the global variables that are also created when this feature is enabled. In other words, in this case we can also use, directly, a global variable that will have the name $retry and whose value will be true.

10.4.3   Logging Out: The Logic of logout.php

There are two situations in which the user may attempt to log out: first, the "normal" case in which the user has in fact logged in, and second, the case in which the user has not logged in. We must be ready for both, since you never know just what a user will do, whether accidentally or intentionally.

The logout page is produced by logout.php, which is available in our web10 subdirectory and is shown in Figure 10.21. The overall file structure seen in this figure is by now quite familiar, so we concentrate on the PHP script at the beginning of the file (lines 3–6) and the one in the div element identified as content.

In line 3 we start up a session as usual and then in line 4 we record in the local variable $notLoggedIn whether or not the user is in fact logged in. We need to record this value in a local variable because the very next thing that we do (lines 5–6) is shut down the session in preparation for logout, and once this happens we will no longer have access to this information that we have recorded locally. The session would be shut down anyway if we closed our browser, but we should always try to be "good programming citizens" and keep our logic "clean" in any case.

In the other script we simply use a PHP if-statement to check the value of $notLoggedIn and activate the appropriate XHTML markup, depending on its value.

Figure 10.22 shows the display a user receives after successfully logging out, while Figure 10.23 is what the user sees if an attempt is made to log out when the user has not yet logged in.

10.5   An E-Store Session After a Successful Login

Once a user has successfully logged in to our website, all subsequent movements through our e-store will be labeled with the user's relevant personal information. Figure 10.24 shows the web page now produced by estore.php, which displays the user's information in the top-right corner. The date and time are included, as before, as well as a new link for logging out, which replaces the previous one for logging in.

```php
<?php
//logout.php
session_start();
if ($_SESSION["customer_id"] == "") $notLoggedIn = true;
session_unset();
session_destroy();
?>
<!DOCTYPE html PUBLIC "-//W3C//DTD XHTML 1.0 Transitional//EN"
    "http://www.w3.org/TR/xhtml1/DTD/xhtml1-transitional.dtd">
<html xmlns="http://www.w3.org/1999/xhtml">
  <head>
    <title>Nature's Source - Logging Out</title>
    <meta http-equiv="Content-Type" content="text/html;charset=utf-8" />
    <link rel="stylesheet" type="text/css" href="css/default.css" />
    <script type="text/javascript" src="scripts/menu.js"></script>
  </head>
  <body>
    <div id="page">
      <?php
      include("common/banner.php");
      include("common/mainmenu.html");
      ?>
      <div id="content">
        <div id="textOnly" class="FeedbackForm">
        <?php if ($notLoggedIn) { ?>
        <p>Thank you for visiting Nature's Source.<br />
        You have not yet logged in.</p>
        <p><a href="login.php" class="noDecoration"> Click here if you wish to
          log in.</a></p>
        <p><a href="department.php" class="noDecoration"> Click here to browse
          our product catalog.</a></p>
        <?php } else { ?>
        <p>Thank you for visiting our e-store.<br />
        You have successfully logged out.</p>
        <p><a href = "login.php" class="noDecoration"> Click here if you wish
          to log back in.</a></p>
        <p><a href = "department.php" class="noDecoration"> Click here to
          browse our product catalog.</a></p>
        <?php } ?>
        </div>
      </div>
      <?php include("common/footer.html"); ?>
    </div>
  </body>
</html>
```

FIGURE 10.21

cdrom/web10/logout.php
PHP code for processing the logout.

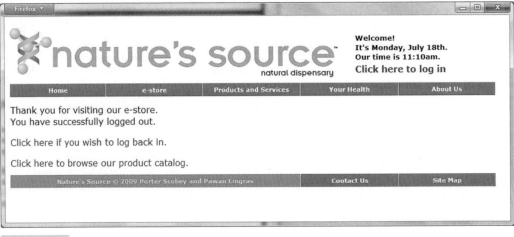

FIGURE 10.22

`graphics/ch10/displaySuccessfulLogout.jpg`
The display indicating a successful logout.

FIGURE 10.23

`graphics/ch10/displayLogoutWithoutLogin.jpg`
The display that results when an attempt is made to log out without having logged in.

At Concordia University College, you choose from a full range of undergraduate and graduate degree programs taught in small classes by some of the finest professors in Canada. You'll be encouraged to set your own course for an exciting career or further studies. If you want a top academic education in a close-knit university community that invites your involvement in every way, you can do that here.

- *Bachelor of Arts*
- *Bachelor of Education*
  (After Degree)
- *Bachelor of Environmental Health*
  (After Degree)
- *Bachelor of Management*
- *Bachelor of Science*
- *Master of Information*
  Systems Security Management

7128 Ada Boulevard,
Edmonton, Alberta, Canada T5B 4E4
Telephone: (780) 479.9220
Toll Free: 1.866.479.5200 ext. 220
Fax: (780) 378.8460
www.concordia.ab.ca

infrastructure that permits us to do this, but we s_____ and modifications to various files, which we now ___ ___ed to take:

____f which `session_start()` needs to be called, ____of those files. This is now essentially all of our ___in our "usual" display at the top of the page. ____on to "persist" in the same location as he or ____ext. In any case, any file that needs to have ___hat is stored in the `$_SESSION` superglobal ___ as its first action.

___ cases, however, we may want a script to have access to this information but choose not to display it. For example, some scripts that we will see later—such as `addItem.php` and `processPayment.php`—may manipulate our database in some way and then redirect the user to a different web page fall into this category. If there is a redirection using the `header()` function, we are not allowed to echo any text.

We can use the global variable `$nodisplay` to help us deal with this situation, as we will see in a moment when we look at `banner.php` in detail.

- Identify all files that need to include our PHP "connection code" from `db.php` to make the connection with our MySQL database, and make sure it is included in the `head` element of each of those files. This will include any files that need to access the database themselves, rather than simply make use of any information that is available from the `$_SESSION` array.

- Revise our `banner.php` file to take care of these new requirements. Recall that our original `banner.php` simply displayed a non-specific `Welcome` message, along with the current date and time. Until the user actually logs in, we essentially want to continue doing this, but also add a strategically placed link in this area of our web pages to facilitate easy login, as we have seen in previous page displays.

   Figure 10.25 shows the revised version of our `banner.php` file. Notice first of all the comment in lines 8–9 pointing out that we should remember to call `session_start()` as the first action in any file that includes this script. Otherwise, we will not be able to extract information from the `$_SESSION` array, which is what the script does as it gets under way. All the necessary `$_SESSION` array values are retrieved and assigned to appropriately named local variables.

   If the global variable `$nodisplay` is `false` we go ahead with a display in the top-right corner of our page. If `$customer_id` is an empty string, we assume that the user has not logged in and display our generic welcome message and a login link. Otherwise, we have a logged-in user whose relevant information has been retrieved and made available to us, so we display that information along with our welcome message and a logout link.

- As we continue to develop our site, adding new pages and associated scripts, we will have to identify those pages on which we do not want the banner information displayed. For those pages we will have to make sure that the key/value pair `nodisplay=true` is passed with the relevant URL when the user is redirected to such a page.

10.6 Browsing Our E-Store Product Catalog

A user who is logged in to our website will likely want to browse through our product catalog. At least we hope so. In fact, we permit this kind of product browsing even if a site visitor is not logged in, and of course in that case we want our login link to be readily available on each page just in case the user decides it's time to buy.

```
1    <!-- banner.php -->
2    <div id="logo">
3      <img src="images/naturelogo.gif" alt="Nature's Source"
4      width="608px" height="90px" />
5    </div>
6    <div id="welcome">
7      <?php
8      //Please make sure that you have called session_start()
9      //at the beginning of the file that includes this script.
10     $salutation = $_SESSION["salutation"];
11     $customer_first_name = $_SESSION["customer_first_name"];
12     $customer_middle_initial = $_SESSION["customer_middle_initial"];
13     $customer_last_name = $_SESSION["customer_last_name"];
14     $customer_id = $_SESSION["customer_id"];
15     if ($nodisplay != true)
16     {
17         if ($customer_id == "")
18         {
19             echo "<h5>Welcome!<br />";
20             echo "It's ".date("l, F jS").".<br />";
21             echo "Our time is ".date('g:ia').".</h5>";
22             echo "<strong><a href = \"login.php\">Click here to log in</a></strong>";
23         }
24         else
25         {
26             echo "<h5>Welcome, " . $customer_first_name . "!<br />";
27             echo  $salutation . " " .
28             $customer_first_name . " " .
29             $customer_middle_initial . " " .
30             $customer_last_name . "<br/>";
31             echo "It's ".date("l, F jS").".<br />";
32             echo "Our time is ".date('g:ia').".</h5>";
33             echo "<strong><a href = \"logout.php\">Click here to log out</a></strong>";
34         }
35     }
36     ?>
37   </div>
```

FIGURE 10.25

cdrom/web10/common/banner.php
The newly-revised version of our banner.php file from the current common subdirectory.

Either the Browse our catalog link under e-store on our main menu or the Product Catalog link under Products and Services on our main menu will take the user to the display shown in Figure 10.26, which is produced by department.php, with the help of the script shown in Figure 10.27. We do not show department.php

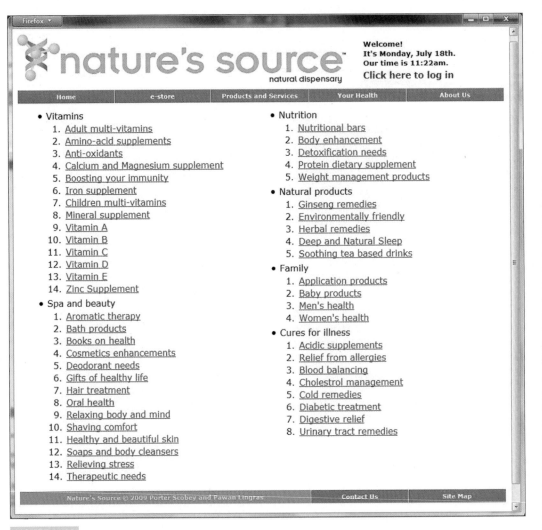

FIGURE 10.26

graphics/ch10/displayDepartmentPhp.jpg
A listing of the departments and product categories in our e-store.

itself, since it is very similar to previous pages and there is nothing new to see there, except to note that we have a new `div` element with `id` value `departmentList`, and a few helpful styles for this `div` have been added to our `default.css` for this chapter. The reader should confirm this by checking out these files in our `web10` directory. In any case we will focus this part of our discussion on the script in `displayDepartments.php`.

```php
<?php
//displayDepartments.php
$query = "SELECT * FROM Ref_Product_Categories
    ORDER BY department_name DESC";
$category = mysql_query($query)
    or die(mysql_error());
$numRecords = mysql_num_rows($category);
$catCount = 0;
$currentDepartment = "";
echo "<table><tr><td><ul>";
for ($i = 0; $i < $numRecords; $i++)
{
    $row = mysql_fetch_array($category);
    if ($currentDepartment != $row["department_name"])
    {
        if ($currentDepartment != "") echo "</ol></li>";
        if ($catCount > $numRecords/2)
        {
            echo "</ul></td><td valign='top'><ul>";
            $catCount = 0;
        }
        $currentDepartment = $row["department_name"];
        echo "<li>$currentDepartment<ol>";
    }
    echo "<li><a href=\"category.php?cat='"
        .$row["product_category_code"] . "'\">"
        .$row["product_category_description"]
        ."</a></li>";
    $catCount++;
}
echo "</ol></li></ul></td></tr></table>";
?>
```

FIGURE 10.27

cdrom/web10/scripts/displayDepartments.php
PHP code for displaying departments and categories.

10.6.1 Displaying a Two-Column List of Products

The script `displayDepartments.php` in Figure 10.27 starts by retrieving the list of all product categories from the table Ref_Product_Categories, ordered by the values of the attribute department_name in descending alphabetical order (lines 3–6). We also save the number of records returned by the query in the variable $numRecords (line 7).

We want to write the names of our product departments as an ordered list, and all the product categories in each department as a nested ordered list under that department. We also want the entire display to appear in two columns, as shown in Figure 10.26. That means our script should create the second column approximately halfway through our listing. We will see how the code in Figure 10.27 produces such a display.

We keep track of the number of categories that have been displayed using the variable $catCount, initialized to 0. When $catCount exceeds $numRecords/2, we will start a new column with the next department. Another variable called $currentDepartment holds the string value of the current department that is being listed. To start, we initialize the value of $currentDepartment to be an empty string.

Once we have initialized our variables, we are ready to start the display, which begins by outputting the opening tags for a table with one row in which the first table cell will contain the first column of a two-column unordered list of departments, so we also output a <ul> tag to mark the beginning of this list. We then enter a for-loop that will go through all the records retrieved by the preceding query. For each record, we retrieve the row as an array called $row. The first thing we do is see if the department for the current record is different from the last value of the department stored in the variable $currentDepartment. If it is different, it is time to do the following:

- First, close the ordered list for the previous department by echoing </ol>. We close the ordered list only if $currentDepartment is not an empty string, since if it is an empty string we are just beginning the first department.

- Next, if the number of categories printed so far is greater than or equal to $numRecords/2, we terminate the first column and first table cell, and start a second table cell containing the second (continuation) column of the unordered list of departments and product categories with the code in line 19:

  ```
  echo "</ul></td><td valign='top'><ul>";
  ```

- Finally, we re-initialize the value of $currentDepartment to the value of departmer in the current record, and then display the name of the current department as a list item in line 23:

  ```
  echo "<li>$currentDepartment<ol>";
  ```

Note that the opening `<li>` tag in the above line of code is not closed until immediately after the order list begun by the `<ol>` tag at the end of the line has been terminated, since the ordered list is nested inside a list element of the unordered list. This structure must be done just so if we want our page to validate.

Each time through the `for`-loop another product category description is listed as an item in one of the (nested) ordered lists via the following code (lines 25–28):

```
echo "<li><a href = \"category.php?cat='"
    .$row["product_category_code"] . "'\">"
    .$row["product_category_description"]
    ."</a></li>";
```

This category description appears as a link to another PHP script named `category` `.php`, which has a key/value pair attached to its URL. The key is named `cat` and its value is the category code for the category of product items we wish to see if we click on that link. Finally, we increment the count of the number of categories that were displayed. When all the retrieved results have been displayed, we exit the `for`-loop and close, in the appropriate order, all the markup elements that remain open (line 31).

10.6.2   Displaying Individual Products within a Category

A click on any of the links shown in Figure 10.26 will provide the user with a display of the details for each of the products in that particular category. For example, clicking on `Deodorant needs`, which is item 5 in the list under the `Spa and beauty` department, brings up the page shown in Figure 10.28. The link itself is a link to the PHP script `category.php`, which is called from the departmental listing with a single parameter called `cat` containing the category code for the desired product. The category code for the category in our example is `DEOD`. This particular category contains only the four products shown in the figure, though many categories will contain a much longer list of items. The information is presented in a tabular format with five columns and these column headers: `Product Image`, `Product Name`, `Price`, `Quantity in Stock`, and `Purchase?`. This last column contains a button link for adding the corresponding product to the shopping cart.

As was the case with `department.php`, the `category.php` file is very similar to previous pages so we do not show it here. Note, however, that once again we have a new `div` element with `id` value `categoryList`, and a few more helpful styles for this `div` have been added to our `default.css` for this chapter. We shall concentrate

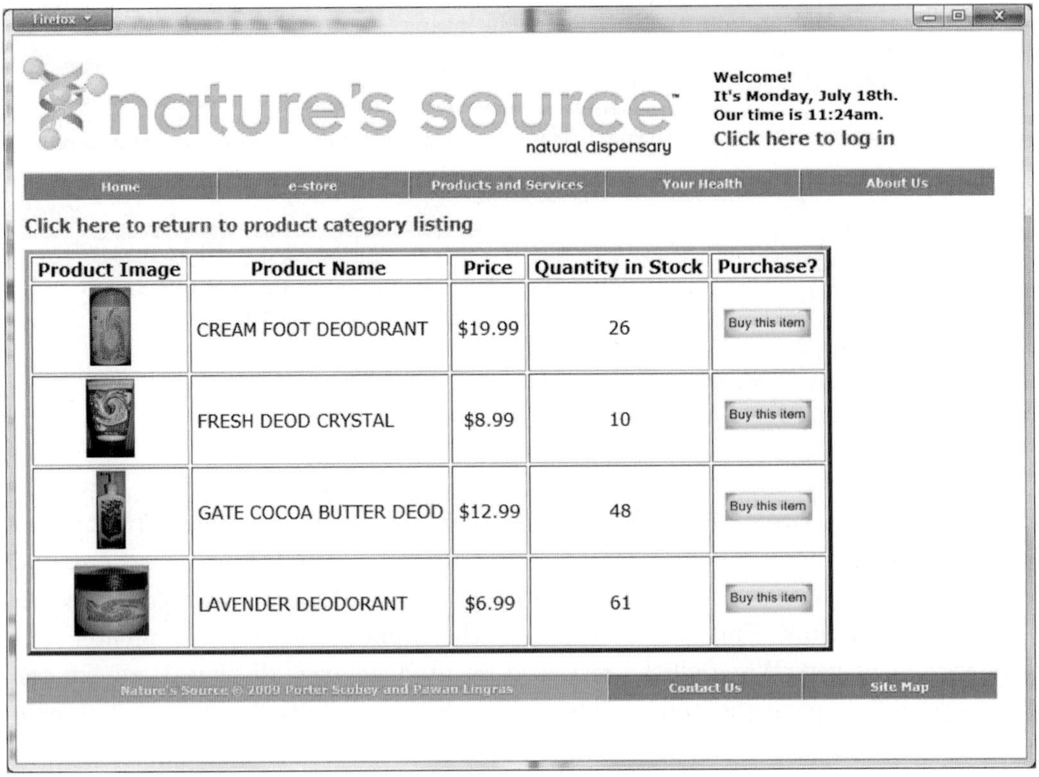

FIGURE 10.28
graphics/ch10/displayCategoryPhp1.jpg
A listing of the individual products in the Deodorant needs category under our Spa and beauty department.

instead on the PHP script `displayCategory.php`, which produces the listing of individual products in a particular category, as shown in Figure 10.28. This script is found in the subdirectory `web10/scripts` and is shown in Figure 10.29.

The first statement in the script `displayCategory.php` uses a built-in PHP function called `stripslashes()`, which removes "slashes" from a string. The reason we need such a function is that the strings that arrive at our script (from a form submission, for example) may well have within them expressions like \' or \" that will cause a problem when they are forwarded to MySQL within a query. For example, in our case, the value of the variable `$cat`, which is supposed to be `'DEOD'` will in fact be `\'DEOD\'` when it arrives at our script. So, we strip out the slashes using `stripslashes()` and restore the variable to its less problematic "slash-free" value.

```php
<?php
//displayCategory.php
$cat = stripslashes($cat);
$query = "SELECT * FROM Products WHERE
    product_category_code = $cat
    ORDER BY product_name ASC";
$category = mysql_query($query)
    or die(mysql_error());
$numRecords = mysql_num_rows($category);
echo "<p><a class=\"noDecoration\"
    href='department.php'><strong>Click here to return to
    product category listing</strong></a></p>";
echo "<table border='4px'>";
echo "<tr><td align='center'><strong>Product Image</strong></td>
    <td align='center'><strong>Product Name</strong></td>
    <td align='center'><strong>Price</strong></td>
    <td align='center'><strong>Quantity in Stock</strong></td>
    <td align='center'><strong>Purchase?</strong></td></tr>";
for ($i = 0; $i < $numRecords; $i++)
{
    echo "<tr>";
    $row = mysql_fetch_array($category);
    echo "<td align='center'>";
    echo  "<img height='70px' width='70px'
        src='".$row["product_image_url"]."'
        alt='Product Image' />";
    echo "</td><td>";
    echo $row["product_name"];
    echo "</td><td align='center'>";
    printf("$%.2f",$row["product_price"]);
    echo "</td><td align='center'>";
    echo $row["product_inventory"];
    echo "</td><td align='center'>";
    echo "<a href=\"purchase.php?prod='".$row["product_id"]."'\">";
    echo "<img src='images/buythisitem.png' alt='Buy this item' /></a>";
    echo "</td></tr>";
}
echo "</table>";
?>
```

FIGURE 10.29

cdrom/web10/scripts/displayCategory.php
PHP code for displaying products in a category.

The following two statements (lines 4–8) retrieve all the products from the Products table that match the category code given by the value of $cat. As before, we assign the number of records retrieved to the variable $numRecords.

The next echo statement (lines 10–12) simply displays a link back to the web page department.php if a user wishes to return to the departmental listing.

The rest of the code in displayCategory.php constructs and displays the table containing the list of products returned by MySQL. The echo statements prior to the for-loop set up the table and display the first row of the table (lines 13–18). The for-loop itself goes through each record returned by MySQL and displays each product (lines 19–37). The statement after the for-loop ends the table with the closing </table> tag (line 38).

Let us look at the for-loop in greater detail. The body of the loop begins with the echoing of the <tr> tag and ends with the echoing of the </tr> tag. In between, as the content of this row element, we display five table cells (table columns) containing the information on a specific product.

First, we retrieve the next record as an associative array called $row. Next, the five columns are displayed by retrieving appropriate row attribute values and placing them within td elements as follows:

1. The first column contains an image of the product, the path to which is stored in the attribute with key value product_image_url, and which we embed in an <img/ > tag.

2. The second column contains the name of the product, found in the array element with key value product_name.

3. The third column contains the product price, from the array element with key value product_price. It uses a built-in function called printf() (for "print formatted") to display a numerical value in an appropriate format. The function takes a variable number of parameters. In our case, we have two parameters:

   ■ The first parameter is a string indicating the format specification. The string "$%.2f" says that we will first print the character $, then display the value given by the second parameter as a floating-point value (real number) with two places after the decimal. For more details on other formatting options, see the end-of-chapter **References** section.

   ■ The second parameter is the actual value that will be printed (the value of product_price in our case).

4. The fourth column contains the quantity of the product in stock (the value in the array element with key value `product_inventory`).

5. The fifth column always displays the same `Buy this item` button link to the same web page, namely `purchase.php`. However, the value of the parameter `prod` that is passed to `purchase.php` is the value of the attribute `product_id` from the record. Clicking on this link will take the customer from "browsing mode" to "shopping mode," which is discussed in the following section.

10.7 Purchasing Products

Processing purchases is probably the most complex logic one needs to handle in an e-commerce website. We have tried to ensure that all of the essential features of the purchasing process are illustrated in our prototype, while keeping the logic of the code involved easy enough to follow.

Once again, the file `purchase.php` is similar in structure and content to several previous files such as `department.php`, so we do not show it. This file includes the script `processPurchase.php` from our `scripts` subdirectory. That is where all the details of managing the shopping cart are handled, and where we will focus our attention. The script is longer and more involved than ones we have seen before, and hence is distributed across multiple figures within the following discussion.

Consider first the display in Figure 10.30, which shows the web page that appears when a user clicks on the `Buy this item` button for a given product in a display like the one shown in Figure 10.28. The assumption is that the customer has logged in and this is the first product that is being added to the cart. A customer who clicks on one of these buttons without having logged in will be transferred to the login page, since logging in is required before purchasing can proceed.

Let us assume that the customer enters the quantity 5 into the textbox provided under the `Quantity` column header, and clicks on the `Buy this item` button. The customer further continues with shopping and clicks on the `Add to cart` link for another product. The resulting web page is shown in Figure 10.31. This time the customer enters a quantity of 15, which happens to exceed the inventory level, which is 9. The system returns with the web page shown in Figure 10.32, asking the customer to enter a quantity that does not exceed the inventory level. When the customer has entered an acceptable quantity, the resulting shopping cart contents are shown in Figure 10.33. Although we do not illustrate the result of doing so, you will note that

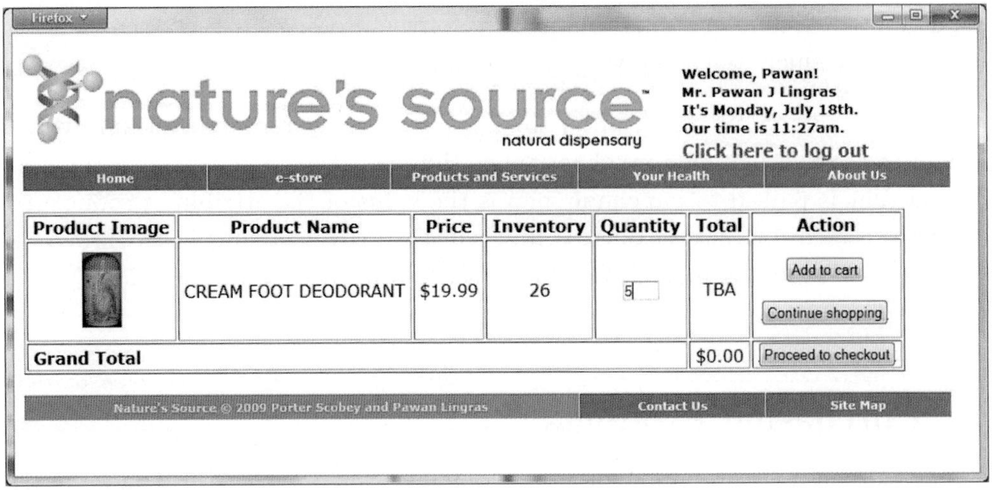

FIGURE 10.30

graphics/ch10/displayPurchasePhp1.jpg
Purchasing a first product.

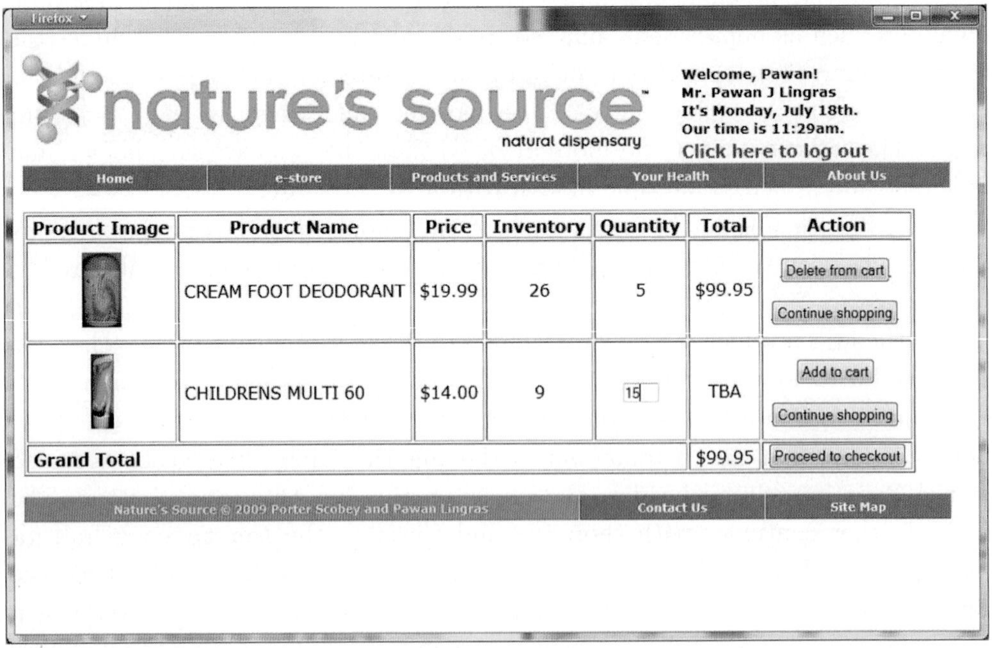

FIGURE 10.31

graphics/ch10/displayPurchasePhp2.jpg
Purchasing an additional product and trying to buy more than the company has in stock.

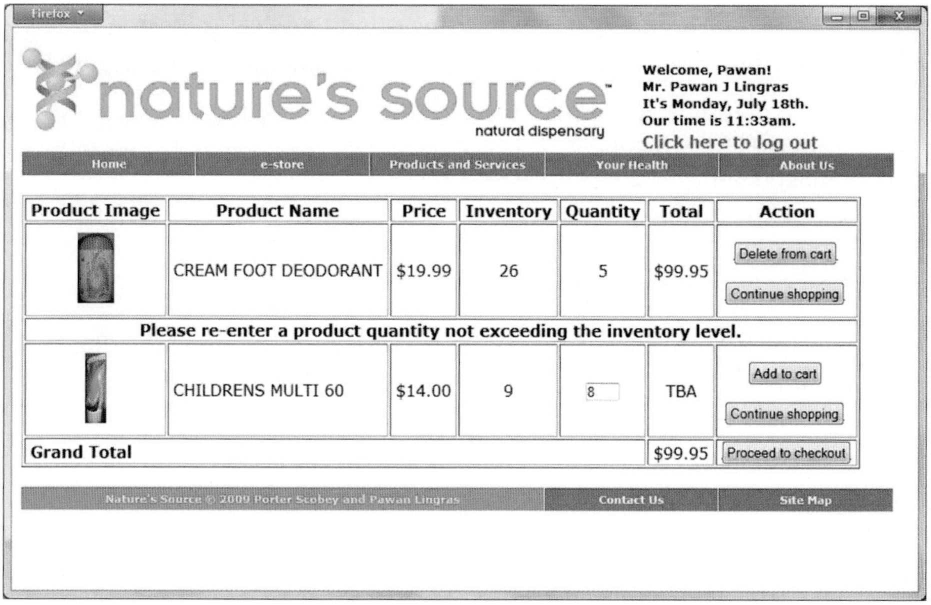

FIGURE 10.32

graphics/ch10/displayPurchasePhp3.jpg
Customer is asked to try again, making sure not to request more than the available number.

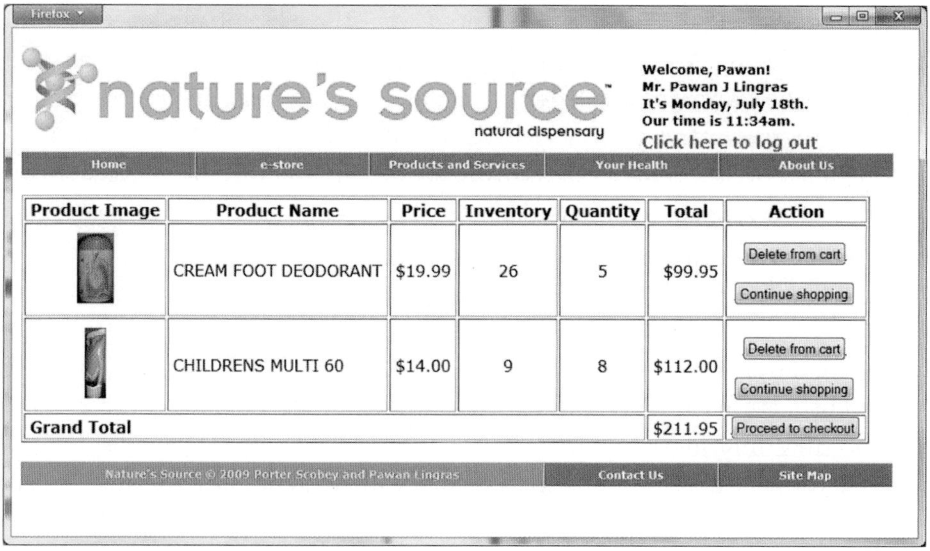

FIGURE 10.33

graphics/ch10/displayPurchasePhp4.jpg
Viewing the shopping cart with two items in it, ready for checkout.

deleting an item from the shopping cart is also possible by clicking on the Delete from cart button in the Action column of the row corresponding to the product to be deleted.

In the following sections we look at the PHP code that handles this kind of shopping cart management.

10.7.1   A High-Level View of the processPurchase.php Script

Figure 10.34 shows the main part of the script for processing the purchase. There is no explicit main() function in a PHP script, so we refer to the portion(s) of the total script that are not part of any function as the "main" part of script. Each of the functions called by this part of the script, and which we simply mention in passing in this section, will be discussed in more detail in the following sections.

As before, we use the stripslashes() function to get rid of any unwanted slashes from the variable $prod that has been passed to the script. The value of $prod is the product code if the customer is adding a product to the cart. Otherwise, $prod is set to view, which means that the customer will be only viewing the existing items in the cart.

A function called getExistingOrder() is called with $customer_id as the parameter. The value of $customer_id is associated with the current session and may be retrieved from $_SESSION on any web page that begins with a call to session_start(). The function getExistingOrder() retrieves all the items in the order that is currently "in progress" (those for which order_status_code='IP') for the customer, and we again store the number of records retrieved in the variable $numRecords.

If $numRecords is zero and the customer is only trying to view the cart, then there is really nothing to display. Therefore, a message to that effect is displayed for the customer, along with a link to estore.php, the start page for our e-store, which returns the customer to browsing mode.

On the other hand, if $numRecords is not zero, or the customer is adding an item to the cart, or both, we have more work to do. We begin by displaying the header for a table of product information with a call to the function displayHeader().

The running total of all the items in the cart will be kept in a variable called $grandTotal, which is then initialized to zero.

If $numRecords is zero, we need to create a new order for the customer using the function createOrder(). Otherwise, we have to display all the items that are currently in the cart using the displayExistingItem() function within a for-loop. This function not only displays one item per call, but also returns the total cost of the item, which is added to $grandTotal.

```php
1   <?php
2   //processPurchase.php
3   /////////////////// main begins ///////////////////////
4   $prod = stripslashes($prod);
5   $items = getExistingOrder($customer_id);
6   $numRecords = mysql_num_rows($items);
7   if ($numRecords == 0 && $prod == "view")
8   {
9       echo "<p><strong>Your shopping cart is empty.</strong></p>
0           <p><a class='noDecoration'
1           href='estore.php'><strong>Please click here
2           to continue shopping ...</strong></a></p>";
3   }
4   else
5   {
6       displayHeader();
7       $grandTotal = 0;
8       if ($numRecords == 0)
9       {
0           createOrder($customer_id);
1       }
2       else //There are existing items to display
3       {
4           for ($i = 0; $i < $numRecords; $i++)
5           {
6               $grandTotal += displayExistingItem($items);
7           }
8       }
9
0       if ($prod != "view") //Display entry row for new item
1       {
2           if ($retry)
3           {
4               echo "<tr><td colspan='7' align='center'>
5                   <strong>Please re-enter a product
6                   quantity not exceeding the inventory
7                   level.</strong></td></tr>";
8           }
9           displayNewItem($prod);
0       }
1       displayFooter($grandTotal);
2   }
3
4   /////////////////// main ends functions begin ////////////////////////
```

FIGURE 10.34

cdrom/web10/scripts/processPurchase.php (Part 1)
PHP code for the main part of the PHP script for processing purchases.

Once all the existing items have been displayed, we check to see if $prod has the value view. If it does not, we have a new item to display. If the variable $retry is true, that means the previous attempt at adding the item to the cart has failed (because the customer tried to add more to the shopping cart than the company has in stock), so we display an appropriate message. Whether or not this message is displayed, we then display a row of the table for this item using the function displayNewItem(). Finally, we display the $grandTotal as well as the rest of the footer of the table using the function displayFooter().

Now that we have looked at the global logic of the main part of processPurchase .php, let's move on to look at some of the lower-level details by studying the various helper functions mentioned above, beginning with those that work with the database tables.

10.7.2   Recalling the Relevant Tables in Our Database Structure

Before we look at performing any database queries by a PHP script, let us review the two relevant tables in our database scheme. The first of the two tables that are used to manage our shopping cart is the Orders table, which contains the following attributes:

- order_id

- customer_id

- order_status_code

- date_order_placed

- order_details

The main purpose of the Orders table is to keep track of information that is common to all the items that are being purchased by a customer at any given time. We assume that there is at most one order in progress for a customer at any given time. If there is such an order in progress, the order_status_code will be IP. The list of items in the order is maintained in the second table of interest, Order_Items, which contains the following attributes:

- order_item_id

- order_item_status_code

- order_id

- `product_id`

- `order_item_quantity`

- `order_item_price`

- `other_order_item_details`

10.7.3 Getting the Product Details of an Existing Order with the getExistingOrder() Function

The function `getExistingOrder()` shown in Figure 10.35 takes `customer_id` as its parameter and retrieves all the items for that customer that are "in progress" (i.e., for which the value of `order_status_code` is IP). The function simply constructs an appropriate query, executes the query, and returns the retrieved results to main.

The essence of the function lies in the query construction. This particular query is a little more complex than previous ones we have seen, as it involves "joining" the two tables `Orders` and `Order_Items`. We retrieve those records satisfying the following criteria (see the `WHERE` clause in lines 53–56 of Figure 10.35):

```
Orders.order_id=Order_Items.order_id and
Orders.order_status_code='IP' and
Orders.customer_id='$customer_id'
```

The query actually retrieves the first three attributes from the `Orders` table (using the wildcard character * in line 52) and all the attributes from the `Orders_Items` tables. The order of the attributes will be as shown below.
Attributes from the `Orders` table:

- `order_id`

- `customer_id`

- `order_status_code`

Attributes from the `Orders_Items` table:

- `order_item_id`

- `order_item_status_code`

- `order_id`

```
44     /////////////// main ends functions begin //////////////////////
45
46     function getExistingOrder($customer_id)
47     {
48         $query = "SELECT
49             Orders.order_id,
50             Orders.customer_id,
51             Orders.order_status_code,
52             Order_Items.*
53             FROM Order_Items, Orders WHERE
54             Orders.order_id=Order_Items.order_id and
55             Orders.order_status_code='IP' and
56             Orders.customer_id = $customer_id;";
57         $items = mysql_query($query)
58             or die(mysql_error());
59         return $items;
60     }
61
62     function createOrder($customer_id)
63     {
64         $query = "INSERT INTO Orders
65         (
66             customer_id,
67             order_status_code,
68             date_order_placed,
69             order_details
70         )
71         VALUES
72         (
73             '$customer_id',
74             'IP',
75             CURDATE( ),
76             NULL
77         );";
78         mysql_query($query)
79             or die(mysql_error());
80     }
```

FIGURE 10.35

cdrom/web10/scripts/processPurchase.php (Part 2)

PHP functions for retrieving product information for an order-in-progress, and for creating a new order.

- product_id

- order_item_quantity

- order_item_price

- other_order_item_details

10.7.4 Creating a New Order with the createOrder() Function

The second database-related function that may be called from the main part of the script creates a new order if the customer does not have an existing order "in progress." This is the createOrder() function, also shown in Figure 10.35. This function receives customer_id as its parameter and inserts a record into the Orders table.

Note that we do not specify the value for the order_id attribute. It is generated automatically by MySQL. The value of customer_id is set to the one that was passed to the function. The order_status_code is set to IP to indicate an in-progress order item. A built-in PHP function called CURDATE() is used to specify the value of the attribute date_order_placed. The order_details attribute is left NULL.

10.7.5 Displaying the Header and Footer of the Shopping Cart Table with the displayHeader() and displayFooter() Functions

Figure 10.36 shows the functions that are used to display the header and footer of the shopping cart table. The function displayHeader() begins by opening a form that can be used to add an item, identified as orderForm. The form is validated by the JavaScript function validateOrderForm() found in the file order.js from the web10/scripts subdirectory.[5] The subdirectory scripts also contains the PHP script addItem.php that will be called when the form is submitted. The rest of the function displayHeader() simply displays the header row of the table that will display the shopping cart contents.

The function displayFooter() is also shown in Figure 10.36. It receives $grandTotal as a parameter, and this value is displayed in the last row of the table at the bottom of the Total column. This function also places a Proceed to checkout button in the Action column of this final row of the table.

Note that the script in the value of the href attribute of the Proceed to checkout button link is, of course, payment.php, but note as well that the parameter nodisplay with a value of true is passed to the script when it is invoked. As we'll see a bit later when we discuss the checkout procedure, this prevents the user information, date, and time from being displayed in the upper-right corner of the receipt page. This information appears elsewhere on that page.

---

[5] All that needs to be validated in this case is the customer's entry for the quantity of product desired. Note that this validation by JavaScript can only determine whether the user has entered a positive integer quantity. JavaScript cannot determine whether the quantity entered exceeds the current inventory level. The quantity must be sent to the server for that determination to be made.

```
82   function displayHeader()
83   {
84       echo "<form id='orderForm' onsubmit='return validateOrderForm();'
85           action='scripts/addItem.php'>";
86       echo "<table border='1px'>";
87       echo "<tr>
88           <td align='center'><strong>Product Image</strong></td>
89           <td align='center'><strong>Product Name</strong></td>
90           <td align='center'><strong>Price</strong></td>
91           <td align='center'><strong>Inventory</strong></td>
92           <td align='center'><strong>Quantity</strong></td>
93           <td align='center'><strong>Total</strong></td>
94           <td align='center'><strong>Action</strong></td>
95           </tr>";
96   }
97
98   function displayFooter($grandTotal)
99   {
100      echo "<tr><td colspan='5'><strong>Grand Total</strong></td>";
101      printf("<td align='right'>\$%.2f</td>", $grandTotal);
102      echo "<td align='center'><a href = 'payment.php?nodisplay=true'>
103          <input type='button' value='Proceed to checkout' /></a>
104          </td></table></form>";
105  }
```

. . .

FIGURE 10.36

cdrom/web10/scripts/processPurchase.php (Part 3)
PHP functions for displaying the table header and footer for the shopping cart display.

Finally, the function then completes the display of the shopping cart information by outputting the closing **</table>** and **</form>** tags.

10.7.6   Displaying the Product Information in the Shopping Cart with the displayFirstFourColumns(), displayExistingItem(), and displayNewItem() Functions

Now we come to the display of the product information for the current contents of the shopping cart. If a new item is being added, this will include a row for that product's information as well, and this row will have a textbox form field into which the customer can enter the desired quantity of this product. As you read the rest of the discussion in this section, you may find it helpful to refer back to the display in Figure 10.31.

```
07   function displayFirstFourColumns($prod)
08   {
09       $prod = stripslashes($prod);
10       $query = "SELECT * FROM Products WHERE product_id = $prod;";
11       $product = mysql_query($query)
12           or die(mysql_error());
13       $row = mysql_fetch_array($product);
14       echo "<tr>\n";
15       echo "<td align = center>";
16       echo  "<img height='70' width='70'
17           src = \"".$row[product_image_url]."\" />";
18       echo "</td><td>";
19       echo $row[product_name];
20       echo "</td><td align='center'>";
21       printf("$%.2f\n",$row[product_price]);
22       echo "</td><td align='center'>";
23       echo $row[product_inventory];
24       echo "</td>";
25   }
```

FIGURE 10.37

cdrom/web10/scripts/processPurchase.php (Part 4)
PHP function for displaying the first four descriptive table columns for each item in the shopping cart.

The first four columns for items already in the shopping cart, as well as the first four columns for any new item, are always the same, so we use a separate function to handle these columns in both cases. That function, shown in Figure 10.37, is called displayFirstFourColumns(), and it receives the product ID as a parameter via the variable $prod. The function first removes any unwanted slashes from $prod. Next, it retrieves the record for the given product from the Products table, which is then converted to an associative array and stored in $row.

Finally, the function outputs a row of information, so it begins with a <tr> tag and follows this with its four columns of information, each displayed inside a td element:

- The first column contains an img element whose src attribute value is given by the value obtained from the associative array $row containing the retrieved record by using the key product_image_url.

- The next three columns simply display the values of the attributes product_name, product_price, and product_inventory, again obtained from the $row array with the corresponding keys.

```
127    function displayExistingItem($items)
128    {
129        $row = mysql_fetch_array($items);
130        $prod = $row[product_id];
131        displayFirstFourColumns($prod);
132        echo "<td align='center'>";
133        echo $row[order_item_quantity];
134        echo "</td><td align='right'>";
135        $total = $row[order_item_quantity]*$row[order_item_price];
136        printf("$%.2f", $total);
137        echo "</td><td align='center'>";
138        echo "<p><a href='scripts/deleteItem.php?order_item=".
139            $row[order_item_id]."&order_id=".$row[order_id]."'>
140            <input type='button' value='Delete from cart' /></a></p>
141            <p><a href='department.php'>
142            <input type='button' value='Continue shopping' />
143            </a></p></td></tr>";
144        return $total;
145    }
```

. . .

FIGURE 10.38

cdrom/web10/scripts/processPurchase.php (Part 5)
PHP function for displaying the last three table columns for each item already in the shopping cart.

The first two statements in the function displayExistingItem(), shown in Figure 10.38, set up and call the displayFirstFourColumns() function that we have just discussed. This involves retrieving product_id from the array $row that is passed to it and then passing it on to the displayFirstFourColumns() function. Once we have displayed the first four columns, the remaining three columns for an existing item are displayed by the rest of the function code as follows:

- The fifth column displays the value of the attribute order_item_quantity, retrieved from the associative array $row.

- The sixth column displays the total cost for the ordered item in the current row. This cost is calculated by multiplying order_item_quantity and order_item_price, which are retrieved from the associative array $row and stored in the variable $total.

- The seventh and final column contains two button links. The first button contains the label Delete from cart, and clicking on it activates the PHP script deleteItem.php, with order_item_id passed as a parameter called order_item. The order_item_id value is retrieved, once again, from the associative array

$row and used in the construction of the link. The second button contains the label Continue shopping and clicking on it activates the script department.php, taking the user back to the view of all of our departments and the product categories within them.

Once we have displayed all the items already in the shopping cart, the final row in the main script may call the function displayNewItem() to display the part of the form that allows a user to add another item to the cart. This function is shown in Figure 10.39. The function receives the value of product_id as a parameter called $prod. The first statement again calls the function displayFirstFourColumns() to display the first four columns. The remaining three columns have the following contents:

- The fifth column displays a textbox field named quantity for accepting the quantity of the product to be added to the order. In addition, a hidden form field called prod is added to the form, which stores the product_id. This hidden attribute is a convenient way of passing this information along to the PHP script addItem.php, where it is needed.

- The sixth column displays the string TBA, since when this row is displayed we do not yet know the quantity of the item the user wants, so we cannot display the total cost for that item.

```
48    function displayNewItem($prod)
49    {
50        displayFirstFourColumns($prod);
51        echo "<td align='center'>";
52        echo "<input type='hidden' id='prod'
53            name='prod' value=\"$prod\">";
54        echo "<input type='text' id='quantity'
55            name='quantity' size='3'>";
56        echo "</td><td align='center'>";
57        echo "TBA";
58        echo "</td><td align='center'>";
59        echo "<p><input type='submit' value='Add to cart' /></p>
60            <p><a href='department.php'>
61            <input type='button' value='Continue shopping' /></a></p>
62            </td></tr>";
63    }
64    ?>
```

FIGURE 10.39

cdrom/web10/scripts/processPurchase.php (Part 6)
PHP function for displaying the last three table columns for a new item coming into the shopping cart.

- The seventh and final column again contains two button links. Remember that the table containing our shopping cart display is also the content of a form, and if the display contains a last row for adding a new item to the cart, we must also have a submit button to send the form data to the server. The first button in the last column, which contains the label `Add to cart`, is actually the submit button for this form. Thus clicking on it submits the form data to the PHP script `addItem.php`, with `order_item_id` passed as a parameter called `order_item`. This `order_item_id` value is retrieved, once again, from the associative array `$row` and used in the construction of the link. The second button contains the label `Continue shopping` and clicking on it activates the script `department.php`, taking the user back to the view of all of our departments and the product categories within them. This is the same button that also appears at the end of each row corresponding to an item already in the cart.

The PHP script `processPurchase.php` that we have discussed so far displays the contents of the cart and creates the form for possibly adding an item. The resulting web page needs two database manipulation scripts, one called `addItem.php` and the other called `deleteItem.php`. We will discuss these two scripts in the following two sections.

10.7.7   Adding an Item to the Shopping Cart

The complete code for the PHP script `addItem.php` is shown in Figure 10.40. The main script begins once again by calling the `session_start()` function. We then include the script `db.php` to connect to our MySQL database. In line 6 we get the `customer_id` value from the `$_SESSION` array and immediately pass it to the `getOrderID()` function to retrieve the "in progress" order for this customer. We will look at this function later in this section.

Next, as usual, we remove any unwanted slashes from the variable `$prod` and then use it to get the record for the desired product from the `Products` table by executing an appropriate query. The results of this query are again stored as an associative array in the variable `$row`.

Now we retrieve `product_inventory` from `$row`. If `product_inventory` is less than `$quantity`, we cannot proceed any further, so we redirect the customer back to `purchase.php` by setting the value of parameter `prod` to the original `product_id` value stored in `$prod`. We also add a parameter called `retry` with a value of `true` to the URL to indicate to the receiving script that this is a repeated attempt. The script will take this as an indication to display the reminder message to the user that we have seen earlier about not exceeding the inventory level.

```php
<?php
//addItem.php
////////////////// main begins //////////////////
session_start();
include "db.php";
$customer_id = $_SESSION["customer_id"];
$order_id = getOrderID($customer_id);
$prod = stripslashes($prod);
$query = "SELECT * FROM Products WHERE product_id=$prod;";
$product = mysql_query($query)
    or die(mysql_error());
$row = mysql_fetch_array($product);
$product_inventory = $row[product_inventory];
if ($product_inventory < $quantity)
{
    header("Location: ../purchase.php?prod=$prod&retry=true");
}
else
{
    $product_price = $row[product_price];
    $query = "INSERT INTO Order_Items
    (
        order_item_status_code,
        order_id,
        product_id,
        order_item_quantity,
        order_item_price,
        other_order_item_details
    )
    VALUES
    (
        'IP',
        $order_id,
        $prod,
        $quantity,
        $product_price,
        NULL
    );";
    mysql_query($query)
        or die(mysql_error());
    header('Location: ../purchase.php?prod=view');
}
//////////////// main ends functions begin //////////////
function getOrderID($customer_id)
{
    $query = "SELECT
            Orders.order_id,Orders.order_status_code,
            Orders.customer_id
        FROM Orders WHERE
            Orders.order_status_code = 'IP' and
            Orders.customer_id = '$customer_id';";
    $order = mysql_query($query)
        or die(mysql_error());
    $row = mysql_fetch_array($order);
    return $row[order_id];
}
?>
```

FIGURE 10.40

cdrom/web10/scripts/addItem.php
PHP code for adding a new item to the cart.

Alternatively, if `quantity` is less than or equal to `product_inventory`, we continue with the code given in the `else` block. This code involves retrieving the value of `product_price`. We know the rest of the values to add a record to the table `Order_Items`. The following statement builds the query string using these values. We do not specify any value for the `order_item_id`, which will be automatically determined by MySQL. The `order_item_status` code is set to IP, and the values of the rest of the attributes are obtained from the available variables, with the `other_order_item_details` set to NULL.

Once the query is executed, the customer is redirected back to `purchase.php`, but with the value of the parameter `prod` set to `view`. This means the customer will only see the items currently in the cart, which will include the recently added item.

Finally, let us take a quick look at the `getOrderID()` function that appears at the bottom of Figure 10.40. This function builds a query string to retrieve a record from the `Orders` table with `order_status_code` equal to IP for the customer given by `$customer_id`. The value of `$customer_id` was passed to the function as a parameter. Once the query is executed, the results are once again stored in an associative array in `$row`. The value of `order_id` from the array `$row` is returned to the main script.

10.7.8   Deleting an Item from the Shopping Cart

The PHP script `deleteItem.php` for deleting an existing item from the shopping cart is shown in Figure 10.41. The script gets a parameter called `order_item`. After executing `session_start()` and connecting to the database with the script `db.php`, the script constructs a query string for deleting the given `order_item` from the table `Order_Items`. The query is then executed and the customer is redirected to the web page `purchase.php` to view the revised status of the cart, thus confirming the deletion. Also, the script checks to see if deleting the given item empties the cart and, if so, the order itself is deleted.

10.8   Checkout

We have now come to the final stage of our e-commerce website's purchase-processing functionality: providing our customers with the ability to "purchase" the items they have added to their shopping carts and then to "check out." Our checkout script will therefore perform the following actions:

- Display a receipt and thank the customer for the business.

```php
1   <?php
2   //deleteItem.php
3   //main begins
4   session_start();
5   include "db.php";
6   $order_item = stripslashes($order_item);
7   $order_id = stripslashes($order_id);
8   $query = "DELETE FROM Order_Items WHERE order_item_id = $order_item;";
9   mysql_query($query)
10      or die(mysql_error());
11
12  $query = "SELECT COUNT(*) AS numItemsStillInOrder
13      FROM Order_Items
14      WHERE order_id=$order_id;";
15  $return_value = mysql_query($query)
16      or die(mysql_error());
17  $row = mysql_fetch_array($return_value);
18  if ($row[numItemsStillInOrder] == 0)
19  {
20      $query = "DELETE FROM Orders WHERE order_id=$order_id;";
21      mysql_query($query)
22          or die(mysql_error());
23  }
24
25  header('Location: ../purchase.php?prod=view');
26  //main ends
27  ?>
```

FIGURE 10.41

cdrom/web10/scripts/deleteItem.php
PHP code for deleting an item from the cart.

- Adjust the proper entries in the Orders and Order_Items tables to indicate payment.

- Reduce inventory as appropriate.

Actually, we do not provide the ability to accept a real payment. The payment mechanism requires a secure communication with a payment gateway site, which is beyond the scope of this text.

So, let us look at the checkout programming that *is* implemented for our prototype website, short of actual payment for products purchased. Figures 10.42 to 10.44 show three web pages that illustrate the checkout process.

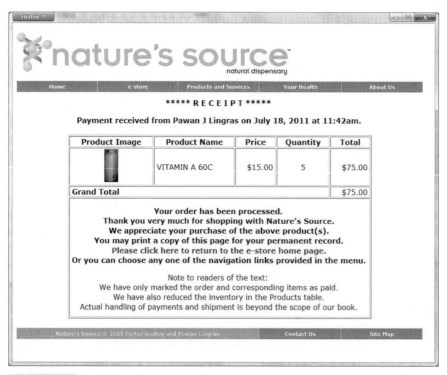

FIGURE 10.42

graphics/ch10/displayPurchasePhp5.jpg
A shopping cart with a single item in it, ready for checkout.

FIGURE 10.43

graphics/ch10/displayPaymentPhp.jpg
The receipt displayed to the customer upon completion of the checkout process.

graphics/ch10/displayCategoryPhp2.jpg
A view, after checkout, of the database product category containing the purchased item, confirming the reduction in inventory.

Figure 10.42 shows a shopping cart containing a single item, which is ready for the user to "proceed to checkout" by clicking the corresponding button at the extreme right in the final row of the table.

Figure 10.43 shows the web page that results when the customer clicks on the `Proceed to checkout` button. There is no intermediate stage in which the customer provides credit card information for the payment and chooses a shipping method, for example. The `payment.php` page, which is activated here simply displays a receipt and a thank-you message.

Figure 10.44 shows the web page we would now see if we proceeded as though we wished to make another purchase of the same product by displaying the product category containing the just-purchased product. The main point here is that we can now verify that the checkout process has indeed made the appropriate reduction of the inventory level for the purchased product by comparing the inventory level for this product in Figures 10.42 and 10.44.

Let us look at how `payment.php` processes the checkout. Most of the XHTML and PHP code in `payment.php` is the same as in some other files we have already looked at, such as `purchase.php`, so in Figure 10.45 we show only the PHP code that is relevant to us at this point.

```
1    <?php
2    //payment.php
3    session_start();
4    if (preg_match('/purchase.php/', $_SERVER[HTTP_REFERER]) == 0)
5    {
6        header('Location: purchase.php?prod=view');
7    }
8    ?>
```

. . .

FIGURE 10.45

cdrom/web10/payment.php (excerpts)
XHTML and PHP code for relevant parts of payment.php.

The file begins with a PHP script that starts by executing session_start(), as usual. It then checks to see whether the HTTP_REFERER was purchase.php. We use the PHP function preg_match() that looks for the pattern /purchase.php/ in the string given by the variable $_SERVER[HTTP_REFERER], which contains the page the browser said it came from to get to the current page. The function preg_match() will return 0 if there was no match, and 1 otherwise. If there was no match, we want the customer to view the shopping cart before purchasing. Hence, we redirect the customer to the web page purchase.php, with the value of the parameter prod set to view, by a call to the header() function.

After setting up the usual page and database-connection "infrastructure," the payment.php page proceeds to include the script processPayment.php, which does the actual checkout processing and which will be discussed next. Recall, however, as we pointed out at the end of section 10.7.6, because this time $nodisplay has the value true, this means that when banner.php is called it only sets variables from the session, it does not display them.

Figure 10.46 shows the (very short) "main" part of the script processPayment.php. This script gives us the value of $customer_id, which is passed to a number of functions that will be used to process the payment. It will be used to retrieve the necessary information for the customer's current order.

The processPayment.php script also includes the receipt.php script, which contains the functions that will print the receipt. The main "driver" function among these is displayReceipt(), with parameter $customer_id as its input parameter, but this function also uses a number of auxiliary "helper" functions to display the header and footer of the receipt, as well as to get and display the necessary infor-

```
1   <?php
2   /////////////// main begins ///////////////////
3   session_start();
4   include "receipt.php";
5   displayReceipt($customer_id);
6   $order_id = orderPaid($customer_id);
7   orderItemPaid($order_id);
8   ////////////// main ends functions begin //////////////
```

. . .

FIGURE 10.46

cdrom/web10/scripts/processPayment.php (Part 1)
PHP code for the "main" part of the script for processing a payment.

mation about the purchased items. This code for displaying the receipt is a stripped
down version of the similar code we saw in processPurchase.php, since here we
display fewer columns and this script does not provide a form for adding new items.
Therefore, we will not discuss this code in detail again or even show it here, but
readers are encouraged to examine the relevant part of the script that is, as usual,
available from the web10/scripts directory on the CD-ROM.

After displaying the receipt, the next step in processing a payment is to mark the
customer's order in the Orders table as paid. This is the purpose of the orderPaid()
function shown in Figure 10.47. The function accepts $customer_id as a parameter
and returns the order_id, which is used in the following call(s) to the function to
mark the individual order item(s) paid as well. It uses its $customer_id parameter to
build a query, which will retrieve the record containing the current order-in-progress
for this customer. This order is indicated by an order_status_code with the value
IP. The record is converted to an associative array and assigned to the variable $row.

Next, we build a query to replace the old record with a new record. All the values
in the new record will be the same as the retrieved record, except for order_status_
code, which is set to PD for paid. The date_order_placed is set to the current date
returned by the function CURDATE(). Finally, order_details is set to NULL. After
executing the query, the function returns the order_id from the retrieved record.

Figure 10.48 shows the code for the function orderItemPaid(), which marks each
individual item in the order as paid. It accepts $order_id as a parameter and builds a
query to retrieve all the records for the corresponding order. The number of records in
the result is stored in the variable $numRecords. We go through all the records via the
subsequent for-loop. Inside that loop, the next record is converted to an associative
array named $row. We then build a query to replace the old record with a new record.

```
10    function orderPaid($customer_id)
11    {
12        $query = "SELECT * FROM Orders WHERE
13            Orders.order_status_code = 'IP' and
14            Orders.customer_id = '$customer_id';";
15        $order = mysql_query($query)
16            or die(mysql_error());
17        $row = mysql_fetch_array($order);
18        $query2 = "REPLACE INTO Orders
19        (
20            order_id,
21            customer_id,
22            order_status_code,
23            date_order_placed,
24            order_details
25        )
26        VALUES
27        (
28            '"
29            .$row[order_id]."','"
30            .$row[customer_id]."',
31            'PD',
32            CURDATE(),
33            NULL"
34            .");";
35        mysql_query($query2)
36            or die(mysql_error());
37        return $row[order_id];
38    }
```

. . .

FIGURE 10.47
cdrom/web10/scripts/processPayment.php (Part 2)
PHP function for marking an order as paid.

All the values in the new record will be the same as the retrieved record, except for order_item_status_code, which is set to PD for paid. Also, order_details is set to NULL. After executing the query, the function calls the function reduceInventory() to make the necessary inventory adjustment for the item that has just been marked as paid.

The function reduceInventory(), which receives the product_id for the purchased item in its $prod aprameter, as well as the number of items purchased in its $quantity, is shown in Figure 10.48. The function builds a query to retrieve the record for the product. The record is converted to an associative array

```
function orderItemPaid($order_id)
{
    $query = "SELECT *
        FROM Order_Items WHERE
        order_id = '$order_id';";
    $orderItems = mysql_query($query)
        or die(mysql_error());
    $numRecords = mysql_num_rows($orderItems);
    for($i = 0; $i < $numRecords; $i++)
    {
        $row = mysql_fetch_array($orderItems);
        $query2 = "REPLACE INTO Order_Items
        (
            order_item_id,
            order_item_status_code,
            order_id,
            product_id,
            order_item_quantity,
            order_item_price,
            other_order_item_details
        )
        VALUES
        ('"
            .$row[order_item_id]."',
            'PD','"
            .$row[order_id]."','"
            .$row[product_id]."','"
            .$row[order_item_quantity]."','"
            .$row[order_item_price]."',
            NULL".
        ");";
        mysql_query($query2)
            or die(mysql_error());
        reduceInventory($row[product_id], $row[order_item_quantity]);
    }
}
```

...

FIGURE 10.48

cdrom/web10/scripts/processPayment.php (Part 3)
PHP function for marking as paid each individual item in a customer's order.

named $row. We subtract $quantity from the value of the array element indexed
by product_inventory. We then build a query to replace the old record with the
new record. All the values in the new record will be the same as the retrieved record,
except for the changed value for product_inventory.

```
78    function reduceInventory($prod, $quantity)
79    {
80        $query = "SELECT * FROM Products WHERE product_id=$prod;";
81        $product = mysql_query($query)
82            or die(mysql_error());
83        $row = mysql_fetch_array($product);
84        $row[product_inventory] -= $quantity;
85        $query = "REPLACE INTO Products
86            (
87                product_id,
88                product_category_code,
89                product_name,
90                product_price,
91                product_inventory,
92                product_color,
93                product_size,
94                product_description,
95                product_image_url,
96                other_product_details
97            )
98            VALUES
99            ('"
100               .$row[product_id]."','"
101               .$row[product_category_code]."','"
102               .$row[product_name]."','"
103               .$row[product_price]."','"
104               .$row[product_inventory]."','"
105               .$row[product_color]."','"
106               .$row[product_size]."','"
107               .$row[product_description]."','"
108               .$row[product_image_url]."','"
109               .$row[other_product_details].
110            "');";
111        mysql_query($query)
112            or die(mysql_error());
113    }
114    ?>
```

FIGURE 10.49

cdrom/web10/scripts/processPayment.php (Part 4)
PHP function for reducing the inventory level after a payment has been made.

10.9   Summary

In a very real sense, PHP and MySQL have "grown up together," at least in the sense that much effort has gone into making the two technologies work well together. The fact that this effort has been successful is reflected in the number of major commercial enterprises that use the combination to handle their database activities.

PHP contains many functions for dealing directly with a MySQL database system and, for that matter, for dealing with many other database systems. You can write your own scripts to connect to a MySQL database system, create and populate tables with data, add and remove data after the fact, modify that data, and retrieve it in various ways. Or, if you are the database administrator, you can use a sophisticated PHP-based front-end GUI-like phpMyAdmin to do all of these things and more.

Exactly what scripts you will need for your own website will depend on what you want your site visitors to be able to do with the data stored in your database. At a minimum, if you are setting up an online store, you will want them to be able to view your offerings, make choices, and pay for them online. Except for the final step of actually making a payment, we have illustrated the steps needed for such transactions. A new concept, called a "session," allows your site to "remember" what is going on as the user browses from one page to another and puts more and more items into a "shopping cart." These items will be "paid for" at "checkout time." This is in contrast to the simple display of one static page after another, a process which "has no memory."

10.10   Quick Questions to Test Your Basic Knowledge

1. Some folks regard the combination of PHP and MySQL as a "marriage made in heaven," and certainly it is widely used on the Web, but there are other competing technologies. Can you name some of them?

2. What is the PHP function you need to use to connect to MySQL from a PHP script, and what are its parameters?

3. Once your PHP script has connected to MySQL, what is the PHP function you need to use to choose a database for subsequent queries, and what are its parameters?

4. What is a good way to keep your MySQL login information out of any PHP script that is going to access your MySQL database, and thus "hide" it from anyone who might be able to view your script?

5. What is the PHP function that sends an SQL query to a MySQL database, and how would you describe the general form of the return value of this function?

6. Suppose your MySQL database contains a table named `Clients`, and suppose among its columns is one named `first_name` and one named `last_name`. Can you quickly perform each of the following tasks?

   - First, compose a query that would retrieve the first and last names (last names first) of all clients whose last name is either `Jones` or `Green`, and then assign the query to a variable named `$query`.
   - Second, send the query to MySQL from a PHP script, assuming the connection has already been made and the database chosen.

7. What PHP function do you use to direct a visitor to one page to another page if, for example, your script on the current page performs a test of some kind and decides the user should go to that other page?

8. What is the PHP technique called that you use to provide a way for certain information to be "remembered" as your site visitors browse from one page to another? And what is the first thing you should do in a PHP script that wants to take advantage of this feature?

10.11   Short Exercises to Improve Your Basic Understanding

1. Write a short PHP script that simply tries to connect to your MySQL database system and reports either success or failure, depending on the outcome of the attempt.

2. Write a short PHP script that connects to your MySQL database system and displays a list of all databases accessible to you. If there is a problem with connection or with generating the list of databases, your script should report the problem, with an appropriate message.

3. Write a short PHP script that connects to your MySQL database system and then displays a list of all tables in all databases accessible to you. If there is a problem with connection or with generating the list of tables, your script should report the problem, with an appropriate message.

4. Create an XHTML form page that lets the user enter the name of a table to be created in a particular MySQL database and the number of fields that this table is to contain. Provide a button that, when clicked by the user, will take

the user to a second form page where the user can choose the data type and size for each field of this table. A button on this page, when clicked, should then connect to the database and create the table.

5. Create an XHTML form page and corresponding PHP script that will let the user enter a single record into the table created in the previous exercise.

6. Create an XHTML page with several links on it. Each link, when clicked, retrieves and displays all or part of the data stored in the table of the previous exercise.

7. Revise the `processRegistration.php` script shown in Figure 10.13 so that in addition to producing displays like those shown in Figures 10.9 and 10.11, it also sends out appropriate e-mail messages to the client.

8. Make the following two improvements to the registration form shown in Figure 10.4:

   ■ Ask the user to enter the password twice, to use at least six alphanumeric characters with at least one capital letter and at least one digit, and validate accordingly.

   ■ Include a separate entry textbox for the zip code, and validate it as well. If you are really ambitious, do a little research to establish the exact possible formats for U.S. and Canadian zip (postal) codes, and validate according to the client's country of origin.

10.12   Exercises on the Parallel Project

In this section of the previous chapter you created some data for your business and entered it into a MySQL database. Thus you now have a business-related database containing several tables that your business website must be able to communicate with so that your users can retrieve, among other things perhaps, at least the information that you would like them to know about what you have to offer them.

Also, for some time now you have had a "Products and Services" link, or a similar link, on the home page of your business. Previously that link would have simply taken you to a static web page display showing what your business offers for sale. Now you must make that page dynamic, as outlined in the following exercises.

1. First, your "Products and Services" link must either be converted to a drop-down menu list or take the user to a new page containing a menu list of options showing the various categories of items or services your business offers for sale. Each of the links on this dropdown menu or menu list will link to a PHP script that connects to your database, retrieves the necessary product and/or service information, and displays it for the user in a sensible format.

2. Design and implement the necessary PHP scripts for the "back-end" processing required for your "Products and Services" link.

3. Depending on the time available, you should also try to pursue the additional features illustrated in this chapter, which include registering with your business and conducting an online session in which several products are chosen for purchase and the user then proceeds to "checkout."

10.13   What Else You May Want or Need to Know

1. There is one aspect of PHP that may cause you some confusion and potentially some problems if you are not aware of how it behaves in this language: *variable scope*. The most important thing to remember is that in PHP if a variable has the same name inside and outside a function, it is *not* the same variable. Where this is most likely to cause you a problem is if you are using a variable inside a function and thinking it is that variable outside the function with the same name and the value you know it to have. You will actually be using a different variable that probably doesn't have any value at all. This is one of the main problems with PHP and many other scripting languages—the lack of strong typing—and though it can be very convenient it is also a minefield around which one must tread very carefully.

2. We have pointed out in this chapter that it is critical to your business that you keep your database secure. In our db.php script, shown in Figure 10.3, the hostname, username, and password are actually in that file, and the file itself is located in the same directory as the scripts that depend on it. This is not a good idea. It may be OK for the file to be there, but the username and password information (at least) should be somewhere else, preferably in a file located in a more inaccessible location on the server that can still be included in the place where it is needed by the PHP include() function.

3. You may have observed, or wondered, along the way, what might happen if several customers are attempting to buy products from us at the same time. This in fact might be a problem if, for example, there are only three of some product left in inventory and one customer has them in his shopping cart when suddenly another customer in more of a hurry shows up and buys the items while they are still in the first customer's cart. Our simple model does not address this problem, but a real-world store would have to deal with it, of course, by ensuring that pending purchases by one customer are "locked down" until that customer's session has finished. A more general discussion of *transaction processing*, which considers this entire problem and how to handle it, is beyond the scope of this text.

4. Sometimes, when you are debugging a PHP script that generates and sends some reasonably complex XHTML markup to the browser that is not appearing in the expected form (nested lists that aren't coming out right, for example), you may want to include the newline character \n in your PHP output. As you know, this will not have any effect on the browser display, but if you do a "view source" to see what your page looks like "behind the scenes," it may be useful to have appropriately placed line breaks to help you read and debug your markup.

5. We have used a PHP *session* to help us "remember" some information about the customer as that customer browses from page to page on our site during the shopping process. Sometimes it is convenient, when a customer comes back to a site, for the site to "remember" that the customer has been there before. This can be done even if the site does not force the user to log in and be identified in that way. The other technique is to use a *cookie*, which is a small piece of text sent by the server to the browser and stored on the customer's computer. When that customer returns, from that same computer, the cookie is sent back to the server and the information in it can be used to identify the visitor and display a "Welcome Back" message (for example). Cookies may be useful, but should not be relied on for anything too serious, since the browser may be instructed not to accept them.

10.14   References

1. The home page of PHP can be found at:

   http://www.php.net

and there you will find the most up-to-date documentation on the latest version of the language, as well as links from which you can download various versions of the software for your particular platform.

2. The part of the PHP home site that deals explicitly with its interface to MySQL can be found here:

   `http://php.net/manual/en/book.mysql.php`

3. Check out this site for a PHP/MySQL tutorial:

   `http://www.freewebmasterhelp.com/tutorials/phpmysql`

4. As always, the `w3schools.com` site is also an excellent resource, and you can start here:

   `http://www.w3schools.com/PHP/php_intro.asp`

5. For the official word on PHP arrays, see:

   `http://php.net/manual/en/book.array.php`

6. The PHP manual on the `printf()` formatting function is found here:

   `http://php.net/manual/en/function.printf.php`

7. Check out this site for tutorials on both PHP cookies and PHP sessions:

   `http://www.tizag.com/phpT/phpcookies.php`
   `http://www.tizag.com/phpT/phpsessions.php`

8. Here is another site with some concise but helpful pages on both cookies and sessions:

   `http://php.about.com/od/advancedphp/qt/php_cookie.htm`
   `http://php.about.com/od/advancedphp/ss/php_sessions.htm`

CHAPTER 11

XML (eXtensible Markup Language) for Data Description

CHAPTER CONTENTS

11.1   Overview and Objectives

XML (*eXtensible Markup Language*) is a relatively simple meta-language derived from the much more complex *SGML* (*Standard Generalized Markup Language*). As a meta-language, it can be used to describe other languages, and we have already seen how it was used to "rewrite" HTML as XHTML. But it can be used for much more than that.

The power, flexibility, and usefulness of XML really does stem from its simplicity. First, it has very few rules that a developer must remember and use. Second, as its name indicates, it is *extensible*. This means that unlike XHTML, say, which has tags that can only be used in the way that XHTML specifies, XML lets you make up your own tags and decide what they mean and how they will be used. In fact, not only *can* you make up your own tags, you *must* make up your own tags, since XML does not have *any* predefined tags. Of course, by now lots of people and organizations have made up their own tag sets to describe their own kinds of data, and you may wish to avoid making up *your* own tags by using those made up by someone else. See the **What Else ...** section at the end of this chapter for more on this.

Thus XML can be used to describe almost anything, and the WWW has embraced it as the best way to describe all kinds of different data on any kind of computing platform. XML has become the *lingua franca* of the Web.

As with the other technologies we have introduced, we will only have time and space to scratch the XML surface. By the end of this chapter you should have a good idea of what XML is all about and why it may be useful, but if you wish to incorporate it into your website in any significant way you will need to spend some additional time and effort delving further into some of the topics we only touch upon here. See the end-of-chapter **References** for some relevant links.

We will first present the main features of XML, and then see how we can represent some of our data using it. If we have several documents containing the same kind of data, we will also want to verify that they all have the same structure, and for this we will use an appropriate *DTD* (*Document Type Definition*). We may also want to put the XML tags and attributes we have chosen to describe our data in an *XML namespace* to prevent them from being confused with the tags and attributes chosen by others.

One of the things we often want to do, of course, is display our data, and we will see how we can use our CSS knowledge to apply some style when we display data stored in XML format. An alternative to this approach, more in keeping with the XML way of doing things, is to use styles in XSL (*eXtensible Style Language*) format and an XSLT (*eXtensible Style Language Transformation*) to "transform" our data into an XHTML page for display in a browser. The power of this simple idea immediately suggests that we might want to use a different XSLT to transform our data into some other useful form, and in fact that is just what the XSLT technology allows us to do.

In this chapter, then, we discuss the following topics:

- The few basic syntax rules you must follow when preparing an XML document

- What it means for an XML document to be *well-formed*, and what happens when it isn't

- What it means for an XML document to be *valid*, and the validation process

- The structure and syntax of a *Document Type Definition* (*DTD*)

- What happens when you view a "raw" XML document in a browser

- How to style an XML document using *CSS* (*Cascading Style Sheets*)

- A brief introduction to *eXtensible Style Language* (*XSL*) and transforming an XML document with *XSL Transformations XSLT* and *XPath*

- XML namespaces

11.2 The Basic Rules of XML

In the next section we actually put XML to work describing some of our data. It's a good idea to get ready for that by acquiring some familiarity with the very few things you need to know about XML in order to begin using it effectively. Here's a short list, and if you are already comfortable with XHTML, you will feel right at home here:

1. XML is just text, so any editor can be used to create and modify XML markup. There are also XML-specific editors available, with varying degrees of functionality and cost. See the end-of-chapter **References** for links to some possible choices.

2. XML lets you create your own tags to describe elements that have content enclosed by a tag pair, as in `<tag>... content ...</tag>`, which must be properly nested. Empty elements are possible as well, and have the form `<tag/>`.

Also, every XML document must contain a single *root element*, within which all of the other elements of the document are contained.

3. XML elements may have attributes. Each attribute must have a value, and that value must be enclosed in quotation marks, as in `<tagname attribute="value">`. Either single or double quotes are OK.

4. XML is case-sensitive, and names must start with a letter or underscore (_), which can then be followed by any number of alphanumeric characters, hyphens, periods, or underscores.

5. XML has only five predefined *entity references* (special characters), and here they are:

```
&lt;    <    less than
&gt;    >    greater than
&amp;   &    ampersand
&apos;  '    apostrophe (single quotation mark)
&quot;  "    quotation mark (double quotation mark)
```

6. XML has comments, as in `<!-- text of comment -->`, just like those of XHTML.

7. XML preserves whitespace (unlike (X)HTML, for example). However, exactly what this means does "depend on the situation."

8. In XML *you have to get it right* if you expect any XML parser (processor), including your favorite browser, to process your document. This will come as a shock to those who have been accustomed to having their (X)HTML trespasses forgiven by most browsers. Getting it right means following all of the above rules, of course, but also having a special line as the first line of an XML document, *before anything else appears*, even a single blank space. More on this when we look at our first example.

See what we mean by simplicity? You are now ready to describe some data, which we begin to do in the next section.

11.3   Describing Our Data with Well-Formed XML

To see how we can use XML to describe our data it is best to begin with an example, so take a look at Figure 11.1, which shows the contents of the file `sampledata.xml`.

The first thing to note is that the file is identified as containing XML data by its `.xml` file extension. Also, the first line of the file is the *XML declaration* (also called the *XML prolog*), which defines the XML version (1.0) and encoding (`ISO-8859-1 =` Latin-1/West European character set) being used. You will often see UTF-8 as the encoding scheme as well. UTF-8 offers many more characters, but for a unilingual English website ISO-8859-1 is fine, and, for all intents and purposes, equivalent to UTF-8.

```
1   <?xml version="1.0" encoding="ISO-8859-1"?>
2   <!-- sampledata.xml -->
3   <supplements>
4     <vitamin product_id="10">
5       <name>Vitamin A</name>
6       <price>$8.99</price>
7       <helps_support>Your eyes</helps_support>
8       <daily_requirement>5000 IU</daily_requirement>
9     </vitamin>
0     <vitamin product_id="20">
1       <name>Vitamin C</name>
2       <price>$11.99</price>
3       <helps_support>Your immune system</helps_support>
4       <daily_requirement>250-400 mg</daily_requirement>
5     </vitamin>
6     <vitamin product_id="30">
7       <name>Vitamin D</name>
8       <price>$3.99</price>
9       <helps_support>Your bones, especially your rate of
0         calcium absorption</helps_support>
1       <daily_requirement>400-800 IU</daily_requirement>
2     </vitamin>
3   </supplements>
4
```

FIGURE 11.1

cdrom/web11/sampledata.xml
Some sample data described using XML tags.

The second line of the file is a comment. Note that XML comments are the same, not surprisingly, as XHTML comments. However, there is an important placement distinction here. The XML declaration *must* be the first line of an XML file, which requires our comment containing the file name to be the second line. We had a similar convention of placing the analogous comment in an XHTML file immediately following the `DOCTYPE` declaration.

Line 3 of `sampledata.xml` contains the *opening tag* of the *root element* of the XML document in the file. This outermost element is the `supplements` element in this case. It corresponds to the `html` element in an XHTML document, since in either case all other elements are contained within the root element.

All XML documents consist essentially of a collection of nested elements, and this one is no exception. Nested within the outermost (root) element `supplements` we have several `vitamin` elements containing information about each available vitamin. This information is, in turn, contained in a sequence of elements nested within each `vitamin` element. Each element in the sequence specifies one further piece of information associated with the corresponding vitamin.

Note that, just like XHTML tags, XML tags can also have attributes, and the rules are the same (each attribute must have a value, and the value must be enclosed in quotes). This is illustrated here by the `product_id` attribute of the `vitamin` tag.

11.3.1   Nested Elements vs. Tag Attributes

One of the more difficult decisions to be made when you are designing an XML document to describe some of your data is the choice of what information should be placed in a nested element and what should be placed in a tag attribute.

For example, in the simple XML document shown in Figure 11.1 we have given the `vitamin` tag an attribute called `product_id`. Although ID numbers often do show up as attributes in XML documents, there is no theoretical, or even practical, reason why we could not have placed this information in another nested element, along with `name`, `price`, and the rest.

So, here are one rule, one guideline, and one "rule of thumb" for what you should do when making these decisions:

> **Rule** Any binary data (such as an image) *must* be specified by placing its location in a tag attribute, since only text can appear in an XML file. This is analogous to the `src` attribute of the XHTML `img` tag.

Guideline If the information in question might, at some later time, need to be subdivided, placing it in an element rather than an attribute will make this much easier. This is because although nothing can be added to an attribute once it is in place, we can easily add nested tags to any existing tag to reflect the growth of complexity in our data. On the other hand, if it is clear that the information will never need to be subdivided, and is simply "information about your information" (in other words, *meta-data*) then an attribute is probably the better choice. Identification information like that contained in the XHTML `id` or `name` attribute will be a likely candidate for an XML attribute.

Rule of Thumb This one may be rather vague, but it is, after all, only a "rule of thumb": Use an attribute for information that you would not likely need or want to display to a user of the information.

For example,

```
<customer>
  <name>Pawan Lingras</name>
  <phone>420-5798</phone>
</customer>
```

is much better than

```
<customer name="Pawan Lingras">
  <phone>420-5798</phone>
</customer>
```

because it is much easier to convert, if necessary, to this:

```
<customer>
  <first_name>Pawan</first_name>
  <last_name>Lingras</last_name>
  <phone>420-5798</phone>
</customer>
```

11.3.2   And What Does It Mean for Our XML to Be "Well-Formed"?

In section 11.2 we listed a number of syntax rules that we have to follow when constructing our XML documents (properly nested tags, consistent capitalization, and so on). XML processors are much more stringent in their expectations than XHTML processors, and will simply refuse to process our XML documents if we break *any* of these rules. If our XML document does in fact conform to all of the required syntax rules, we say that it is *well-formed*.

11.4   Viewing Our Raw (Unstyled) XML Data in a Browser

We are by now very familiar with the fact that whatever browser we use to "surf the Web" contains a *rendering engine* that reads the contents of a web page document and displays it in a browser window for us to view. We also know that this rendering engine is a very "forgiving" machine, since it will often overlook markup errors in a web page and simply do its best to interpret what it sees and try to produce a reasonable display of the content.

It turns out that most modern browsers are also capable of reading and displaying an XML document, although as of this writing the way that various browsers display an XML document is not consistent. Fortunately, however, two of the most widely used browsers, Firefox and Internet Explorer, do show an XML page in more or less the same way.

Figure 11.2 shows what our `sampledata.xml` file looks like when displayed by the Firefox browser. We refer to this as a display of "raw" XML data, in the sense that we have not applied any styling information to the data in the file, and because we have made up the tags ourselves there is no possible way for the browser to know how we would like to see the information displayed. In fact, it informs the viewer of this in the grey box above the display of the XML markup. The markup itself is shown with syntax highlighting, and all tags are explicitly displayed. One handy feature, at least in Firefox and Internet Explorer, is the minus signs (or dashes) at the left. Clicking on any one of these will "collapse" the corresponding portion of the code to a single line and replace the minus sign with a plus sign, indicating that the line may be expanded once again by clicking on that plus sign.

Viewing our XML in this way can be helpful when we are developing the document, but it is really not much of an improvement over the corresponding view in an editor, especially if we are using an XML-aware editor for development. Most likely we will want to style our XML data in much the same way as we have done with our XHTML web pages, and in fact we shall see how to do this very shortly. In the meantime, however, let us discuss the question of determining whether or not our documents are in fact well-formed XML.

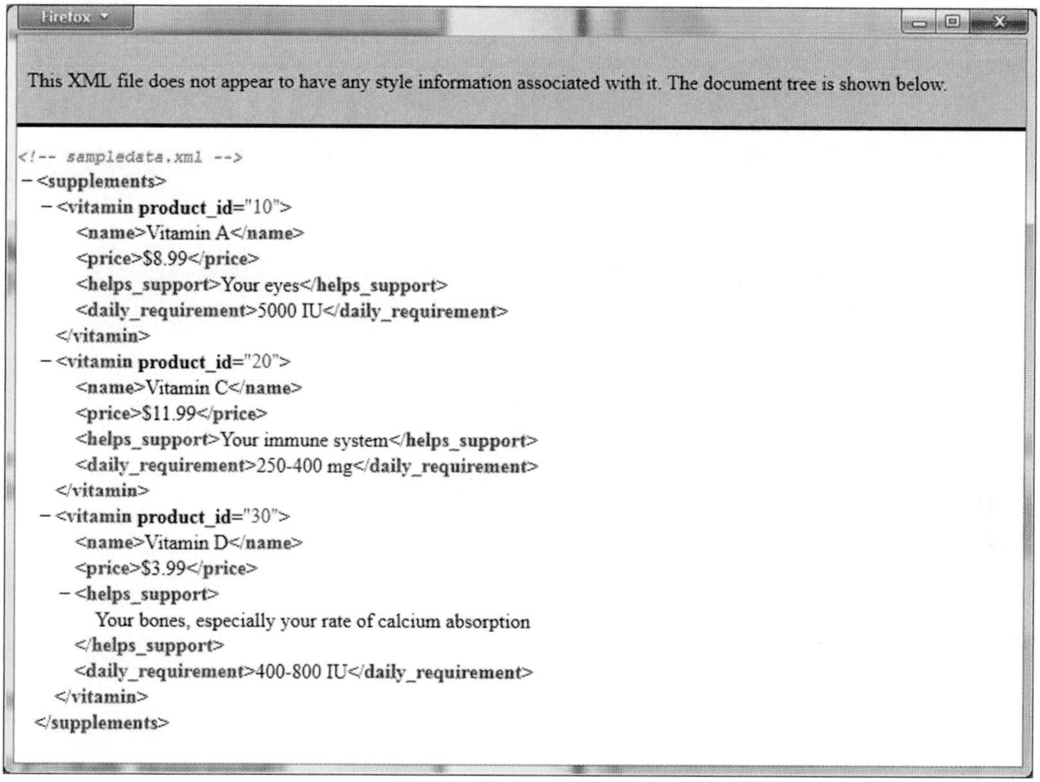

FIGURE 11.2

graphics/ch11/displaySampledataXml.jpg
A Firebox browser display of the XML document in `sampledata.xml`.

11.4.1 What Happens if Our XML Document Is Not Well-Formed?

Even a simple spelling mistake in one closing tag of an XML document, causing a mismatch between the opening and closing tags, will prevent the browser from displaying an XML document. For example, Figure 11.3 shows the error generated and displayed by the browser if we make the closing tag of the first vitamin element `</vitamine>` instead of `</vitamin>`. It should be clear from this example that using an XML-aware editor to prepare your XML documents will be highly advantageous and will help to keep such errors to a minimum.[1]

A file called `sampledataError.xml`, which is identical to the `sampledata.xml` file of Figure 11.1 except that it contains this error, is available in the `web11` directory

---

[1] As noted earlier, a good choice would be **Exchanger XML Lite** from **Cladonia**, a free version for non-commercial use of their professional product, but a Google search will turn up others that you might wish to investigate before making a final choice.

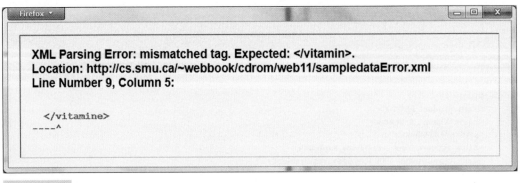

FIGURE 11.3

`graphics/ch11/displaySampledataErrorXml.jpg`
A Firefox browser display of the error message displayed when the XML document in `sampledata.xml` has a misspelled closing tag.

of your CD-ROM. You should browse to that file with whatever browsers you have available to see their reaction when asked to display an XML file that is not well-formed.

11.5   Validating Our XML Data with a Document Type Definition

OK, so now we know what a well-formed XML document is—one that does not violate any of the basic XML syntax rules. But we have a researcher friend who's just discovered several new vitamins, and he wants to describe them in an XML document just like the one we've been using. What to do?

Well, we could send him a copy of our document, which he could study and whose tags and attributes he could try to replicate when he prepares his own document. That might even work for a simple document like ours, but for a larger and more complex XML data description, this approach would be iffy at best. We need a better way.

One such "better way" is to prepare a *Document Type Definition (DTD)*, which describes in unambiguous terms what a document such as ours is allowed to contain, and the form in which its contents must appear. Then we give this DTD to our researcher friend and it is up to him to make sure his document conforms to the specifications that it contains. In fact, he and anyone else using our tag set and our

DTD can and should validate their XML documents against our DTD to ensure that they do in fact conform to the required specifications for such documents.

Thus a *Document Type Definition* is a collection of rules, called *declarations*, that describe the structure of a particular kind of XML document. That is, it specifies what elements and attributes are allowed to appear, the order in which they may appear, what elements are allowed to have which attributes, and so on.

The Document Type Definition is just one method we can use to specify how our XML document must be constructed. Another approach is to use an *XML schema*, which we will not discuss here, since at the time of writing DTDs are more widely used and supported than XML schemas for this purpose. It is likely, however, that eventually XML schemas will replace DTDs, so you should at least be aware of them. For one thing, they are more powerful, more flexible, and more expressive when it comes to describing the kinds of data we can place in our XML documents. For another, DTD syntax is quite different from the syntax of XML itself so it cannot be processed by the same processor that is processing the XML. An XML schema, on the other hand, is itself written in XML, so both the schema and the XML it describes can be processed by the same processor.

The best way to get an initial feeling for what a DTD looks like and how it is used is to look at an example. Figure 11.4 shows a very simple DTD that could be used for the XML data in the `sampledata.xml` file of Figure 11.1. Just as CSS styles and JavaScript code can appear in an XHTML document, so can a DTD appear in the same file as the XML data it describes. However, just as we have argued that placing CSS styles and JavaScript code in separate files is a good idea, we will make the same argument for keeping our DTD in a file separate from the XML code, and for pretty

```
<!-- sampledata_with_dtd.dtd -->
<!ELEMENT supplements (vitamin+)>
<!ELEMENT vitamin (name, price, helps_support, daily_requirement)>
<!ELEMENT name (#PCDATA)>
<!ELEMENT price (#PCDATA)>
<!ELEMENT helps_support (#PCDATA)>
<!ELEMENT daily_requirement (#PCDATA)>
<!ATTLIST vitamin product_id CDATA #REQUIRED>
```

FIGURE 11.4

cdrom/web11/sampledata_with_dtd.dtd
A simple DTD file for validating the file `sampledata_with_dtd.xml`.

much the same reasons. For example, a separate DTD file can be referenced by many different XML files, provided they all need to conform to that particular DTD.

11.5.1 Connecting an XML Document to Its DTD: DOCTYPE Revisited

Before we study Figure 11.4 in detail, take a look at Figure 11.5, which shows the first few lines of the file `sampledata_with_dtd.xml`. This file has the same contents as `sampledata.xml`, except for the DOCTYPE declaration in line 3:

```
<!DOCTYPE supplements SYSTEM "sampledata_with_dtd.dtd">
```

If you now think back to the DOCTYPE declarations you have been seeing and using for some time in XHTML files, you will notice a distinct similarity, and that whole DOCTYPE business may finally begin to make sense. Here, the outermost element in your file is **supplements**, so the **supplements** tag now takes the place of the **html** tag in your XHTML DOCTYPE. Furthermore, the PUBLIC part of the XHTML DOCTYPE, which referred to some mysterious URI for its information about what should be in the XHTML document, is now replaced by the SYSTEM keyword (which refers to the local system) and the name of a DTD file located in the same directory as the XML file itself. As we know, *this* is the file that says what has to be in the XML document, and the one we now look at in more detail.

11.5.2 A Simple DTD Anatomy Lesson

Now let's take a closer look at what's in the DTD file of Figure 11.4.

The first line is a comment containing the name of the file, as usual. Note that comments in a DTD file are the same as those in an XML (or XHTML) file.

The rest of the document contains information, using DTD syntax, to describe what an XML document must "look like" if it is to be a valid document according to this DTD. Each line consists of a *declaration* having the following form:

```
<!keyword additional_information >
```

```
1   <?xml version="1.0" encoding="ISO-8859-1"?>
2   <!-- sampledata_with_dtd.xml -->
3   <!DOCTYPE supplements SYSTEM "sampledata_with_dtd.dtd">
4   <supplements>
```

FIGURE 11.5

`cdrom/web11/sampledata_with_dtd.xml` (excerpt)

A file with the same contents as `sampledata.xml`, except for the DOCTYPE declaration in line 3, which links this file to its DTD.

Line 2 of the file is

```
<!ELEMENT supplements (vitamin+)>
```

which tells us that the highest-level element in our file must have a tag named **supplements**. The (**vitamin+**) part of the declaration tells us that there must be *at least one* element called **vitamin** nested within the supplements element (i.e., in the body of the **supplements** element). The **+** is thus used here as a numerical qualifier in much the same way it is used in regular expressions. The ***** (for zero or more) and the **?** (for zero or one) qualifiers may also be used.

Line 3 of the file is

```
<!ELEMENT vitamin (name, price, helps_support, daily_requirement)>
```

which specifies that a **vitamin** element must, in turn, contain four nested elements—**name**, **price**, **helps_support**, and **daily_requirement**—and *they must be in the order listed*, because they appear in a comma-separated list.

Line 4 of the file is

```
<!ELEMENT name (#PCDATA)>
```

which specifies that the content (body) of a **name** element will be of type **#PCDATA**. This is Parsable Character **DATA**. You can think of such data as ordinary text that may (or may not) contain XML entities (such a **&**) that need to be "parsed" and replaced by their equivalent characters when the file is processed. Lines 5–7 are analogous to line 4.

Line 8 of the file is

```
<!ATTLIST vitamin product_id CDATA #REQUIRED>
```

and it specifies that the **vitamin** element *must have*, because it has **#REQUIRED** in the *default value* position for the attribute called **product_id**, whose value will be of type **CDATA**.[2] Think of this kind of data as just ordinary text containing nothing that needs to be "parsed."

---

[2]If you are wondering why, for example, **#PCDATA** has a **#** at the beginning and **CDATA** does not, you are not alone. The **#** is a *Reserved Name Indicator* (*RNI*). Although XML does not have "reserved words" in the same sense as programming languages like Java or C++, it does have terms that are used in special ways, and it appears to be convention that some but not all of them are preceded by the **#** to ensure there is no ambiguity created by a developer deciding to use the same name for some other purpose. The bottom line: having a **#** in front of a term effectively makes the combination a keyword.

11.5.3   More DTD Anatomy

The simple DTD document analyzed in the previous section did not illustrate a great deal about DTDs. In this section we mention a few additional features that you may find useful in your own documents.

User-defined entities   In addition to the five predefined XML entities listed earlier, you can define your own by using the following syntax:

```
<!ENTITY va "Vitamin A">
```

This `ENTITY` declaration is similar to the `ELEMENT` and `ATTLIST` declarations discussed above. It defines the entity `va` so that if we have an XML document that uses the DTD in which this `ENTITY` declaration appears, everywhere we use the entity reference `&va;` it will be replaced by the string "Vitamin A".

> *Moreover, when we use a DTD, the five predefined XML entities are no longer defined, so if we want to use one or more of them, we have to redefine them ourselves in our DTD.*

Finally, if an entity's definition is not just a word or two but contains a lot of text, you may want to remove it from the main DTD document to reduce clutter. You can do this using the following syntax:

```
<!ENTITY name_of_entity SYSTEM "path/file_containing_definition">
```

CDATA sections   Since any data of type `CDATA` is not parsed, it may contain meta-symbols like < or &, which would otherwise have to appear as entities. Also, any entities that appear in a `CDATA` section will simply remain as themselves. Thus if you have some character data in your XML document that contains a lot of these kinds of items, it is convenient to be able to place this data in a `CDATA` section. Here is an example, which illustrates both the syntax and some typical content:

```
<![CDATA[
A section like this can contain things like << or >>, as well as
& if we wish to use it for "and". This is convenient, since we
don't have to use entities like &lt;, &gt; and &amp;.
]]>
```

Note that neither the 9-character opening delimiter `<![CDATA[`, nor the 3-character closing delimiter `]]>`, has to be placed on a line by itself in the way we've done in the example, but doing so may enhance readability. In any case, neither delimiter may contain any blank spaces.

Other element data types In addition to `#PCDATA` and `CDATA` data types, a DTD will let you specify `EMPTY` as a data type to indicate that an element does not contain any data (like an XHTML `img` tag, for example). There is also an `ANY` data type, signifying that an element's content can be most anything. This is not very helpful, except perhaps during development as a placeholder until you have decided just what you want the content to be. If you want more comprehensive control over the permissible data types for your elements than can be provided by DTDs, you need to use an XML schema.

Other attribute data types In addition to using the `CDATA` data type for an attribute value, XML provides a number of other choices. We mention only the `ID` type (an XML name to be used as a unique identifier) and the `ENUMERATED` type (a list of possible values for an attribute, with values in the list separated by a vertical bar rather than the usual comma or space).

Default attribute values When giving an XML element an attribute, we can also give the attribute a value or specify some criterion that the value must satisfy. The general syntax of the `ATTLIST` declaration is

```
<!ATTLIST element-name attribute-name attribute-data-type
attribute-default-value>
```

We have already seen `#REQUIRED` used in the `attribute_default_value` position to insist that the `product_id` attribute of the `vitamin` element must actually have a value (of type `CDATA`). There are other possibilities for the `attribute_default_value` as well. These include

```
#FIXED
```

which means that in every element having the attribute with this default value, the attribute will in fact have this value (which cannot be changed), as well as

```
#IMPLIED
```

which means that, in effect, no default value is specified, so the value may (or may not) be supplied in a given element. You can also simply supply a default value for an attribute without preceding it by a keyword like `#FIXED`. In this case, the supplied value is used unless another value is given in a particular element.

Numerical qualifiers We have seen how `vitamin+` was used to specify that at least one (i.e., one or more) `vitamin` elements was the requirement for the content of a `supplements` element. Just as the `+` is used to mean one or more (required and repeatable), the `*` may be used to mean zero or more (optional and repeatable), and the `?` may be used to mean zero or one (optional and *not* repeatable).

Finetuning your choices A comma-separated, parentheses-enclosed list like `(a, b, c)` requires the sequence `a`, `b`, and `c` (in that order), while `(a|b|c)` simply requires a choice of `a`, `b`, or `c`.

Note that numerical qualifiers may be combined with the sequence and choice indicators to construct some reasonably complex descriptors, such as

```
<!ELEMENT person (parent+, spouse?, child*, (brother|sister)*)>
```

which would be interpreted to mean that a person has one or more parents, possibly a spouse, zero or more children, and any number of brothers and/or sisters.

11.5.4   Do You Really Need a DTD for Your XML Document?

That depends. If your document is just a one-of-a-kind standalone document, maybe not. But if you are going to be creating several or a large number of similar documents, and especially if other people are going to be creating and using similar documents, then you should seriously consider having a DTD against which you and others can test all such documents to ensure that each one conforms to the same set of rules.

In any case, remember that to be useful your document must at the very least be well-formed, even if it has not been validated against a DTD.

11.5.5   Validating Your XML Document Against Your DTD, if You Have One

As we know, most any browser will recognize an XML file that is not well-formed and display an appropriate error. But that is a far cry from actually validating an XML document against its associated DTD, and at the time of writing it seems that most browsers are not, by default, *validating parsers*. That is, they parse, but they don't validate.

At the time of writing, you could validate your XML file against a DTD on the w3schools.com site, but only if it was an internal DTD and only if you were using Internet Explorer. See the **References** at the end of this chapter for links to other, perhaps more convenient, validators.

11.6 Styling Our XML Data with CSS

When you load an XHTML document into your browser, the browser has prior knowledge of all the XHTML tags you've used and can display your document with all the headings, paragraphs, lists, and other items in their proper places and with their default styling. If we wish to change or enhance that styling, as we often do, we know that we can use CSS to do so.

On the other hand, when it comes to XML we have made up our own tags, so there is no way any browser can have prior knowledge of what those tags mean or how we would like to have their content displayed. That's why, by default, the browser simply shows a stylized display of the raw XML markup itself when asked to "display" an XML file.

However, it turns out that we can leverage our knowledge of CSS to help us display our XML data with our choice of fonts, colors, indentation, and other styling features, in much the same way we did in the case of XHTML. We now illustrate this by using a CSS file to provide the style for a display of our sampledata.xml file. To do so, we have yet another minimally modified version of this file in sampledata_with_css .xml, the first few lines of which are shown in Figure 11.6.

The CSS file itself is called supplements.css and is shown in Figure 11.7. You should by now be familiar with everything in this file. Note, however, that instead of styling XHTML selectors like h1 and p, we are now styling the element tags we have chosen for our own data.

The output of the data content of sampledata_with_css.xml, styled with the CSS in supplements.css, is shown in Figure 11.8.

```
1   <?xml version="1.0" encoding="ISO-8859-1"?>
2   <!-- sampledata_with_css.xml -->
3   <?xml-stylesheet type="text/css" href="supplements.css"?>
4   <supplements>
```

FIGURE 11.6

cdrom/web11/sampledata_with_css.xml (excerpt)
A file with the same contents as sampledata.xml, except for the xml-stylesheet processing instruction in line 3, which links this file to its CSS file.

```
1    /*supplements.css*/
2
3    supplements
4    {
5      background-color: #ffffff;
6      width: 100%;
7      font-family: Arial, sans-serif;
8    }
9
10   vitamin
11   {
12     display: block;
13     margin-top: 10pt;
14     margin-left:0pt;
15   }
16
17   name
18   {
19     background-color: green;
20     color: #FFFFFF;
21     font-size: 1.5em;
22     padding: 5pt;
23     margin-bottom:3pt;
24     margin-right:0;
25   }
26
27   price
28   {
29     background-color: lime;
30     color: #000000;
31     font-size: 1.5em;
32     padding:5pt;
33     margin-bottom:3pt;
34     margin-left:0
35   }
36
37   helps_support
38   {
39     display: block;
40     color: #000000;
41     font-size: 1.2em;
42     padding-top: 3pt;
43     margin-left: 20pt;
44   }
45
46   daily_requirement
47   {
48     display: block;
49     color: #000000;
50     font-size: 1.2em;
51     margin-left: 20pt;
52   }
53
```

FIGURE 11.7

cdrom/web11/supplements.css
The CSS file used to style sampledata_with_css.xml.

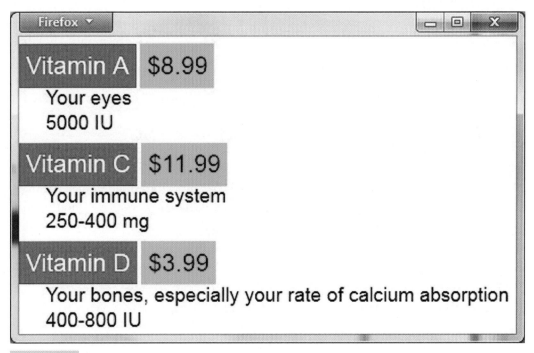

FIGURE 11.8

graphics/ch11/displaySampledataWithCssXml.jpg
A Firebox browser display of the XML document in `sampledata_with_css.xml` styled by the CSS in
`supplements.css`.

11.7 Isolating Our XML Tag Sets within XML Namespaces

Many programming languages have the following problem: Two or more different developers working on the same project choose the same names for different things and when their work is combined they experience a *name clash*. Different languages solve the problem in different ways—Java with *packages* and C++ with *namespaces*, for example. Similar problems, if they occur in languages like JavaScript or PHP, may have to be solved "after the fact," since these languages do not provide elegant facilities for helping developers avoid the problem in the first place.

The same sort of problem can happen with XML. Suppose some developer creating his own tag set decides to use one or more names that we have used in our tag set. Then a third developer decides he likes, and wants to use, both tag sets. Once again ... a name clash, a problem of ambiguity that an XML parser will not be able to resolve on its own.

We can avoid this problem if each developer places his tag set in an *XML namespace*, which is just a particular collection of element and attribute names that has been assigned a name.

You may have forgotten, but we are already familiar with XML namespaces. Do you remember the following line, containing the opening `html` tag, from virtually all of our XHTML files?

```
<html xmlns="http://www.w3.org/1999/xhtml">
```

Here, `xmlns` is the *XML namespace attribute* and its value, `"http://www.w3.org/ 1999/xhtml"`, is the URL of an actual document that describes, among other things, the tags and attributes that can be used for XHTML. However, we should note immediately that the value of `xmlns` need *not* be a URL; it need only be a URI, which is to say it can have the same form as a URL without referring to an actual document. Making it a URI is one way of ensuring that the namespace name will itself be unique. In fact, even though there is a document at `http://www.w3.org/1999/xhtml`, it is better to think of this simply as a name for the namespace.

Thus, if we had a large collection of health supplements with XML tags and attributes to describe them all, we might want to place them in an XML namespace, perhaps like this:

```
<supplements xmlns="http://cs.smu.ca/nature/source/supplements">
```

We say more about namespaces in the next section, where we actually see how they can be used to help avoid conflicts.

11.8   Transforming Our XML Data with XSL, XSLT, and XPath

XSL is the acronym for *eXtensible Style Language*, and the moment you hear that you might suspect that XSL is an XML replacement for CSS. In a way, that may even be true. But XSL is capable of much more than styling the presentational aspects of our XML documents, though that is indeed one of the things it can be used for.

More generally, we should think of an XSL document as describing how we want one of our XML documents to be "transformed" into another kind of document, possibly an XML document but not necessarily. An XHTML document is just one of many things that other kinds of document could be.

Thus we have another acronym, *XSLT*, which stands for *XSL Transformation*. XSLT is more of a programming language[3] than a markup language, and its transformations (functions) are what convert our XML document from one form to another. We can think of an XSLT processor (and many browsers have this capability) as a "black box" taking two inputs and producing a single output, like this:

```
XSLT processor(XML file, XSLT file) => some_kind_of_output
```

Here, `some_kind_of_output` could be anything from plain ASCII text to (X)HTML to another XML document of some kind. We illustrate the process with the XHTML output shown in Figure 11.9, which is once again based on the same input from `sampledata.xml` that we have been using all along, but this time "transformed" by an appropriate XSLT.

More specifically, as you can see from Figure 11.10, we have yet another minimally modified version of the original `sampledata.xml` file in `sampledata_with_xsl.xml`. The only change we have made in the original file this time is to associate it with the `supplements.xsl` file containing our XSLT code. This file is shown in Figure 11.11.

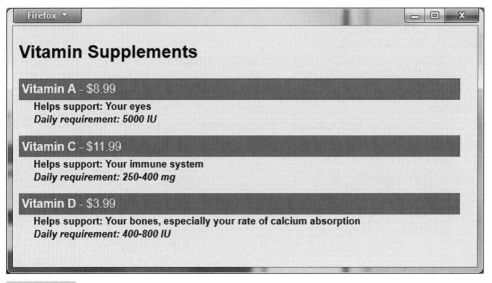

FIGURE 11.9

graphics/ch11/displaySampledataWithXslXml.jpg
A Firebox browser display of the XML document in `sampledata_with_xsl.xml`, styled by the XSLT in `supplements.xsl`.

---

[3]But not a language you might be used to, like Java or C++. It is more like a "functional" language such as LISP.

```
1    <?xml version="1.0" encoding="ISO-8859-1"?>
2    <!-- sampledata_with_xsl.xml -->
3    <?xml-stylesheet type="text/xsl" href="supplements.xsl"?>
4    <supplements>
```

FIGURE 11.10

cdrom/web11/sampledata_with_xsl.xml (excerpt)

A file with the same contents as sampledata.xml, except for the xml-stylesheet declaration in line 3, which links this file to supplements.xsl.

```
1    <!-- supplements.xsl -->
2    <xsl:stylesheet version="1.0"
3      xmlns:xsl="http://www.w3.org/1999/XSL/Transform"
4      xmlns="http://www.w3.org/1999/xhtml">
5    <xsl:output method="html"/>
6      <xsl:template match="supplements">
7      <html>
8        <head>
9          <title>Vitamin Supplements</title>
10       </head>
11       <body style="width:600px;font-family:Arial;font-size:12pt;background-color:#EEEEEE">
12         <h2>Vitamin Supplements</h2>
13         <xsl:for-each select="vitamin">
14           <div style="background-color:teal;color:white;padding:4px">
15             <span style="font-weight:bold"><xsl:value-of select="name"/></span>
16             - <xsl:value-of select="price"/>
17           </div>
18           <div style="margin-left:20px;margin-bottom:1em;font-size:10pt;font-weight:bold">
19             Helps support: <xsl:value-of select="helps_support"/><br />
20             <span style="font-style:italic">
21               Daily requirement: <xsl:value-of select="daily_requirement"/>
22             </span>
23           </div>
24         </xsl:for-each>
25       </body>
26     </html>
27     </xsl:template>
28   </xsl:stylesheet>
```

FIGURE 11.11

cdrom/web11/supplements.xsl

The XSLT file used to style sampledata_with_xsl.xml.

11.8.1   How Does XSLT Compare with CSS for Styling?

The simple answer to this question is this: XSLT is much more powerful than CSS and gives you more control over the appearance of your document. However, at the time of writing CSS is better supported by the most commonly used browsers.

For a simple example of the kind of problem one faces, consider this. CSS can essentially be used only for styling what appears as content in the elements of your XML document. Even if you want to do something as simple as add a label to that content, you cannot do this using CSS.

Perhaps "cannot" is a bit harsh, but the "generated content" feature of CSS that would allow you to do this is so poorly or infrequently implemented in today's browsers that trying to use it in a production-level website would be more of a gamble than most web developers would be willing to take.

The really bizarre thing is that *XSL-FO—XSL-Formatting Objects*, the part of XSL that would take over from CSS if the browser folks would just implement it—is in fact in even worse shape across today's browsers than CSS itself, so when you look at file with a `.xsl` extension, you will still see CSS mixed in with the XHTML among the XSLT code. Oh, well....

11.8.2   Our Example in Detail: How Does XSLT Use XML Namespaces and XPath to Do Its Job?

Note first that in this file we can place the comment containing the name of the file as the first line, since this is not, strictly speaking, an XML file, but an XSL (or XSLT) file.

Second, note that the file contains an `xsl::stylesheet` element as its highest-level container, and the opening tag for this element contains two `xmlns` attributes. The URI value of the first one is

`"http://www.w3.org/1999/XSL/Transform"`

and the `xsl` suffix that is appended to this `xmlns`, and separated from it by a colon (`:`), provides us with a shorthand way of referring to anything that we use in the file and that lives in that namespace (`xsl:output`, `xsl:template`, `xsl:for-each`, `xsl:value-of`). In fact, such a shorthand, provided it is unique in the current context, ensures that any names in this namespace do not conflict with the names in any other namespace we may be using.

And in fact we *are* using another namespace, the one with this URI value:

`"http://www.w3.org/1999/xhtml"`

This is the usual XHTML namespace we have been using in our XHTML files for some time, and we could give it a shorthand suffix as well. The fact that we choose not to do so simply means that for this file this namespace is the default. In other words, for example, any element not qualified with a prefix (`html`, `head`, `body`, and so on) is assumed to come from this namespace.

The (empty) `xsl:output` element with its `method` attribute value of `html` simply indicates that the output from the XSLT in this particular file should be (X)HTML markup (for display in a browser, for example).

The `xsl:template` element with its `match` attribute value of `supplements` indicates that the processor should look for an element called `supplements` and then process that element according to the "instructions" in the body of the `xsl:template` element. Actually, it's a little more involved than we've let on. The value of the `match` attribute (`supplements`, in this case) is actually part of an *XPath path*, which starts at the root of the document (represented by /, so XPath paths tend to look a lot like regular paths on many systems, particularly Unix-like systems). Thus we can think of `supplements` as short for `/supplements`, and the same goes for values of the `select` attribute that appears several times later on in the file.

Now, the "processing" that goes on in the body of this template involves the output of some XHTML to set up our web page, followed by the "execution" of the XSLT looping construct `xsl:for-each`, which loops over each of the vitamin elements in the `sampledata_with_xsl.xml` file. On each iteration, this loop sets up a new vitamin for display by adding some text of its own, extracting the corresponding content of the nested elements within each `vitamin` element using the `xsl:value-of` function, and styling the result with CSS.

Thus we see a simple XML data file "transformed" by XSLT into an XHTML file, ready for browser display. It should be clear from what you see here that many other kinds of transformations may be possible, depending on what other functions like `xsl:for-each` and `xsl:value-of` are provided by XSLT. Of course, there are many other such functions, so many other kinds of transformations are in fact possible.

11.9   Summary

The *eXtensible Markup Language* (*XML*) is a meta-language that has a variety of uses. We have already pointed out how it was used to "rewrite" HTML as XHTML. In this chapter we have seen how it can be used to describe virtually any kind of data with which our business may wish to deal.

XML has only a very few rules that must be followed, but what rules it does have must be followed very strictly, or your XML markup will not be processed by any XML processor. As with XHTML, tags must be capitalized consistently and nested properly, all tags except empty tags must have a closing tag, and all tag attributes must have a value that is enclosed in quotation marks.

Any XML document that follows these simple syntax rules is said to be *well-formed*. We may also create a Document Type Definition that describes the structure of an XML document in terms of what tags and attributes it must or may contain and where they may be placed and what kind of content the elements may have. We may then validate an XML document against such a DTD, which is one way of ensuring that the structure of all XML documents describing a particular kind of data is consistent. A DTD may be *internal* or *external*, but an external DTD is much more useful since it may be linked to an unlimited number of XML documents.

CSS may be used to style our XML data in much the same way it was used to style (or alter the styling of) our XHTML documents. XSLT (eXtensible Style Language Transformation) code may be used to transform our XML documents into other kinds of documents, such as plain text, (X)HTML, or alternate XML formats.

11.10   Quick Questions to Test Your Basic Knowledge

1. If you already know XHTML, you will probably feel right at home with XML. How would you explain this statement?

2. What are the five entities (special characters) in XML?

3. What does the acronym DTD stand for, and what exactly is a DTD?

4. What is the difference between a well-formed XML document and a valid XML document?

5. What is the syntax of a typical `DOCTYPE` declaration you would find in an XML document if its DTD is located in the same directory as the XML document itself?

6. What is the major difference between a CSS file used to style one of your XHTML documents and one used to style one of your XML documents?

7. How do you connect an XML file with a CSS file containing the styles that are being used to style the data in the XML file?

8. What is the difference in the placement of the file-naming comment in an XML file compared to a file containing XSLT code?

9. How do you connect an XML file with a file containing the XSLT code that will be used to transform the XML markup in the XML file, and what extension is used, by convention, for such a file?

10. What does an XPath path resemble?

11. What does the `xsl:for-each` function do?

12. What does the `xsl:value-of` function do?

11.11   Short Exercises to Improve Your Basic Understanding

1. Load the file `sampledata.xml` into several different browsers to see how each one deals with an XML file in "raw" form. In some cases you may have to choose the browser's `View Source` option to actually see the XML markup.

2. Introduce several XML syntax errors, but only one at a time, into the `sampledata.xml` file and try to load the file into one or more browsers after the error is in place. In each case the browser should give you a reasonably helpful message about what is wrong. Be sure to correct each error before introducing the next one. Finally, introduce several errors at once after having introduced each one individually, load the file into a browser, and then remove the errors one at a time until the file displays properly again.

3. Validate the XML file `sampledata_with_dtd.xml` against the DTD in the DTD file `sampledata_with_dtd.dtd` to confirm that it does in fact validate. Then make a change in the XML file that will cause the validation to fail. Re-validate to confirm that it does in fact fail.

4. In line 19 of the file `sampledata.xml`, replace the comma and space after the word "bones" with the XML entity `&amp;` and re-load the file into your browser to show that the entity is replaced with the & symbol. Make the same replacement in line 20 of the file `sampledata_with_dtd.xml` and then load this file into

the browser to confirm that you get an error, showing that the predefined XML entities are no longer in effect when you use a DTD. Put the entity definition necessary to correct the problem into the DTD file and reload the XML file to confirm that the problem has been corrected.

5. In line 20 of the file `sampledata_with_dtd.xml`, replace the comma and space after the word "bones," as well as the word "especially", with the XML entity `&ae;` and re-load the file into your browser to show that an error is generated because this entity is unknown to the XML processor in the browser. Then put a declaration in the DTD file `sampledata_with_dtd.dtd` that defines this entity to be the string "and especially". Now reload the file `sampledata_with_dtd.xml` again to show that the entity is now replaced with the content of the definition you gave it.

11.12   Exercises on the Parallel Project

1. Choose at least ten of the products and/or services of your business, and then choose some XML element tags and attributes that will describe these items adequately.

2. Create an XML file that contains full descriptions of each of the items, using the XML tags and attributes you chose in the previous exercise. Make sure that your file is well-formed.

3. Create a corresponding DTD file and place an appropriate `DOCTYPE` declaration for this DTD in your XML file.

4. Create a CSS style file that contains styles for displaying each of your items. Place these styles in a separate style file and place a corresponding stylesheet link in your XML file.

5. Check your XML file to make sure it is well-formed and then validate it against your DTD file to make sure it passes that test.

6. Finally, display your XML file in several browsers to confirm that your CSS styles are also performing as they should on your data.

11.13   What Else You May Want or Need to Know

1. XML is a W3C standard. The first version, XML 1.0, was published in February, 1998. The second, XML 1.1, was published in 2004, but as of this writing is still not widely supported.

2. If you are planning to create a set of XML tags to describe some of your own data, it might be a good idea to see if you can save yourself some trouble. Do a Google search using a string like "XML tag sets your_subject_keywords" to see what turns up.

3. In this chapter we have only discussed external DTDs. An *external DTD* is one located in a file separate from the XML file(s) it describes. This is similar to the CSS files and JavaScript files that we separated from our XHTML files in earlier chapters; we make the separation here for the same kinds of reasons. However, as with CSS and JavaScript files, we can have an *internal DTD* as well. That is, we can place our DTD right in the document it describes. If you do this, you must place the entire DTD in the `DOCTYPE` declaration of the XML file, using the following syntax:

```
<!DOCTYPE highest_level_tag_name
[
   ... DTD content ...
]>
```

In this context of internal and external DTDs we should mention the (optional) `standalone` attribute of the `xml` tag that appears in the `xml` declaration that opens every XML file. In particular we should note that the `standalone` attribute has two possible values, `yes` and `no`, the default is `no`, and also:

   (a) If the value is `yes`, the document should not depend on any external DTD, though it may (or may not) have an internal DTD.

   (b) If the value is `no`, the document may or may not actually depend on an external DTD, but if it does it must have a `DOCTYPE` declaration specifying the location of that DTD.

4. Just another quick reminder here. As we mentioned earlier in this chapter, the DTD is only one way of describing how our XML documents should be constructed. A major drawback of a DTD is that it is not itself an XML document.

That is why using an XML schema for this purpose provides a more consistent approach, and in that case both an XML document and the XML schema describing it can be processed by the same parser. DTDs are simpler, but if you wish to pursue XML seriously, you will need to learn something about XML schemas. Alternatively, you may wish to investigate something called *RELAX NG (REgular LAnguage for XML Next Generation)*, which is a schema that specifies a pattern for the structure and content of an XML document but which, compared to other popular schema languages, is relatively simple.

5. We mentioned in section 11.2 that whitespace is "significant" in XML, but just what that means "depends on the situation," so let's say a bit more about this now. First, note that in XML whitespace consists of the blank space, the carriage return, the line feed, and the tab, as well as any combination of them.

The essential thing to remember is that an XML parser should send all whitespace in an XML file through to any application (such as a browser) that is going to process that file, and leave it up to the application to deal with the whitespace in whatever way the application deems appropriate.

Thus, for example, an application processing XML may or may not choose to treat

```
<name>Vitamin A</name>
```

the same as

```
<name>
    Vitamin A
</name>
```

or not, but an XML parser should send the four spaces in front of "Vitamin A" in the second version through to that application and let it decide what to do with them.

6. Just like there was an XHTML DOM whose nodes and other properties could be accessed and manipulated by JavaScript, there is also an XML DOM that is subject to the same access and manipulation by JavaScript.

7. If you have XML data that you wish to manipulate in any way, and if you are already using PHP, then you should investigate *SimpleXML*, which is a PHP extension that permits easy processing of XML data in various ways. You will need to have version 5 or later of PHP to use it. You can, of course, process

XML by "rolling your own" PHP code to do whatever you like, but a package like SimpleXML is quite likely to have built-in facilities to perform the most common operations that you would normally require, so using it instead would probably save you both development time and debugging agony.

11.14   References

1. The w3schools.com site has a section on XML. Start here:

   http://www.w3schools.com/xml/default.asp

2. One very good XML editor that you can pay for, but which also has a free version, is **Exchanger XML Lite**. If you plan to do a lot of XML editing, you might do well to check out this program at the following site:

   http://www.freexmleditor.com/

3. A simple XML editor called XML Notepad 2007 is available from this Microsoft site::

   http://www.microsoft.com/download/en/details.aspx?displaylang=en&id=7973

4. The sites listed below provide some additional XML editor choices. The Altova XML Spy option is not free, but comes highly recommended by the folks at W3Schools:

   http://free.editix.com/
   http://www.firstobject.com/dn_editor.htm
   http://www.altova.com/simpledownload1.html

5. To check out the XML standard itself, start here:

   http://www.w3.org/XML/

6. For information on the standard for XML namespaces, look here:

   http://www.w3.org/TR/REC-xml-names

7. Here is where you will find the standard for eXtensible Stylesheet Transformations:

   ```
   http://www.w3.org/TR/xslt
   ```

8. The standard for XPath is here:

   ```
   http://www.w3.org/TR/xpath
   ```

9. You can check an XML document for well-formedness at the w3schools.com site, but if you wish to check the document for validity you may wish to look elsewhere, since at the time of writing to use that one you had to be using Internet Explorer with an internal DTD. Although the in-your-face advertising is a bit off-putting, this site appears to be quite useful:

   ```
   http://www.xmlvalidation.com/
   ```

   And here is another:

   ```
   http://www.stg.brown.edu/service/xmlvalid/
   ```

10. Many programming languages, including PHP, have special facilities for dealing with XML. For example, see the following:

    ```
    http://php.net/manual/en/book.xml.php
    ```

11. Here are the home page link, a tutorial link, and the Wikipedia link for RELAX NG:

    ```
    http://relaxng.org/
    http://relaxng.org/tutorial-20011203.html
    http://en.wikipedia.org/wiki/RELAX_NG
    ```

CHAPTER 12

Collecting, Analyzing, and Using Visitor Data

CHAPTER CONTENTS

12.1   Overview and Objectives

The information age is gradually causing the accumulation of vast quantities of data in various repositories large and small around the world. Extracting useful information from such mountains of data is sometimes referred to as *data mining*.

Web-based businesses generate even larger quantities of information than do regular businesses. A physical store may record purchases by a customer, but it does not record the customer's browsing experience. A Web-based store, on the other hand, can record not only the items purchased, but also the sequential order in which the customer visited various departments and looked at different products. Such a store can also keep a record of items that a customer put in his or her shopping cart and later chose not to buy. Information like this can be used to increase sales by analyzing the causes of aborted purchases.

This challenging area is termed *web mining*—data mining applied to web-data repositories (Ramadhan et al., 2005). Web mining may be subdivided into three areas (Cooley et al., 1997 and Akerkar and Lingras, 2007):

- *Web-content mining*, which deals with primary data on the Web, meaning the actual content of web documents.

- *Web-structure mining*, which is concerned with the "topology" of the Web, focusing on data that organizes the content and facilitates navigation. The principal source of information in web-structure mining is the hyperlinks that connect one page to another.

- *Web-usage mining*, which does not deal with the contents of web documents, but instead has the goal of determining how a website's visitors use web resources and the study of their navigational patterns. The data used for web-usage mining is essentially secondary, and is generated by users' interactions with the Web. The data sources include web-server access logs, proxy-server logs, browser logs, user profiles, registration data, user sessions and transactions, cookies, user queries, bookmark data, mouse clicks, and scrolls (Kosala and Blockeel, 2000).

Akerkar and Lingras (2007), in their book entitled *Building an Intelligent Web: Theory and Practice*, provide a detailed introduction to web mining. This chapter contains excerpts from that book that pertain to the analysis of web-server access logs, an initial step in web-usage mining, and we discuss the following topics:

- Web-server access logs and their formats, including an Apache web-server example

- Analysis of web-server access logs, including summarization with Analog, click-stream analysis with Pathalizer, and visualization of individual user sessions with StatViz

- Some cautions to keep in mind when interpreting web-server access logs

12.2   Web-Server Access Logs

A *web-server access log*, also referred to simply as a "server log," "web log," or "access log," is generally defined as a set of files containing the details of an activity performed by a server (Wikipedia, 2006). Usually these files are automatically created and maintained by the server. The activity of a web server mainly consists of servicing the page requests; therefore, one of the important logs maintained by a web server is the history of page requests.

The World Wide Web Consortium (W3C) has specified a standard format for web-server access log files. In addition to this format specified by the W3C, there are other proprietary formats for web logs. Most of them contain information about each request, such as:

- The IP address of the client making the request

- The date and time of the request

- The URL of the requested page

- The number of bytes sent to serve the request

- The user agent (the program that is acting on behalf of the user, such as a web browser or web crawler)

- The referrer (the URL that triggered the request)

Server logs typically do not collect user-specific information. The logs of activities of a web server can all be stored in one file; however, a better alternative is to separate the log into different categories such as an access log, an error log, and a referrer log. An access log typically grows by more than 1MB for every 10,000 requests (Apache, 2006). This means that even on a moderately busy server, these log files tend to be fairly large. Consequently, it is usually necessary to periodically rotate the log files by moving or deleting the existing logs.

Depending on the duration of an analysis, it may be necessary to use data from multiple log files. On most servers, the log files are not accessible to general Internet users. Only web-server administrators and system administrators have the necessary permissions to read, modify, and delete the log files. In some cases, users with an account on the system that hosts the web server may be able to read the access logs. These server logs contain a wealth of information that can be statistically analyzed to reveal potentially useful traffic patterns based on the time of day or day of the week.

This information can be useful for planning system maintenance and load balancing. System maintenance could be scheduled during times when the server is less in demand. Similarly, elective computing jobs and network traffic emanating from the server could also be suspended during peak times.

In addition, looking at traffic patterns based on referrer and user agents can be useful for developing web strategies. For example, the look and feel of a website could be made more consistent with frequent referrer sites, and more visible links may also be placed on the referrer sites to further facilitate navigation.

Furthermore, knowledge of the most frequent user agents could be helpful in optimizing the site for that user agent. For example, if most users are using Firefox, the web developers should ensure that their web pages are properly displayed in Firefox.

Thus, analysis of web logs can facilitate efficient website administration, scheduling of adequate hosting resources, and the fine-tuning of sales efforts.

A wide variety of tools are available for analyzing web logs. It is important for marketing personnel from organizations that facilitate business through their websites to understand these powerful tools. In this chapter we will discuss how three of these tools—Analog, Pathalizer, and StatViz—work, and also look at the theoretical basis for them. The enclosed CD-ROM contains links to these software packages.

12.2.1   Format of Web-Server Access Logs

The common log format of records in web-server access log files is supported by most web servers. Similarly, a majority of log analyzers are designed to work with the common log-file format. Table 12.1 shows the general format of a common log file described on the W3C website. The following are examples of entries in the common log format:

```
140.14.6.11 - pawan [06/Sep/2001:10:46:07 -0300] "GET /s.htm HTTP/1.0" 200 2267
140.14.7.18 - raj [06/Sep/2001:11:23:53 -0300] "POST /s.cgi HTTP/1.0" 200 499
```

The first entry is a GET request that retrieves a file named s.htm. The second entry is a POST request that sends data to a program called s.cgi.

Let us describe each field of the first request:

1. The first field tells us that the request came from a computer (client machine) identified with the IP address of 140.14.6.11.

2. The dash (-) for the second field tells us that the information for that field is unavailable. In this case, the missing information is the RFC 1413 identity of the client, which is determined by a program (daemon) called identd running on the client's machine. This information is highly unreliable and should almost never be used except on tightly controlled internal networks (Apache, 2006).

Format:	remotehost rfc931 authuser [date] "request" status bytes
remotehost	Remote hostname (or IP number if DNS hostname is not available or if DNSLookup is Off)
rfc931	The remote logname of the user
authuser	The username the user has used to authenticate himself
[date]	Date and time of the request
"request"	The request line exactly as it came from the client
status	The HTTP status code returned to the client
bytes	The content length of the document transferred

Table 12.1

Common log format.
See http://www.w3.org/Daemon/User/Config/Logging.html#common-logfile-format.

3. The third field tells us that the name or ID of the user is **pawan**. This ID is determined by HTTP authentication for documents that are password protected. This entry will be a dash (-) for documents that are not password protected.

4. The fourth entry provides the time of the request as [06/Sep/2001:10:46:07 -0300]. The first part of the time is rather obvious. The request came just after 10:46 a.m. on September 6, 2001. The -0300 tells us that the time zone is three hours behind Greenwich Mean Time (GMT), which in this case makes it Atlantic Canadian Daylight Saving Time.

5. The fifth field, given by "GET /s.htm HTTP/1.0", lists the request from the user. In this case, the request is to GET the document s.htm using the protocol HTTP/1.0.

6. The sixth field is the status code sent back to the user by the server. Codes beginning with 2 mean that the request resulted in a successful response. In our example, the code is 200, which means the request was successfully served. The codes that start with 3 tell us that the request was redirected to another server. If the user makes an erroneous request (for example, requesting a non-existent page), codes beginning in 4 will be returned to the user. Finally, an error in the server leads to codes starting with 5.

7. The seventh and last field in the request indicates that 2267 bytes were transferred as a result of the request.

12.2.2   An Extended Log-File Format

While the common log format is standard, and supported by all servers, information contained in these records is fixed and rather limited. Many web-server administrators find it necessary to record more information, which has created a need for an extended log-file format. However, due to legislation related to the protection of websites, certain servers may want to omit certain data that may directly or indirectly make it possible to identify users. In addition, servers may need to change the field separator character if the standard field separator occurs in their fields. The extended log-file format is designed to overcome some of the shortcomings of the common log format by providing the following features (Hallam-Baker and Behlendorf, 1996):

- Permits control over the data recorded

- Supports the needs of proxies, clients, and servers in a common format

- Provides robust handling of character-escaping issues

```
#Version: 1.0
#Date: 12-Jan-1996
#Fields: time cs-method cs-uri
00:34:23 GET /foo/bar.html
12:21:16 GET /foo/bar.html
12:45:52 GET /foo/bar.html
12:57:34 GET /foo/bar.html
```

FIGURE 12.1

An example of a log file in extended format.
(Hallam-Baker and Behlendorf, 1996)

■ Allows exchange of demographic data

■ Allows summary data to be expressed

The extended log-file format makes it possible to customize log files. Because the format of log files may vary from server to server, a header specifies the data types of each field at the start of the file. The format is readable by generic log-analysis tools, which we will discuss later in this chapter.

Hallam-Baker and Behlendorf (1996) describe the format of the extended log file in great detail. The following is a summary of their specifications.

An extended log file consists of a sequence of lines, each containing either a directive or an entry. Figure 12.1 shows a simple example of an extended log file reproduced from Hallam-Baker and Behlendorf (1996). The lines starting with a hash mark (#) are directives, while the rest are entries.

Directives record information about the logging process itself. The type of a directive starts with a hash mark (#) and is followed by the name of the directive. Types are shown in Table 12.2.

The directives **#Version** and **#Fields** are mandatory and must appear before all the entries. Other directives are optional. The **#Fields** directive specifies the data recorded in the fields of each entry by providing the list of fields. Each field in the **#Fields** directive can be specified in one of the following ways:

■ By an identifier; for example, **time**.

■ By an identifier with a prefix separated by a hyphen; for example, the method in the request sent by the client to the server is specified as **cs-method**.

■ By a prefix followed by a header in parentheses; for example, the content type of the reply from the server to the client is given by **sc(Content-type)**.

#Version:	version of the extended log-file format used
#Fields:	fields recorded in the log
#Software:	software that generated the log
#Start-Date:	date and time at which the log was started
#End-Date:	date and time at which the log was finished
#Date:	date and time at which the entry was added
#Remark:	comments that are ignored by analysis tools

Table 12.2

Directive types in the extended log-file format.

cs	client to server
sc	server to client
sr	server to remote server (this prefix is used by proxies)
rs	remote server to server (this prefix is used by proxies)
x	application-specific identifier

Table 12.3

Identifier prefixes for use in the extended log-file format.

The possible identifier prefixes in Table 12.3 and Table 12.4 show the identifiers that must be used with a prefix, while Table 12.5 shows a list of identifiers that do not take a prefix.

ip	IP address and port
dns	DNS name
status	status code
comment	comment returned with status code
method	method
uri	URI
uri-stem	stem portion alone of URI (omitting query)
uri-query	query portion alone of URI
host	DNS hostname used

Table 12.4

Identifiers that must be used with a prefix in the extended log-file format.

date	date at which transaction was completed
time	time at which transaction was completed
bytes	bytes transferred
cached	records whether a cache hit occurred (1 means a cache hit and 0 indicates a cache miss)

Table 12.5

Identifiers without prefixes for use in the extended log-file format.

The entries in a log file consist of a sequence of fields as specified in the #Fields directive corresponding to a single HTTP transaction. Fields are separated by white-space, usually a TAB character. If information for a field is either unavailable or not applicable for a given transaction, a dash (-) is used.

12.2.3   An Example: Apache Web-Server Access Log Entries

In the previous section we looked at the generic description of web-access log formats. Different web servers will have their own peculiarities in logging HTTP requests. In this section, we will look at the web-logging process employed by Apache, one of the most popular web servers. See the **References** section for a link to more detailed information.

For the Apache server, the LogFormat directive is used to specify the selection of fields in each entry. The format is specified using a string that is styled after the printf format strings in the C programming language. For example, the common log format entry

```
140.14.6.11 - pawan [06/Sep/2001:10:46:07 -0300] "GET /s.htm HTTP/1.0" 200 2267
```

discussed earlier can be represented using the following LogFile directive:

```
LogFormat "\%h \%l \%u \%t \"\%r\" \%>s \%b" common
```

This directive defines the format of the log and associates it with the nickname "common." The format string consists of "percent directives," each of which tells the server to log a particular piece of information. Literal characters in the format string will be copied directly into the log output. If we want the quote character (") to appear as a literal, it must be escaped by placing a backslash before it, so that it is not interpreted as the end of the format string. The format string may also contain the special control characters \n for newline character and \t for a TAB. Table 12.6 gives the meaning of the various format parameters.

%h	IP address of the client (remote host)
%l	RFC 1413 identity of the client
%u	userid of the person requesting the document
%t	time when server finished processing the request
\"%r\"	request line from the client is given in double quotes
%>s	status code that the server sent to the client
%b	number of bytes returned to the client

Table 12.6

Parameters in the Apache common log-format example.

Here the time is in the following format:

```
[day/month/year:hour:minute:second zone]
day = 2*digit
month = 3*letter
year = 4*digit
hour = 2*digit
minute = 2*digit
second = 2*digit
zone = (+ | -) 4*digit
```

An example of another commonly used format, the combined log format, is

```
140.14.6.11 - pawan [06/Sep/2001:10:46:07 -0300] "GET /s.htm HTTP/1.0" 20(
"http://cs.smu.ca/csc/" "Mozilla/4.0 (compatible; MSIE 5.5; Windows NT 5.(
```

for which the corresponding format string is

```
LogFormat "%h %l %u %t \"%r\" %>s %b \"%{Referer}i\" \"%{User-agent}i\""
```

which has the two additional fields shown in Table 12.7.

In this example, the referrer is `http://cs.smu.ca/csc/`, and it has a link to the file `s.htm`. The software that was used for the request was `Mozilla/4.0 (compatible;`

\"%{Referer}i\"	site that the client was referred from, enclosed in quotes
\"%{User-agent}i\"	software that made the request, enclosed in quotes

Table 12.7

Additional fields in the combined log format.

`MSIE 5.5; Windows NT 5.0)`, which is, in fact, the web browser Microsoft Internet Explorer 5.5 for Windows NT 5.0.

The server configuration also specifies the location of the log file using the `CustomLog` directive. The path for the access log file is assumed to start from the server root unless it begins with a slash. For example, the directive `CustomLog logs/access_log combined` will store logs, in the combined log format, in a file called `access_log` in the subdirectory `logs` under the server root.

Apache (2006) cautions server administrators about the large sizes of access-log files, even on a moderately busy server. As we mentioned before, such a file typically grows by 100 bytes per request; therefore, it is periodically necessary to rotate the log files by moving or deleting the existing logs.

12.3   Analysis of Web-Server Access Logs

The formatting information about web-server access logs in the previous section can be used to write programs to analyze web usage for your website, as well as for running data-mining tools. However, prior to applying data-mining techniques, it is necessary to understand the data set. This is typically done by creating multiple summary reports and, if possible, using visual representations.

Before writing your own software for analyzing web-server access logs, you may want to consider one of the analysis tools already available. One or more of these tools may provide answers to most of your questions regarding usage of your website. Figure 12.2 tabulates a large number of freeware and open-source web-access analysis tools listed on the Open Directory Project site `http://www.dmoz.org/`. In addition to the freeware and open-source tools, you can also find a listing of commercial tools on that site. In this section, we discuss how to obtain summary reports as well as visualization of aggregate clickstream and individual user sessions from web-server access logs.

12.3.1   Summarization of Web-Server Access Logs Using Analog

One of the more popular tools for analyzing web-server access log files is called Analog (`http://www.analog.cx`). This software is available for free and includes full C source code as well as executables for the Windows and Mac platforms. One should, in fact, be able to compile it for almost any operating system. The website for Analog also has links to precompiled versions for a variety of other operating systems. The developers claim that it is designed to be fast and to produce

Analog	http://www.analog.cx
AWStats	http://awstats.sourceforge.net
BBClone	http://bbclone.de
The Big Brother Log Analyzer	http://bbla.sourceforge.net
BlibbleBlobble LogAnalyser	http://www.blibbleblobble.co.uk/Downloads/LogAnalyser
Dailystats	http://www.perlfect.com/freescripts/dailystats
GeoIP	http://www.maxmind.com/geoip
High Speed Merging	http://www.whurst.net/programming/hHSM/index.php
HitsLog Script	http://www.irnis.net/soft/hitslog
Http-Analyze	http://www.http-analyze.org
Kraken Reports	http://www.krakenreports.com
Logfile	http://www.ratrobot.com/programming/shell
LogFile Analyse	http://www.jan-winkler.de/dev
LogReport Foundation	http://logreport.org
MagicStats	http://www.nondot.org/MagicStats
Modlogan	http://www.modlogan.org
NedStat	http://www.nedstat.com
Pathalizer	http://pathalizer.bzzt.net
phpOpenTracker	http://www.phpopentracker.de
PowerPhlogger	http://pphlogger.phpee.com
RCounter	http://rcounter.noonet.ru
Realtracker Website Statistics	http://free.realtracker.com
Relax	http://ktmatu.com/software/relax
Report Magic for Analog	http://www.reportmagic.com
RobotStats	http://www.robotstats.com/en
Sevink Internet Advertising	http://www.sevink-2.demon.nl
Sherlog	http://sherlog.europeanservers.net
Snowhare's Utilities	http://www.nihongo.org/snowhare/utilities
Superstat	http://www.serversolved.com/superstat
VISITaTOR- a free web mining tool	http://visitator.fh54.de
Visitors	http://www.hping.org/visitors
WebLog	http://awsd.com/scripts/weblog
Webtrax Help	http://www.multicians.org/thvv/webtrax-help.html
W3Perl	http://www.w3perl.com/softs
Wwwstat	http://www.ics.uci.edu/pub/websoft/wwwstat
ZoomStats	http://zoomstats.sourceforge.net

FIGURE 12.2

Web access log analyzers.
(`http://dmoz.org/Computers/Software/Internet/Site_Management/`
`Log_Analysis/Freeware_and_Open_Source/`)

accurate and attractive statistics. One can also combine Analog with Report Magic (`http://www.reportmagic.org`) for better graphical analysis.

Getting and Installing Analog

Although Analog is free software, its distribution and modification are covered by the terms of the GNU General Public License. You are not required to accept this license, but nothing else gives you permission to modify or distribute the program (Turner, 2006).

The zipped version of Analog 6.0 for Windows can be downloaded from the Analog site. Create a folder on your hard drive called Chapter12 and copy the zip file to that location. If you right-click on the zip file and choose Extract All, you will be able to access all the files. This should create a folder called `analog_60w32`. Double-clicking on that folder will take you to another folder called `analog 6.0`, which has the Analog 6.0 package for Windows. The `docs` subfolder has all the documentation for the package. The best place to start is the `Readme.html` file, which can be opened using your web browser. In what follows we provide a summary of the essentials of this documentation, and a brief tutorial.

Getting Input for Analog

In section 12.2, we discussed the format and location of log files for the Apache web server. If you cannot easily locate these log files for your web server, you may wish to contact your administrator. In order to run Analog, you need read access to these log files. The Analog package comes with a small log file called `logfile.log` with 50 HTTP requests. The file is located in the Analog 6.0 folder but is too small for us to explore the real power of this analysis tool. Hence, we have included another log file from an educational site.

The data we will study was obtained from the web-server access logs of an introductory first-year course in Computing Science at Saint Mary's University in Halifax, Nova Scotia over a 16-week period. The initial number of students in the course was 180. That number fell over the course of the semester to 130–140 students. Certain areas of the website were protected, and users could access them using only their IDs and passwords. The activities in the restricted parts of the website consisted of submitting a user profile, changing a password, submitting assignments, viewing the submissions, accessing the discussion board, and viewing current class marks. The rest of the website was public and contained course information, a lab manual, class notes, class assignments, and lab assignments.

If users accessed only the public portion, their IDs would be unknown. For the rest of the entrants, the usernames were changed to **user** to protect their privacy. The zipped version of the log file is available under Chapter12 on the CD-ROM as **classlog.zip**. Copy the file to the Analog 6.0 folder and extract the log file. Make sure that the file is expanded in the Analog 6.0 folder. The extracted file should have the name **classlog.txt**. Notice that the file is rather large (67MB) and has 361,609 lines. It is in the combined log format, which was discussed previously.

We are now ready to explore the power of Analog, which will involve the following three steps:

- Edit the **Analog.cfg** file.

- Run Analog by double-clicking on the icon (a command window pops up momentarily).

- Read the **Report.html** file.

Configuring Analog

You can configure Analog by putting commands in the configuration file, **Analog.cfg**. This may seem a little tedious for users who prefer a graphical user interface (GUI); however, the package comes with a default configuration file that may simplify the process. Moreover, the configuration file allows users more flexibility than a GUI. You can edit **Analog.cfg** using any plain-text editor, even Notepad.

First, copy the existing configuration file **Analog.cfg** to **origAnalog.cfg** as a backup. Now we are ready to make changes to **Analog.cfg**. Note that any text following a hash mark (#) on a line is ignored by Analog as a comment.

One command you will need to change right away is

```
LOGFILE logfilename      # to set where your logfile lives
```

The log file must be stored locally on your computer, because Analog is not designed to use FTP or HTTP to fetch the log file from the Internet. As mentioned previously, the supplied **logfile.log** file contains only 50 HTTP requests, so we will use our own log file, **classlog.txt**. The rest of the configuration already contains many of the essential configuration commands to get us started. We will leave these commands unchanged and see what happens when we run Analog. Later on in this section, we will discuss the significance of these commands.

Running Analog

There are two ways to run Analog: either from Windows by double-clicking on its icon or from the DOS command prompt. If you run it from Windows, it will create a DOS window, which will flash on your screen momentarily during its execution (this usually takes a couple of seconds). When Analog is finished, it will produce an output file called `Report.html` and some graphics. A file called `errors.txt` will contain any errors that may have occurred during the analysis of the log file.

If you run Analog from the DOS command prompt, you can specify the configuration-file commands via the command-line arguments. These are specified on the command line after the program name and are simply shortcuts for configuration-file commands. The use of command-line arguments may save you the trouble of editing the configuration file every time you want to change the nature of the reporting. The command-line arguments can also be specified from a batch file. Refer to the documentation in the `docs` folder to learn more about the command-line arguments.

Checking the Output from Analog

Look at the `Report.html` file from the Analog 6.0 folder by opening it using a web browser. If you double-click on `Report.html`, Windows should open it using your default browser. If that does not work, you may want to open the file explicitly through your browser. The file `docs/reports.html` provides a list of all possible reports. Usually you will get only a subset of these reports, depending on what information is recorded in your log file. Our report is divided into sections, listed in Table 12.8 and shown in Figures 12.3–12.15.

The following are some definitions from `docs/defns.html` that will aid in understanding the reports obtained:

- The *host* is the computer that is making the request for information (also called the *client*). The request may be for a *page* or another file, such as an image. By default, filenames ending in `.html`, `.htm` or `/` are considered pages. We can tell Analog to count other files as pages using the `PAGEINCLUDE` command.

- The *total requests* consist of all the files that were requested, including pages and graphics. Total requests corresponds to the traditional definition of number of hits. The *requests for pages* include only those files that are defined as pages.

- The *successful requests* are those with HTTP status codes in the 200s or with the code 304. Codes in the 200s correspond to requests in which the document was returned. The code 304 results when the document was requested but was not needed because it had not been recently modified, and the user could use a cached copy. You can configure the code 304 to be a redirected request instead of a successful request with the 304ISSUCCESS command. *Successful requests for pages* are the subset of successful requests, limited to pages.

1	**Report or Summary**	**What it Contains**
1	General Summary	overall statistics
2	Monthly Report	activity for each month
3	Daily Summary	activity for each day of the week over all weeks
4	Hourly Summary	activity for each hour of the day over all days
5	Domain Report	countries from which files were requested
6	Organization Report	organizations that requested files
7	Search-Word Report	words used by search engines to find the site
8	Operating-System Report	operating systems used by the visitors
9	Status-Code Report	HTTP status codes of all requests
10	File-Size Report	sizes of all requested files
11	File-Type Report	extensions of all requested files
12	Directory Report	all directories from which files were requested
13	Request Report	all requested files from the site

Table 12.8

Types of summaries and reports output by Analog.

```
Successful requests: 303,511
Average successful requests per day: 2,285
Successful requests for pages: 101,655
Average successful requests for pages per day: 765
Failed requests: 24,571
Redirected requests: 33,495
Distinct files requested: 1,441
Distinct hosts served: 2,800
Corrupt logfile lines: 32
Data transferred: 2.09 gigabytes
Average data transferred per day: 16.15 megabytes
```

FIGURE 12.3

General summary from Analog.

Each unit (☐) represents 1,000 requests for pages or part thereof.

month	reqs	pages	
Aug 2001	1974	904	
Sep 2001	67218	30136	
Oct 2001	111887	35054	
Nov 2001	96688	28603	
Dec 2001	25744	6958	

Busiest month: Oct 2001 (35,054 requests for pages).

FIGURE 12.4

`graphics/ch12/analogMonthlyReport.pdf`
Example of a monthly report from Analog.

Each unit (☐) represents 800 requests for pages or part thereof.

day	reqs	pages	
Sun	33863	10455	
Mon	55616	17777	
Tue	75579	28509	
Wed	35883	10525	
Thu	55132	20155	
Fri	23087	7120	
Sat	24351	7114	

FIGURE 12.5

`graphics/analogDailySummary.pdf`
Example of a daily summary from Analog.

- *Redirected requests* are those with codes in the 300s with the exception of 304. These codes indicate that the user was directed to a different file. This may happen because of an explicit redirection. Another common cause is an incorrect request for a directory name without the trailing slash. Redirected requests may also result from their use as "click-thru" advertising banners.

- *Failed requests* are those with codes in the 400s (error in request) or 500s (server error). These failed requests generally occur when the requested file is not found or is not readable.

- The *requests returning informational status code* are those with status codes in the 100s. These status codes are rarely recorded at this time.

- The corrupt log file lines are those that could not be parsed by Analog. It is possible to list all the corrupt lines by turning debugging on.

- There are a few other types of log file lines not included in our example that may be listed in the General Summary. The term *lines without status code*

Each unit (▫) represents 250 requests for pages or part thereof.

hour	reqs	pages	
0	6246	2143	
1	4065	1143	
2	1836	627	
3	1115	413	
4	599	267	
5	473	143	
6	1711	277	
7	2986	718	
8	10876	3648	
9	12466	4439	
10	10039	3070	
11	26922	10236	
12	21000	6990	
13	13248	4318	
14	27175	10176	
15	22683	7719	
16	19579	7227	
17	15645	5204	
18	19042	5773	
19	24002	8315	
20	18215	5823	
21	18097	5208	
22	14495	4332	
23	10996	3446	

FIGURE 12.6

graphics/ch12/analogHourlySummary.pdf
Example of an hourly summary from Analog.

refers to those log-file lines without a status code. *Unwanted logfile entries* are entries that are explicitly excluded.

Figure 12.3 shows the general summary for our `classlog.txt` file. Out of a total of 361,609 requests, there were 303,511 successful requests; that is, 84% of all requests were successful. Roughly one-third (101,655) of the successful requests were for pages. The average data transfer was a little over 16MB per day. The average data transfer can be used to determine the bandwidth of the connection to your server.

The general summary report can be turned on or off with the `GENERAL` command. The `GENSUMLINES` command controls which lines are included in the summary. The `LASTSEVEN` command can be used to include or exclude the figures for the last seven days.

reqs	%bytes	domain
303511	100%	[unresolved numerical addresses]

FIGURE 12.7

Example of a domain report from Analog.

The remaining 12 reports (other than the general summary) can be divided into three categories: time reports (Figure 12.4: monthly report), time summary report (Figures 12.5 and 12.6: daily and weekly summary), or non-time reports (Figures 12.7–12.15). Most of the following reports include only successful requests in calculating the number of requests, requests for pages, bytes, and last date, with the exception of reports on redirection or failure. You can control whether each report is included or not with the most appropriate ON or OFF command. You can control which columns are listed with the COLS commands.

The time reports describe the number of requests in each time period. They also identify the busiest time period. The monthly report given in Figure 12.4, which provides monthly statistics, is an example of a time report. The report shows the number of requests and how many of those were pages. The number of pages is also represented using a bar chart to make it easier to compare. The month of August has the lowest traffic because classes do not start until September. The report lists October as the busiest month, which makes sense because that is when the midterm examination is held. There is a decline in traffic in November as the number of students in the course goes down after the midterm. The final examinations are over by the middle of December; therefore, December traffic is the second lowest.

In the time and time summary reports you can make the following adjustments:

- Measurement for the bar charts and the "busiest" line can be changed using the GRAPH commands.

- The number of rows displayed can be changed with the ROWS commands.

- Lines can be displayed backward or forward in time by the BACK commands.

- The graphic used for the bar charts can be changed with the BARSTYLE command.

- The time zone is usually the server's local time. In some cases, it may be GMT. You can get Analog to report based on another time zone with the LOGTIMEOFFSET command.

Time-summary reports are different from time reports because a given time period may occur multiple times in a log file. For example, there are multiple Sundays

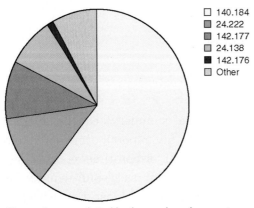

☐	140.184
■	24.222
■	142.177
☐	24.138
■	142.176
☐	Other

The wedges are plotted by the number of requests.

Listing the top 20 organizations by the number
of requests, sorted by the number of requests.

reqs	% bytes	organization
178914	62.54%	140.184
35737	12.22%	24.222
34127	9.99%	142.177
30520	8.49%	24.138
5489	1.25%	142.176
2333	0.45%	129.173
1949	0.34%	165.154
1895	0.70%	140.230
1500	0.20%	198.166
1391	0.46%	154.5
1283	0.22%	209.73
1273	0.44%	209.148
509	0.11%	216.239
429	0.19%	209.167
408	0.10%	209.226
372	0.16%	207.107
339	0.20%	64.10
322	0.03%	66.77
292	0.13%	172.149
248	0.06%	205.188
4181	1.72%	*

* [not listed: 211 organizations]

FIGURE 12.8

graphics/ch12/analogOrganizationReport.pdf
Example of an organization report from Analog.

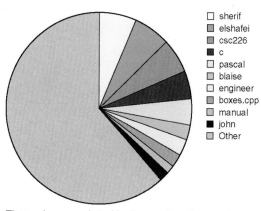

The wedges are plotted by the number of requests.

Listing the top 30 query words by the number
of requests, sorted by the number of requests.

reqs	search term
12	sherif
12	elshafei
11	csc226
9	c
8	pascal
5	blaise
5	engineer
4	boxes.cpp
...	...

FIGURE 12.9

graphics/ch12/analogSearchWordReport.pdf
Example of a search-word report from Analog.

in our log file; therefore, the daily report provides a sum of traffic for all the Sundays. The daily summary given in Figure 12.5 is an example of a time-summary report. It specifies the total number of requests in each day of the week. From Figure 12.5, we can see that the highest traffic was on Tuesday, because classes and labs are held on those days. Thursday has the second highest traffic. Assignments are due on Monday, which explains traffic increases on Sunday and Monday. The hourly summary given in Figure 12.6 describes the hourly variation in the traffic. The three peak hours, 11 a.m., 2 p.m., and 7 p.m., correspond to the laboratory times.

Now look at the non-time reports given in Figures 12.7–12.15. The domain report given in Figure 12.7 is supposed to list all the domains that visited our site. Unfortunately, our report has very little useful information. All the domains are listed as "unresolved numerical addresses," which means that the domain server records only

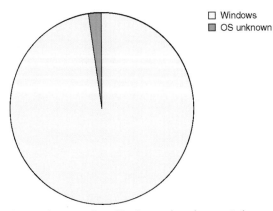

☐ Windows
■ OS unknown

The wedges are plotted by the number of requests for pages.

Listing operating systems, sorted by the number of requests for pages.

no	reqs	pages	OS
1	296266	99236	Windows
	157564	60126	Windows 2000
	70373	19427	Windows 98
	48870	13763	Windows ME
	8804	3085	Windows 95
	6682	1738	Windows XP
	2602	607	Windows NT
	1371	490	Unknown Windows
2	6867	2327	OS unknown
3	224	49	Macintosh
4	118	42	Unix
	74	26	Linux
	43	16	SunOS
	1	0	HP-UX

FIGURE 12.10

graphics/ch12/analogOSReport.pdf
Example of an operating-system report from Analog.

the numerical IP addresses of the hosts that contact you, not their names. Recording names of the hosts requires a time-consuming lookup process, which is why many server administrators choose to not record the domain names.

The organization report in Figure 12.8 shows all the organizations that the host computers belong to. The organizations are identified by the first two numbers of their IP addresses. More than 62% of hosts are from Saint Mary's University (140.184). The next four listings correspond to IP numbers from cable and phone companies in Halifax and account for 32% of requests. The organization report not only tells us

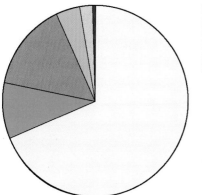

- ☐ 200 OK
- ◼ 301 Document moved permanently
- ◼ 304 Not modified since last retrieval
- ◼ 401 Authentication required
- ☐ 404 Document not found
- ◼ Other

The wedges are plotted by the number of requests.

Listing status codes, sorted numerically.

reqs	status code
237631	200 OK
1529	206 Partial content
33258	301 Document moved permanently
237	302 Document found elsewhere
54351	304 Not modified since last retrieval
6	400 Bad request
15174	401 Authentication required
466	403 Access forbidden
8428	404 Document not found
427	405 Method not allowed
21	408 Request timeout
5	416 Requested range not valid
44	500 Internal server error

FIGURE 12.11

`graphics/ch12/analogStatusCodeReport.pdf`
Example of a status-code report from Analog.

where our clientele comes from, but also gives us an opportunity to improve network connections for these organizations.

The search-word report (Figure 12.9) tells us which words the user typed in a search engine to get to our site. Most of the traffic in the `classlog.txt` file is from students registered in the class, who would typically bookmark the page instead of searching for it through a search engine; therefore, the search-word report is not very relevant in our case. However, for other organizations, it may reveal many interesting facts. If you look at the `Analog.cfg` file, you will notice the use of the `SEARCHENGINE` command to identify requests from search engines.

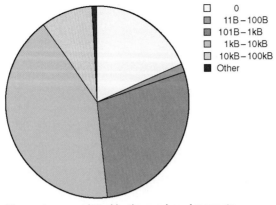

☐	0
◼	11B–100B
◼	101B–1kB
◻	1kB–10kB
◻	10kB–100kB
◼	Other

The wedges are plotted by the number of requests.

size	reqs	%bytes
0	56699	
1B–10B	117	
11B–100B	4576	0.01%
101B–1kB	86091	1.85%
1kB–10kB	126223	20.09%
10kB–100kB	27746	31.79%
100kB–1MB	2059	46.25%

FIGURE 12.12

`graphics/ch12/analogFileSizeReport.pdf`
Example of a file-size report from Analog.

The operating-system report (Figure 12.10) tells us that most of the users came from Windows-based computers. It also lists the number of requests that came from robots. The ROBOTINCLUDE command in Analog.cfg is used to identify known robots.

The status-code report from Figure 12.11 can be used to determine if the users are finding it difficult to navigate through the site, and the data from the report can be used as a means of improvement. If traffic from the site is unduly high, the file-size report (Figure 12.12) will allow us to determine if the problem is caused by many requests for small files or a small number of requests for large files. Based on this report, one may start looking for the offending files. In our case, the largest frequency of requests is for files of fewer than 10 kilobytes.

Figure 12.13 shows the popular file types by number of requests and size. GIF files (a type of image) were most frequently requested. On the other hand, EXE files (executable programs) accounted for the largest amount of data transfer. This report

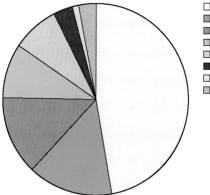

.exe [Executables]
[directories]
.doc [Microsoft Word document]
.pl [Perl scripts]
.htm [Hypertext Markup Language]
.gif [GIF graphics]
.cpp
Other

The wedges are plotted by the amount of traffic.

Listing extensions with at least 0.1% of the traffic,
sorted by the amount of traffic.

reqs	% bytes	extension
3040	47.49%	.exe [Executables]
82003	14.61%	[directories]
14440	13.39%	.doc [Microsoft Word document]
12908	9.17%	.pl [Perl scripts]
18907	8.19%	.htm [Hypertext Markup Language]
129170	3.32%	.gif [GIF graphics]
23231	1.03%	.cpp
745	0.81%	.html [Hypertext Markup Language]
349	0.66%	.zip [Zip archives]
2484	0.59%	.js [JavaScript code]
4976	0.43%	.php [PHP]
4618	0.13%	.cgi [CGI scripts]
6640	0.18%	[not listed: 8 extensions]

FIGURE 12.13

`graphics/ch12/analogFileTypeReport.pdf`
Example of a file-type report from Analog.

can be useful in devising a strategy to reduce the data transfer; for example, if it were possible to reduce the size of EXE files, we could reduce the data transfer.

Figure 12.14 identifies two directories as the most popular ones in the directory report. The directory /~csc226/ corresponds to the root for the course and /~pawan/ corresponds to the instructor for the course. A small portion of the request report is shown in Figure 12.15. In addition to the request for the home page for the course (/~csc226/), the home page for the bulletin board (/~csc226/cgi-bin/yabb.pl) is also a popular page.

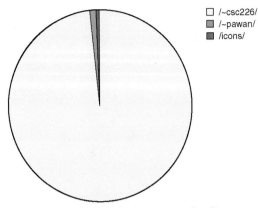

	□ /~csc226/
	■ /~pawan/
	■ /icons/

The wedges are plotted by the amount of traffic.

Listing directories with at least 0.01% of the traffic, sorted by the amount of traffic.

reqs	% bytes	directory
248972	98.56%	/~csc226/
2054	1.04%	/~pawan/
52460	0.40%	/icons/
25		[not listed: 4 directories]

FIGURE 12.14

graphics/ch12/analogDirectoryReport.pdf
Example of a directory report from Analog.

There are many commands that can change the non-time reports. You can make the following adjustments:

- Control how many items are listed with the **FLOOR** commands

- Control whether to show charts and how the pie charts are plotted (if you choose to show them) with the **CHART** commands

- List the time period covered by each report with the **REPORTSPAN** command

- Include or exclude individual items with the output **INCLUDE** and **EXCLUDE** commands

- Change the names of items in the reports with the output alias commands

- Control which files are linked in the reports with the **LINKINCLUDE** and **LINKEXCLUD** commands

- Change the links with the **BASEURL** command

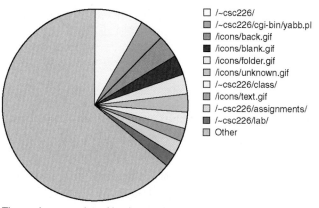

☐ /~csc226/
■ /~csc226/cgi-bin/yabb.pl
■ /icons/back.gif
■ /icons/blank.gif
☐ /icons/folder.gif
☐ /icons/unknown.gif
☐ /~csc226/class/
■ /icons/text.gif
☐ /~csc226/assignments/
■ /~csc226/lab/
☐ Other

The wedges are plotted by the number of requests.

Listing files with at least 20 requests, sorted by the number
of requests.

reqs	%bytes	last time	file
24304	9.25%	16/Dec/01 04:00	/~csc226/
11545	8.84%	15/Dec/01 22:47	/~csc226/cgi-bin/yabb.pl
1996	2.28	15/Dec/01 21:53	/~csc226/cgi-bin/yabb.pl?board=general
...	...	...	...

FIGURE 12.15

graphics/ch12/analogRequestReport.pdf
Example of a request report from Analog.

- The "not listed" line at the bottom of the majority of non-time reports counts those items that did not get enough traffic to get above the **FLOOR** for the report. It does not include items that were explicitly excluded using various **EXCLUDE** commands in the configuration file

12.3.2 Clickstream Analysis: Studying Navigation Paths with Pathalizer

In the previous section we studied various summarizations of web-access logs, which can be used to get insight into the web usage for a particular site. In this section, we will use the same logs to study how users navigate through the site. There are a number of commercial and free software packages available for studying navigation on the site. We will look at a free program called Pathalizer for this purpose.

Pathalizer (2006a) is a visualization tool that shows the paths most users take when browsing a website. This information can be useful for improving the navigation within a site. In conjunction with the summarization of web logs, the visual representation of navigation can also be used to determine which parts of the site need most attention. Pathalizer generates a weighted directed graph from a web-server access log in the combined format favored by Apache servers; however, it can be configured to analyze web logs in other formats.

Getting and Installing Pathalizer

The software can be downloaded from `http://pathalizer.sourceforge.net/` (Pathalizer 2006b). The software usage is subject to the standard GNU Public License (GPL). It is written in C++ and can be compiled using a GNU C++ compiler (g++) for any platform; however, end users may want to directly download the graphical user interface (GUI) versions for Linux, Windows, or Mac. Under Chapter12 on the CD-ROM there are links to two software packages—Graphviz and Pathalizer—and you should install Graphviz before running Pathalizer. Graphviz (also subject to the GPL) is used to create graphical versions of navigation graphs.

We will now assume that you have already created a folder called Chapter12 on your hard drive. Next, create another folder under Chapter12 called Pathalizer. Then download the latest Windows executables of Graphviz from `http://www.graphviz.org/` and of Pathalizer from `http://pathalizer.sourceforge.net/` to the Pathalizer folder. Once these two programs are installed, you are ready to run `pathalize.exe`.

Running Pathalizer

Double-clicking on `pathalize.exe` will launch Pathalizer. The top window in Figure 12.16 shows the screenshot of what you will see when you launch Pathalizer. (If you wander around, you can come back to this screen by clicking on `Input` in the left panel.) Under the box for `Log files:`, click on the `Add ...` button, and you will see the window shown at the bottom of Figure 12.16 for choosing the log file.

Next, go up one level to select the file `classlog.txt`. You will have to pick `All files` from `Files of type:` to see the files that do not have the `.log` extension. You may also want to click on the `Add ...` button under the `Hostnames:` box to add the domain name `http://cs.stmarys.ca`. This addition of hostname simplifies the output by not explicitly listing the prefix `http://cs.stmarys.ca`.

Now, click on `Filter` in the left panel to specify display criteria. If you choose to see every link in the log file, you will get a cluttered graph; therefore, specify a reasonable number of links to be displayed. The default is 20, but change it to 7 as shown in Figure 12.17. (Pathalizer always displays one more edge than what is specified.)

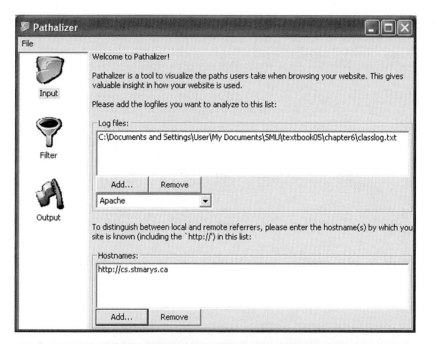

FIGURE 12.16
graphics/ch12/pathalizerLogFile1.pdf and
graphics/ch12/pathalizerLogFile2.pdf
Choosing the logfile for Pathalizer.

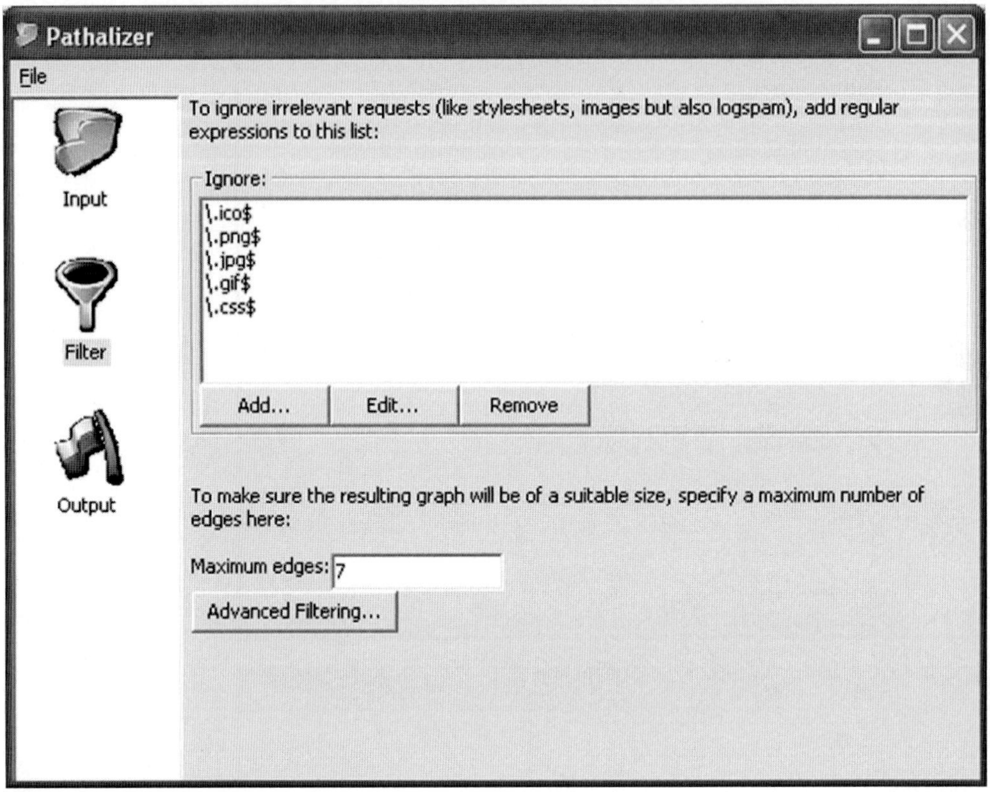

FIGURE 12.17

`graphics/ch12/pathalizerFilters.pdf`
Specifying filters for Pathalizer.

Clicking on `Output` in the left panel will bring up the top window shown in Figure 12.18. Choose an appropriate file type. We have chosen the `png` file type. Under `Action:`, click on `Save as ...` and choose a filename as shown in the bottom window in Figure 12.18. Note that we have to explicitly add the extension `.png` to the filename.

Now that we have all the essential information, click on the `Start!` button and wait for Pathalizer to finish its computation. Generally, there is a barely perceptible flashing of the window to signify computing. You can then go to the directory where you asked Pathalizer to store the file and launch it by double-clicking on it. Figure 12.19 shows the output, and we now provide an explanation of the graph drawn by Pathalizer:

- Every node is a page. The path/URL for the page and the number of hits on the page are listed inside these shapes.

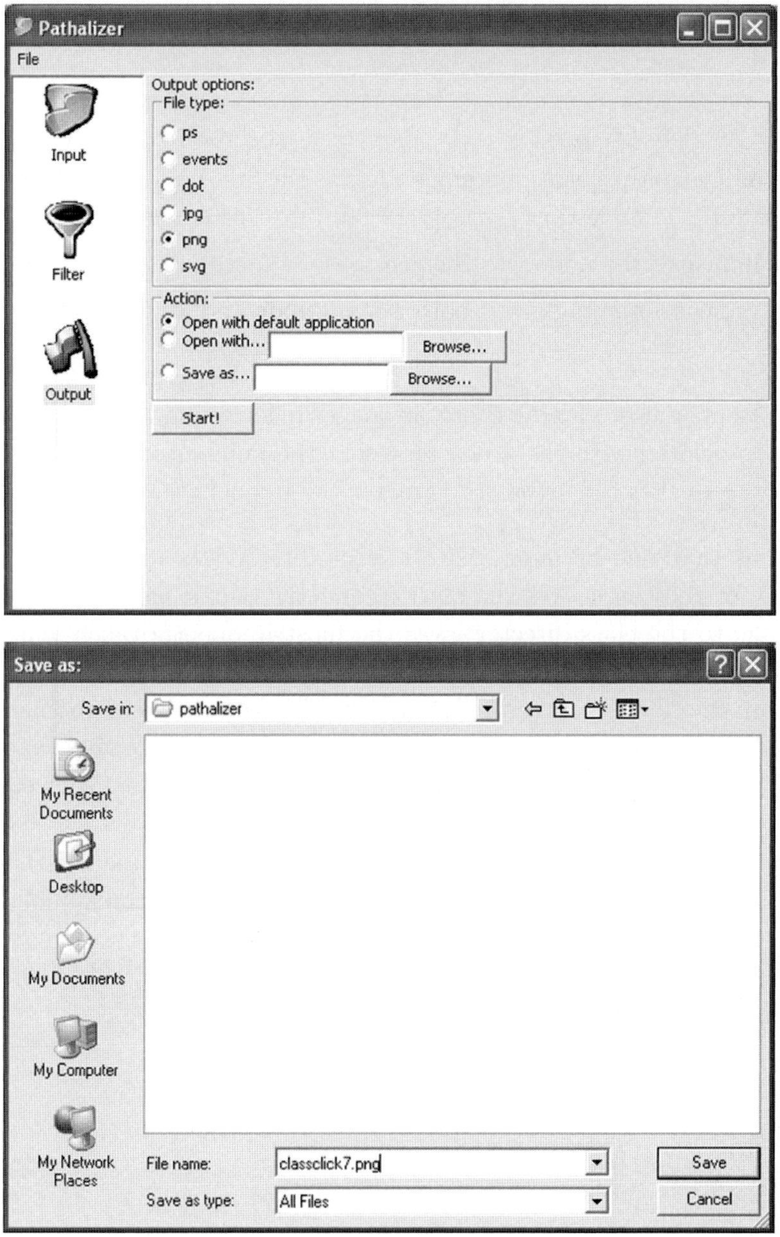

FIGURE 12.18

graphics/ch12/pathalizerFormatAndFile1.pdf and
graphics/ch12/pathalizerFormatAndFile2.pdf
Specifying output format and file for Pathalizer.

- Although all the nodes in our figure are rectangles, nodes can have various shapes:

  - An *ellipse* is the default.
  - A *rectangle* indicates the corresponding node was the first node of a session at least once (all the nodes in Figure 12.19 fall into this category).
  - A *diamond* indicates the node was the last node of a session.
  - An *octagon* indicates the node was both a start-node and an end-node at least once.

- Every arrow represents a user visiting those two pages in succession. The width and the number associated with the arrow represent the number of times that path was taken (the thicker the arrow, the greater the frequency).

Figure 12.19 tells us that one or more visitors went directly to all five pages shown. The home page for the course was the most frequently visited page, and the link from the home page to the class directory was the most frequently taken. The link from the home page to the assignment page was the second-most popular path, followed by the link from the home page to the lab folder. This knowledge of popular pages and links tells us that every page should have a link to the home page, and that links to the class folder, assignments, and lab folder should be prominently displayed on the home page.

The specification of seven links to Pathalizer gave us only a bird's eye view of the website. If we wish to have a more detailed analysis, we need to increase the number of edges in the filter section. Figure 12.20 shows a more detailed analysis with 20 edge specifications. As the number of edges increases, it is difficult to read the graph because of the large amount of information as well as the smaller text size.

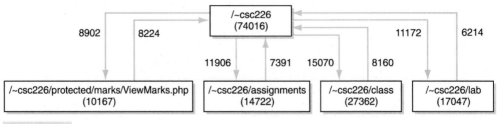

FIGURE 12.19

graphics/ch12/pathalizer7LinkClickstream.pdf
Clickstream using Pathalizer with seven-link specification.

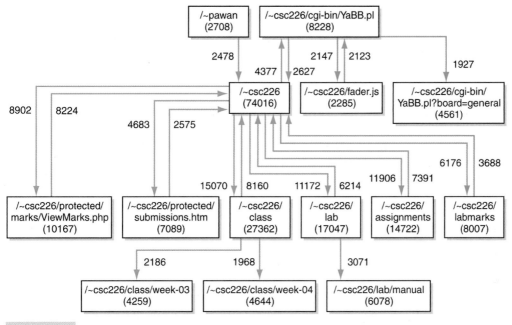

FIGURE 12.20

graphics/ch12/pathalizer20LinkClickstream.pdf
Clickstream using Pathalizer with 20-link specification.

You may want to experiment with different output-file types to determine the best type for your usage. We found the use of postscript files (converted to pdfs) makes it possible to view as many as 100 edges easily. These pdf files are available in the folder Pathalizer under Chapter12 on the CD-ROM. The filenames are classclick7.pdf, classclick20.pdf, and classclick100.pdf. It will be necessary to magnify and then analyze the graph in pieces by scrolling horizontally and vertically. The graph in Figure 12.20 uncovers additional important pages (such as the bulletin board and the submissions page) and links (such as ~pawan→csc226 and lab page→manual). This information can be used to design other pages on the site.

Now that we have some idea of what Pathalizer does, let us see how it works. The computation of paths is based on a list of hits with referrer fields. Consider two requests from a user session (from the same computer in a reasonably short time interval):

```
Requested URL: /~csc226/class/ Referer URL: /~csc226/
Requested URL: /~csc226/class/week-03/ Referer URL: /~csc226/class/
```

Clearly, we should have the following edges:

`/~csc226/`→`/~csc226/class/` and
`/~csc226/class/`→`/~csc226/class/week-03/`

The following case uses a bit of heuristics to model user behavior:

`Requested URL: /~csc226/class/ Referer URL: /~csc226/`
`Requested URL: /~csc226/assignment/ Referer URL: /~csc226/`

Again, assume that it is the same user making these two requests. In this case, it is reasonable to assume that the user used the `Back` button from `/~csc226/class/` to `/~csc226/` after the first request, before making the second request. Therefore, Pathalizer creates three edges:

`/~csc226/`→`/~csc226/class/`
`/~csc226/class/`→`/~csc226/` and
`/~csc226/`→`/~csc226/assignment/`

12.3.3   Visualizing Individual User Sessions with StatViz

In the previous two sections, we looked at two different aggregate web-usage analytical tools. The first one (Analog) created a variety of reports on web usage. The second (Pathalizer) provided a visualization of pages that are in high demand as well as being the most popular paths.

It is also possible to look at an individual user's interaction with a website. Because a site will have a large number of visitors, it will be practically impossible to analyze each one of them in great detail; but one can randomly pick sessions of various sizes to study how individual visitors traverse through a site. Such an analysis should always be a precursor to the application of a data-mining technique. Sometimes such a visualization process may also be conducted after uncovering interesting navigational patterns from the data-mining exercise. For example, if one notices a certain category of users aborting their sale, the site manager may choose a session from a list of such pre-emptive users and study the visual representation of their navigation patterns.

Again, there are a number of commercial and free software programs that can help track individual user sessions. We will look at a free software package that is available under the MIT license `http://www.opensource.org/licenses/mit-license.php`. The software is available from `http://sourceforge.net/projects/StatViz/`. The description of the software can be found at `http://StatViz.sourceforge.net/`. The software is written in PHP.

StatViz produces two types of output: an aggregate clickstream analysis similar to that of Pathalizer and an individual session track. Because we have already looked at aggregate clickstream analysis using Pathalizer, we will look only at the individual session tracks.

StatViz keeps track of the movements from page to page within an individual session stored in the log file. A session is simply associated with an IP address. That means all the requests from a given computer are considered to be for the same session. This is not a good assumption, especially for a public computer. The developer indicates that it is possible to configure the definition of a session. You can easily configure StatViz to use a different column as the "unique session ID." The unique session IDs can be obtained from **mod_usertrack** or a custom session ID logged via the Apache notes mechanism.

The session-track reporter from StatViz graphs the exact clickstream for the longest sessions in the log. The number of clicks, not time, determines the length of the session. The configuration file is used to specify how many sessions should be graphed. The session-track reporter will produce one graph per session. Each graph is designed to give a good sampling of how visitors move around the site.

Tracking individual sessions is a computationally intensive activity. Moreover, it is difficult to study all the user sessions individually; therefore, we selected a 1.25-hour snapshot from our **classlog.txt**. The time period that was chosen was from 11:30 a.m. to 12:45 p.m. on a Tuesday (October 9, 2001). Usually, this time reports fairly intensive activity on the course website, because it follows the class, and there are two labs scheduled in parallel during that time. We picked three sessions of different lengths, which are shown in Figures 12.21–12.23.

The following is a brief explanation of a StatViz "session tracks" graph (StatViz, 2006):

- The graph shows movement through the website as links from one page to another. Each node is a web page, and each solid line is a "click" from one page to the other as indicated by the arrow.

- Each line has a number next to it representing the number of that particular "click" in the session track. The time of the "click" is also shown next to the number.

- In some cases you will also see a dashed line with the same number as another click. These **BACK** links indicate that the visitor went back to that page using the **Back** button before proceeding.

- Pages that are not on our site (external referrers) are shown as blue ovals.

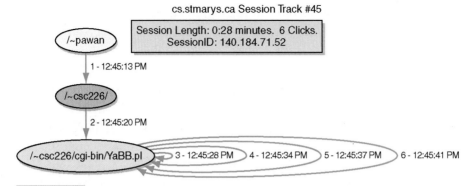

FIGURE 12.21

graphics/ch12/statVizBriefOnCampus.pdf
A brief on-campus session identified by StatViz that browses the bulletin board.

- The "entry" page is colored green. The "exit" page is colored red. If the entry and exit pages are the same, that page will be red.

Graphical display of individual session tracks allows us to understand how people successfully or unsuccessfully navigate through a site. Studying them will not only help us understand the information needs of our visitors but also provide insight into how we could better present information on the site to facilitate easier navigation. Let us try to interpret the StatViz graphs from Figures 12.21–12.23.

The session #45 depicted in Figure 12.21 lasted less than half a minute and involved six clicks. The user came from the instructor's home page, /~pawan/, to the home page for the class, /~csc226/, and immediately proceeded to the bulletin board. He quickly looked at various messages posted on the board and exited from the bulletin board. It is clear that he knew exactly what information he was looking for, and did not waste any time wandering around. The IP number starts with 140.184, which means it was an on-campus computer.

Figure 12.22 shows an off-campus session (#31), which was equally brief, lasting a little over 1.5 minutes. The IP number starting with 142.177 tells us that the user came from an Internet service provided by the local phone company. Again, the user seemed to know what she was looking for. She either used a bookmark or typed the URL directly to get to the entry page, /~csc226/. She then proceeded with three clicks to look at the assignment for week-05, came back to the lab folder with the Back button, and used two clicks to look at the assignment from the previous week (week-04). She then used the Back button to get to the course home page. Clicks 7–10 were used to browse the bulletin board. Finally, she checked the marks and then exited the site. As with the previous user (Figure 12.21), this user also knew the

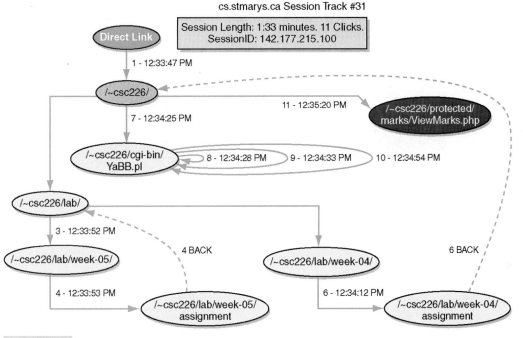

FIGURE 12.22
graphics/ch12/statVizBriefOffCampus.pdf
A brief off-campus session identified by StatViz with three distinct activities.

structure of the site very well. That is why she managed to conduct three separate activities in a relatively short period of time:

- View two lab assignments

- Browse the bulletin board

- View marks

The third session (#9), depicted in Figure 12.23, is a little more leisurely than the previous two, lasting almost half an hour. (It is possible that this in fact is a combination of two distinct sessions.) While the user accesses the lab manual for sample programs, he does not seem to be directly working on the lab assignment, because he is not looking at any lab assignment. There is a flurry of activity from 11:45 to 11:50 a.m., when he looks at the two programs `fileio.cpp` and `shell.cpp` from the lab manual, and checks the bulletin board. Presumably he uses the information to do some course-related activity, such as an assignment. The activity picks up again after about 20 minutes (12:12 p.m.) as the user looks at the class folder and has another look at the two sample programs before exiting.

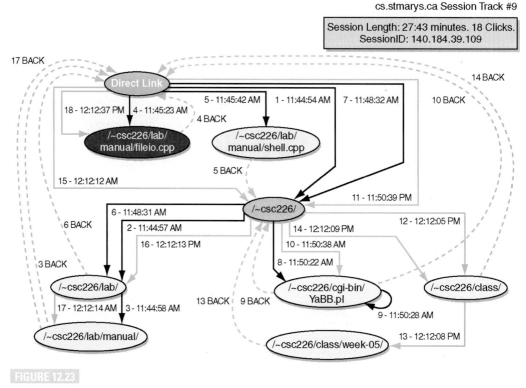

graphics/ch12/statVizLongOnCampus.pdf

FIGURE 12.23

graphics/ch12/statVizLongOnCampus.pdf
A long on-campus session identified by StatViz with multiple activities.

There are two possible explanations to these two distinct sets of activities. One possibility is that the last bit of activity involves double-checking the work that was done in the previous 20 minutes. Another possibility is that the graph is representing two distinct visits. They may very well be from the same user or from two different users, because the IP address corresponds to an on-campus public-access computer. This discussion underscores the difficulties in interpreting web-access logs. The next section articulates these difficulties in greater detail.

12.4   Caution in Interpreting Web-Server Access Logs

In previous sections we have now discussed how information in web-server access logs can help us learn about the usage of a website. While the information in these logs can be very useful, the developer of Analog throws cold water on our excitement by pointing out many pitfalls in an optimistic interpretation of these logs (Turner

2004). This section provides a brief summary of Turner's arguments. Sometimes his arguments are copied verbatim in order to avoid misinterpretation.

Web-server access logs record information such as the date and time of page requests, the requested page, the Internet address (IP number) of the user's computer, which page referred the user to the site, and the make and model of the user's browser. Unless specifically programmed, the user's name and e-mail address are not recorded.

First, in addition to requesting the web page itself, the browser will generate additional requests unbeknownst to the user for any graphics on the page. If a page has 10 pictures, for example, there will be 11 requests. In reality, the user asked for only one page.

Turner (2004) also points out that the reality is not as simple as described above, due to caching. There are two major types of caching. First, the browser automatically caches files when they are downloaded. This means that if the same user revisits the page, there is no need to download the whole page again. Depending on the settings, the browser may check with the server that the page has not changed. If such a check is made, the server will know and record the page access. If the browser is set to not check with the server, the access log will have no entry of the page reuse.

The other type of cache is implemented by Internet Service Providers (ISPs). The ISP proxy server will not forward a request to a server if some other user from the same ISP has already downloaded the page, because the ISP proxy server will cache it. The user browser settings cannot overrule the proxy server caching. This means that even though the server served and recorded the page request only once, many people can read the same page. With web-server access logs, the only information we know for certain is the number of requests made to our server, when they were made, which files were asked for, and which host asked for them. We also know what browsers were used and what the referring pages were.

Moreover, Turner also cautions about the browser and referrer information. Many browsers deliberately lie about what sort of browser they are, or even let users configure the browser name (Turner 2004). Moreover, some proponents of protection of privacy use "anonymizers" to deliberately send false browser and referrer information.

Turner (2004) emphasizes that you do not really know any of the following:

- *The identity of your readers*, unless you explicitly program the server to receive their identities.

- *The number of your visitors*, because the number of distinct hosts is not always a good measure, for the following reasons:

  - ISP proxy server caching will not show some of the requests.

- Many users may use the same IP number.

- The same user may appear to connect from many different hosts. For example, AOL allocates a different hostname for every request. This means if an AOL user downloads a page with 10 pictures, the server may think that there were 11 visitors.

■ *The number of visits*, since programs that count visits define a visit as a sequence of requests from the same host until there is a significant gap between requests. This assumption may not always be true. Some sites try to count their visitors by using cookies, which may provide better estimates. However, in order for the cookies to be effective, you will have to mandate that users accept them and assume that they don't delete them.

■ *The user's navigation path through the site*, since the use of the Back button and caching gives only a partial picture. Programs will have to use the kind of heuristics employed by Pathalizer to guess the complete path.

■ *The entry point and referral*, since if the home page was retrieved from the cache, the first request may actually be somewhere in the middle of the true visit.

■ *How users left the site or where they went next*, since there is no way to know the next request made by the user after leaving the site.

■ *How long people spent reading each page*, since after downloading a page, they might read some (unrecorded) cached pages before a new request is recorded. They might step out of the site and come back later with a new request to the site.

■ *How long people spent on the site*, since in addition to the problems with recording time for each page, there is no way to tell the time spent on the final page. In most cases, the final page may take the majority of the time of the visit, because the user has finally found what he or she was looking for, but there is no way to verify this.

We end this (somewhat discouraging) section with the following quote from Turner (2004):

I've presented a somewhat negative view here, emphasizing what you can't find out. Web statistics are still informative: it's just important not to slip from "this page has received 30,000 requests" to "30,000 people have read this page". In some sense these problems are not really new to the web—they are just as prevalent in print media. For example, you only know how many magazines you've sold, not how many people have read them. In print media we have learnt to live with these issues, using the data which are available, and it would be better if we did on the Web too, rather than making up spurious numbers.

12.5 Summary

Many businesses, both large and small, have websites, and some of them are quite elaborate. Still, you hear many people complaining about how hard some websites are to use. If you have a business, you don't want your website to be one of those, and it is unlikely you will get enough relevant feedback from your users via a direct, but optional, feedback form like the one we discussed earlier to help you improve your site in any significant way.

Help is not far away, however, and in this chapter we have touched briefly on the topic of web-usage mining to illustrate some of the many software tools that are available, as well as the kinds of data that can be recorded by web servers and processed by these tools to provide information that can aid with the task of site improvement. The process begins with the web-server access log, a file in which the web server records a great deal of information about website visits (though not necessarily about website visitors).

These "web logs" are generally recorded in a standard format (a *common log format*) and can be read and processed by many different tools that can read this format, including these:

- Analog, which can produce various kinds of summary information about visits to your website.

- Pathalizer, in conjunction with Graphviz, which can perform *clickstream analysis* to show how users navigate through your website.

- StatViz, which allows you to visualize an individual user session at your website.

As useful as these tools and others like them may be in helping us analyze our website traffic, we should not be overly confident about what we think they may be telling us. It will always be necessary to treat the information they provide with (perhaps) a grain of salt, and certainly with more than a grain of common sense.

12.6   Quick Questions to Test Your Basic Knowledge

1. Can you name three types of *web mining*, and describe each briefly?

2. What is a *web-server access log*, and what are some of the shorter terms used to refer to the same thing?

3. What is the *common log format*, and how many entry fields does it contain?

4. How many of the entry fields in the common log format can you describe?

5. What is the *combined log format*, and how many additional entry fields does it have, over and above those of the common log format?

6. What are the contents of the additional entry fields of the combined log format?

7. For what purpose would you use Analog?

8. For what purpose would you use Pathalizer, and what other piece of software should you install along with it?

9. For what purpose would you use StatViz?

10. What cautions would you pass along to someone who was about to use one or more of the above-mentioned tools for the first time?

12.7   Short Exercises to Improve Your Basic Understanding

Actually these exercises may not be all that short, unless you have already installed the relevant software.

1. Install the Analog software and experiment with the supplied `logfile.log` sample file, or with any web-log file that you can obtain from your local web server administrator.

2. Install Pathalizer and Graphviz and experiment with any web-log file that you can obtain from your local web server administrator.

3. Install Statviz and experiment with any web-log file that you can obtain from your local web server administrator.

12.8 Exercises on the Parallel Project

If you have completed the **Short Exercises** of the previous section, then you will already have installed the Analog, Pathalizer with Graphviz, and StatViz software. If not, then you will need to do that now.

The next step is to give some thought to what you might like to learn about the traffic on your own website. A reasonable approach here might be to design a fairly intensive browsing experience on your own site that you, and perhaps some friends, can carry out. Having full knowledge of how your site is laid out, you could write a script that you, or someone else, could follow. This would include a list of which links to click on, and which order, for example.

Before executing this script, it might be wise to confirm with your web server administrator that the activity you will be performing will in fact be recorded, and that you will have access later to the appropriate web server access log data.

The main purpose of this exercise may be described as follows. First, the script that you use to perform the browsing activity gives you a complete and accurate record of the activity performed. Once you have the web server access log file, your task is to determine how much of that known activity you can deduce from the output of the software tools mentioned above and discussed in this chapter.

Perform the activities described above, and then prepare a report on the outcome. This report should include your assessment of how effective these tools are.

12.9 What Else You Might Want or Need to Know

If you are business owner and your business has a website, or is planning to have one, the question of how much of your effort and resources can be devoted to its development and maintenance is an important one. Whether this is handled in-house, or outsourced, the business should be comfortable that both the developer and maintainer know what they are doing.

A website can be an important means of attracting clients and even selling directly to them, as we have seen. However, a poor website is probably worse than no website at all, so some attention needs to be devoted to it by those who own and care about the business.

A small business owner may very well not have the time, energy, or financial resources to engage in the kind of traffic analysis we have discussed in this chapter, and certainly this is not the first order of business. It will be much more important to have an interesting, useful, and easy-to-use site with no annoying features, such as broken links and obviously out-of-date information.

12.10   References

The end-of-chapter **References** sections of previous chapters contained exclusively links to online resources. Some of these references are of the more traditional form, and we use here a more traditional format.

1. Akerkar, R., and P. Lingras. 2007. Building an intelligent web: theory and practice. Boston: Jones and Bartlett Publishers.

2. Agrawal, R., and R. Srikant. 1994. Fast algorithms for mining association rules. In Proceedings of the 20th VLDB Conference, 487–499. Santiago, Chile.

3. Apache. 2006. Log files. `http://httpd.apache.org/docs/2.2/logs.html`.

4. Cooley, R., B. Mobasher, and J. Srivastava. 1997. Web mining: Information and pattern discovery on the World Wide Web. In Proceedings of International Conference on Tools with Artificial Intelligence. Newport Beach, CA, 558–567.

5. Hallam-Baker, P.M., and B. Behlendorf. 1996. Extended log file format. `http://www.w3.org/pub/WWW/TR/WD-logfile-960221.html`.

6. Kosala, R., and H. Blockeel. 2000. Web mining research: A survey. *SIG KDD Explorations*, 2 (15): 1–15.

7. Pathalizer 2006a. Project details for Pathalizer. `http://freshmeat.net/projects/pathalizer/`.

8. Pathalizer 2006b. Pathalizer download. `http://pathalizer.sourceforge.net/`.

9. Ramadhan, H., M. Hatem, Z. Al-Khanjri, and S. Kutti. 2005. A classification of techniques for Web usage analysis. *Journal of Computer Science*, 1 (3): 413–418.

10. StatViz. 2006. StatViz - Graphical clickstream/path analysis of web traffic. `http://statviz.sourceforge.net/`.

11. Turner, S. 2006. Analog. `http://www.Analog.cx`

12. Turner, S. 2004. How the Web works. `http://www.Analog.cx/docs/Webworks.html`.

13. Wikipedia. 2006. Server logs. `http://en.wikipedia.org/wiki/Server_log`.

List of Figures

Index

Credits

Chapter 2

2.1-2.2 Courtesy of Nature's Source; **2.3** Courtesy of PuTTY; **2.4** Courtesy of WinSCP.

Chapter 3

3.1-3.2 Courtesy of Nature's Source; **3.4** Courtesy of Nature's Source; **3.6** Courtesy of Nature's Source; **3.8-3.10** Courtesy of Nature's Source; **3.15-3.16** © W3C.

Chapter 4

4.3 Courtesy of Nature's Source; **4.5** Courtesy of Nature's Source; **4.8** Courtesy of Nature's Source; **4.15** Courtesy of Nature's Source, (inset) © Kim Pan Tan/ShutterStock, Inc.; **4.18** Courtesy of Nature's Source, (inset) © Kim Pan Tan/ShutterStock, Inc.; **4.19-4.20** Courtesy of Nature's Source; **4.23-4.24** © W3C.

Chapter 5

5.2 Courtesy of Nature's Source; **5.4-5.5** Courtesy of Nature's Source; **5.8-5.9** Courtesy of Nature's Source; **5.11** Courtesy of Nature's Source.

Chapter 6

6.2 Courtesy of Nature's Source; **6.7** Courtesy of Nature's Source; **6.14** Courtesy of Nature's Source; **6.17** Courtesy of Nature's Source; **6.19** Courtesy of Nature's Source; **6.22** Courtesy of Nature's Source.

Chapter 7

7.1 Courtesy of Nature's Source, (inset) © Photos.com.

Chapter 8

8.2 Courtesy of Nature's Source; **8.3** Courtesy of Nature's Source, (inset) © Photos.com; **8.6** Courtesy of Nature's Source; **8.11** Courtesy of Nature's Source; **8.13-8.14** Courtesy of Nature's Source.

Chapter 9

9.2-9.4 © phpMyAdmin; **9.6-9.7** © phpMyAdmin; **9.9-9.12** © phpMyAdmin; **9.15-9.16** © phpMyAdmin; **9.18-9.19** © phpMyAdmin; **9.21** © phpMyAdmin; **9.23-9.24** © phpMyAdmin; **9.32** © phpMyAdmin; **9.33** Courtesy of Firefox; **9.38** © phpMyAdmin; **9.39** © phpMyAdmin.

Chapter 10

10.1 Courtesy of Nature's Source, (inset) © Photos.com; **10.2** Courtesy of Nature's Source; **10.4** Courtesy of Nature's Source; **10.8-10.11** Courtesy of Nature's Source; **10.15** Courtesy of Nature's Source; **10.20** Courtesy of Nature's Source; **10.22-10.24** Courtesy of Nature's Source; **10.26** Courtesy of Nature's Source; **10.28** Courtesy of Nature's Source; **10.30-10.33** Courtesy of Nature's Source; **10.42-10.44** Courtesy of Nature's Source.

Chapter 11

11.8 Courtesy of Nature's Source; **11.9** Courtesy of Nature's Source.

Unless otherwise indicated, all photographs and illustrations are under copyright of Jones & Bartlett Learning, or have been provided by the author(s).

Some images in this book feature models. These models do not necessarily endorse, represent, or participate in the activities represented in the images.